TRUMAN AND THE DEMOCRATIC PARTY

TRUMAN AND THE
☆ ☆ ☆ ☆ ☆
DEMOCRATIC PARTY

SEAN J. SAVAGE

THE UNIVERSITY PRESS OF KENTUCKY

Publication of this volume was made possible in part by a grant from the National Endowment for the Humanities.

Scholarly publisher for the Commonwealth,
serving Bellarmine College, Berea College, Centre
College of Kentucky, Eastern Kentucky University,
The Filson Club Historical Society, Georgetown College,
Kentucky Historical Society, Kentucky State University,
Morehead State University, Murray State University,
Northern Kentucky University, Transylvania University,
University of Kentucky, University of Louisville,
and Western Kentucky University.

Editorial and Sales Offices: The University Press of Kentucky
663 South Limestone Street, Lexington, Kentucky 40508-4008

01 00 99 98 97   5 4 3 2 1

Library of Congress Cataloging-in-Publication Data

Savage, Sean J., 1964–
    Truman and the Democratic Party / Sean J. Savage.
        p.   cm.
    Includes bibliographical references and index.
    ISBN 0–8131–2003–9 (cloth : alk. paper)
    1. Truman, Harry S., 1884–1972.   2. Democratic Party (U.S.)—
    History—20th century.   3. United States—Politics and
    government—1945–1953.   I. Title.
E814.S28   1997
973.918′092—dc21   96–49954

This book is printed on acid-free recycled paper
meeting the requirements of the American National Standard
for Permanence of Paper for Printed Library Materials.

Manufactured in the United States of America

☆ ☆ ☆ ☆ ☆

CONTENTS

Illustrations follow page 136

☆ ☆ ☆ ☆ ☆

Preface
A REFORMER AND A REGULAR

No previous book exclusively and comprehensively devotes its content and purpose to a detailed analysis of Harry S. Truman's relationship with the Democratic party and his presidential behavior as a party leader. In particular, this is the first book that contains separate chapters on the Democratic National Committee during Truman's presidency and on his relationships with machine bosses. It further introduces my own concept of Democratic dissensus. I have benefited from personal interviews with former Truman administration and DNC officials—as well as an examination of neglected archives from the Truman Library, Library of Congress, Joseph W. Martin Jr. Institute, and the University of Kentucky Library.

Truman's approach to and behavior as a party leader reflected the internal conflicts that he experienced in his own relationship with the Democratic party and in his goals for the party. These conflicts partially resulted from the fact that Truman was both a party regular and a liberal reformer. As a party regular, he overemphasized the importance of unconditional party loyalty to Democratic allies and subordinates and did little to co-opt liberal Republicans and independents into the Democratic party or cultivate a significant liberal Republican bloc of supporters for his domestic policy agenda, as FDR had done.

Likewise, Truman as a party regular initially behaved passively and even complacently to the growing evidence of corruption by administration officials. He criticized the Kefauver committee hearings' public disclosures of collusion between gangsters and Democratic machines for weakening the Democratic party electorally in the 1950 and 1952 elections. As a regular Democrat, Truman sought internal harmony and cooperation within his party's apparatus, especially by ensuring that White House aides did not usurp the Democratic national chairman's authority and responsibilities, as had happened under Roosevelt. Likewise, he wanted a more harmonious, deferential relationship with leading Democrats in Congress than FDR had.

Despite Truman's desire for a more internally cohesive, smoothly function-ing Democratic party, he experienced significant intraparty discord. To a certain extent, this discord resulted from the second and equally influential quality of Truman's party leadership and political behavior—that is, his status as a liberal reformer. Influenced by agrarian populism, Wilsonian progressivism, and his own record as a New Deal senator, Truman possessed a simple yet sincere lib-eral ideology that partially motivated him to pursue policy goals that often weak-ened and divided his party, especially among southern Democrats in Congress. Truman's Twenty-one Point Program, submitted to Congress in 1945, was a more detailed and extensive compilation of social welfare and economic reform proposals than FDR's 1944 Economic Bill of Rights. In particular, Truman's advocacy of civil rights for blacks, the legal foundation for a desegregated mili-tary, a national health insurance proposal, federal aid to elementary and second-ary education, and repeal of the Taft-Hartley Act are evidence of this belief in maintaining and further enhancing the Democratic party as a distinctly liberal party in its ideology and policy agenda.

This theme of vacillation, conflict, and occasional symbiosis between Truman's two roles is evident throughout the book. Consequently, unlike biog-raphies of Harry Truman and histories of his presidency, this book is arranged in topical, not always chronological, order. For example, while the last chapter includes a section on the 1952 presidential campaign, various elements of the 1952 Democratic presidential campaign, such as the tactics of the DNC's appa-ratus and the role of Jacob Arvey, are addressed previously in the book. Through-out, Truman's political behavior in general and as party leadership in particular are frequently assessed according to the criteria of ideology, coalition, and policy agenda as the major characteristics of a party. I hope that such an analysis of Truman's party leadership is useful to both historians and political scientists.

I thank Saint Mary's College and the Harry S. Truman Library Institute for awarding me grants that enabled me to conduct interviews and extensive archi-val research from a variety of collections. I also thank the following student assistants for thier help in researching and preparing this book's manuscript: Nicole M. DeMatteis, Rachel I. Lamb, Mary Beth Wilkinson, Mary K. Moreland, and Stefanie L. Kyte. The typing skills and diligence of Mary Beth Dominello were instrumental in enabling me to submit the completed manuscript punctu-ally. I was honored to have the manuscript reviewed by political scientists John K. White, Mark J. Rozell, Frank J. Sorauf, William J. Crotty, John S. Jackson III, William C. Binning, and Howard L. Reiter.

Finally, I dedicate this book to my sisters, Marguerite and Kathleen.

1

☆ ☆ ☆ ☆ ☆

TRUMAN AND HIS PARTY

Harry S. Truman's identification and prepresidential involvement with the Democratic party were shaped by two often conflicting value systems: his ethos as a party regular and his ethos as a liberal reformer. The ethical, attitudinal, and behavioral compromises that Truman made to reconcile these two conflicting value systems enabled him to satisfy his political ambition and advance his career. These compromises and self-imposed internal changes by Truman sometimes manifested themselves through severe headaches, nervous exhaustion, and penitent letters to his wife in the short term.[1] But such stress induced Truman to eventually adapt his political character and behavior to changes in his political environment.

TRUMAN THE DEMOCRAT

Truman's chronic internal conflicts and political changes closely paralleled those of the Democratic party. Truman first knew the organization as a southern- and rural-dominated minority party loosely affiliated with a few urban machines and often lacking a unifying domestic policy agenda and ideology beyond states' rights, minimal government, low tariffs, and an inflated currency. During his lifetime it became a northern- and urban-dominated majority party whose liberal policy objectives and philosophy were committed to using a big, activist, innovative federal government for reforming and regulating big business and focusing on the special policy interests of blacks, organized labor, and major cities. Consequently, Truman's values and political experiences prior to his presidency gave him the perspective to understand this evolution of the Democratic party and the diversity of opinions and demands among its members —for example, those of the southern segregationists, blacks, union officials, farm leaders, and machine bosses—once he assumed the role of party leader.

This same political background, however, would also limit and hamper Truman's party leadership by impelling him to inconsistently alternate between two personas: the liberal reformer who permanently committed the national Democratic party to such policy goals as civil rights and national health insurance, regardless of interest group pressure and intraparty discord, and the inflexibly and sometimes blindly loyal regular, who would make and excessively defend unsuitable appointments as rewards for party service. Likewise, Truman would criticize and even try to obstruct legitimate investigations of Democratic corruption.[2] Such vacillation in Truman's party leadership would raise doubts among the public, media, and his fellow Democrats, including the most determined segregationist Democrats and the most devoted Roosevelt liberals, about the direction, clarity, and sincerity of his leadership behavior.

What is a good Democrat? Is he an ideologically motivated reformer who wants to use his party to achieve far-sighted, humanitarian, progressive policy goals in government according to the ideals of Jefferson, Jackson, and Wilson?[3] Or is he a pragmatic political actor unconditionally loyal to his party's nominees and officials and tolerant of spoils, favoritism, and corruption in his party as an inevitable and even necessary part of the political process?[4] These questions would plague Truman from Jackson County, Missouri, to the White House.

Truman's family life and self-education in history provided the foundation for his Democratic affiliation and a value system that oriented him toward populism and later liberalism. Truman's parents, Martha and John Truman, instilled their son with an enthusiastic, unquestioning identification with the Democratic party. Their southern ancestry, resentment of Republican tight money and high tariff policies, and suspicion of Wall Street combined to form a Democratic family tradition subscribing to the agrarian populism of Thomas Jefferson and Andrew Jackson.[5] Like Jefferson and Jackson, the Trumans believed that political and economic freedom could best be preserved in a nation of independent small farmers. For the Truman family, the Republican party represented forces of big business and economic centralization, which threatened to concentrate economic and political power in an eastern elite and destroy the basis of American democracy, a broad, agricultural middle class.[6]

John Truman was financially ambitious and engaged in livestock trading and grain speculation, but his business ventures often failed. Despite the example of his father's financial reverses, Harry Truman entered into his own get-rich-quick schemes in oil and mining investments in 1916, but he sold his shares shortly before joining the army in 1917.[7] Like his father, Harry Truman had an entrepreneurial spirit but failed to achieve his goal of being a leading, prosperous businessman in Jackson County. Despite the popularity of Truman's haberdashery with the comrades from his World War I artillery battery, he and his business partner, Eddie Jacobson, closed their store after sales suffered from the 1921-22 recession. Even as an elderly man, Truman bitterly blamed his haberdashery's failure on Republican economic policies. A Republican president, he believed, will "look out for the rich and squeeze out the farmer and the small businessman."[8]

Truman's status as a well-liked, respected former army captain, however, did prove to be a political asset. James M. Pendergast was a nephew of Kansas City machine boss Tom Pendergast and had been a lieutenant in Truman's artillery unit. He and his father, Alderman Mike Pendergast, approached Truman in 1922 about running in the Democratic primary for county judge for the eastern district of Jackson County, which included Truman's hometown of Independence.[9] Jim and Mike Pendergast persuaded Boss Tom that Truman's status as a Mason, Baptist, veteran, and former farmer and small businessman would attract rural voters to their circle within the Jackson County Democratic party, known as the Goats. Mike Pendergast had known Truman as a member of the Tenth Ward Democratic Club and had secured his appointment as Grandview postmaster and road overseer in 1915.[10]

Truman was certainly familiar with the Goats. His father had participated in their Democratic faction. John Truman had attended Democratic national and state conventions as a Goat, and was rewarded with an appointment as road overseer in Grandview. He was equally enthusiastic about the Democratic presidential candidacies of Grover Cleveland, a conservative, and William Jennings Bryan, an agrarian populist. Harry Truman had briefly served as his father's successor as road overseer and as a clerk in the Grandview voting precinct.[11]

When he agreed to run as the Goats' candidate for county judge on the three-member court (which actually presided over public works projects and county institutions), Harry Truman was familiar with both organization politics and the reputation of the Pendergast machine in Kansas City.[12] Tom's brother, James Pendergast, had begun his machine as a ward organization, but Tom gradually expanded the machine's power throughout the city and now wanted to gain political influence in eastern, rural Jackson County. The Pendergast machine derived its wealth, power, and success from a combination of ballot fraud, distribution of informal welfare services, patronage, jobs, and public contracts. It also benefited from collusion with brothels, bootleggers, and other illegal activities, and favors to business interests.[13] Even after blacks and various immigrant groups settled in Kansas City, it still had a large white, middle-class, Protestant community. The Irish Catholic Pendergasts recognized the need to provide a diversity of services and favors throughout the city and county and to satisfy the middle class and business community through impressive improvements in the public infrastructure.[14]

Besides the need to satisfy a diversity of needs and interests, the Goats also had to contend with a rival Democratic faction, the Rabbits, led by Joseph Shannon. Shannon was a handsome, distinguished Irish Catholic who bore a striking resemblance to Republican President Warren G. Harding.[15] Shannon was a conservative, states' rights Democrat who fancied himself an expert on Thomas Jefferson and his political philosophy.[16] He was outraged when Pendergast built a hotel and named it after Jefferson. In the late 1920s, the two feuding party bosses agreed to cooperate against the Republicans, and Tom Pendergast helped elect Shannon to the House of Representatives in 1930.[17] As a congressman, Shannon asserted himself as an opponent of the New Deal and charged that Franklin D. Roosevelt's big government liberalism betrayed the Jeffersonian principles of the Democratic party.[18]

But in 1922 the Goats and Rabbits apparently opposed each other for the eastern district judgeship. The Rabbits promoted the candidacy of Emmett Montgomery, a banker from Blue Springs. Initially, though, the Pendergasts' nominal backing of Truman was actually a sham because Tom Pendergast had agreed privately with Shannon to electorally support Montgomery on primary day if the Rabbits supported Henry F. McElroy, the Goats' candidate for western district judge.[19]

In fact, as early as January 1922, the *Independence Examiner* wrote about Truman as an "independent" candidate.[20] Truman promoted this image as an independent reform candidate in his rhetoric and campaign literature, despite the June endorsement of him by the Tenth Ward Democratic Club. The endorsement was arranged by Mike Pendergast. As the August primary day neared, however, the Rabbits suspected that Tom Pendergast had betrayed them as Truman proved to be a surprisingly effective campaigner who threatened the nomination of Montgomery, the front runner among the five candidates for this judgeship.[21]

Truman was not an eloquent or inspiring orator. Instead, Truman's success in his first campaign can primarily be attributed to two assets: his network of friends, relatives, and associates in various fraternal, veteran, and civic organizations of voters, campaign volunteers, and contributors in eastern Jackson County and his straightforward advocacy of honest, efficient "good government" practices in the administration of the county government's finances, hiring practices, and construction projects. He promised the voters a "square deal" in which he would reduce payroll costs and improve the extent and quality of paved roads at lower costs.[22] Miles Bulger, the presiding judge of the court, who was neither a Goat nor a Rabbit at this time, acquired the reputation as a corrupt administrator who had preferred construction companies contracts for high-priced, low-quality "pie crust" roads that crumbled easily. Thus, Truman's "good government" platform was especially attractive to voters and won him the endorsement of the Triangle Club, a mostly Republican business organization interested in civic improvements.

With no electoral support from the Pendergast-controlled voters, Truman defeated Montgomery by a margin of 279 votes.[23] He then defeated his Republican opponent in the general election by emphasizing the adoption of sound business practices even more. Truman's proven ability as a vote getter on his merits impressed the Pendergasts and embittered Joe Shannon.

Truman's fairly self-sufficient victorious campaign gave him a degree of political autonomy in fulfilling his duties of office that he would never have again. The presiding judge, E.W. Hayes, was a Rabbit, but McElroy and Truman gave all the county's patronage jobs to Goats. While giving such patronage discretion to the Pendergasts, Truman asserted that he would not tolerate the incompetence and absenteeism of county employees that characterized the Bulger administration. Although he and McElroy were Goats, Truman differed with McElroy, closely affiliated with Tom Pendergast and the contractors favored by the boss, on one key policy decision. Truman defeated the attempt of McElroy to move the Jackson County courthouse from Independence to Kansas City.[24]

During his two-year term, though, Truman focused on reducing the county's debt by nearly $700,000 and improving its credit. This accomplishment won Truman high marks from the business community and the endorsement of an anti-Pendergast Republican newspaper, the *Kansas City Star*. Angry over their loss of county patronage and power on the court and Truman's unexpected victory in 1922, Shannon's Rabbits collaborated with the local Ku Klux Klan and the Republicans to defeat Truman in 1924.[25] It was the only campaign Truman ever lost.

Although earning a prosperous income selling automobile club memberships, Truman was determined to stay in politics.[26] He approached Tom Pendergast about running for the well-paying position of county tax collector in 1926. Stating that this job had been promised to another Goat, Boss Tom suggested that Truman run for presiding judge of the county court. Truman agreed. Because of an agreement between Tom Pendergast and Joe Shannon, Truman ran unopposed in the Democratic primary and easily defeated his Republican opponent. He was elected to another four-year term in 1930.[27]

Truman's eight-year tenure as presiding judge of Jackson County provided the basis of the conflict between Truman's reformist and regular value systems.

With Henry McElroy serving as city manager of Kansas City, Truman had the authority and dominance of the court to more fully express and accomplish his reformist objectives.[28] Truman respected and often followed the proposals and studies of the Kansas City Civic Research Institute to modernize the county's accounting methods and administration of its services. He oversaw the appointment of two civil engineers, carefully ensuring that one was a Republican and the other a Democrat, to conduct a study of the county's defective roads and submit a plan for building a modern, thoroughly paved road system.[29] Despite the skepticism of Tom Pendergast, Truman persuaded most of the county's voters to approve a bond issue over $12 million, $6.5 million for the proposed road system and the rest for a new county courthouse and other institutions.[30]

Even though some of Boss Tom's favored contractors lost bids and some Goats lost patronage jobs because of Truman's drive for greater cost efficiency and personnel competence, the machine boss realized that good government could be good politics, provided that good government methods and objectives were implemented by a loyal Goat.[31] Tom Pendergast grudgingly and gradually began to respect the bespectacled former haberdasher recruited by his brother Mike, whose political judgment Boss Tom rarely valued.[32] Truman's conscientious, business-like, selfless devotion to improving the county's public infrastructure and finances conveyed the image of a machine that, despite its graft and voting irregularities, could professionally accomplish major policy objectives.[33]

This opportunity to express his reformist values strengthened Truman's self-esteem and political ambitions. Increasingly, Truman was not perceived as merely another docile functionary of the Pendergast machine. Instead, his administrative accomplishments as presiding judge and reputation for personal integrity and decisive, far-sighted leadership in public construction projects and their maintenance conveyed a public image that appealed to the middle-class ethos of good government reformers and mostly Republican business leaders. Truman's proven success in the county's structural improvements helped to convince the voters of Kansas City to pass the bond issue for a $40 million, ten-year public construction plan for Kansas City in 1931.[34] From 1930 to 1931, Truman encouraged a movement that promoted his candidacy for governor in 1932, known as the Truman for Governor Club.[35] Several Missouri newspapers and Democratic county judges were especially important in disseminating Truman's name recognition throughout the state. But Truman abruptly dissolved this exploratory campaign organization when Tom Pendergast informed him that the machine would promote Judge Guy B. Park for the gubernatorial nomination.[36]

It was now evident that Truman's first campaign in 1922 was the first and last time that he could enter and win a race without strong machine support.

Lacking personal wealth and a charismatic personality and speaking style, Truman needed the votes, campaign services, financial contributions, and alliances throughout Missouri that the Pendergast machine could provide if he wanted to be nominated and elected to higher offices. While Boss Tom was willing to give Truman a degree of administrative and fiscal discretion as county judge, when Truman's policy accomplishments served his machine well, he had made it clear to Truman that the machine would determine the Independence Democrat's political future when Truman's second term as presiding judge expired in 1934.[37] Likewise, as 1934 approached, Tom Pendergast rejected another request by Truman to run for the lucrative position of county tax collector.

The limitations, timing, and controls that the machine boss imposed on Truman's political career proved to be frustrating to Truman's ambition, demeaning to his reformist values, and burdensome to his competing ethos as a loyal party regular. Truman's good government, reformist liberalism was especially troubled by the professional and ethical compromises that he made as a Pendergast Democrat on the county court. He felt compelled to ignore the corruption of his machine colleagues and political allies, the use of ballot fraud to insure the election of himself and other Pendergast officials on a county-wide basis, and the more blatant collaboration that was developing between organized crime and the Pendergast machine by the late 1920s.[38] By the early 1930s, Boss Tom's political power extended throughout Missouri as ambitious Democrats sought the machine's electoral support in the at-large congressional elections of 1932. The boss emerged as a power broker at the 1932 Democratic national convention.[39]

Truman prided himself on his abstinence from the graft in which other machine officials indulged and his strenuous efforts to lessen the pernicious influence of partisan, machine politics in the administration of the county government.[40] Nevertheless, Truman's reformist and party regular value systems collided to the extent that the presiding judge of Jackson County began to suffer periods of mental and physical exhaustion and question his status as a public official. While resting and recovering from apparently psychosomatic headaches and stomach pains at the Pickwick Hotel in 1934, Truman expressed this constant clash between his two value systems more openly than at any other time. After reviewing policy accomplishments and the moral and legal compromises that he had made for the machine at great length and great detail, Truman asked with exasperation, "Am I an administrator or not? Or am I just a crook to compromise in order to get the job done? You judge it, I can't."[41]

Ironically, this dualistic and seemingly incompatible nature of Truman's political character and behavior would actually further his political career by making him more attractive to Boss Tom as a senatorial candidate in 1934 and irresistible as a vice presidential candidate in 1944. After his requests to run for county collector and then for a newly created congressional seat in 1934 had been rejected by Tom Pendergast, Truman was astonished that the boss offered his endorsement for U.S. senator.[42] Actually, Boss Tom had previously offered his support in the Senate race to Joe Shannon and then James Aylward, the Democratic state chairman, both of whom declined this offer.[43]

Again, Tom Pendergast's choice of Truman as a candidate was not an act of generosity to the failed haberdasher. Truman had repeatedly proven his ability as a loyal machine member to attract the votes of Masons, farmers, the reform-minded, civic groups such as the Kansas City Civic Research Institute, and other middle-class and rural voters and organizations that were often skeptical of or antagonistic toward the Pendergast machine. Furthermore, Truman had already developed as an ardent New Dealer while serving as federal re-employment director in Missouri. Through this position, Truman had established a cooperative relationship with administrator Harry Hopkins of the Works Progress Administration (WPA).[44] Truman and later Matthew Murray, a Pendergast Democrat who was appointed WPA director of Missouri in 1935 at Boss Tom's and Truman's request, ensured that Kansas City received a disproportionate share of WPA and Civil Works Administration jobs and funds allocated for Missouri.[45]

While Truman possessed these broadly appealing vote-getting qualities, he still needed the Pendergast machine's financial, organizational, and electoral resources, and network of political alliances throughout Missouri in order to win the closely contested Democratic senatorial primary of 1934. He confronted three powerful opponents. Truman defeated his closest rival, Congressman John Cochran of St. Louis, by a margin of 39,255 votes.[46] In November, he easily defeated his Republican opponent, winning 60 percent of the votes.[47]

Immediately after his primary victory, Truman characteristically became ill from nervous and physical exhaustion. Jonathan Daniels, a journalist and a former White House aide to Roosevelt and Truman, observed, "It was an odd thing to become at once sickened and a senator."[48] Truman was also tormented by the accusation of his Democratic primary opponents, especially Jacob Milligan, that the county judge was a Pendergast stooge who provided a wholesome facade for the machine's seamy operations.[49]

The machine's efforts for Truman's campaign provided credibility to these charges. Guy Park, the pro-Pendergast governor, pressured state employees to work for, financially contribute to, and vote for Truman in the primary. Combined with WPA job holders, postmasters, and other federal employees, the state employees were a reliable source of votes for Truman.[50] Foster W. Amick, a federal relief official in Independence, forced applicants for public works jobs to sign cards pledging to vote for Truman.[51]

In the primary, 146,966 of the 276,850 votes that Truman received came from Jackson County.[52] In 1936 a state election commission found more than eighty-five thousand ghost votes on the voter registration rolls of Kansas City in that year and approximately sixty thousand for 1934.[53] As usual in Kansas City, the day of the 1934 primaries was characterized by the machine henchmen's use of repeat voters and violence against anti-Pendergast organizations and voters.[54]

Upon entering the Senate in 1935, Truman, tainted by the machine's unscrupulous tactics in his primary campaign, was derisively known as the "Senator from Pendergast" and snubbed by most of his colleagues. They regarded him as a shabby, mediocre political hack. Truman, though, quickly recognized his powers and duties in the Senate as an opportunity to express his reformist values in the New Deal policy agenda.[55]

As a senator, Truman developed a reputation as an amiable, conscientious, border-state senator respected for his integrity and deference to the norms of the Senate, generally supportive of the Roosevelt administration's legislation, and later consulted for his knowledge about railroad and utility regulations.[56] His Democratic friends and political allies ranged from southern conservatives, such as Byron "Pat" Harrison and Tom Connally, to 100 percent New Dealers, such as Sherman Minton and Alben Barkley, and maverick progressives, such as Burton Wheeler, a Montana Democrat who later led the opposition to Roosevelt's court-packing bill in 1937.[57]

Through Max Lowenthal, Truman's staff aide on the Interstate Commerce Committee, the Missouri senator immersed himself in the study of railroad and aviation regulation. Truman would help write the Civil Aeronautics Act of 1938 and later coauthor the Transportation Act of 1940 with Burton Wheeler, his committee's chairman.[58] His research and committee work investigating abusive, monopolistic practices by railroads, banks, insurance companies, as well as other big business interests motivated the once mute, junior senator to unleash fiery, populist rhetoric. In a Senate speech given on June 3, 1937, Truman described the railroads as bigger thieves than Jesse James and his outlaw gang.[59] On December 20 that year, the Missourian gave a speech on the Senate floor denouncing Wall Street and insurance companies. Using biblical allusions, the senator chastised them for centralizing so much wealth and power and contributing to the misery of the Depression.[60]

Earlier, despite lobbying pressure exerted by utility companies allied with the Pendergast machine, Truman voted against amendments weakening the regulatory bill that became the Public Utility Holding Company Act of 1935.[61] As business interests in Missouri and those lobbying in Washington sought to prevent or weaken the regulatory reforms of the New Deal, Truman's liberal, reformist value system became more suspicious and hostile toward the motives, objectives, and even the mere size of big business. Truman, who once aspired to become a wealthy businessman and later prided himself on applying business practices to county government, increasingly perceived national politics and policymaking as a struggle between a Republican party mostly devoted to the protection and promotion of big business interests and a Democratic party whose liberalism would develop and implement reform policies that would empower wage earners, farmers, and small businessmen and provide a broader distribution of wealth and economic and political power.[62]

Throughout his Senate career, this more strident liberal antagonism toward big business would develop a partisan rhetoric for Truman that swayed to the left of Roosevelt's earlier diatribes against "economic royalists." In the 1948 presidential campaign, Truman referred to the GOP as "Gluttons of Privilege," and as a party that "favors the privileged few and not the common everyday man."[63] During his retirement, Truman expressed his outrage in a 1962 memo that the Democratic party would become exclusive and oriented to wealthy elites with John F. Kennedy's adoption of $1,000 a plate fund-raising dinners. "When the party of the People goes high hat on a cost basis, it no longer represents the common everyday man—who is the basis of the Democratic Party."[64]

Truman's liberal reformism was further refined by his extended conversations with Louis Brandeis, a former Supreme Court justice appointed by Woodrow Wilson, one of Truman's presidential mentors and Democratic icons.[65] Introduced to Brandeis by Lowenthal, Truman solidified his respect for the civil liberties of individuals and his belief in reforming the economy through stricter regulations to counteract the power of Wall Street. In a December 13, 1937, letter to his wife, Truman remarked how interested Brandeis was in his committee's work on railroad and insurance company regulations and how honored the Missourian was to be invited to "a rather exclusive and brainy party" at the erudite jurist's home.[66]

Despite his fairly dependable loyalty to the New Deal's social welfare and regulatory policy objectives, Truman felt snubbed by the Roosevelt administration. Senator Bennett Clark of Missouri, a more conservative Democrat, was granted control of most of Missouri's federal appointments by Roosevelt and Chairman James Farley of the Democratic National Committee (DNC).[67] This preference continued even after Clark openly opposed Roosevelt's controversial, unsuccessful "court packing" bill of 1937, while Truman supported it.[68] Taking Truman's vote for granted on its legislation, the Roosevelt administration was startled when it failed to persuade Truman to vote for Alben W. Barkley, a New Deal loyalist, instead of Byron "Pat" Harrison, an increasingly anti–New Deal conservative from Mississippi, as Senate majority leader in 1937.

Truman resented Roosevelt's use of White House lobbyist Tommy Corcoran and Tom Pendergast's intervention to pressure him to support Barkley. Although friendly with both Harrison and Barkley, Truman had decided that the bitter competition for a new Senate majority leader was not a matter of personal friendship or fidelity to New Deal liberalism. It was an internal, institutional decision based on the norms of the Senate subculture. Harrison had more seniority than Barkley, and Truman had previously pledged his vote to the Mississippian. He would not renege on his word.[69]

While some New Deal liberals in the Roosevelt administration and Congress still derided Truman for his machine roots and friendships with conservatives, they were impressed by the national recognition, media praise, and bipartisan respect that he gained as chairman of the Special Committee Investigating the National Defense Program.[70] More commonly known as the Truman committee, it investigated and revealed waste, fraud, and mismanagement in defense contracts and submitted recommended reforms for Congress and the Roosevelt administration.[71] The committee estimated that its activities saved $15 billion and countless lives.[72] In chairing this committee, Truman applied his liberal, reformist value system. Specifically, he combined his 1920s good-government belief in using administrative reforms to inspire efficiency in the cost and quality of government purchases with his growing populist rage against what he regarded as abusive, cynical practices by large corporations receiving defense contracts.[73] As a veteran and an anti–Wall Street populist, Truman was horrified to learn that some defense contractors fraudulently sold defective airplanes and spare parts at excessive prices.[74] Like Roosevelt, Truman feared a sharp, permanent growth in the economic power and political influence of major defense contractors because of the war boom.[75]

Far from the Pendergast machine in Kansas City, Truman enjoyed the discretion to carve out a policy specialty in the New Deal and distinguish himself as a leading border state conciliator among the increasingly factionalized Democratic senators. But he was still grateful to his machine mentor and was careful to defer to Boss Tom on federal appointments and the distribution of New Deal relief funds and public-works projects and jobs in Missouri.[76] This political arrangement with the Pendergast machine paralleled his career as presiding judge, during which he impressed the voters with more efficient county services and high-quality public construction accomplishments while granting patronage and most contracts to machine-favored companies (especially Boss Tom's concrete and oil companies) and relying on the machine for his votes in Kansas City. As a senator with no strong personal following throughout his state, it appeared that the Pendergast machine, its resources, and its state-wide alliances would be just as indispensable for Truman's renomination campaign in 1940 as they had been in the 1934 primary.

Consequently, Harry Truman's value system as a party regular and organization Democrat was confronted with its greatest challenges from 1938 to 1940. After the 1936 election, Democratic governor Lloyd Stark, who had been rebuffed by Tom Pendergast in 1932 when Stark sought the boss's endorsement for governor, began a relentless and eventually successful effort to destroy Boss Tom and his machine through a state investigation of ballot and insurance fraud. Sensing that the political power in the Missouri Democracy was shifting toward Stark, Roosevelt directed U.S. Attorney Maurice Milligan and the Bureau of Internal Revenue (BIR) to aggressively investigate and prosecute Tom Pendergast and leading machine members for ballot fraud and income tax violations.[77] Boss Tom was in prison by 1939, an anti-machine ticket was subsequently elected to Kansas City's municipal offices, and Truman's renomination and reelection in 1940 seemed hopeless.

Truman's reputation in the Senate had gradually emerged from that of a colorless machine hack to a sincere, diligent, liberal reformer in regulatory policy and, therefore, an asset to the New Deal. But Truman vehemently manifested his competing ethos as a party regular when he refused to disassociate himself from the dying Kansas City machine. As Truman's Senate speeches in 1937 denouncing the greed and monopolistic practices of railroads and insurance companies expressed his reformist values, his speech of February 15, 1938, revealed most clearly his unyielding belief in and loyalty to the now crumbling, irreparably discredited machine to which he owed his Senate seat.

Privately, Truman had already tried to dissuade Roosevelt from reappointing Maurice Milligan as U.S. Attorney for western Missouri. After promising the president that he would not ask his Senate colleagues to reject Milligan as a senatorial privilege, Truman delivered a speech accusing the Republican federal judges of Kansas City of being motivated by partisan vengeance and Maurice Milligan of being corrupt.[78] Truman dramatically concluded "that a Jackson County Democrat has as much chance of a fair trial in the Federal District Court of Western Missouri as a Jew would have in a Hitler court or a Trotsky follower before Stalin."[79] Shortly thereafter, with the imprisoned, ailing Tom Pendergast powerless, Truman even asked Burton Wheeler if he should resign instead of completing his term in the Senate.[80]

Truman realized that he needed to develop a new strategy and coalition of allies in order to be renominated in 1940.[81] Fortunately for Truman, the anti-Pendergast voters in the Democratic senatorial primary were divided between Maurice Milligan and Governor Lloyd Stark. To win this raucous, highly competitive primary, Truman had to fully benefit from his pro–New Deal Senate record. Also, Truman had to distinguish his fairly liberal policy behavior and rhetoric from that of his more conservative colleague from Missouri, Bennett Clark, while also gaining Clark's support or at least his neutrality in the primary race.

Truman's state-wide foundation of active campaign support in 1940 consisted of Works Progress Administration officials, many of whom also served as chairmen or members of Democratic state, county, and precinct committees.[82] These officials and other Truman allies and friends, such as two of his military associates, Harry Vaughan and John Snyder, met at the Statler Hotel in St. Louis in January 1940.[83] Harry Easley, who served as personnel director of the WPA in Missouri, organized this meeting and recognized that Truman had been "in a position to pretty well set up the WPA organization in Missouri, and most of the people in key positions were Truman people when it came to the showdown."[84] Jimmy Miller, one participant at this meeting, assured Easley, "We vote them out where I live like a machine."[85]

Strong campaign support for Truman by WPA employees, however, was a limited campaign asset. As a reaction against the political exploitation of the WPA in 1938 campaigns, the Hatch Act of 1939 imposed limitations and prohibitions on the political activities and campaign contributions of federal employees. While the *St. Louis Post-Dispatch* later accused Harry Vaughan, the Truman campaign's treasurer, of illegally soliciting contributions from WPA employees, Truman's campaign literature urged Missouri Democrats not to violate the Hatch Act.[86]

Truman also located a major campaign headquarters in St. Louis, partially to seek electoral support from that city's ward leaders. For the purposes of voter mobilization, the two leading Democrats in St. Louis were Mayor Bernard Dickmann and Robert E. Hannegan, chairman of the St. Louis Democratic Committee.[87] Dickmann and Hannegan supported Stark for senator but were concentrating their campaign efforts on the gubernatorial candidacy of Larry McDaniel. Dickmann and Hannegan finally and suddenly switched their endorsements and voter mobilization to Truman shortly before the August 6 primary.

Other than the desire of Dickmann and Hannegan to secure support for McDaniel from pro-Truman voters and politicians, they eventually swung the electoral support of their machine-controlled wards to Truman because of pressure from Senator Bennett Clark. Victor Messall, Truman's secretary and campaign chairman, had failed to persuade Clark to actively support Truman's renomination either through speeches or Clark's influence over voting blocs and factional leaders. Clark's initial apathy toward Truman's apparently inevitable defeat was not surprising.[88] While Truman had remained a steadfast New Dealer, Clark had become increasingly conservative and antagonistic toward further liberal legislation since the 1936 election.

Senator Carl Hatch of New Mexico, though, succeeded in persuading Clark to openly endorse Truman through speeches and to secure Hannegan's and Dickmann's electoral support for Truman. Hatch's intervention on Truman's behalf illustrated another crucial element of his successful campaign strategy—the vigorous assistance of his Senate allies. In addition to Hatch, Senators Alben Barkley, Sherman Minton, and Lewis Schwellenbach traveled to Missouri and urged voters to renominate Truman as a senator who was instrumental in supporting and furthering New Deal policies for the nation's welfare.[89] Likewise, Max Lowenthal, Truman's chief aide on the Interstate Commerce Committee, successfully lobbied A.F. Whitney, president of the Brotherhood of Railroad Trainmen, to provide campaign contributions, a voter mobilization drive, and promotion of Truman's candidacy in *Labor,* his union's newspaper. While other unions endorsed Truman and urged their members to vote for him, the railroad unions were most active and effective in their support for Truman.[90]

The intervention by Truman's Senate colleagues and A.F. Whitney reminded Missourians that Truman was no longer derided and dismissed in Washington as the "Senator from Pendergast." Truman's ethos and skills as a liberal New Deal reformer and as a conciliatory, border-state senator were highly valued in the Senate and by a major interest group of the New Deal coalition, organized labor. In addition to campaign support from his fellow senators, labor unions, farm organizations, and the machine-controlled wards of St. Louis, black voters constituted the final foundation of Truman's campaign strategy.

Harry Truman had to carefully and tactfully solicit the votes of black Missourians. He especially could not risk alienating white Democrats in southeastern Missouri, probably the most culturally southern region of the state concerning race relations. On June 15, 1940, Truman officially began his primary campaign by delivering a speech on civil rights in Sedalia, Missouri. The senator asserted government's obligation to protect blacks from lynching and other mob violence and specified how New Deal policies had improved education and employment for blacks. Truman was careful, though, not to imply support for racial integration.[91] One month later, Truman addressed an organization of black Democrats in Chicago and clarified this distinction. "I am not appealing for social equality of the Negro. . . . Negroes want justice, not social relations."[92] With endorsements from the *Call,* a major black newspaper in Missouri, and the delivery of heavily black wards in St. Louis by Dickmann and Hannegan, Truman received the bulk of black votes in the primary.[93]

Truman won a plurality in the Democratic senatorial primary of August 6, 1940, by a margin of 7,976 votes.[94] Evidently, the most important ingredient of Truman's primary victory was the support of Hannegan and Dickmann. Truman carried fourteen wards in St. Louis, enabling him to carry that city by 8,411 votes.[95] With the demise of the Pendergast machine, Truman won a plurality of about twenty thousand votes in Jackson County, in sharp contrast to the more than one-hundred-thousand-vote margin that he had received there in 1934.[96]

A few days after the primary, Truman was greeted in the Senate by colleagues who enthusiastically congratulated him. To his wife, he wrote: "Both floor leaders and all the Democrats made a grand rush. . . . I thought Wheeler and Jim Byrnes were going to kiss me."[97] Truman enjoyed the greater status, recognition, and, in particular, the greater independence from his Pendergast roots that his primary victory had given him. In a letter to his wife written on September 15, 1940, Truman asserted his pride in his proven vote-getting skills. "I've spent my life pleasing people, doing things for 'em, and putting myself in embarrassing positions to save the party and the other fellow, now I've quit. To hell with 'em all. Now I feel better anyway."[98]

The remainder of Truman's prepresidential career, however, did not reveal the defiant independence from his ethos as a party regular that this letter suggests. After all, the basis of Truman's network of campaign workers was formed by his shrewd distribution of WPA patronage to Democratic committee chairmen throughout Missouri. One month after Truman's primary victory, Dorsey H. Watson, chairman of the Jasper County Democratic Central Committee, wrote to the senator, "In return for our united efforts in your behalf, our committee organization has only this to ask; that after your election, you cooperate and work with our organization on matters of patronage."[99] One week later, Truman replied to Watson, "I don't belong to the class of public officials who forgets the Democrats after the election.[100] As Harry Truman continued to reward Democrats actively loyal to him, his values and behavior as a party regular continued to both advance and limit his political career.

Reelected to the Senate by a margin of less than forty-five thousand votes, Truman turned his attention to the investigation of defense contracts.[101] Truman, as the chairman of this select committee, received most of the favorable analyses and national recognition from the press.[102] Especially after the United States entered World War II and defense spending rapidly increased—along with public concern about waste, fraud, and inefficiency by national defense contractors—Truman's image evolved from that of a bland, docile party hack beholden to machine politicians for his Senate seat to that of a scrupulously impartial, judicious, and respected yet unassuming Senate leader who quietly and diligently served the war effort without self-promoting grandstanding. Devoting a cover story to Harry Truman's investigatory success, *Time* concluded in a 1943 issue that "Harry Truman and his committee . . . seemed the best living proof that democracy, even when imperfect, can be a success."[103]

Truman's chairmanship of this select committee was one of the clearest and most complete examples of his reformist value systems. Just as he had done with his well-planned and expertly executed road-building and courthouse projects as a county judge, Truman manifested his "good government" ethos. The Missouri Democrat made sure that his fellow committee members and their staffs be impartial and accurate in their research, hearings, and recommendations. Big business, small business, labor unions, federal agencies, and even the president were not exempt from the Truman committee's inquiries and constructive criticisms in the conduct of defense contracts.[104] In particular, the Truman committee criticized the president's use of "dollar a year" business executives serving in federal agencies because of the frequent conflicts of interest concerning the receipt of defense contracts.[105] Journalists Robert S. Allen and William V. Shannon claim that Truman was well suited to chair this particular committee because "Truman was a regular Democrat with whom the people in the executive offices could readily cooperate, but at the same time he could safely criticize the administration on grounds of war efficiency without seeming to attack the President or incurring his wrath."[106]

The bipartisan respect and national recognition that Truman received as an investigator, however, did not diminish his attitudes and behavior as a regular Democrat in intraparty affairs. Besides continuing to concern himself with the electoral health and internal harmony of the Missouri Democratic party, Truman became more assertive and persistent in seeking the intervention of the Democratic national chairman. By doing so, the Missouri senator was more frank in his criticism of the president for neglecting himself and other New Deal liberals in his state regarding patronage as Republican electoral strength grew there since 1940. In a 1941 letter to DNC Chairman Edward J. Flynn, Truman complained to Flynn about Roosevelt's apparent favoritism toward Senator Bennett Clark and other conservative Democrats regarding federal patronage. According to Truman, Roosevelt "has done everything possible to break up any organization of Missouri liberals" and "never has been able to appreciate that the majority of Democrats in Missouri are liberal and are for him."[107]

Despite Truman's more open criticism of Roosevelt's party leadership, Roosevelt began to grant a larger share of federal patronage to Truman as the senator's national and institutional status grew.[108] As Frank Walker prepared to resign as Democratic national chairman at the end of 1943, Roosevelt first asked Truman to succeed Walker. After discussing this offer with Senator Carl Hatch of New Mexico and other Democratic senators, Truman declined Roosevelt's offer and suggested Bob Hannegan as the next Democratic national chairman.[109]

Grateful for Hannegan's mobilization of crucial votes for him in the 1940 senatorial primary and impressed by the St. Louis Democrat's political acumen, Truman secured Hannegan's appointment as collector of internal revenue for eastern Missouri in 1942 and as Commissioner of Internal Revenue in 1943.[110] A few days after Hannegan's election as DNC chairman on January 22, 1944, the *St. Louis Post-Dispatch* already perceived a link between Hannegan's new position and the possibility of Harry Truman becoming vice president, since Hannegan's chairmanship "boosts Truman's stock for the vice presidential nomination."[111]

TRUMAN AND THE VICE PRESIDENCY

As early as March 2, 1943, Harry Truman felt compelled to assert to a Chicago journalist that he was not seeking the vice presidency in 1944 and that he was "not a candidate for anything but reelection to the United States Senate in 1946, and I am announcing that right now."[112] Publicly, Truman always insisted that he did not seek the vice presidency and that he had promised to support Jimmy Byrnes, director of the Office of War Mobilization, for this office.[113] Truman always claimed that he only reluctantly agreed to be Roosevelt's running mate after the president virtually insisted that Truman accept the vice presidential nomination as a wartime duty to his party and nation.

By contrast, some scholars and journalists, especially those unfavorable to Truman, have portrayed Truman as shrewdly and duplicitously building support for his nomination at the 1944 Democratic national convention while dividing and minimizing delegate support for Jimmy Byrnes, Sam Rayburn, and Alben Barkley by publicly encouraging their candidacies.[114] While not attributing any devious or ruthless qualities, some of Truman's Missouri friends and political associates, such as Harry Easley and Victor Messall, claimed that the senator had wanted and sought the vice presidential nomination long before Roosevelt's offer during the July 1944 Democratic national convention.[115]

Sam Wear, whom Truman appointed as U.S. attorney for western Missouri in May 1945, later wrote, "I was in Washington in March, 1944, and was told by some of then-Senator Truman's staff, that the Senator was going to be nominated for vice-president."[116]

This perception of Truman as an ambitious, calculating candidate for the vice presidential nomination regards his efforts to have Hannegan chosen as DNC chairman as an example of his machinations, since Hannegan proceeded to promote Truman by scheduling him to speak at Democratic state conventions and fund raising dinners.[117] New Deal liberals who disliked Truman later suspected that Hannegan and such leading party regulars as Frank Walker and Edward Flynn, his predecessors as DNC chairman, Edwin Pauley, the DNC's secretary-treasurer, and machine bosses Edward Kelly and Frank Hague pressured an ailing and internationally preoccupied Franklin D. Roosevelt to dump Henry Wallace as vice president and replace him with a mediocre party hack amenable to their interests.[118] Senator Claude Pepper of Florida, a Wallace ally, claimed that Hannegan manipulated Roosevelt and the conduct of the 1944 Democratic national convention in order to "put over his crony Truman."[119]

Both Truman's argument that he was an unwilling, passive actor who did nothing to promote his candidacy for vice president and the anti-Truman thesis that Truman and Roosevelt were pawns manipulated by an inner circle of party regulars are somewhat inaccurate and misleading.[120] Truman's written and spoken words in 1943 and 1944 rejecting any interest in the vice presidency were contradicted by his intraparty behavior during this time period. Truman increased his name recognition and stature among organization Democrats by regularly addressing Democratic state conventions and fund-raising dinners. Truman rarely rejected speaking engagements that Bob Hannegan arranged for him.[121] Edwin Pauley, a wealthy California oil executive and secretary-treasurer of the DNC, especially valued Truman's popularity as a speaker with Democratic state leaders and financial contributors.[122]

A more complex yet persuasive explanation of Harry Truman's role in his selection as the Democratic vice-presidential nominee of 1944 is that Truman, however hesitantly and ambivalently, increased his appeal as a running mate through these speaking engagements and kept himself available for the nomination despite his frequent statements of disinterest. By being coy and discreet about his ambitions, Truman made himself more attractive to Roosevelt than the brazenly opportunistic Jimmy Byrnes.[123] Despite his claim that Roosevelt had initially preferred him as the Democratic vice presidential nominee of 1944, Byrnes overlooks the fact that Roosevelt had rejected him as a running mate for the 1940 campaign because Byrnes, as an ex-Catholic Southerner, was perceived as unacceptable to many Catholics, blacks, and union members.[124]

Furthermore, the role of Franklin D. Roosevelt as an active, deliberative, cognizant, and calculating decision maker in the selection of Harry Truman should not be underestimated. Several accounts of Truman's selection as Democratic vice presidential nominee portray Roosevelt as so ill and preoccupied with the military strategy and diplomacy of World War II that he apathetically deferred this important decision to a clique of party insiders led by Bob Hannegan.[125] Roosevelt's rhetoric and behavior as a presidential party leader clearly indicated that he wanted the Democratic party to endure as an electorally successful, distinctly liberal majority party after his presidency.[126]

This desire required the replacement of Henry Wallace with a New Deal liberal who was a proven vote-getter and respected by Democrats in Congress, especially in the Senate, for the purpose of treaty ratification. Despite Henry Wallace's sincere liberal convictions and political following among Congress of Industrial Organization (CIO) union members and liberal intellectuals, he had become a political liability to Roosevelt.[127] As president of the Senate, Wallace had little influence over the Senate's legislative behavior, especially when Roosevelt lost some major Senate votes.[128] Eccentric, politically inept, and expressing a tendency for publicly airing conflicts with fellow Democrats, Wallace had especially embarrassed Roosevelt in 1943, when the vice president publicly criticized Secretary of Commerce Jesse Jones's policies.[129]

Consequently, Hannegan and other party insiders did not have to induce Roosevelt to dump Henry Wallace. They merely had to confirm his already existing desire.[130] Ed Pauley took the initiative in providing this confirmation.[131] Realizing how unpopular Wallace was with DNC contributors and Democrats who would control delegate blocs at the 1944 convention, Pauley made an arrangement with Edwin "Pa" Watson, Roosevelt's appointments secretary. Watson gave anti-Wallace delegates, whom Pauley recommended, invitations to see Roosevelt and urge that Wallace not be renominated.[132] As for Wallace's replacement, Pauley, Flynn, and other members of the "dump Wallace" clique concluded that a southern running mate would not be feasible because of black voters.

Even North Carolina newspaper publisher Josephus Daniels, who was Roosevelt's superior as secretary of the navy during World War I, wrote to the president that "it will not be deemed good politics to place a Southernor [*sic*] in the ticket this year, in view of the tricky race question."[133] This consideration helped to disqualify the three most likely southern running mates—Jimmy Byrnes, Speaker of the House Sam Rayburn of Texas, and Senate majority leader Alben Barkley of Kentucky.[134] For Rayburn, there was the additional liability that Texas Democrats were so rancorously divided in choosing delegates for the national convention that Rayburn could not even control his own state's delegate votes.[135] Barkley was a reliable New Deal liberal whose legislative record on antilynching, the poll tax, and the Fair Employment Practices Committee was acceptable to blacks. The Kentucky senator, though, had embarrassed Roosevelt in 1943 by opposing the president's veto of a tax relief bill and was derided by many southern senators as Roosevelt's lap dog.[136]

Roosevelt casually mentioned Supreme Court Justice William O. Douglas as a possible running mate because of the jurist's youth and cerebral liberalism.[137] Douglas was preferred by Sidney Hillman, vice president of the CIO, as a replacement for Wallace. Despite his personal affection for Douglas, Roosevelt had enough political acumen to realize that the jurist would have little appeal to the delegates, most of whom would be party regulars. Thus, regardless of whether the President definitely implied a preference for Truman in the letter that he gave Hannegan stating that he would be "very glad" to run with either Truman or Douglas, this letter was a vital asset to Hannegan and his allies in organizing delegate votes behind Truman.[138]

Roosevelt's selection of Truman as a consciously chosen running mate, rather than as a compromise candidate hastily foisted upon an indifferent president, is bolstered by a comment that Harry Hopkins made to his biographer, Robert Sherwood. Hopkins, the former WPA administrator and one of Roosevelt's closest confidantes, stated: "People seemed to think that Truman was just pulled out of a hat—but that wasn't true. The President had had his eye on him for a long time."[139] Hopkins especially emphasized the favorable publicity and accomplishments of the Truman committee and Truman's presumed ability as a vice president who would help gain Senate ratification of postwar treaties because of his popularity in the Senate.[140]

Hopkins's analysis corresponds with Roosevelt's primary reason for denying renomination to Henry Wallace. Wallace had proven himself to be an unpopular and ineffective president of the Senate for administration bills. Also, Truman, unlike Wallace, had proven himself to be an impressive vote-getter in his upset victory in the 1940 Missouri primary, a campaign in which Roosevelt implicitly supported Lloyd Stark and assumed that Truman would not win. Truman's legislative record would be acceptable to all major liberal interest groups and voting blocs in the Democratic party—organized labor, blacks, and urban ethnics. Despite his voting record on race-related legislation, Truman's border-state origins and his popularity among southerners in the Senate would deter any significant opposition to his nomination from southern delegates.

In short, Harry Truman was far more than merely the least objectionable running mate who would do the least damage to Roosevelt's reelection campaign. The Missouri senator could satisfy the numerous and conflicting needs that a new vice president had to fulfill better than any other prospective candidate.[141] Harry Truman's value systems and political behavior as both a party regular and liberal reformer had served his own ambition and the political needs of Roosevelt's party leadership equally well.

For his part, Truman behaved more cautiously and shrewdly about discerning Roosevelt's actual intentions and the probability of his vice presidential nomination than Byrnes, Barkley, and Wallace had. Truman understood that a statement from Roosevelt merely claiming that Roosevelt would be happy to have him as a running mate did not mean that Roosevelt had definitely and exclusively chosen him and that his nomination by the delegates was assured.[142] During his nearly ten-year Senate career, Truman had become jaded about how complex, contradictory, evasive, and even duplicitous Roosevelt could be in his decision making as a party leader.[143]

Consequently, Truman waited at the 1944 Democratic convention in Chicago until Roosevelt virtually insisted by telephone that Truman be his running mate and until delegate support for Henry Wallace and other rivals subsided enough so that he would most likely be nominated for vice president.[144] After a rousing and aggressive pro-Wallace demonstration was instigated by CIO activists at the convention, Ed Kelly and Ed Flynn asked CIO President Philip Murray to inform Truman that he may have to withdraw his vice presidential candidacy. Truman reputedly told Murray: "I know what you want me to do, and I'm not going to do it. There is no use talking about it. I'm not going to withdraw."[145] However hesitant and ambivalent Truman appeared before Roosevelt's phone call, he was determined not to relinquish the vice presidential candidacy once he accepted it.

THE 1944 CAMPAIGN AND VICE PRESIDENCY

Because Roosevelt only gave eight major campaign speeches and concentrated on the war effort, vice presidential nominee Harry Truman served as an important spokesman and defender of Roosevelt's record after the 1944 national conventions. During an August 18 lunch, Roosevelt briefly discussed the campaign with Truman. The Missourian wrote his wife that Roosevelt "gave me a lot of hooey about what I could do to help the campaign and said he thought I ought to go home for an official notification and then go to Detroit for a labor speech and make no more engagements until we had had another conference."[146] Throughout the general election campaign, however, Roosevelt gave Truman little direction. Bob Hannegan, the DNC staff, and two of Truman's

Senate committee aides, Hugh Fulton and Matthew Connelly, scheduled the candidate's train trips and helped him prepare speeches.[147] Truman's campaign speeches in 1944 were often fairly predictable, cautiously worded addresses that emphasized the need to maintain the continuity and success of American foreign policy by reelecting Roosevelt.[148]

The Republican campaign and journalists hostile to Roosevelt and Truman exploited Truman's greatest political liability—his affiliation with the notorious and discredited Pendergast machine.[149] Responding to this criticism about his machine origins, Truman frankly and proudly admitted his Pendergast affiliation.[150] Instead of being grudgingly complimented for his honesty, Truman was denounced for being blatantly cynical about his machine roots. An editorial in the *Pittsburgh Sun-Telegraph* stated, "It is the utter CYNICISM of Senator Truman that discredits and disqualifies him. . . . Political morality and honesty do not consist merely of candor and frankness."[151] Columnist Westbrook Pegler, after commenting on the vices and electoral fraud of the Pendergast machine, argued that if the Roosevelt-Truman ticket won and Roosevelt died in office, "his successor would be a man of the same, if not possibly lower, moral and ethical standards, equipped by character and experience to carry on the New Deal in the same contempt for decency in politics and office."[152]

Truman subsequently avoided any more public statements about his association with the Pendergast machine. Truman publicly expressed one of the strongest principles of his ethos as a party regular—his unequivocal and everlasting gratitude and loyalty to the machine boss and organization that had developed his political career. This principle was certainly a crucial factor in the promotion of Truman's vice presidential nomination by the inner circle of machine bosses and current and former DNC officials who advised Roosevelt. Biographer David McCullough wrote, "Again at Chicago, as so consistently through the Truman career, it had been the system of politics, the boss system, that counted in deciding his fate."[153]

As a party regular, Truman revealed a certain naïveté by assuming that he could convince the press and public opinion that he could be affiliated with and politically supported by a notorious machine without compromising his personal integrity and his competing value system as a liberal reformer. A skeptical public and press wondered why the Pendergast machine—infamous for graft, bloated payrolls of patronage jobs, protection of vice rackets, and electoral fraud—would nurture Harry Truman's political career and never ask him, as Truman claimed, "to do a dishonest deed."[154] Maintaining this loyalty, though, was not easy for Truman. According to Margaret Truman, her father "never revealed the inner agony he suffered as he struggled to retain his principles and at the same time build a political career within the domain of Boss Tom Pendergast."[155]

Harry Truman's election to the vice presidency signified the complete independence of his political career from the Pendergast machine. Truman, nonetheless, refused to ignore his machine roots when Tom Pendergast died six days after he became vice president in January 1945. The vice president dramatically illustrated his eternal gratitude and affection for the deceased, deserted, and convicted boss by attending Pendergast's funeral, despite widespread criticism.[156]

During his brief vice presidency, Truman capably served one of Roosevelt's requirements in choosing his last vice president—an effective liaison between the White House and Senate while presiding over that chamber. Truman's most difficult legislative task as president of the Senate was the Senate confirmation of Henry Wallace as the next secretary of commerce.[157] Roosevelt wanted to both remove Jesse Jones, a conservative Texas banker, from this position and compensate Henry Wallace for the termination of his vice presidency.[158] As Truman actively lobbied senators for Wallace, the fulfillment of Truman's task was threatened by a coalition of conservative Democrats and Republicans who distrusted the ultraliberal Wallace's economic views, especially since the secretary of commerce also served as federal loan administrator.[159] After Senator Walter George introduced legislation separating these two positions, Truman was able to assure Wallace's confirmation.[160]

TRANSITION TO PARTY LEADERSHIP

While Roosevelt expected Truman to cultivate and organize support in the Senate for the treaties and domestic legislation that he anticipated after the war, he rarely informed the vice president of crucial policy matters.[161] Truman felt uneasy about his lack of preparation and knowledge, given the possibility that he might suddenly succeed Franklin D. Roosevelt. During the 1944 campaign, Truman confided to his World War I army buddy Eddie McKim that the prospect of soon becoming president "scares the hell out of me."[162] Shortly after his inauguration as president on April 12, 1945, Harry Truman diligently educated himself on his new duties and sought to assure the public that there would be continuity with Roosevelt's foreign and domestic policies.[163]

As Harry Truman struggled to master his tasks as an international leader and an economic manager in the immediate postwar era, he was more confident in his ability to serve as presidential party leader. His two political value systems as a party regular and a liberal reformer provided a guiding foundation for his perceptions, decisions, and behavioral patterns as a party leader. These two value systems, though, would alternate between complementing and conflicting with each other.

Matthew Connelly served as Truman's appointments secretary and unofficial liaison with party regulars. He summarized Truman's values as a party regular in 1968: Truman "believed that you had to be a member of a party or you could stay out of it. He liked political organization. . . . And he didn't like so-called independent groups."[164]

As a liberal reformer, however, Truman spent his first few years as presidential party leader trying to satisfy and co-opt liberal intellectuals, activists, and Roosevelt administration members who disdained Truman or at least doubted the sincerity and efficacy of his liberalism.[165] As a presidential party leader socialized in and influenced by the party regular values of unconditional party loyalty, the widespread use of patronage to reward services to the party, and backing for strong party organization, Harry Truman assumed that he would enjoy the loyalty and political support of the big-city machine bosses who shared these values.[166] Unfortunately for Truman, most machine bosses would prove to be less loyal and supportive of his party leadership than he had hoped.[167]

2

☆ ☆ ☆ ☆ ☆

TRUMAN AND THE MACHINE BOSSES

As a young Democratic politician, Franklin D. Roosevelt had entered politics as an antimachine progressive crusader with a rural orientation in his policy emphasis. But as a president and party leader, Roosevelt developed symbiotic political and programmatic relationships with the Democratic mayors of major cities.[1] By the end of his presidency, it was clear that nationally prominent Democratic machine bosses and their working-class constituents were the most loyal and politically effective supporters of the type of liberal, inclusive, pluralistic, electorally successful Democratic party that Roosevelt sought to develop. The voting results of the 1932 and 1944 presidential elections revealed that the percentage of Roosevelt's winning plurality of votes derived from the nation's twelve largest cities had increased from 25 percent to 65 percent.[2]

FDR, HST, AND THE BOSSES

A major factor in Roosevelt's choice of a running mate in 1944 was the appeasement of Democratic machine bosses and urban policy interests. Most major machine bosses—including Ed Kelly of Chicago, Ed Flynn of the Bronx, Frank Hague of Jersey City, and David Lawrence of Pittsburgh—actively promoted Truman's vice presidential candidacy at the Democratic National Convention.

In addition to the economic benefits that Roosevelt's domestic policies had provided to their cities and working-class constituents, Democratic machine bosses highly valued Roosevelt's status as a proven vote-getter to provide coattail effects to their Democratic candidates.[3] The machine bosses readily recognized Harry Truman's importance as a running mate who was acceptable to their constituents and other major Democratic interest groups and voting blocs. Likewise, it is not surprising that early in 1948 certain Democratic machine bosses sought to deny Truman renomination when they concluded that his presidential candidacy would lose votes for their Democratic slates.

Upon Harry Truman's assumption of the presidency in 1945, however, he appeared to be the ideal president and party leader from the perspective of most Democratic bosses.[4] More so than that of any other president in the twentieth century, Truman's career path was influenced and advanced by machine politics. No matter how controversial and notorious the Pendergast machine had been, Truman never dissociated himself from it. He was always grateful for this machine's crucial organizational and voter mobilization resources, which enabled him to become a county judge and U.S. senator. As a senator, Truman accepted and understood his transactional relationship with the Pendergast machine in which he supported New Deal programs beneficial to Kansas City and urban policy interests in general and tried to discourage an aggressive federal investigation and prosecution of Tom Pendergast and the machine members.

In short, Truman, unlike Roosevelt, not only favored liberal domestic policies that helped the cities and electoral coalitions of the Democratic bosses but also shared their values and experiences as a party regular and machine politician. Roosevelt had occasionally circumvented the Democratic party by implicitly supporting maverick liberal Republicans like Fiorello LaGuardia and the formation of a leftist minor party in New York, the American Labor party, in order to promote or satisfy liberal electoral or programmatic needs. Furthermore, Roosevelt had not declined to vigorously apply the full investigatory and prosecutorial powers of the Justice and Treasury departments against Democratic bosses, such as Tom Pendergast and James Michael Curley of Boston, after he regarded them as liabilities.[5] It was reasonable, therefore, for the Democratic bosses to assume that Harry Truman as president and titular leader of the Democratic party would behave more loyally and predictably as a party regular in these matters and in the distribution of federal patronage.

FEDERAL-URBAN RELATIONS

Even by the end of Franklin D. Roosevelt's presidency, it was clear that a Democratic president could no longer sustain harmonious, mutually advantageous political relationships with the Democratic mayors and voters of major cities simply through a shrewd distribution of federal patronage, financial aid, and broad discretion to local governments in the implementation of urban-oriented federal programs, such as public housing. World War II had rapidly imposed policy burdens and stresses on major cities that were staggering in number, severity, and complexity. Machine-run cities, such as Chicago and Pittsburgh, that were major industrial centers experienced sharp increases in population. In particular, blacks and poor whites from the South migrated to northeastern and midwestern cities due to the attraction of defense plant jobs.[6] During the war, support for federal civil rights legislation became a higher priority for the bosses as their cities' populations became increasingly black while racial conflicts grew and occasionally, as in Detroit in 1943, led to riots.[7]

Besides the sharp growth and changing racial composition of their cities' populations, the urban leaders faced a myriad of rising policy needs in public health, education, police protection, sanitation, mass transit, zoning for new industries, water and sewer systems, and housing. The end of the war only interrupted and complicated the programmatic and political responsibilities of big city mayors as millions of returning veterans began families and sought scarce housing and jobs while most of the recently arrived, former defense industry workers and their families remained. Democratic mayors and the Truman administration realized that cooperative federalism—which had emerged during the New Deal in order to enable local governments and their neediest residents to survive the Great Depression—would not end, even though the nation was relatively prosperous in the immediate postwar era. It became increasingly evident that urban residents, especially the younger, better educated veterans, were demanding that the domestic policies and leadership of cooperative federalism improve conditions in public education, housing, employment, health care, and urban redevelopment and planning both quantitatively and qualitatively. Dissatisfaction among these urban voters in particular contributed to certain Republican congressional victories in 1946, the decision of Jacob Arvey and other Chicago Democratic machine politicians to deny renomination to mayor Ed Kelly in 1947, and the decline of the Hague machine in Jersey City.[8]

In general, more domestic policy matters that had once been regarded as mostly or entirely the concerns of state and local governments were now regarded by the Truman administration as permanent national political responsibilities that the federal government would share with state and local governments. In his 1946 State of the Union Address, Harry Truman announced, "Specifically, the Federal Government should aid state and local governments in planning their own public works programs, in undertaking projects related to Federal programs of regional development, and in constructing such public works as are necessary to carry out the various policies of the Federal Government."[9]

Thus, the federal government would not merely provide financial aid to cities. It would also seek to improve policy expertise and guidance to the cities in urban planning, urban redevelopment (later renamed urban renewal by the

Eisenhower administration), public housing, and the development of highway systems connecting major cities to their rapidly growing suburban communities.[10] More broadly, the federal government's role under Truman in cooperative federalism had evolved to the point that it regarded the major cities' quality of public infrastructure, living conditions of its residents, and economic health to be issues of national interest. It felt obliged to fulfill an active role as an equal partner in policy formation and leadership with state and local governments.

The most astute major Democratic machines during the Truman presidency, namely those of Chicago and Pittsburgh, understood and used this changing federal-city relationship to bolster their political longevity by adapting to and exploiting this greater federal intervention rather than resisting it and perceiving it as a threat to their local political power. The growth and diversification of federal aid after World War II enabled the Chicago and Pittsburgh machines in particular to satisfy the social welfare, public employment, and public housing needs of lower-income constituents. Simultaneously, it helped meet the demands of home owners and business interests for fewer property-tax increases, urban renewal, and structural improvements conducive to commerce and industry.[11] While greater federal funding to cities was accompanied by greater federal requirements for compliance with regulations and oversight, shrewder big city mayors capitalized on their new roles as implementers of new federal programs for their constituents and as brokers between their constituents and federal officials.[12] Steven Erie convincingly revealed that after World War II "machine building required vertical alliances to sympathetic state and national leaders . . . in order to monopolize public sector resources, starve factional opponents, and reward party functionaries and voters."[13]

In addition to being the only major Fair Deal policy proposal to become law, the Housing Act of 1949 was the most significant form of federal aid to urban governments that illustrated the growth of federal intervention in cities during the Truman administration. Sponsored by Senator Robert Wagner, a Tammany Hall Democrat, the Housing Act of 1937 created the U.S. Housing Authority to oversee the construction and management of federally funded public housing and to assist local governments in slum clearance.[14] This 1937 law further stipulated that each unit of slum housing demolished had to be replaced with one unit of public housing.

However, the potential of the Housing Act of 1937 for revolutionizing the role of the federal government in public housing and, more broadly, in helping local governments reduce poverty and urban blight, was severely diminished by inadequate appropriations from Congress and effective lobbying by real estate and construction interests against the building of a significant level of public housing.[15] Furthermore, local governments were reluctant to engage in the slum clearance provision of the 1937 law because of the strict unit-per-unit replacement provision regarding public housing. This replacement provision was not included in the Housing Act of 1949.[16]

Besides the omission of a unit-per-unit replacement requirement, the 1949 housing law's wording and policy content reflected the compromises that were made due to bipartisan cooperation and concessions to real estate and construction interests. Led by Senator Robert A. Taft of Ohio, Republicans in Congress who supported this legislation wanted to ensure that federally funded public housing would not interfere with the construction, sale, and rental of private housing. Southern Democrats in Congress ensured that the law's wording would implicitly allow the racial segregation of public housing residents by local housing authorities. Cities had to submit detailed project proposals that complied with their master plans for long-term planning in order to receive federal funds for slum clearance and urban redevelopment under this 1949 statute. But broad discretion was granted to local governments and business interests in the formulation of project proposals.[17]

The Housing Act of 1949 authorized the construction of 810,000 units of public housing over six years. The construction of public housing under this law, though, fell far short of this goal. This failure can be mostly attributed to the economic regulations imposed because of the Korean War; the sluggish and complex proposal, approval, and implementation requirements of the law; insufficient appropriations from Congress; and the hostility toward public housing by real-estate brokers and home builders at the local level.[18]

Despite the limitations and shortcomings of the Housing Act of 1949 and subsequent federal housing laws, federally funded public housing, slum clearance, and urban renewal helped some urban Democratic machines. Especially in Chicago and Pittsburgh, housing projects enabled machine governments to maintain the de facto residential and educational segregation demanded by many of their white, working-class constituents while public housing projects facilitated the geographic delivery of the votes of their low-income black constituents.[19] Also, the almost $30 million in federal loans and grants derived from the 1949 Housing Act contributed to Pittsburgh's implementation of the first major comprehensive urban renewal program in the nation.[20] In New York City, Mayor William O'Dwyer appointed Parks Commissioner Robert Moses to chair his committee on slum clearance and generally granted Moses broad powers over urban renewal and public housing as well. Moses was able to use Title I of the Housing Act of 1949 to seize and purchase private property for the sake of slum clearance, the creation and expansion of the public infrastructure, and the advancement of private economic interests.[21]

TRUMAN AND FOUR BOSSES

Toward the end of the Roosevelt presidency, Charles Van Devander wrote, "In general it can be said that the bossed delegations from the nation's big cities have provided the most consistent and effective support to the 'liberal' domestic programs of the New Deal and, usually, for the Administration's foreign policy as well."[22] Van Devander's observation continued to be true during the Truman administration. Northern machine-supported Democratic members of Congress, such as Senators Francis Myers of Pennsylvania and Robert Wagner of New York, enthusiastically supported such Fair Deal proposals as civil rights legislation, national health insurance, and repeal of the Taft-Hartley Act and such foreign policy measures as the Marshall Plan and recognition of Israel.[23] Like Roosevelt, Truman was grateful for this machine-based political support and was usually sensitive and deferential toward the preferences and interests of Democratic urban bosses and machine-affiliated members of Congress in patronage distribution and the selection of Democratic national chairmen. Truman disliked Senator Estes Kefauver's televised committee hearings investigating organized crime, partially because of their potential political damage to Democratic machines in the 1952 election.

Harry Truman's political relationships with Democratic machine bosses differed according to how well-organized and powerful their machines were and how supportive they were of Truman's domestic policies and his 1948 presidential campaign. When analyzed according to these two criteria, the four most significant major urban Democratic bosses during the Truman presidency were David Lawrence of Pittsburgh, Edward Crump of Memphis, Jacob Arvey of Chicago, and William O'Dwyer of New York City. Regarding their political relationships with Harry Truman, Lawrence and Crump in particular proved to be quite distinct from each other.

Among the four bosses, David Lawrence was the most consistent, loyal, and effective in providing political support for Harry Truman and his domestic policies. At the 1944 Democratic National Convention, Lawrence played a role in helping Truman to become Roosevelt's running mate by submitting a pre-arranged motion to the convention chairman to adjourn until enough pro-Truman delegates could be organized to nominate him.[24] Unlike the other three bosses, Lawrence never opposed Truman's presidential nomination in 1948 and was the only nationally prominent machine mayor to skillfully and energetically mobilize voters for Truman in his bailiwick.[25] As Democratic national committeeman for Pennsylvania, Lawrence was a source of loyal influence for Truman within the DNC.[26] The Pittsburgh mayor sought to ensure that the 1948 Democratic National Convention in Philadelphia ran as smoothly as possible by securing the reelection of Senator Francis Myers, a Pennsylvania Democrat supported by Lawrence's machine, as chairman of the Platform Committee. After the 1948 election, Lawrence used his influence within the Democratic National Committee to expel DNC members who had supported Dixiecrat J. Strom Thurmond for president.[27]

By contrast, Ed Crump's persistent, vocal opposition began at the 1944 Democratic national convention. Through his pervasive control of the votes of the Tennessee delegates, Crump refused to support Truman's nomination for vice president, even on the final ballot.[28] Crump regarded Truman as unfit for the vice presidency and later the presidency because of the Missourian's association with the Pendergast machine. Ironically, Crump, despite the fact that he ran one of the most autocratic, centralized urban machines in the nation, disliked his public image as a machine boss. Vain and eccentric, he wanted to be perceived as a civic-minded businessman active in civic and party affairs because of his own notion of noblesse oblige.[29] After Truman announced his civil rights proposal, Crump became an even more strident critic of the president and became the only major machine boss to support J. Strom Thurmond's Dixiecrat presidential candidacy.

Unlike David Lawrence and Edward Crump, Jacob Arvey and William O'Dwyer experienced more ambiguous relationships with Harry Truman. Both Arvey and O'Dwyer initially opposed Truman's presidential nomination in 1948. They feared that Truman's nomination would damage the electoral appeal of their own Democratic slates. After the 1948 Democratic convention, however, both Democrats reconciled themselves with Truman's nomination. The Chicago machine in particular fervently mobilized its city's Democratic voters for Truman.[30] Both Democratic bosses harshly criticized Truman's initial vacillation regarding the recognition of Israel but also provided crucial rhetorical assistance and congressional lobbying for the 1949 Housing Act and civil rights legislation.[31] More detailed, individual analyses of these four bosses, however, are necessary to explain their impact on Harry Truman's party leadership and national Democratic policies during his administration.

LAWRENCE THE LOYALIST

The mutually beneficial, trusting political relationship that Harry Truman and David Lawrence shared was enhanced by the personal and political traits that they held in common. Both men became seriously nearsighted at a young age. They compensated for their lack of college degrees by assiduously educating themselves on public policy and public administration and carefully sought the counsel of well-educated appointees for their major policy decisions. During their careers in local government, they believed that machine politics was compatible with the development and implementation of ambitious, farsighted projects of urban planning and major improvements in public infrastructure. Truman and Lawrence also shared an enduring interest and participation in strengthening the apparatus of the Democratic party and stressed the party regular's ethos of placing intraparty harmony, unity, and electoral success above individual ambition.

Like other northern Democratic machine bosses, David Lawrence was reared in an Irish Catholic working-class home in a multi-ethnic industrial city. His father, Charles Lawrence, was a Democratic ward committeeman in Pittsburgh. Although his formal education ended at the tenth grade, David Lawrence became a law clerk and protégé of William Brennen, an influential attorney and the Democratic chairman of Allegheny County.[32] Since the Democratic party was often the minority party in the politics and government of his home city and state, Lawrence recognized and emphasized the importance of subordinating personal political ambition to the organizational, consensual, and electoral welfare of his party.[33] Throughout the 1930s and early 1940s, he repeatedly rejected requests that he run for mayor or governor. As he struggled to develop the Pennsylvania Democratic party as the majority party of his city and state during the New Deal era, Lawrence believed that his Catholicism would repel some voters and electorally weaken entire Democratic slates.

While David Lawrence avoided being a candidate for major elective governmental offices during this period, he sought and was elected to several positions in the organization of the Pennsylvania Democratic party. As Democratic chairman of Allegheny County and the state party committee and as Democratic national committeeman for Pennsylvania, Lawrence gradually built an expanding, vibrant organizational and electoral base by closely linking the distribution of federal, state, and local patronage jobs to a recipient's loyalty to the Democratic party apparatus and his proven efficacy in delivering Democratic votes. His appointed positions as a federal income tax collector for western Pennsylvania and later as secretary of the commonwealth as well as his crucial campaign activities for Democratic Governor George Earle and U.S. Senator Joseph Guffey, both first elected in 1934, had greatly enhanced his power of patronage distribution when combined with his various party leadership roles.

Unlike machine politicians with less foresight and concern for their party organization's long-term political strength, Lawrence realized that he should closely identify his party—the evolving, pro-union, urban-based Pennsylvania Democracy—with New Deal liberalism and the party leadership of Franklin D. Roosevelt. This was especially important for realigning previously Republican blacks, Italians, and blue-collar Protestants with the Pennsylvania Democratic party.[34] Shortly after his election as Democratic state chairman in 1934, Lawrence declared that "beneath the banners of the Roosevelt New Deal we have formed our columns for the final march upon the last trenches of Toryism and special privilege."[35]

Despite his lack of an elective position in Pittsburgh's local government, Lawrence was widely recognized as the de facto "boss" of that city for twelve years before his election as mayor in 1945. The Democratic mayors and most of the aldermen who served since the 1933 local elections owed much of their electoral success to David Lawrence's power and skill as a campaign organizer, mobilizer of voters, patronage dispenser, and broker of conflicting interests and ambitions among the Democratic politicians of Allegheny County. Besides helping to elect a Democratic governor, U.S. senator, and Democratic-controlled state legislature in 1934, Lawrence played a key role in promoting and enacting Pennsylvania's "Little New Deal" policies of strict work safety regulations, workmen's compensation, union rights, higher corporate taxes, and prohibition of racial discrimination from 1935 to 1939.[36] In 1936, with Allegheny County delivering a large Democratic plurality of votes, Pennsylvania voted mostly Democratic for president for the first time since 1856.[37]

Lawrence's most important ally in rapidly expanding the Pennsylvania Democracy was Senator Joseph Guffey. Lawrence, however, resented Guffey's abrasive personal ambition and suspected that the senator was inadequately concerned about the state party's unity and long-term welfare. Supporting different Democratic candidates in the 1938 gubernatorial primary, the rivalry between Lawrence and Guffey became more public and contributed to the Democratic loss of the governorship and of control of the state legislature in the general elections of 1938.[38] David Lawrence's influence in statewide politics was further diminished by two highly publicized trials during 1939 and 1940 in which he was prosecuted for a variety of corruption charges, including padding state payrolls and forcing state employees to kick back portions of their salaries for campaign funds.[39] Lawrence was acquitted of all charges, but his hostile rivalry with Joe Guffey continued until the senator's defeat for reelection in 1946.[40]

David Lawrence's emergence as the most powerful Democrat in Pennsylvania with the most influence on the White House began with his support of Harry Truman for vice president in 1944. Although he had previously and briefly met the Missouri senator in Washington on a few occasions, Lawrence became an early and enthusiastic supporter of Truman as Roosevelt's running mate after Truman visited Pennsylvania in April 1944 to deliver several speeches. As a machine politician and party regular acquitted of corruption charges, Lawrence especially respected Truman's staunch loyalty to Tom Pendergast.[41] Since Joe Guffey and the CIO unions of Pennsylvania were die-hard supporters of Henry Wallace's renomination, Lawrence managed to deliver only twenty-four of Pennsylvania's seventy-two delegate votes for Truman on the first convention ballot.[42]

But through his position as Democratic national committeeman for his state and mayor of Pittsburgh, Lawrence maintained close relations with the Truman White House and received control of all federal patronage in Pennsylvania after Guffey's defeat in 1946.[43] According to Truman's memoirs shortly after the Missourian became president in April, 1945, Lawrence assured him "of the solid support" of the Pennsylvania Democracy and said "something about supporting me in 1948."[44]

David Lawrence's greatest services and demonstrations of unwavering loyalty to Harry Truman occurred during the presidential campaigns of 1948 and 1952, especially at the Democratic national conventions. Despite the Republican congressional victories in 1946 and the general assumption that Truman would lose the 1948 election, Lawrence did not join the effort of bosses Jacob Arvey, William O'Dwyer, Ed Flynn, and Frank Hague to dump Truman and draft Dwight Eisenhower.[45] While most delegates and party leaders at the beginning of the 1948 Democratic National Convention only reluctantly supported Truman's nomination, Lawrence unequivocally asserted his enthusiasm for Truman's party leadership and presidency in his welcoming address to the delegates. He urged his fellow Democrats to "continue the Democratic Party as the nation's party of liberalism" under Truman and praised the president's "courageous showdown with the Republican 80th Congress."[46] During the convention's votes on platform positions, Lawrence sternly ordered all of his state's delegates to be present to vote for the Americans for Democratic Action (ADA)–sponsored civil rights plank.[47] Despite a major campaign speech by Truman in Pittsburgh and his receipt of 55 percent of Allegheny County's votes, he failed to carry Pennsylvania in the electoral college.[48]

Throughout the rest of Harry Truman's presidency, David Lawrence best served the Democratic National Committee and Truman's party leadership as a mediator of regional and procedural conflicts within the party and as a nationally-recognized spokesman of urban policy interests.[49] As a leading DNC member, Lawrence alternated between promoting intraparty harmony and punishing DNC members who openly opposed Truman in the 1948 general election.[50]

While he was willing to appease southern Democrats with a more moderately worded civil rights plank at the 1952 Democratic National Convention, Lawrence aggressively pursued and helped to execute the expulsion of Dixiecrats from the DNC in 1949.[51] As a member of the DNC's Credentials Committee, the Pittsburgh Democrat asserted that a DNC member who refused to support his party's presidential nominee should not "serve on the National Committee, when he is not in accord with the Party."[52]

Greatly impressed by the statesmanlike demeanor and patrician eloquence of Adlai Stevenson, David Lawrence was second only to Jacob Arvey of Chicago among machine bosses in his active promotion of Stevenson's presidential candidacy during and after the 1952 Democratic National Convention.[53] Mostly through the efforts of Lawrence and former senator Francis Myers, Pennsylvania was the only large state other than Illinois that gave Stevenson a majority of its delegation's votes on the first ballot.[54] By networking with his nationwide contacts in the DNC, in organized labor, and among southern moderates and urban liberals, Lawrence played a crucial role in assuring Adlai Stevenson's nomination for president on the third ballot.[55] During Dwight Eisenhower's presidency, Lawrence used his position on the DNC to try to enhance the national Democratic party's public image and policy agenda as a distinctly liberal party.[56]

Perhaps, David Lawrence's greatest contribution to the urban liberalism that had begun to characterize the Democratic party under Roosevelt and Truman was his success in implementing the first major, comprehensive urban redevelopment program in the immediate postwar period.[57] In contrast to his reputation as a highly partisan Democratic machine boss, Lawrence readily joined Richard Mellon and other Republican business leaders in an ambitious, long-term project to revitalize the central business district of Pittsburgh immediately after his inauguration as mayor in 1946. With businessmen providing investment funds and construction proposals, Lawrence provided the political leadership necessary to secure the cooperation of the Democratic-controlled city council and labor unions and secure an adequate amount of funds for slum clearance, public housing, and urban planning derived from the state government and later the Federal Housing Act of 1949. Federal loans and grants to Pittsburgh derived from this law would total nearly $30 million by the late 1950s.[58]

Known as the Pittsburgh Renaissance, this multi-purpose urban renewal plan's achievements included a substantial reduction in air pollution, an improvement in flood control through federal aid and expertise, numerous skyscrapers, a major new airport, a more diverse tax and employment base, and major improvements in traffic control, recreational and cultural opportunities, and downtown parking. Pittsburgh, a city which, by 1944, had been "the dirtiest pile of slag in the United States" was "Exhibit A of the new style of municipal politics" by the last year of Lawrence's mayoralty in 1958.[59]

During his tenure as governor of Pennsylvania from 1959 until his sudden death in 1966, David Lawrence continued to represent his state on the Democratic National Committee. Within the DNC and during the Democratic national conventions of 1960 and 1964, Lawrence continued to use his influence and mediation skills to develop the type of national Democratic party that Harry Truman had sought—a party that was pluralistic, cohesive, electorally successful, and committed to liberal policy objectives. Like Truman, Lawrence believed that the ethos of a party regular could be conducive, rather than detrimental, to successful public administration. In 1954 Lawrence wrote, "The canniest political leadership will serve no good public purpose if it does not put itself wholeheartedly into the cause which the political party is organized to serve— the advancement of the people who vote it into responsibility."[60]

THE MEMPHIS MAVERICK

David L. Lawrence and Edward H. Crump provided the sharpest contrast as urban bosses in terms of political styles and relationships with Harry Truman. Lawrence had sought to make the Pennsylvania Democracy an electorally successful, competitive party in what had been a virtually one-party Republican state since the Civil War. He generally avoided publicity, preferring to work behind the scenes to promote intraparty unity and cooperation, and successfully developed a lasting relationship with Roosevelt and Truman that mutually benefited their political and policy interests. Determined to develop the Pittsburgh Democratic machine as a party organization that could succeed without his personal leadership, Lawrence recognized the importance of distinguishing himself as a national spokesman for urban policy interests within the DNC and at Democratic national conventions as one method of assuring enough federal aid to revitalize Pittsburgh and strengthen the longevity of his party's machine.

By contrast, Ed Crump devoted his political career to building and maintaining a machine that made Memphis and the rest of Shelby County, Tennessee, a personal fiefdom heavily dependent on his political skills and autocratic control for its survival and success in an overwhelmingly Democratic state. By collaborating with Republican politicians in East Tennessee and Democratic county bosses throughout the state, Crump was the most powerful single influence in statewide elections from 1936 until 1948. His almost scientific micromanagement mobilized and delivered votes in Shelby County. Through his close alliance with Senator Kenneth D. McKellar and early endorsement of Franklin D. Roosevelt's presidential nomination at the 1932 Democratic National Convention, Crump was able to ensure a generous flow of federal aid for Memphis. In particular, the Public Works Administration spent nearly $8.5 million in Memphis while the Crump Stadium, a large zoo, and an airport expansion were built by the Works Progress Administration (WPA).[61] Likewise, the Tennessee Valley Authority provided Memphis with low-cost electricity, flood control, and additional patronage jobs for the machine. Crump's enthusiastic support for Roosevelt in all four of the president's campaigns, his ability to generate an incredibly high pro-Roosevelt voter turnout in Shelby County, and his influence in Congress through most of Tennessee's congressional delegation enabled Crump to ignore the demands of Harry Hopkins that Memphis pay a larger share of matching funds for WPA aid.[62]

While federal aid bolstered the Crump machine and helped Memphis to keep its property taxes low, the New Deal was not essential to the Crump machine's power. First elected mayor of Memphis in 1909, Ed Crump had previously entered politics as a self-made young businessman who opposed the machine of Mayor Joe Williams and advocated the "good government" idea of using business practices to improve municipal services and the economic and moral climate of Memphis.[63] Although he resigned as mayor shortly after his reelection in 1915 and served as a U.S. representative from 1931 to 1935, Ed Crump was the de facto chief executive of Memphis's local government for the rest of his life, acting through a series of hand-picked mayors and commissioners. Crump's only long-term elective office was the chairmanship of the Memphis Democratic party, which he held from 1922 until his death in 1954.

Throughout his long reign, Crump and his supporters credited the machine's success with the substantial improvements in municipal services, economic growth, and the general quality of life in Memphis that had occurred under his leadership. During the Crump era, the professionalism and efficacy of the city's police, fire, sanitation, and public health departments significantly improved so that Memphis's rates of murder, fire insurance, and contagious diseases substantially declined.[64] Illegal gambling was suppressed, and prostitution was limited to a few brothels tolerated by the machine.[65] During World War II, the population of Memphis rapidly grew from approximately 250,000 to nearly 400,000 as industrialization significantly increased and diversified due to defense contracts and the attraction of Memphis's relatively low property taxes, riverfront location, public infrastructure, and its machine's suppression of CIO organizing efforts.[66]

While Crump thus gained the support of most of Memphis's businessmen, he cultivated a personal following among poor and working-class Memphis residents, both black and white, by promoting a highly publicized image as a ubiquitous benefactor of the underprivileged. By expanding the number of public charitable institutions for orphans, the disabled, and the elderly of both races, Crump regularly organized and led highly publicized steamboat rides, picnics, and trips to circuses and amusement parks. Discouraging membership drives by CIO officials through police harassment, the Crump machine co-opted the local American Federation of Labor (AFL) unions through its hostility to their CIO rivals and its selection of Oscar Williams, an AFL official, as commissioner of public works.[67] Crump also succeeded in appealing to the small yet noticeable Catholic and Jewish minorities of Memphis through the machine's inclusion of such prominent members of these faiths as police commissioner Joe Boyle and prosecutor Will Gerber. Catholic Democrats also admired Crump's open, active support for the 1928 Democratic presidential nominee Al Smith when most Protestant Democratic politicians in Tennessee abandoned the Catholic governor of New York.

The role of blacks in the Crump machine combined both the northern urban practice of mobilizing and rewarding blacks as loyal voters and the southern practice of racial segregation and white supremacy. Comprising over 40 percent of Memphis's population by 1940, blacks were rewarded by the Crump machine for their reliable electoral support through patronage jobs, relief, cash and liquor distributed on election days, and an expansion in the number of schools, parks, and other public institutions reserved for blacks. Crump was also careful to cultivate the political support of prominent black businessmen, ministers, and educators, and to have some black policemen patrol black neighborhoods.[68]

The Crump machine's major asset, though, in controlling and delivering impressive numbers of votes to its candidates in Shelby County was Tennessee's poll tax law. During the 1930s and 1940s, voter turnout in statewide Democratic primaries and general elections averaged approximately 25 percent of Tennesseans eligible to vote.[69] In Shelby County, however, most eligible adults voted due to the Crump machine's comprehensive system of paying poll taxes for lower-income whites and blacks, and transporting them en masse to the polls with clear instructions on voting for Crump-endorsed candidates. City and county employees sold poll-tax receipts and were required to provide 10 percent of their salaries to the machine for a poll tax fund. Poll-tax receipts were even bought and sold by brothels tolerated by the machine.

By the late 1930s, Ed Crump was able to deliver more than one hundred thousand votes in Tennessee due to his machine's voter mobilization system, the poll tax, and his alliances with Democrats and Republicans in East Tennessee. Despite several attempts by anti-Crump forces in the state legislature to repeal the poll tax, Tennessee's poll tax was not ended until anti-Crump Governor Gordon Browning signed anti-poll-tax legislation in 1951.[70] Jennings Perry, a reporter for the *Nashville Tennessean,* a newspaper whose publisher crusaded against the Crump machine, concluded in 1944, "Crump was a city boss who made himself a state boss, sharing control of Tennessee with no one and attaining a degree of authority which the regimes of Pendergast, Hague, and . . . Chicago . . . never quite laid hold of."[71]

Roosevelt received more than 80 percent of Shelby County's votes in 1944 and asked Crump to see him in Washington shortly before his death in 1945. Roosevelt perceived Senator Kenneth D. McKellar as an increasingly conservative obstacle to his policy goals in Congress and urged Crump to refuse to support his longtime ally for renomination in the 1946 Democratic primary. Crump refused and asserted that McKellar would win another Senate term in 1946.[72]

Ed Crump's rejection of Roosevelt's request and his persistent vocal opposition to Harry Truman from Truman's vice presidential candidacy until the end of his presidency revealed the degree of independence that he enjoyed from presidential party leadership. Truman relished the opportunity to firmly reject Crump's application for a Reconstruction Finance Corporation loan in 1948, and Memphis was one of the few major cities which did not apply for federal urban renewal aid from the Housing Act of 1949.[73]

While David Lawrence used his positions as mayor and Democratic national committeeman to promote Harry Truman's party leadership, Ed Crump used his power within the Tennessee Democracy to thwart it. At the Tennessee democratic Convention of 1948, Crump advocated an unsuccessful resolution that would have required Tennessee's delegates to leave the 1948 Democratic national Convention in protest if Truman were nominated.[74] Instead, Crump had to satisfy himself with a personal boycott of the national convention and with Tennessee's delegates voting to nominate Georgia Senator Richard Russell for president.[75]

Denouncing Truman for his roots in the Pendergast machine and his civil rights proposals, Crump endorsed the presidential campaign of Dixiecrat J. Strom Thurmond. But the Crump machine managed to deliver only a narrow majority of votes for Thurmond in Shelby County while Truman received all but one of Tennessee's electoral-college votes.[76] Even the Crump-affiliated McKellar, concerned about federal patronage, supported Truman.

Most of Ed Crump's political activity in 1948, however, focused on the Democratic gubernatorial and senatorial primaries. Crump supported the incumbent governor, James McCord for renomination against former governor Gordon Browning, once a Crump ally but now a bitter enemy. For the Democratic senatorial nomination, Crump opposed both incumbent Senator Thomas

Stewart and Representative Estes Kefauver while endorsing John Mitchell, an obscure judge.[77]

The 1948 Democratic primary in Tennessee soon became a dramatic battle between Crump and Kefauver. Supported by the Nashville Tennessean and CIO unions, Kefauver capitalized on Crump's well-publicized depiction of him as a scurrilous raccoon by donning a coonskin cap as a symbol of defiant independence from the Crump machine. Although John Mitchell beat Kefauver by a margin of almost ten thousand votes in Shelby County, Kefauver easily won the primary and about two-thirds of the black vote in Memphis.[78] Likewise, in the gubernatorial primary, Governor James McCord, Crump's candidate, carried Shelby County by a margin of nearly thirty thousand votes but lost the primary to Gordon Browning by a statewide margin of more than fifty thousand votes.[79] Boss Crump's image of electoral invincibility was permanently shattered.

Except for his home state of Missouri, Harry Truman had a policy of not openly intervening in Democratic primaries to support preferred Democratic candidates for party nominations. Truman, however, directed Attorney General Tom Clark to comply with Estes Kefauver's request for the posting of FBI agents in the Tennessee primary to prevent ballot fraud and voter intimidation by the Crump machine.[80] Truman's memoirs later referred to Ed Crump's machine as a prominent example of one of the "big evils" and "a vicious arrangement in both parties" that "exercised undue influence over the selection of candidates."[81]

Apparently, though, Harry Truman never perceived the Crump machine to be a serious threat or burden to his party leadership. He did not promote aggressive federal investigations and prosecutions, as Roosevelt had toward Tom Pendergast and Boston boss James M. Curley. Despite Truman's desire to continue and enhance modern liberalism in the Democratic party and attract support in Congress for Fair Deal legislation, the president continued to adhere to senatorial courtesy by granting most federal patronage in Tennessee to Senator Kenneth D. McKellar, Crump's conservative ally, rather than to the distinctly more liberal Estes Kefauver after his inauguration in the Senate in 1949.

Determined to destroy the Crump machine and a faithful supporter of most Fair Deal bills, the junior senator expressed his frustration regarding Truman's passive neutrality in the ongoing conflict between liberals and conservatives in the Tennessee Democracy. "Mr. President, we are trying to build up a progressive real Democratic Party in Tennessee. We will either do this or the old Crump forces will take over again. It means much to you and to our administration to have a condition in Tennessee where liberals can run on the Democratic slate and be elected."[82]

A few months later, Kefauver reminded Truman of this situation and again asked the president to defer most federal patronage to him in order to strengthen liberal Democrats in Tennessee loyal to Truman.[83] In his reply, Truman firmly stated the limits of his powers and appropriate actions as a party leader. "I don't think it is my job to straighten out factional fights in every State in the Union."[84]

Harry Truman's aloof indifference to the Crump machine and Kefauver's efforts to destroy it seemed justified. From the results of the 1948 Democratic primary in Tennessee until Ed Crump's death in 1954, the Crump machine gradually declined and then disintegrated due to a variety of forces and events peculiar to Tennessee politics. In 1952 Senator Kenneth D. McKellar was defeated for renomination by liberal Representative Albert Gore Sr. With his power and status in Tennessee improved by his crime investigations and 1952 presidential candidacy, Kefauver was easily reelected in 1954.[85]

Furthermore, the repeal of the poll tax, the end of vote-trading deals by East Tennessee Republicans, and the use of voting machines greatly reduced the Crump machine's ability to decide statewide primaries and elections. In the 1959 municipal elections of Memphis, antimachine candidates were elected to the mayorship and most commissioners' seats.[86] Unlike David Lawrence of Pittsburgh and Jacob Arvey of Chicago, Ed Crump lacked the foresight and ideological flexibility to discern and adapt to the political changes of the postwar era, especially the growing demand by blacks for civil rights legislation, and the increasing opposition of urban voters to the anachronistic, autocratic political style that Crump personified. Crump, though, unlike other Democratic urban bosses, was secure and independent enough in his machine power to defy Harry Truman's party leadership and the increasingly liberal composition and policy agenda of the national Democratic party.[87]

THE CHICAGO POWER BROKER

Jacob Arvey was never elected mayor of Chicago. But Arvey combined his positions as alderman, Democratic chairman of Cook County, and later Democratic national committeeman with his skills as an intraparty mediator and consensus builder to become a nationally recognized, influential figure in the Democratic party during Truman's presidency. Like David Lawrence, Arvey realized that the political survival, success, and influence on federal policy of his city's Democratic machine depended on its identification with the increasingly liberal national Democratic party that had emerged since the New Deal and its active participation in national party affairs, especially the presidential nomination and platform-making processes.[88]

Early in his political career as an alderman and Democratic committeeman from the almost entirely Jewish twenty-fourth ward of Chicago, Arvey distinguished himself by being able to deliver almost all of his constituents' votes for any candidate endorsed by his machine superiors. After Mayor Ed Kelly endorsed Herman Bundesen for the Democratic gubernatorial nomination in 1936, Arvey faithfully delivered more than 90 percent of his ward's votes for Bundesen, despite pressures from rabbis for him to support fellow Jewish Democrat Henry Horner, who won the Democratic primary for governor.[89] After the 1936 election, Franklin D. Roosevelt personally congratulated Arvey for delivering 26,112 votes in his ward to Roosevelt—Republican nominee Alf Landon got only 974—and for having "the number one ward in the entire Democratic party."[90]

Arvey assiduously used the WPA and other New Deal programs to increase patronage jobs and government benefits available to his constituents. Unlike other ward bosses, Arvey realized that the New Deal and Roosevelt's party leadership served a purpose for the Chicago machine and other urban Democratic machines that extended beyond providing more patronage jobs and relief for their electoral bases. For Arvey, they provided a longterm, coherent, liberal policy agenda and ideological identity that superseded the immediate political interests of machine bosses. After interviewing Arvey in 1977, journalist Ralph Whitehead described him as a "cosmopolitan" machine boss who "helped to conserve the domestic political legacy of Franklin Roosevelt" and "kept the Roosevelt legacy going just long enough for it to become the conventional wisdom."[91]

As a leading member of the Democratic National Committee for twenty years, Arvey's contributions to the national Democratic party included his indispensable promotion of Adlai Stevenson's gubernatorial and presidential candidacies, his aggressive lobbying for Truman's recognition of Israel and the ADA's civil rights plank at the 1948 Democratic national convention, and his support for the Democratic Advocacy Council to protect and express a liberal identity for the Democratic party during the Eisenhower presidency.[92] But before Arvey could serve and influence his party nationally, he had to ensure the longevity of Chicago's Democratic machine. Its survival appeared to be in jeopardy shortly after World War II.

Despite the fact that Ed Kelly was both mayor and Democratic chairman of Cook County in 1946, Democratic aldermen increasingly looked to Arvey for political guidance and counsel. Ed Kelly's status and credibility with other machine politicians and their constituents had eroded during World War II. Chicagoans increasingly complained about the deteriorating quality of public education, garbage collection, and public transportation. Democratic ward committeemen also believed that as party chairman Kelly had not chosen the best possible slate of candidates for the 1946 election. Many Chicago Democrats believed the ailing, aging Ed Kelly should be removed from both positions as quickly and smoothly as possible. Renowned and respected for his proven skills as a campaign manager and mediator of intraparty conflicts, Arvey was given the task of persuading and pressuring Kelly to resign as Democratic county chairman before the 1946 general elections and to not seek another term as mayor in 1947.

Elected Democratic chairman of Cook County on July 19, 1946, Arvey did not hold this position long enough to prepare for the elections in November. Partially benefiting from the national Republican trend in voting behavior and local disenchantment with the Kelly administration, the Republicans won five of the ten contested congressional seats in the Chicago area and several Cook County offices, including county sheriff. Fortunately for Arvey, the ward bosses did not blame the recently elected party chairman for the Democratic machine's staggering electoral losses, which included the defeat of the Democratic nominee for sheriff, Richard J. Daley, the future mayor and undisputed boss of the Chicago machine.

Arvey believed that the Democratic machine's revitalization, and even its survival, would depend on its ability to promote the successful campaigns of candidates for mayor in 1947 and for governor and U.S. senator in 1948. The party chairman realized that it needed to endorse electable Democratic candidates for these offices who had reputations for integrity and apparent independence from the machine, or else the machine would disintegrate into its ward-level baronies known only for their petty corruption, collusion with gangsters, patronage distribution, and fiscal irresponsibility. In short, if the Chicago machine wanted to remain an influential actor in national, state, and even mayoral politics, it would have to compromise and moderate some of its more scandalous behavior.

Consequently, Arvey persuaded his fellow Democratic ward bosses to reluctantly accept the mayoral nomination of Martin Kennelly. A self-made executive of a moving and storage firm, Kennelly had been active in civic affairs through his positions on the Chicago Crime Commission and his volunteer efforts for the Red Cross. But he held no party position in the Cook County Democratic organization, and he publicly reminded Arvey and the other Democratic ward committeemen that he had opposed the machine's gubernatorial candidate in the 1936 Democratic primary and had opposed Ed Kelly's renomination for mayor in 1939. Kennelly concluded his speech by boldly promising that, if elected mayor, he would continue his independence from the machine.[93]

Attracting favorable comments from the *Chicago Tribune,* a Republican newspaper, and the support of some antimachine voters, Kennelly was easily

elected mayor in 1947. To the shock and anger of the aldermen, Kennelly focused on civil service reform and reduced the number of patronage jobs available to them from approximately thirty thousand to eighteen thousand.[94]
Kennelly's vigorous suppression of the policy-wheel gambling rackets in black
neighborhoods tolerated by Ed Kelly aroused the opposition of black aldermen
led by Representative William Dawson. It was only the intervention of white
aldermen that persuaded Dawson to grudgingly endorse Kennelly for a second
term in 1951.[95]

    Despite his success in expanding the civil service coverage of municipal
jobs and improving the administration of the Chicago public school system,
Kennelly proved to be a well-intentioned but politically inept mayor since Arvey
remained Democratic county chairman and the de facto boss of the city's government and Democratic politics. After Kennelly's election in 1947, Arvey then
focused on choosing and supporting attractive gubernatorial and senatorial candidates for the 1948 campaign. Since Cook County Republicans had made substantial gains in the 1946 congressional, state, and county elections and the
1947 aldermanic elections, Arvey recognized the machine's need to support
"blue-ribbon" candidates who had public reputations of integrity and independence from the ward bosses. Such "blue-ribbon" candidates were needed to
attract independent and antimachine voters, especially from rural downstate Illinois, in order to be elected in a year that many assumed would see another
Republican sweep.

    Under Arvey's leadership, the ward bosses supported the candidacies of
Adlai Stevenson for governor and Paul Douglas, an economics professor and
reform-minded alderman, for senator. Although Stevenson originally preferred
running for senator, Arvey induced the aristocratic Protestant Democrat to run
for governor by promising him the machine's electoral support with the freedom to run a clean administration. Arvey knew that his machine colleagues
would have resisted a gubernatorial candidacy for Douglas since they feared
that the economist would not cooperate on patronage matters and might seek to
eventually destroy them through aggressive investigations and prosecution.[96]

    Despite the enthusiasm of ADA activists, independents, and antimachine
Democrats for the Douglas and Stevenson candidacies, Arvey initially perceived
Harry Truman's presidential candidacy to be a liability to the Illinois Democratic ticket. Unlike southern conservatives and some liberal activists, the Democratic chairman of Cook County did not briefly oppose Truman's nomination
because he opposed the president on policy issues or doubted his ideological
convictions as a New Deal liberal. Although he was somewhat exasperated with
Truman's waffling on the recognition of Israel, Arvey simply believed that the

machine's political resurgence required an attractive vote-getter as the Democratic presidential nominee of 1948.

Arvey coalesced with ADA activists such as Franklin D. Roosevelt Jr., Joe
Rauh, New York City Mayor William O'Dwyer, and Jersey City boss Frank
Hague in urging Dwight Eisenhower to seek the Democratic presidential nomination. From the urban politicians' perspective, Eisenhower's immense bipartisan popularity as a war hero would make him the ideal nominee to carry their
Democratic slates.[97] After Eisenhower made it clear that he was definitely not
interested in the nomination, Arvey joined the ADA and the other urban party
regulars such as O'Dwyer, David Lawrence, and Bronx boss Edward Flynn in
lobbying for and securing passage of the ADA's civil rights plank by the delegates of the Democratic National Convention.[98] With the ADA-written plank
more liberal and objectionable to southern conservatives than the plank that
Truman had proposed, Arvey and other machine politicians hoped that their
prominent, crucial support for the ADA plank, dramatized by the walk-out of pro-
testing Dixiecrats, would attract more black voters to their Democratic tickets.[99]

On October 25, shortly before the election, Arvey organized a huge rally
and motorcade for Harry Truman in Chicago. At the insistence of Arvey, Mayor
Kennelly reluctantly introduced the underdog presidential candidate to the over-
flowing crowd at Chicago Stadium. In this nationally broadcast speech, Truman
sharply distinguished the two major parties from each other. He accused the
Republicans of giving "lip-service to the principles of democracy" and of opening "the gate to forces that would destroy our democracy."[100] The machine-
organized crowd was the ideal audience for applauding such an aggressively
partisan speech.

Like David Lawrence and unlike O'Dwyer, Flynn, and Hague, Jacob Arvey,
despite his earlier endorsement of Eisenhower, diligently sought to mobilize as
many voters as he could for Harry Truman so that the beleaguered Democratic
president could carry Illinois in the electoral college.[101] With the indispensable
Democratic votes of Cook County, Truman carried the state by a margin of
33,612 votes while Stevenson and Douglas won by respective margins of 572,067
and 407,728 votes.[102] Since Stevenson and, to a lesser degree, Douglas were
able to attract the votes of significant numbers of antimachine Democrats, independents, and liberally inclined Republicans, the machine-delivered Democratic
votes of Chicago were especially necessary for Truman's razor-thin margin of
victory in Illinois.[103]

From the results of the 1948 election until the aftermath of the 1950 midterm election, Jacob Arvey was at the peak of his power as the Democratic
chairman of Cook County and the de facto boss of Chicago. Arvey expected

Governor Stevenson to appoint well-qualified machine Democrats to state positions, such as ward boss and future mayor Richard J. Daley as state revenue
director. In general, though, Arvey kept the following promise of independence
that he made to Stevenson during the 1948 campaign. "You're our showcase. If
you do well, then we'll look good. All I ask is that you be loyal to the party—
don't make an alliance with the Republicans."[104]

Other Chicago ward bosses grumbled when Stevenson reduced the amount
of state patronage by expanding civil service coverage of state jobs.[105] What
was even more threatening to the political and financial bases of several aldermen and ward committeemen, especially those from Chicago's west side, was
Stevenson's sponsorship of legislation and state police raids aimed at illegal
gambling, especially slot machines.[106] Although some West Side bosses tried to
defeat Democratic state legislators who supported Stevenson on the issues for
renomination in the 1950 Democratic primaries, Arvey refused to intervene and
pressure Stevenson to abandon his policies against criminal rackets often involving machine politicians.

In the short term, though, Arvey's protection of Stevenson's independence
from the machine's political interests contributed to the Chicago machine's severe losses in the 1950 midterm election. Stevenson's anticrime efforts combined with the Senate investigation of organized crime in Chicago and other
cities chaired by Estes Kefauver highly publicized and graphically reminded
Illinois voters of the regular, blatant collusion between several machine politicians and notorious members of organized crime. After analyzing such evidence
in Chicago, Kefauver concluded that "in fact there could be no big-time organized crime without a firm and profitable alliance between those who run the
rackets and those in political control."[107]

The greatest damage to Arvey's reputation as a shrewd selector of electable
candidates was his choice of Daniel Gilbert as the Democratic nominee for
county sheriff. Gilbert, a police captain, testified before the Kefauver committee in October 1950 and admitted that he had amassed his wealth through illegal
gambling. Scathing newspaper headlines and stories labeling Gilbert as "the
world's richest cop" helped to defeat Gilbert and the reelection bid of Scott
Lucas, a U.S. senator and Democratic majority leader.[108]

Having succeeded Ed Kelly as Democratic national committeeman, Jacob
Arvey resigned as the Democratic chairman of Cook County shortly after the
1950 election. He would never again dominate the Chicago machine, especially
after Richard J. Daley was elected Democratic county chairman in 1953 and
mayor in 1955. Instead, Arvey used his position on the DNC and influence with
Illinois delegates and other states' urban delegates, especially those controlled

by David Lawrence of Pittsburgh, to promote Adlai Stevenson's presidential candidacy in 1952. Like Truman, Arvey perceived Kefauver's highly publicized crime hearings to have been a political gimmick to initiate his own presidential campaign, especially since no Tennessee cities known for illegal gambling operations were investigated by the Kefauver committee.[109] But it was apparent that in the wake of the Senate investigation of organized crime Stevenson's independence from the most unsavory links among several Chicago machine politicians and gangsters strengthened the viability of the governor's presidential candidacy while Arvey could quietly serve as Stevenson's liaison with urban party regulars and DNC members.

Although Stevenson repeatedly insisted to Truman and Arvey that he would not seek the Democratic presidential nomination in 1952, Arvey quietly organized a coalition of northern urban party regulars, southern moderates, and liberal activists to support Stevenson's nomination if the governor were pressured to accept a nomination sponsored by a draft movement. Inspired by Stevenson's eloquent, highly principled welcoming address and the Draft Stevenson Committee's lobbying, most delegates eventually supported the moderate, dignified governor as the only presidential candidate acceptable to most factions of the party. After reluctantly accepting the Democratic presidential nomination, Stevenson relied on Arvey to galvanize electoral support from Chicago Democrats and Jewish organizations throughout the nation. Arvey intervened on Stevenson's behalf among ward bosses disgruntled about Stevenson's aloofness as governor and aware of Dwight Eisenhower's popularity among their constituents. Even so, Stevenson lost Illinois by a margin greater than four hundred thousand votes in Eisenhower's decisive victory of 1952.[110]

After the 1952 election, Jacob Arvey devoted most of his efforts within the DNC to sustaining a liberal ideological and programmatic identity for the national Democratic party. Arvey joined Harry Truman, David Lawrence, and other liberal Democrats determined to prevent control of their party's policy positions by southern conservatives in Congress during the Eisenhower administration.[111] Arvey was one of the leading members of a DNC executive council, which instituted the Democratic Advisory Council (DAC) after the 1956 presidential election to suggest policy proposals that would reflect the "progressive, forward-looking platform" of the national Democratic party.[112] Until its dissolution in 1961, the DAC formulated and advocated liberal legislation, especially on civil rights, voting rights, urban renewal, and federal aid to education, and influenced several domestic programs of the Kennedy and Johnson administrations. Although Richard Daley replaced Arvey as the boss of the Chicago machine after 1952, Arvey's legacy to the Chicago machine in national Democratic politics was to solidify its position as a key actor in the selection of Democratic presidential tickets and as the supporter of policy positions favorable to urban interest groups.

O'DWYER AND NEW YORK POLITICS

During and shortly after his successful mayoral campaign of 1945, William O'Dwyer projected a convincing image to the public and the press of an antimachine Democratic reform mayor. In his rhetoric, he claimed to be both independent of and antagonistic toward Tammany Hall, the legendary Democratic organization of New York County based in Manhattan. O'Dwyer repeatedly used his public statements to denounce "the sinister elements of Tammany Hall" and referred to this organization as "nothing but a gutter club."[113]

With the charismatic maverick Republican Fiorello LaGuardia retiring as mayor of New York City in 1945, O'Dwyer defeated his Republican opponent, Nathaniel Goldstein, by more than 685,000 votes.[114] Having been defeated by LaGuardia in the 1941 mayoral election, O'Dwyer had greatly benefited from the fact that both the Democratic and American Labor (ALP) parties had nominated him in 1945. The ALP had supported LaGuardia in 1941. O'Dwyer appeared to be a Democratic mayor with a broad enough coalition that would enable him to defy, if not destroy, Tammany Hall in the Democratic politics of New York City.

O'Dwyer's background suggested that he would be the type of reform mayor that anti–Tammany Hall Democrats wanted. O'Dwyer was an Irish immigrant who settled in Brooklyn and studied law while he was a police officer. As a prosecutor and judge in Brooklyn, he gained a citywide reputation as an honest, aggressive enemy of police corruption and criminal activities in Brooklyn, especially through the convictions of gangsters belonging to "Murder, Inc."[115] These credentials—combined with his World War II record as a general in charge of relief efforts in Italy, his insistence that Italian-born Vincent Impellitteri be the Democratic nominee for president of the city council, his formal independence from the Irish-dominated Tammany Hall in Manhattan, and his own ethnicity—seemed to make O'Dwyer the ideal Democratic leader for harmonizing a citywide Democratic party increasingly divided between Irish and Italian voters and politicians.

After O'Dwyer resigned as mayor in August 1950, the Kefauver committee hearings and other revelations indicated that O'Dwyer's actual political behavior and relationships were those of a machine boss rather than an antimachine reformer. Bert Stand, who had been removed as secretary of Tammany Hall at O'Dwyer's insistence, testified before the Kefauver committee in 1951 that "O'Dwyer's actions were always confusing, contradictory and irrational. He changed the leadership in Tammany Hall as often as he changed his mind. The public, however, was apparently misled by all his artful double talk into believing that O'Dwyer sought to reform the organization when, actually, his only objective was to control it."[116]

Stand's testimony was an accurate summary of the contrast between William O'Dwyer's shrill public denunciations of Tammany Hall and his private efforts to seek the political support of the Manhattan organization for his 1945 campaign and his efforts as mayor to manipulate and dominate it as his own personal machine. Despite his later campaign image as a heroic "gang buster," O'Dwyer met Tammany Hall leader Michael Kennedy and Bert Stand in the home of gangster Frank Costello in 1942. O'Dwyer was opposed for the Democratic nomination for mayor at that time by Edward J. Flynn and Frank Kelly, the respective Democratic county leaders of the Bronx and Brooklyn.

O'Dwyer clearly needed, and was given, Tammany Hall's support in order to attract most Democratic politicians to his candidacy by 1945.[117] O'Dwyer asserted to the Kefauver committee that he, as an Army Air Corps general, only went to Costello on military business.[118] O'Dwyer implied to the Kefauver committee, however, that he was willing to accept campaign contributions from a gangster like Costello, which he later received through his confidant James Moran.[119] O'Dwyer stated to the Senate committee, "It doesn't matter whether it is a banker, a businessman, or a gangster, his pocketbook is always attractive."[120]

Frank Costello, Joe Adonis, and other organized crime figures influenced most Tammany Hall district leaders and especially members of Tammany's executive committee, which chose the leader and other officers of this party organization. Through the influence of Costello and the shrewd distribution of city patronage jobs to certain Tammany members, O'Dwyer orchestrated the removal of Edward Loughlin as Tammany Hall leader and replaced him with Frank Sampson. Loughlin was a figurehead for the actual control of Tammany Hall by secretary Bert Stand and Clarence Neal, chairman of Tammany's committee on organizations and elections. Stand and Neal were the source of influence for Vito Marcantonio, the controversial leftist congressman who opposed O'Dwyer in 1949 as the ALP's mayoral nominee.[121]

Although Sampson remained loyal to O'Dwyer's wishes, he was removed as leader in July 1948 by an executive committee vote engineered by Greenwich Village district leader Carmine DeSapio and supported by Costello. In retaliation against the replacement of Sampson with Hugo Rogers as leader of

Tammany Hall, O'Dwyer fired two Tammany district leaders from their city jobs.[122] When Tammany Hall elected DeSapio as its leader on July 20, 1949, it was clear that O'Dwyer could no longer dominate the Manhattan organization. Costello had supported the 1948 removal of Sampson, O'Dwyer's choice, led by DeSapio and supported DeSapio's own assumption of Tammany Hall's leadership.[123]

Despite his own connections with Frank Costello, DeSapio sought to improve Tammany Hall's public image. He soon rivaled O'Dwyer as the most prominent figure in local Democratic politics. Unlike his predecessor, DeSapio frequently held press conferences, gave guest lectures at colleges and civic organizations, and asserted that the "new" Tammany Hall would be an honest, progressive-minded organization identified with "the humane and liberal records" of Franklin D. Roosevelt and Harry S. Truman.[124]

Claiming that Tammany Hall would now focus on liberal ideas and policy goals, DeSapio prominently supported and lobbied New York City's congressmen for such Truman policy proposals as a permanent FEPC and national health insurance.[125] While Tammany Hall had opposed the successful Liberal party candidacy of Franklin D. Roosevelt Jr., in a special 1949 congressional election, DeSapio assured Tammany's endorsement and the Democratic nomination to Roosevelt in 1950 and 1952. After actively supporting the unsuccessful presidential candidacy of the aristocratic diplomat, W. Averell Harriman, at the 1952 Democratic National Convention, DeSapio quickly joined fellow machine politicians Jacob Arvey and David L. Lawrence in providing crucial delegate support for the nomination of Adlai Stevenson.[126]

Throughout his 1949 mayoral campaign, O'Dwyer maintained his public aloofness and disdain toward Tammany Hall. He rejected an invitation to a Tammany Hall fund-raising dinner and instead spoke to a meeting of the Fair Deal Democrats, an anti-Tammany Democratic organization on the same night.[127] Emphasizing his alleged independence from Tammany Hall and the policy accomplishments of his administration in the areas of housing, highway construction, and public education, O'Dwyer easily won a second term. During the campaign, O'Dwyer especially relied on his running mate, City Council President Vincent Impellitteri, to minimize the appeal of Vito Marcantonio, the ALP mayoral nominee, among the city's Italian voters.[128]

Just as he had secretly sought gangster and Tammany Hall support for his 1945 campaign and shrewdly used Impellitteri's ethnic status to counteract Marcantonio in his 1949 campaign, O'Dwyer likewise initially sought to reject Harry Truman as the 1948 Democratic presidential nominee since the then unpopular president appeared to be a liability for his own Democratic slate of candidates in 1948. The New York City mayor joined bosses Jacob Arvey of Chicago and Frank Hague of Jersey City in promoting Dwight Eisenhower for the Democratic presidential nomination.[129] Unlike Arvey, though, O'Dwyer did not loyally and assiduously mobilize the Democratic voters of his city on behalf of Truman's candidacy. O'Dwyer, Ed Flynn, and other Democratic politicians assumed that the New York governor and Republican presidential nominee Thomas E. Dewey would carry his own state and that Henry Wallace's Progressive party candidacy would ensure Dewey's victory by attracting ALP and other leftist voters who usually voted Democratic in presidential elections. Dewey, however, defeated Truman by a margin of only 60,959 votes, a margin of 1 percent, in New York State.[130] Two of Truman's White House aides, Donald Dawson and Eben Ayers surmised, however, that a more vigorous voter mobilization effort by O'Dwyer would have enabled Truman to carry New York.[131]

During his first term as mayor, O'Dwyer did not seek a close political relationship with Harry Truman and allowed Bronx Democratic county leader Ed Flynn, who also served as New York's Democratic national committeeman, to be his liaison with Truman. Considering O'Dwyer's support for Eisenhower and his lethargy toward Truman's campaign after the president was nominated at the convention, Truman certainly did not owe O'Dwyer any political assistance. Most federal patronage jobs for New York City were directed to Ed Flynn, who shared control of these appointments with Carmine DeSapio after DeSapio became Tammany leader.[132]

O'Dwyer had been reluctant to run for a second term and was partially pressured to do so by James Moran, a deputy fire commissioner and his closest political aide.[133] Shortly after the mayor's inauguration to a second term in 1950, Harry Gross, a flamboyant Brooklyn gambler, was arrested and claimed that he regularly paid protection money to more than three hundred police officers and was a major financial contributor to O'Dwyer's campaign through the intercession of Moran.[134] The Kefauver committee later disclosed that John Crane, the president of the New York City Firefighters' Union, claimed to have personally given O'Dwyer $10,000 and Moran $55,000, as illegal campaign contributions for O'Dwyer and gifts to Moran.[135] Moran was convicted in 1952 and imprisoned for seven years for accepting bribes from businessmen seeking to influence fire department permits and inspections.[136]

O'Dwyer wanted to resign as mayor as the seamier side of his mayoralty began to be revealed. Flynn perceived an opportunity to use Truman's intervention to enable O'Dwyer to resign gracefully while timing O'Dwyer's resignation so that a special mayoral election would be held on the same day as the 1950 state and congressional elections in November. Flynn hoped that a special mayoral election would increase Democratic voter turnout in New York City enough so that Democratic Senator Herbert Lehman would win a full term to the Senate and the Democratic nominee for governor could defeat Republican Governor Thomas E. Dewey's reelection bid. According to journalist Warren Moscow, Flynn "convinced Truman that the razzle-dazzle would help the New York Democrats elect a governor and that Truman, as a good party man, should forgive O'Dwyer's disloyalty."[137]

As a former DNC chairman and key actor in persuading Roosevelt to accept Truman as a running mate, Flynn knew how to appeal to Truman's ethos as a party regular. It was apparent that the electoral welfare of New York's Democratic slate in 1950 was at stake. Although, according to Warren Moscow, Flynn met Truman in the White House months before O'Dwyer announced his resignation on August 1, 1950, Truman already anticipated media and public speculation about the real political reasons for O'Dwyer's appointment as ambassador to Mexico shortly after his resignation.

According to White House press assistant Eben Ayers, one White House aide asked the president about how to address "the possibility that someone might raise the point as to the politics involved."[138] Ayers claimed that, in reply, Truman "laughed and said that was one question he could not answer truthfully."[139] Truman's role in Flynn's elaborate election strategy would certainly be hard to believe at this time. During his August 17, 1950, press conference, Truman simply told the press that "for several months Mayor O'Dwyer has been considering the Ambassadorship to Mexico. When I found out that he was in a favorable frame of mind, I sent for him and offered it to him."[140]

Unfortunately for Flynn, his campaign plan failed to achieve its electoral objectives. After Flynn, DeSapio, and other Democratic leaders secured the Democratic mayoral nomination for Ferdinand Pecora, Acting Mayor Vincent Impellitteri ran as an independent. Truman accepted Tammany Hall's invitation to visit New York City and have a photo opportunity with Pecora and followed its advice not to have a publicized meeting with Mayor Impellitteri.[141] Impellitteri skillfully exploited Tammany Hall's opposition to him by denouncing the Manhattan organization as corrupt and gangster-controlled and describing himself as "unbossed and unbought."[142] Having intensified the public's already aroused antipathy toward Tammany Hall, Impellitteri defeated Pecora by a margin of more than 219,000 votes.[143] Dewey easily defeated the Democratic gubernatorial nominee by a margin of more than 572,000 votes while Lehman won narrowly with the help of Liberal party votes.[144]

Although Impellitteri developed a rapprochement with Flynn and several Tammany district leaders, he continued to feud with DeSapio and made sure that DeSapio received no city patronage.[145] Although DeSapio asserted during the Kefauver committee hearings in New York City in 1951 that Frank Costello was "not a power in Tammany Hall," the Senate committee concluded from its investigation and its questioning of Costello and Ambassador O'Dwyer that a "pattern of connections between crime and politics is well established in New York City."[146]

After providing his testimony, William O'Dwyer returned to Mexico City and continued to serve as ambassador until the end of Truman's presidency. Despite the unfavorable publicity toward O'Dwyer that the Kefauver committee's report provided, Truman repeatedly refused to remove O'Dwyer as ambassador and asserted to the press his "confidence in Ambassador O'Dwyer."[147] The president proved to be far more steadfast and unconditional in his loyalty to O'Dwyer than the former mayor had been to him during the 1948 presidential campaign. Throughout the rest of Truman's presidency, Democratic politics in New York City continued to be characterized by bitter factionalism and conflict, especially between Mayor Vincent Impellitteri and Tammany Hall leader Carmine DeSapio.[148]

TWILIGHT OF MACHINE POWER

The mutually beneficial relationship that Franklin D. Roosevelt had forged with major Democratic machine bosses was partially based on the ability of urban machines to deliver substantial Democratic pluralities in presidential elections. The total Democratic plurality in the twelve largest American cities increased from nearly 1.8 million votes in 1932 to more than 2.2 million votes in 1944.[149] During Harry S. Truman's presidency, however, this aggregate Democratic plurality decreased to approximately 1.5 million votes in 1948 and to barely 1 million in 1952.[150]

The ability of urban Democratic machines to mobilize significant Democratic pluralities in presidential elections and even survive in local politics declined after World War II while the population and voting power of surrounding suburbs grew rapidly. The proportion of Americans living in central cities remained at 32 percent from 1940 to 1950 while the number living in the suburbs increased from 15 percent to 23 percent.[151] More specifically, while New York City and Chicago provided approximate, respective, Democratic pluralities of 360,000 and 161,000 votes in the 1952 presidential election, the suburbs of New York City and Chicago provided approximate, respective Republican pluralities of 376,000 and 277,000 votes in that election.[152]

With the electoral power of central cities diminishing, Harry Truman generally remained sensitive and responsive to the political and public policy needs
of urban Democratic leaders. Having served as a county judge in charge of
public works and as a federal unemployment official prior to his Senate career,
Truman could empathize with mayors and ward bosses concerned with the public infrastructure of their cities and the economic needs of their working-class
and unemployed constituents. Democratic mayors like David L. Lawrence and
William O'Dwyer were among the most vigorous advocates of the Employment Act of 1946 and the Housing Act of 1949.[153]

While the Housing Act of 1949 provided local officials and private devel-
opers with the authority and funds to clear slums and begin private construction
projects to revitalize downtown economies, it proved to be disappointing and
inadequate in providing public housing for low-income urban residents. The
1949 law authorized the construction of 810,000 units of public housing by
1955, but only 356,203 units were built by July 1, 1964.[154] The Pittsburgh and
Chicago Democratic machines, which were the most successful and enduring in
the postwar era, nonetheless, effectively used the 1949 law and subsequent federal urban renewal and public housing policies to help them maintain their power.
Mayor David Lawrence was able to use the Housing Act of 1949 to facilitate
and supplement an impressive, consensus-building urban renewal program for
Pittsburgh that he had begun in 1946.[155] Especially in Chicago, machine politicians used federally subsidized public housing to simultaneously satisfy the
housing needs of their low-income black constituents and the demands of their
white supporters for de facto segregation from blacks in housing and public
education.[156]

In general, though, federal domestic policies tended to be more detrimental
than beneficial to machine politics. Federally subsidized FHA and VA mort-
gages and expressway construction encouraged many white central city residents to move to nearby suburbs and become home-owning commuters. With
their federal benefits enabling them to receive college educations and become
white-collar, suburban professionals and business managers, young veterans
were more likely to reject the political ethos of the party regulars that Harry
Truman, machine politicians, and older, urban working-class voters shared and
become Republicans, independents, or Democrats more likely to be split-ticket
voters.[157] The Democratic voters most enthusiastic about Adlai Stevenson's presidential candidacy in 1952, for example, were often young well-educated professionals, some of whom became active in antimachine reform efforts. They
were attracted to Stevenson's idealistic, eloquent rhetoric rather than to his party
affiliation.[158]

Among the machines' remaining working class, poor, and minority constituents, the expansion of federal social welfare benefits begun during the New
Deal weakened the transactional relationship in which these constituents in particular exchanged their electoral support of machine-endorsed candidates for
minor patronage jobs and informal welfare benefits. Since federally regulated
and funded social welfare benefits were entitlements and legal rights, ward bosses
could not easily manipulate and exploit their administration in order to elicit
voting behavior loyal to machine-supported slates of candidates.[159] Also, the
extension of civil service coverage to more jobs in federal, state, and local government after World War II steadily reduced the supply of patronage jobs that
machine politics could use to reward and maintain the political loyalty of their
campaign workers and lower-level organization members.[160] Even Mayor Martin Kennelly of Chicago, whose candidacy was supported by Jacob Arvey and
other machine ward bosses, significantly reduced the number of municipal patronage jobs through civil service reforms. Despite his understanding of the
importance of federal patronage for machine politicians, Harry Truman implemented reforms to reduce the number of political appointments in the Post Office and the Bureau of Internal Revenue, the predecessor of the Internal Revenue
Service.[161]

Harry Truman, though, was careful to consult Democratic machine politicians loyal to him and concerned about major federal appointments within their
cities.[162] Truman also used his presidential power to grant pardons and commute
prison sentences for the benefit of convicted machine politicians. Truman com-
muted the prison sentence of James M. Curley, the colorfully roguish mayor of
Boston, for mail fraud and pardoned Curley's previous conviction for taking a
federal civil service exam for a friend.[163] Likewise, Truman's appointment of
William O'Dwyer as ambassador to Mexico during growing revelations of
O'Dwyer's dealings with the gangster-controlled Tammany Hall and appointments of organized crime figures in the mayor's administration was widely perceived as a virtual exemption from any possible, future criminal investigations.[164]
In 1953, journalist Jules Abels contended, "No one had ever conceived of the
diplomatic service as a sanctuary for corrupt politicians until Harry Truman
entered the White House."[165]

Truman's ethos as a party regular experienced in the subculture and internal behavior of urban machines influenced his decisions to assist Democratic
machine politicians through federal policies favorable to urban needs, legal favors, federal appointments, and neutrality in local intraparty conflicts between
promachine and antimachine Democrats. Nevertheless, apparently inevitable
and irreversible demographic, economic, and political forces withered most major

urban machines after World War II. The increasing intolerance of American voters for the anachronistic, self-contained urban autocracies of Ed Crump in Memphis and Frank Hague in Jersey City was evident in the nomination and subsequent election of anti-Crump Democratic candidates for senator and governor in 1948 and the defeat of Hague's nephew and personally chosen successor in the mayoral election of 1949.[166] Tammany Hall and the Chicago machine also suffered significant defeats in the 1950 elections.[167]

With their weakened ability to nominate and elect their own candidates for local offices, it was not surprising that most Democratic machine politicians initially scorned Truman as a disastrous liability for their slates of candidates in 1948. The ethos of a party regular, shared by Harry Truman and urban machine politicians, was increasingly rejected by voters and activists who cared more about policy issues and candidates' personal qualities than consistent party loyalty.[168] With most major Democratic machines eroding as sources of reliable, effective electoral support and bases of internal party organization, Harry Truman's party leadership sought to use the chairmen, staff, and resources of the Democratic National Committee headquarters to instill his party regular and liberal reformist values within the national Democratic party.

3

★ ★ ★ ★ ★

TRUMAN AND THE DEMOCRATIC NATIONAL COMMITTEE

Columnist Drew Pearson had a conversation with former President Harry Truman in 1959 in which Truman told Pearson that he had recently reprimanded DNC Chairman Paul Butler. According to Pearson, Truman stated that he told Butler that the DNC chairman's job is "to keep the party together, not stir up trouble. The party platform is adopted at each convention and it's the job of the chairman to carry it out. . . . I told him that it's up to the chairman to see that there is harmony in the party."[1] More specifically, the former president had scolded Butler for his publicized comments with Democratic leaders in Congress, especially Senate Majority Leader Lyndon Johnson and Speaker of the House Sam Rayburn, concerning the programmatic and ideological identity of the national Democratic party during the Eisenhower presidency. Johnson and Rayburn wanted a more moderate Democratic party that would cooperate with President Eisenhower while Butler wanted to develop and articulate a more distinctly, consistently, and combatively liberal Democratic party.[2]

HST'S CONCEPT OF THE DNC'S ROLE

In his criticism of Butler, Harry Truman was expressing his ethos as a party regular. As such, Truman evidently believed that a DNC chairman should concentrate on this position's traditional duties of fund raising, organizational leadership, and enhancing intraparty harmony and unity rather than focusing on divisive ideological and programmatic issues that could cause intraparty conflict and thus weaken the party's electoral performance in congressional and presidential campaigns.[3] In his explanation of the four "factional types" of presidential partisanship, political scientist Ralph Goldman has categorized Truman as "partisan." For Goldman, "partisan" presidents are those who "have been

explicit, articulate, and even unabashedly proud of their party affiliation, relatively active in the party's management, and willing to solicit and to campaign
on behalf of the party."[4]

While Harry Truman's nonideological, pragmatic ethos as a party regular
led him to criticize Paul Butler's behavior as DNC chairman, his other ethos as
a liberal reformer induced him to readily accept Butler's appointment of him in
1956 to the Democratic Advisory Council (DAC).[5] Ironically and paradoxi-
cally, Truman as a DAC member served in a DNC-affiliated organization that
developed and articulated a distinctly liberal ideological and programmatic identity for the Democratic party on such divisive issues as civil rights, federal aid to
education, and federal health care policy.[6] Despite his prominence on the DAC
and Sam Rayburn's bitter opposition to the DAC, Truman sympathetically wrote
to Rayburn in 1959 that "I know that you are as unappreciative as I am" of
Butler's behavior as DNC chairman.[7] A further irony and contradiction is that,
while he was president, Truman opposed the formation of a policy advisory
council like the DAC when such a council was proposed by the American Political Science Association's report, "Toward a More Responsible Two-Party
System," in 1950.[8]

These contradictions in Harry Truman's behavior and comments regarding
Paul Butler's chairmanship, Sam Rayburn, and his own activism within the
liberally inclined DAC illustrate conflicts between Truman's two value systems
as a party regular and liberal reformer. More specifically, they also reveal his
own perceptions of the purposes of the DNC chairmen, staff, special divisions,
and the DNC members during his presidency. Through his rhetoric and behavior as party leader that pertained to his relationships with these various elements
of the DNC, Truman often hoped that the DNC could both improve and maintain intraparty harmony in an increasingly divided, factionalized party. Yet he
also articulated and promoted the liberal identity that he wanted to enhance and
perpetuate for the party.[9]

But, of course, it was the DNC chairmen's expression of Truman's liberalism, especially on such policy positions as civil rights, the Taft-Hartley Act, and
national health insurance, that alienated conservative Democrats and intensified intraparty conflict.[10]

Truman's qualities as both a party regular attractive to machine bosses and
southern conservatives in the Senate and as a New Deal loyalist acceptable to such
liberal interest groups as organized labor and blacks were recognized by Franklin D.
Roosevelt when he asked the Missouri senator to succeed Frank Walker as DNC
chairman in 1944. Truman declined the offer and suggested Robert E. Hannegan,
who was then serving as commissioner of internal revenue.[11] Later in 1944, it

was evident to Hannegan, Walker, and Ed Flynn, who had preceded Walker as DNC chairman, that Harry Truman's status as a New Deal liberal from a machine background was also acceptable to more conservative Democrats in Congress. This made him the ideal compromise nominee for vice president.[12]

While Roosevelt increasingly neglected to consult his DNC chairmen after 1936, Harry Truman usually met with the DNC chairman every Wednesday throughout his administration.[13] Political scientist Sidney M. Milkis concluded that "Truman was far more appreciative of party organization than his predecessor."[14] Furthermore, unlike Roosevelt, Truman established a well-defined division of labor and responsibilities among his White House staff and cabinet members regarding relations with the DNC chairmen and staff in order to avoid overlapping, conflicting lines of jurisdiction and communication.[15] Truman deferred patronage matters concerning the DNC to White House personnel director Donald Dawson, and other matters affecting relations between the DNC headquarters and the White House to Matthew Connelly, his appointments secretary.[16] According to presidential scholar James W. Davis, Harry Truman thus began "the practice of designating a staff assistant as the president's personal liaison or contact with party officials and political leaders throughout the country, including national committee members."[17]

Harry Truman's passion for order, efficiency, and a minimum of internal disputes was also found in his choice of DNC chairmen. All four DNC chairmen who served during Truman's presidency were Irish Catholics who had success and experience in such political fields as campaign management, voter mobilization, and fund raising. Such political skills were crucial to party regulars like Truman. All of the DNC chairmen under Truman fit the following characterization that V.O. Key Jr., provided in 1950: "The national chairman is, in effect, a technician, a specialist in campaign management and machine tending, who exercises his power only so long as he enjoys the confidence of the presidential nominee."[18]

Truman's consistent selection of Irish Catholics as DNC chairmen also reflected continuity and precedent. All four DNC chairmen chosen by Roosevelt had also been Irish Catholics. Besides sharing the ethnic and church affiliation of many Democratic politicians and party activists in northeastern and midwestern industrial states, Irish Catholics had traditionally been prominent in the Democratic party for their organizational and liaison skills within the party structure.[19] In 1947 Truman reputedly wanted Clinton Anderson, a Protestant and his first secretary of agriculture, to succeed Bob Hannegan as DNC chairman. Hannegan and Edwin Pauley, a former secretary of the DNC and a major Democratic contributor, urged Anderson to decline the offer.

They claimed that only an Irish Catholic should serve as DNC chairman in order to appease the mostly Irish Democratic machine politicians.[20] Eleanor Roosevelt also opposed Anderson as a possible successor to Hannegan and wrote to Truman, "I consider him a conservative and I consider that the only chance the Democratic party has for election in 1948, is to be the liberal party."[21] With such opposition to Anderson based on both religious and ideological grounds, Truman the regular prudently designated Senator J. Howard McGrath, a Catholic liberal, as Hannegan's successor.

While Truman's selection of DNC chairmen reflected a certain organizational conservatism, the president's reformist ethos expressed itself in his vigorous support of the innovative campaign and publicity techniques and organizational changes suggested by the DNC's chairmen, staff, and special divisions. For example, during the 1948 campaign, Truman was impressed by the comic book about his life and administration that the DNC's publicity division had produced and distributed. Also, during the campaign, Truman adopted the White House staff's suggestion that DNC Chairman J. Howard McGrath establish, fund, and staff a Research Division that would provide the information and outlines necessary for his 1948 whistle-stop campaign.[22]

Truman likewise thought that annual party conventions sponsored by the DNC would be beneficial to the party, if the DNC could afford to finance them.[23] To symbolize the beginning of racial integration within the DNC's apparatus, Truman directed McGrath to end the DNC's Negro Division and hire black staff members during the 1948 campaign.[24] According to her autobiography, Truman offered India Edwards, who served as executive director of the DNC's Women's Division during most of Truman's presidency, the DNC chairmanship in 1951.[25] Edwards declined the offer to succeed William M. Boyle Jr., by telling Truman, "I do not think the men of our party are ready to have a woman chairman."[26]

Truman confirmed his preference for Edwards as Boyle's successor during his press conference of Oct. 25, 1951.[27] If India Edwards had agreed to chair the DNC, Harry Truman would have made history as a party leader by choosing the first woman to chair the Democratic National Committee. While Truman the regular eventually chose Frank McKinney, another Irish Catholic experienced in fund raising and other intraparty committee functions, Truman the reformer evidently had been willing to use the DNC chairmanship to symbolize a more inclusive, progressive, and evolving Democratic party. In Truman's relationships and decisions concerning DNC chairmen and other organizational elements and political issues concerning the DNC, Truman's party leadership would often reveal a mixture of, and occasional conflict between, his value systems as a party regular and as a liberal reformer.

DNC CHAIRMEN, 1945-1952

"To be ideal, a chairman would have to be an organizer of the first quality, a financier of rare ability, a peace-maker of unusual charm, and a diplomat par excellence," according to political scientist Marie Chatham.[28] In his analysis of the national party chairmen's rise in status and influence during the early to mid-twentieth century, political scientist Harold F. Bass Jr., concluded that the national party chairman "was the party's representative in the presidency and the president's liaison with the party."[29] None of the four DNC chairmen who served under Harry Truman fulfilled Chatham's ideal, but all of them loyally and effectively served as Truman's liaison with the DNC and the Democratic party in general.

Serving as DNC chairman from 1944 until 1947, Robert E. Hannegan had been instrumental in organizing enough votes in St. Louis to provide Truman's narrow plurality in his 1940 senatorial primary victory. After securing Hannegan's appointment as collector of internal revenue for eastern Missouri in 1943, Truman then urged Roosevelt to select Bob Hannegan as DNC chairman in 1944.[30] Prior to the 1944 Democratic national convention, Hannegan energetically promoted Truman for the vice presidential nomination by scheduling him as a speaker at Democratic fund raising dinners throughout the nation and reminding Roosevelt about Truman's assets as a running mate.[31]

More so than the following three DNC chairmen who served under Truman, Bob Hannegan solidified and projected a pro-union, liberal identity for the national Democratic party, especially for gaining the political support of CIO unions.[32] This was especially important due to the appeal of Henry Wallace's Progressive party to the more leftist union leaders and the initial alienation of some labor leaders from Truman after the president threatened to draft striking railroad workers in 1946.[33] As postmaster general, Hannegan warily observed the potential of Secretary of the Treasury John Snyder to influence Truman to become more conservative, and thus possibly anti-union, on economic issues. According to columnist Drew Pearson, Hannegan warned Truman that "these men are bad for the country and they're bad for the party. . . . the Democratic Party can thrive only if and when it is the liberal party."[34]

Just as Hannegan was determined to perpetuate pro-union New Deal liberalism to define Truman's party leadership and domestic policy agenda, the *St. Louis Democrat* was equally determined to revitalize the DNC staff, operations, and fund-raising ability. Hannegan assumed that combining a liberal identity for the party with more effective methods of publicity, fund raising, and liaison work with state and local Democratic committees as well as with Congress would continue the Democratic party's electoral and policy success. Shortly after becoming DNC chairman in 1944, Bob Hannegan found that the DNC headquarters was underfunded, understaffed, complacent, and lethargic.[35] Hannegan hired an energetic staff led by publicity director Paul Porter, established close communications with state and local Democratic committees, and conducted an extensively micromanaged voter turnout effort during the 1944 presidential campaign in order to prevent an upset Republican victory caused by low Democratic voter turn-out and organizational inertia by the Roosevelt campaign.[36]

Hannegan's commitment to an ideologically liberal, electorally successful Democratic party also manifested itself in his desire to be more influential in the formation of domestic policy within the Truman administration. Besides using his position as postmaster general to advocate liberal, pro-union positions during cabinet meetings, Hannegan repeatedly asked to regularly attend White House staff meetings.[37] According to White House aide Eben A. Ayers, the White House staff firmly opposed Hannegan's presence, and Truman agreed that Hannegan would not be invited.[38] As the 1946 congressional elections approached, Hannegan was increasingly frustrated by the policy influence of Truman's more conservative White House aides, such as John Steelman. In his column of Sept. 14, 1946, Drew Pearson wrote, "All the money he raises from Jackson Day dinners, all the organization work he does with local Democrats can't win a victory, argues Hannegan, as long as fumblers mess up policy around the White House."[39]

Despite Hannegan's efforts to minimize the disenchantment of liberal activists toward Truman and increase Democratic voter turnout, Republicans won control of both houses of Congress in 1946. Even more important than the substantial Republican numerical gains in congressional seats was the apparent public rejection of the pro-labor, social welfare liberalism that Hannegan promoted.[40] Due to the desire of many Democratic congressional nominees to avoid campaign appearances with the currently unpopular president, Truman declined to campaign, and Hannegan's publicity stressed the Democratic party's continuing identification with Roosevelt and the New Deal.[41] Hannegan even produced radio commercials using tape recordings of Roosevelt's voice.[42] In the immediate aftermath of the 1946 congressional elections, however, the results seemed to indicate a widespread public repudiation of the bureaucratic meddling, meat shortages, favoritism toward socially irresponsible labor unions, high taxes, and excessive economic regulations that the Republicans associated with the Democratic party under Truman.[43]

Truman, however, did not insist that Hannegan resign as DNC chairman because of the 1946 election results.[44] As postmaster general, Hannegan continued to advocate pro-union policy positions at cabinet meetings. He and Secretary of Labor Lewis Schwellenbach were the only cabinet members who privately advised Truman to veto the Republican-sponsored Taft-Hartley bill of 1947.[45] Hannegan hoped that the enactment of this bill, despite Truman's veto of it, would minimize defections of labor leaders from Truman in the 1948 presidential campaign.[46]

Hannegan's time and attention to his duties as party chairman, however, were limited by his efforts to modernize the postal system and by his failing health. Gael Sullivan, an assistant postmaster general and a protégé of Chicago boss Ed Kelly, resigned his federal position on Feb. 12, 1947, to become executive director of the DNC.[47] In contrast to the ailing Hannegan, Sullivan exuded boundless physical energy, new ideas for revitalizing the dispirited Democratic party, and a rousing speaking style.

Like Hannegan, Sullivan wanted to forge cooperative political relationships with CIO unions and improve the Democratic party's appeal to veterans and the youngest voters. Sullivan was brimming with ideas for simultaneously keeping the Democratic party and Truman's domestic policies committed to New Deal liberalism and union interests and promoting the electoral strength of the party for the 1948 campaign through frequent speaking trips and regular radio publicity. For example, the DNC's Publicity Division announced on August 22, 1947, that Sullivan would coordinate a nationally broadcast "radio rally of the Democratic Party" on September 2, 1947, with local Democratic committees throughout the nation. The Publicity Division claimed that this event "will mark the first time that a major political party has used the radio as a means of conducting a meeting of the party nationally."[48] When the DNC's Publicity Division announced another radio rally to be held on January 2, 1948, it claimed that during the radio rally of September 2, 1947, "more than 4,000 individual gatherings were held in counties all over the nation."[49]

From 1947 until his resignation in April 1948, Sullivan developed an enthusiastic following among Democratic activists through his morale boosting speeches. He achieved the admiration of some DNC members and Democratic state chairmen by periodically polling them for their opinions about whether Truman should sign or veto certain bills.[50] As a party speaker, though, Sullivan was willing to occasionally engage in shrill demagoguery. In a 1947 Maryland speech, he compared the 1946 Republican sweep of Congress to the rise of the former Nazi party in Germany and the contemporary Communist party in Hungary.[51] While addressing the Kansas Democratic Club on Feb. 21, 1948, he argued, "One flank of the peoples' [*sic*] battle-line for human advancement is exposed to the Tories of the Status Quo who put money before mankind—and the other flank is exposed to the Commies of Godless Government who would make every individual a chattel of the State."[52]

Upon Bob Hannegan's announcement of his retirement as DNC chairman in August 1947, a growing number of Democrats urged Truman to nominate Sullivan as the new DNC chairman.[53] Impressed by Sullivan's speech at a convention of Young Democrats in Indianapolis, Pleas E. Greenlee, chairman of the Indiana Democratic state committee, urged Truman to select Sullivan as the next DNC chairman. Greenlee told the president that Gael Sullivan "is what we call in Indiana a real Democrat with the Party's interest at heart."[54] Throughout August 1947, Truman was inundated with letters and telegrams urging the selection of Gael Sullivan as Hannegan's successor.[55]

One of Sullivan's most enthusiastic supporters was A.F. Whitney, the president of the Brotherhood of Railroad Trainmen. Sullivan had reconciled Whitney with Truman since the union leader had previously vowed to oppose Truman in the 1948 campaign because of the president's 1946 proposal to draft striking railroad workers.[56] Likewise, Congressman Michael Kirwan of Ohio praised Sullivan for "the enthusiasm and determination with which he meets the problems that concern our Congressional Committee."[57]

While Bob Hannegan had been somewhat reluctant to accept Roosevelt's offer to become DNC chairman, Gael Sullivan yearned for the position.[58] Sullivan's opportunity to become the next DNC chairman was destroyed, however, by an automobile accident in which Sullivan was initially charged with drunken driving, then pleaded no contest to reckless driving.[59]

Upon the resignation of Bob Hannegan as DNC chairman on September 27, 1947, Truman designated Senator J. Howard McGrath of Rhode Island as Hannegan's successor.[60] The DNC formally elected him on October 29, 1947.[61] At the request of McGrath, Sullivan continued as executive director of the DNC.

In a 1968 interview, White House appointments secretary Matthew J. Connelly claimed that he had persuaded Harry Truman to select J. Howard McGrath.[62] Connelly had known McGrath since 1935, when McGrath was a U.S. attorney in Providence, Rhode Island. Besides his status as an Irish Catholic, McGrath was a proven vote getter and organizer. Having been elected governor of Rhode Island three times, he won a Senate seat in 1946, despite the national Republican landslide.

He had also been prominent as vice chairman and then the chairman of Rhode Island's Democratic state committee and as a protégé of Rhode Island's Senator Theodore F. Green during Green's efforts to strengthen the Democratic party organization of their state.[63] Under Green's tutelage, McGrath learned how to build and balance multi-ethnic coalitions. McGrath's 1946 platform and brief Senate record indicated that he was a staunch, pro-union liberal. In short, McGrath seemed to have all the necessary qualities and political skills for preparing and conducting Truman's upcoming presidential campaign.

During his service as DNC chairman from October 1947 until August 1949, J. Howard McGrath faced the greatest obstacles and challenges of all the Truman-era DNC chairmen. Kenneth Birkhead, a member of the DNC's Research Division during the 1948 campaign, sympathized with McGrath, given the problems with a faction-ridden, demoralized party and underfunded campaign treasury. Birkhead recalled that McGrath "worked in the worst possible conditions for a chairman to work under. The Party had taken a beating in '46 in the off-year elections; we were short as heck of money. . . . I know they had a heck of a time keeping up money to get the President on the radio and what little television he got, and keep the train going."[64]

Birkhead's synopsis of the problems that McGrath confronted, however, is an understatement. Before and after McGrath struggled to plan, finance, and execute Truman's presidential campaign, the Rhode Island Democrat was beset by a variety of dangers to Truman's party leadership. In late 1947 and early 1948, McGrath was faced with the movement to nominate Dwight Eisenhower for president (led by such nationally prominent Democrats as California state committee Chairman James Roosevelt and Senator Claude Pepper of Florida), Henry Wallace's Progressive party campaign for president, and southern reaction against Truman's civil rights proposals that stimulated the States' Rights Democratic or "Dixiecrat" presidential candidacy of Governor J. Strom Thurmond of South Carolina.[65] As the party spokesman for Truman's policy positions, McGrath's most challenging task regarding strengthening intraparty unity behind Truman was his efforts to maintain the active support of southern Democrats who were loyal to Truman's candidacy but who also opposed the party's civil rights platform adopted at the 1948 Democratic national convention.[66]

Meanwhile, McGrath had to legally challenge efforts of anti-Truman Democrats in several southern states to prevent Truman from being listed as the official Democratic presidential nominee on their states' ballots.[67] There was even a southern revolt within the DNC headquarters. Shortly after Harry Truman delivered his civil rights message to Congress, George B. Hamilton, the DNC's director of finance, resigned from this position in protest.[68]

Like Bob Hannegan, McGrath was frustrated by the fact that he did not exert more influence on the president's patronage decisions or with the White House staff. The DNC chairman was especially angry that in the election year of 1948 Truman appointed Thomas B. McCabe, a Republican, as chairman of the Federal Reserve Board and Jesse Donaldson, a career civil servant, as Post-master General without consulting him.[69] McGrath had especially wanted to appease southerners by having a southern Democrat appointed chairman of the Federal Reserve Board instead of McCabe. The *Providence Evening Bulletin* commented, "Even before the election of McGrath to the chairmanship of the Democratic National Committee last summer, it was known that party head-quarters was seriously dissatisfied with the role it was playing in matters of party policy."[70]

The White House staff, likewise, was not satisfied with the quality of DNC staff operations in the initial period of McGrath's DNC chairmanship. In a November 19, 1947, memo to Truman proposing a campaign strategy, special counsel Clark M. Clifford provided the following complaints and constructive criticism:

> The current "organization" pours out reams of publicity . . . but there seems to be hardly anyone out "beating the bushes" to harmonize where possible and desirable. . . . [T]he one essential is to have the new Chair-man of the National Democratic Committee, as soon as possible— working to rebuild the Party organization from the ground up. . . . [T]he practice of today's Democratic organization in spending almost all its time in raising money and doing favors for "the faithful" may be useful but it does little to rebuild the Democratic Party—and that is what it needs."[71]

Not surprisingly, it was primarily the White House staff led by Clifford, rather than the DNC chairman, that provided Truman with most of the advice for the content of his campaign speeches, especially during his whistle-stop train trips. Perhaps the most innovative contribution of DNC headquarters to the whistle-stop campaign was the DNC's Research Division. This staff division provided Truman and his aides on the campaign train with information on policy con-cerns, historical facts, and political figures peculiar to the communities in which Truman delivered speeches on a daily basis. Although the DNC's Research Di-vision was part of the DNC headquarters and technically under McGrath's au-thority, the idea for a research division originated with the White House staff. It maintained direct communications with the DNC's Research Division, thus cir-cumventing McGrath. Most of the research staff sensed that McGrath perceived their division as a waste of meager DNC funds.[72]

Following Truman's upset electoral victory of 1948, McGrath had the un-enviable responsibility to explain and implement Truman's vacillating patronage policy toward pro-Dixiecrat members of Congress. Shortly after the election, Truman the reformer asserted to his White House staff, "I don't want any fringes in the Democratic party . . . no Wallace-ites or states' righters."[73] In his memoirs, Truman seemed liberated as a party leader from the southern conservatives. "I was happy and pleased to be elected by a Democratic party that did not depend upon . . . the southern bloc."[74]

During the first few months of 1949, Truman and McGrath publicly stated that federal patronage would be distributed to Democrats in Congress according to their party loyalty and voting records on current legislation, especially Truman's goal of repealing the Taft-Hartley Act. Such a policy would have the effect of denying patronage to such Dixiecrat members of Congress as Senator James Eastland of Mississippi and Representative F. Edward Hebert of Louisiana.[75]

The president, however, also tried to downplay the significance of the Dixiecrat revolt by euphemistically referring to it as "the late unpleasantness." Reflecting Truman the regular's rhetorical attempts at reconciliation with southern conservatives, McGrath referred to the Dixiecrat campaign, in which several southern states denied Truman the ballot designation as the presidential nominee of the Democratic party, as a "venial" rather than a "mortal" sin against the national Democratic party.[76]

During the remainder of McGrath's chairmanship, he and Truman pursued a more conciliatory, moderate patronage policy in which they simply preferred the granting of federal patronage to pro-Truman southern Democrats rather than former Dixiecrats. Thus, to the consternation of more liberal southern Democrats, some former Dixiecrats and their sympathizers received federal appointments recommended by McGrath and approved by Truman.[77] McGrath and pro-Thurmond Mississippi Senator John Stennis consulted Truman by April 1949 about federal patronage.[78] Compared to the more combatively liberal Bob Hannegan, who periodically antagonized and alienated southern conservatives, McGrath later stated that as DNC chairman he wanted to influence federal appointments in order to unite and placate Democrats of all kinds in Congress.[79]

By the summer of 1949, however, McGrath increasingly concentrated on his Senate duties until Truman announced in August 1949 that he would nominate McGrath to succeed Tom Clark as attorney general. McGrath's most significant final action as DNC chairman was to refuse to invite Dixiecrat DNC members from Mississippi and Louisiana to the next DNC meeting, in which McGrath's successor would be chosen.[80] In lengthy meetings conducted on August 23 and 24 of 1949, DNC members who belonged to the Credentials Committee subsequently voted to expel five Dixiecrat DNC members from South Carolina, Alabama, Mississippi, and Louisiana by using Rule 11 of the DNC.[81]

The transition of the chairmanship of the DNC from J. Howard McGrath to his successor, William M. Boyle Jr., was smooth, gradual, and predictable. Truman selected Boyle as executive vice chairman of the DNC on February 8, 1949, and Boyle began to perform most of McGrath's administrative duties as DNC chairman at DNC headquarters. A Kansas City Democrat and veteran of the Pendergast machine, Boyle was more of an alter ego for Truman's party leadership than any other DNC chairman who served under Truman. A former police chief and a prosperous lawyer, Boyle came to Washington, D.C., in 1941 to serve as assistant counsel for Truman's committee for investigating defense spending. In 1942 Truman hired Boyle as his personal secretary and then had Hannegan appoint Boyle as an executive assistant to the DNC chairman so that Boyle could manage Truman's 1944 vice presidential campaign.[82] During Truman's 1948 whistle-stop campaign, Boyle likewise managed the president's train schedule.[83]

On August 24, 1949, the same day on which five Dixiecrats were expelled from the DNC, the DNC formally elected Bill Boyle as chairman. Truman used his address at the DNC dinner honoring Boyle to implicitly state that while the South would no longer dominate the national Democratic party it was welcome as a member of a more nationally integrated, less regional party. "The Democratic Party is a national party, and not a sectional party any more. The tail no longer wags the dog."[84]

Compared to the two previous DNC chairmen, Boyle assumed more of a lobbying role for the president in his relationship with Democrats in Congress. Shortly after Boyle was elected DNC chairman, Harry Truman nominated Leland Olds for a third term on the Federal Power Commission. Led by Democratic Senator Robert Kerr of Oklahoma, a coalition of Republicans and southern moderate and conservative Democrats opposed the confirmation of Olds by the Senate. Olds was a controversial economic liberal perceived as hostile to the interests of the oil industry and as a closet Marxist.[85]

Undaunted, Truman expressed his ethos in his party leadership as a liberal reformer by explicitly telling the press on October 6, 1949 that the Olds nomination was a matter of party loyalty and that he expected Democratic senators to confirm Olds's nomination. Truman stated that Boyle's publicized lobbying of Democratic state chairmen to pressure Democratic senators from their states to vote for Olds's confirmation was "customary, . . . proper, and it should be done."[86] On the topic of party leadership in general, Truman stated, "You have got to have party discipline, if you are going to transact the business of the Government. . . . A man is elected on a party platform, and he ought to carry out what the party promises to do."[87]

Political scientist Ralph Goldman later concluded that Truman's remarks on presidential party leadership regarding Olds's nomination were "possibly the strongest and clearest affirmation to date of presidential prerogatives as party leader."[88] In addition to lobbying by Boyle, Truman asked Eleanor Roosevelt to actively support the reappointment of Leland Olds and submitted a public letter to the Senate urging Olds's confirmation.[89] In addition to contacting Democratic governors and mayors to generate public support for Olds, Boyle urged Olds's confirmation in a radio broadcast.[90]

On the day before the Senate vote on Truman's nomination of Leland Olds, *Washington Star* columnist Lowell Mellett praised Boyle's lobbying for revolutionizing the DNC's role:

What most people failed to realize was that chairman Boyle's action was in keeping with the character the National Committee has assumed since Mr. Truman became President. The National Committee has become an instrument of party policy. There's no longer merely a political machine at the service of any person calling himself a Democrat. It is dedicating itself to the double purpose of carrying out the party's platform and the achievement of party responsibility.[91]

Despite the praise that Truman received from the ADA and liberal columnists, the Senate rejected Olds by a vote of 53 to 15 on October 12, 1949.[92]

In 1950, though, Truman was more successful in using Boyle as a lobbyist for advocating liberal policy positions in Congress for key legislation. When Truman was initially uncertain about whether to sign or veto a bill passed by the bipartisian conservative coalition, such as Robert Kerr's bill to weaken the Natural Gas Act of 1938, Boyle's intervention partially influenced his decision.[93] Generally critical of the Truman administration, columnists Robert S. Allen and William V. Shannon admitted that "Boyle worked hand in glove with militant Democrats . . . to obtain a presidential veto on boodle bills that they couldn't defeat in Congress."[94]

Regardless of whether Truman wanted to express his values as a liberal reformer or a party regular, Bill Boyle was a loyal, skillful instrument of Truman's party leadership. For the most part, though, Boyle focused his DNC chairmanship on improving the internal harmony, campaign finances, and electoral strength of the Democratic party for the 1950 mid-term elections. To achieve the first of these three objectives, Boyle and the DNC periodically organized regional conferences. In a radio interview conducted on October 28, 1949, Boyle stated, "The Democratic National Committee acts as a sort of line of communications to the country."[95] Boyle elaborated that regional party conferences would be one DNC method of informing Democrats about federal policies that especially affected their regions. He announced that the first DNC-sponsored regional conference would be held in Boston on December 20 and 21, 1949, for New England Democrats.[96]

The largest and most politically significant Democratic regional conference during Boyle's chairmanship was held in Chicago on May 15, 1950. Seeking to unite and energize party officials and activists for the 1950 midterm elections, Truman told the Democrats at this conference that the "Democratic Party, today, is the mainstream of American life. It is the party of progressive liberalism."[97] Truman then reaffirmed the liberal identity of the Democratic party as defined by its 1948 platform and his Fair Deal legislation. In particular, Truman's address in Chicago reasserted the commitment of his party leadership to the repeal of the Taft-Hartley Act and the enactment of federal aid to education and civil rights legislation.[98]

Boyle was especially successful in improving the financial health of DNC headquarters. Helped by the favorable impression of Truman's campaign skills among wealthy Democratic contributors following his upset victory in 1948, Boyle announced that by the end of 1949 the DNC had a surplus of $431,169. By contrast, the Republican National Committee (RNC) suffered a deficit of $509,809 by the end of 1949.[99] The DNC raised $1,696,192 in 1950 and $1,318,574 in 1951 compared to the respective RNC amounts of $828,164 and $679,157.[100] Furthermore, during the 1950 campaign, Boyle announced that the DNC would spend $250,000 to purchase a new building for its headquarters.[101]

Despite Boyle's impressive fund-raising and organizational efforts, the Democrats lost five Senate seats, including that of Senate majority leader Scott Lucas of Illinois, and twenty-eight House seats.[102] Truman, though, did not ask for Boyle's resignation. In a November 29, 1950, letter to a Kansas City supporter, the president claimed that, except for the Democratic gains of 1934, "the returns from the election of 1950 are the best off year returns for the Party in power" and that the Republican electoral success in 1950 was due to "vilification and untruths," especially McCarthyism.[103]

While Truman retained his faith in Boyle as chairman, several White House aides partially attributed the extent of Democratic losses in the 1950 election to Boyle. White House aides Ken Hechler, George Elsey, David Lloyd, and Charles Murphy believed that Democratic losses would have been fewer if Boyle had created and maintained an effective full-time DNC Research Division, similar to the one that operated during the 1948 presidential campaign.[104]

Throughout 1951, Boyle was increasingly perceived as a lethargic and ineffective DNC chairman by both White House staff and Democratic members of Congress. During a White House luncheon for Congressional Democrats held in July 1951, Democratic Representative Wayne Hays of Ohio surprised Truman by denouncing Boyle's management of the DNC headquarters. Hays stated: "I personally think it's a disgrace to the Democratic Party and ought to be reorganized from top to bottom. . . . The only time the Democratic National Committee shows any signs of life is at the cocktail hour."[105] In particular, Hays complained that while RNC headquarters efficiently provided Republicans with damaging publicity against the Democrats the DNC headquarters failed to effectively counteract the Republican efforts.

Accusations of organizational ineffectiveness, however, were less serious for Boyle than accusations of corruption or, at the very least, a conflict of interest regarding the relationship between his law firm and his position as DNC chairman. During the summer of 1951, Senate investigation of the Reconstruction Finance Corporation (RFC) examined allegations that Boyle had used his political influence to obtain an RFC loan for the American Lithofold Corporation, a former client of his law firm, in exchange for a fee.[106] In another Senate committee investigation chaired by Democratic Senator Clyde Hoey of North Carolina, Boyle's testimony denied lobbying the RFC for the loan to this company. The Hoey committee concluded that while Boyle had not "engaged in any activities which were either illegal or immoral" his "conduct was not such that it would dispel the appearance of wrongdoing."[107]

Despite Truman's staunch public defense of Boyle, the DNC chairman announced his resignation on October 13, 1951, citing poor health.[108] In his highly publicized letter of resignation, Boyle assured Truman: "Affairs of the Democratic National Committee are in excellent condition. The party organization throughout the country is strong and imbued with confidence in the rightness of our program."[109]

Truman the reformer was initially inclined to nominate a successor to Boyle who would project a fresh, bold, innovative image as DNC chairman. Consequently, instead of just offering the DNC chairmanship to another wealthy, Irish Catholic organization Democrat, Truman asked India Edwards to serve.[110] Edwards turned down the offer but asked Truman to consult her about the choice of Boyle's successor and suggested Senator John Sparkman of Alabama, former Colorado Congressman John Carroll, and Director of Price Stabilization Michael DiSalle as candidates for DNC chairman.[111]

Instead of the men recommended by Edwards, Bill Boyle announced on October 29, 1951, that he and the president were nominating Frank E. McKinney as the next DNC chairman. Outraged that she had not been consulted by Truman,

Edwards protested by briefly vacating her position as DNC vice chairman. In her October 30 letter to Truman, Edwards stated, "I am resigning because it is borne in me too poignantly and unhappily that the Vice Chairmanship is an empty title and that woman's [sic] status in the Democratic Party and Committee has not risen."[112]

Pressured by several DNC members, Truman apologized to Edwards and persuaded her to remain as DNC vice chairman. While the DNC quickly elected Frank E. McKinney as its chairman on October 31, 1951, some Democrats were chagrined that Truman the party regular cautiously chose another self-made Irish Catholic businessman who might have financial conflicts of interest with the federal government that might further tarnish the ethical image of the Truman administration and the Democratic party as they prepared for the 1952 campaign. On November 14, 1951, Ed Brown, a DNC staff member who served as assistant manager of the 1948 Democratic national convention, resigned to protest the selection of McKinney.[113] In a December letter to Truman, W.O. Edwards, a Democratic state representative in Illinois, wrote, "The average Democrat is getting fed up on having to defend a party with so many irregularities by the men in the important positions and if much more dirt is dug up by committees, the road to 1952 will be exceptionally rugged."[114]

Truman had designated Frank E. McKinney due to the recommendations of Frank McHale, Indiana's Democratic national committeeman, and Matthew Connelly, the president's appointments secretary.[115] McKinney, a self-made Indianapolis banker with a variety of business interests, had distinguished himself as a fund raiser in Indiana's Democratic party structure.[116] In his acceptance speech before the DNC, McKinney vowed to fully devote his time to his duties as DNC chairman while not accepting the chairman's salary.

McKinney also promised to improve the ethical reputation of DNC headquarters by ensuring that its staff employees would not lobby federal agencies for private interests.[117] On the following day, November 1, 1951, McKinney announced that the DNC chairman would no longer recommend appointments to the Bureau of Internal Revenue, an agency under an ethical cloud.[118]

In addition to improving the ethical image of DNC headquarters, McKinney promised "to re-establish the political research, publicity and informational activities of the Committee which once received such a high level of effectiveness."[119] Compared to Boyle, McKinney proved to be more receptive to new ideas and more likely to implement them. His spirit of innovation, especially in approving and generously funding a substantial DNC Research Division for the 1952 campaign, pleased White House aides critical of Boyle.[120] The DNC's Research Division in the 1952 campaign also included a pollster, statistician

Louis Bean from the Department of Agriculture, who had predicted Truman's unexpected victory in 1948.

Under McKinney's chairmanship, the DNC established an eleven-member executive committee. With three at-large members and two members from each one of the four regions of the nation, the executive committee's purpose was to improve inter-regional communications and coordination among DNC members and Democratic state organizations.[121] McKinney also sought to improve communication between the DNC headquarters and the Democrats in Congress by establishing a Congressional Liaison Division and appointing Lawrence Westbrook as its director.[122] In general, though, McKinney focused on fund raising and preparing for the Democratic national convention and campaign of 1952.

Unfortunately for McKinney and Truman, McKinney had questionable financial transactions with Frank Cohen, a New York industrialist with an enduring reputation for seeking to buy influence in the federal government. When Cohen, as chairman of the Empire Ordnance Corporation, testified before the Senate Committee to Investigate the National Defense Program in 1941, committee chairman Harry Truman stated to Cohen,"You were after anyone with influence, a distinctly unethical thing."[123] When Cohen underwent a bankruptcy hearing in December 1951, his records revealed that Frank McKinney and Frank McHale had each invested $1,000 in Cohen's Empire Tractor Company in 1947. Each earned a profit of approximately $68,000 when Cohen then bought their shares of stock ten months later.[124]

McKinney was never accused of any financial crimes, but this quick profit combined with revelations of his high expenses charged to the DNC contributed to the image of an unethical "mess in Washington" that the Republicans effectively exploited in 1952. In May 1952 William S. Bradley, the DNC's budget officer, resigned to protest what he claimed were excessive and irregular charges, including $40,000 sent by McKinney to the Cook County Democratic Committee to weaken Senator Estes Kefauver's electoral performance in the Illinois presidential primary.[125]

Supported by the DNC's executive committee, McKinney refuted Bradley's charges. He contended that his personal expenses as DNC chairman were reasonable and legitimate and that he had merely sent the Cook County Democratic committee its share of a DNC fund-raising dinner.[126] Three days after the DNC's May 19 press release, Truman firmly stated at a press conference: "I have every confidence in Frank McKinney. He is a good chairman."[127]

Truman did not perceive McKinney as a liability for the 1952 presidential campaign. But Adlai Stevenson did. Shortly after Stevenson became the Democratic presidential nominee, the governor of Illinois replaced McKinney with

Stephen Mitchell, an antimachine Chicago lawyer acceptable to Jacob Arvey. According to Wilson Wyatt, Stevenson's campaign manager, Stevenson unfavorably associated McKinney with the "political phases" of the Truman administration.[128] Stevenson also chose to locate his main campaign headquarters in Springfield, Illinois, rather than at DNC headquarters in Washington.

Angry that Stevenson had replaced McKinney and conducted a campaign that distanced itself from Truman's party leadership, Truman wrote a memo to Stevenson in August 1952. Though never sent, it scolded Stevenson for having "fired McKinney, the best chairman of the National Committee in my recollection."[129] In another unsent memo to Stevenson written a few weeks later, Truman castigated Stevenson for having "fired and balled up the Democratic Committee Organization that I've been creating over the last four years."[130] In general, Truman was dismayed that Stevenson conducted what Truman perceived as a virtually independent, candidate-centered presidential campaign that was detrimental to the traditional party apparatus.[131]

By the end of his presidency, Harry Truman had not perceived the trend toward atrophy for the role of national party chairmen and national party organization in presidential campaigns.[132] Despite the public assurances of Stevenson and Mitchell that Stevenson's presidential campaign was not distancing itself from Truman and the DNC headquarters, the National Volunteers for Stevenson was formed after the 1952 Democratic national convention. In many localities this independent organization was more important for raising funds and providing campaign services for Stevenson than the DNC's apparatus.[133] Truman's values as a party regular and liberal reformer had led him to hope that, through his careful selection of DNC chairmen and constant modernization of the DNC's apparatus and activities, the DNC headquarters could serve as a powerful instrument in developing and strengthening an electorally successful, cohesively liberal Democratic party.[134] Unfortunately for Truman, the significance of the DNC's chairman and staff operations would weaken during the Eisenhower presidency and diminish further during the Democratic presidential campaigns and administrations of John F. Kennedy and Lyndon B. Johnson.[135]

MAJOR STAFF DIVISIONS

The DNC's Research and Publicity divisions were the most innovative staff divisions of the DNC apparatus during the Truman presidency. The DNC headquarters funded and staffed a Research Division for the 1948 and 1952 presidential campaigns. To the dismay of liberal party activists and some White House aides, especially Ken Hechler and Charles Murphy, the DNC headquarters did not maintain an active, permanent Research Division throughout the Truman administration. Confronted by mostly Republican-owned major daily newspapers and newsmagazines concentrating on allegations of corruption and Communist subversion in the federal bureaucracy, Truman's White House staff believed that a well-funded, professional research operation by the DNC in conjunction with the DNC's Publicity Division and the White House was necessary to counteract Republican charges with policy facts and to reveal Republican votes in Congress against popular policy positions.[136]

Despite Truman's endorsement of a full-time DNC Research Division, Bill Boyle did not adopt such a permanent expansion of the DNC staff after the 1948 campaign. Philip Dreyer, a member of the DNC's Research Division in 1948, surmised that Boyle distrusted the permanent inclusion of liberal intellectual "amateurs" at DNC headquarters.[137]

When the DNC staff did include an active, multimember Research Division in the 1948 and 1952 campaigns, this division proved to be a vital source of effective ideas for speeches, defenses of Democratic policy positions, governmental facts, well-informed attacks of Republican platforms, analyses of Republican roll call votes in Congress, and, especially in 1948, crucial facts about communities in which presidential campaign speeches were delivered. In a January 5, 1952, letter to Truman, Bertram Gross, the director of the DNC Research Division for the 1952 campaign, reminded Truman about what the president had told him in 1950. "'What we need over there at the National Committee,' you said, 'is a research staff that digs out the facts. If we get the facts to-gether, we'll keep on winning elections—because the truth is on our side.'"[138]

It was due to the unexpected success of the relatively small, austerely budgeted 1948 DNC Research Division that Harry Truman and Frank McKinney made sure that the Research Division for the 1952 campaign was larger and better funded. The idea to create a DNC Research Division for the 1948 presidential campaign was introduced by the White House staff, not by DNC Chairman J. Howard McGrath or the staff of DNC headquarters. Led by counsel to the president Clark M. Clifford, the White House staff realized that a full-time, multimember research operation was necessary to constantly provide Truman's speech writers and campaign organizers with a constant supply of policy facts and information peculiar to the communities in which Truman spoke. Thus, the DNC Research Division maintained direct communications with Truman's train staff instead of McGrath and DNC headquarters. But, to the occasional irritation of McGrath and DNC publicity director Jack Redding, the DNC Research Division was funded by DNC headquarters. William L. Batt Jr., the director of

the Research Division in 1948, claimed that such a formal yet misleading affiliation with DNC headquarters was established so that the press and public would
not suspect that White House staff funds were used to finance such a research
unit for campaign purposes.[139]

The de facto independence of the DNC Research Division from DNC headquarters was further symbolized by its location in an office in the Hamilton
Bank Building, rather than in the Ring Building, which housed the DNC headquarters.[140] Batt and the six other researchers also lived in the same apartment
during the summer of 1948 and shared many characteristics. Most of them were
in their twenties and early thirties, World War II veterans, well-educated, and
committed to liberal policy positions, such as civil rights for blacks, national
health insurance, and an internationalist American foreign policy to maintain
peace.[141] Perhaps more significantly, most were also members of the ADA, which
had recently been antagonistic toward Truman, and had no experience in party
organizations.

Besides performing their formal duties of researching and providing policy
facts from federal agencies, damaging facts about Henry Wallace and Thomas
Dewey, and information about communities scheduled for Truman's whistle-
stop campaign, the DNC's Research Division of 1948 also provided two crucial
elements of Truman's campaign strategy. Democratic Congressman A.S. Mike
Monroney of Oklahoma told Batt about farmers in his district complaining about
inadequate storage space for their surplus grain provided by the Commodity
Credit Corporation (CCC). Batt suggested to Truman's campaign staff that the
president should repeatedly criticize the Republicans in Congress for reducing
appropriations to the CCC when he campaigned in farm states. Truman's rhetorical focus on this issue helped him to win the electoral college votes of several grain-growing states in 1948 that Dewey had carried in 1944.[142]

An even more important campaign tactic suggested by the DNC Research
Division was that Truman should unexpectedly call Congress into special session during his acceptance speech at the Democratic National Convention.[143]
Bill Batt's wife contributed Truman's blunt statement during this speech, "We're
right and they're wrong," in asserting the clear programmatic differences between the Truman administration and the Republicans in Congress.[144] Batt later
commented, "We concluded that one way in which this could be dramatized
would be for the President to call Congress and ask them to do what the Republican convention endorsed."[145] Truman's call for a special session, therefore,
enabled him to portray the Republicans in Congress as not only inert on domestic policy needs but also hypocritical by revealing a contrast between their platform positions and legislative behavior.

Shortly after the convention, Harry Truman told the mother of Frank Kelly, one of the researchers, "You know, Mrs. Kelly, those boys really helped me win that election."[146] In complimenting the Research Division, Truman may have exaggerated the importance of this small division among all the elements of his campaign and of the reasons for his upset victory. The DNC Research Division's contribution to Truman's victory in 1948, however, impressed several White House aides enough that they regularly recommended the continuation of a permanent, active research unit at DNC headquarters to Truman, J. Howard McGrath, and then Bill Boyle. Despite Truman's endorsement of this recommendation, a DNC Research Division was not established until 1952 because of Boyle's hostility to the idea.[147]

The DNC's Research Division for the 1952 presidential campaign had more personnel, funds, and a broader purpose than its predecessor. Headed by Bertram Gross, former staff director for the Council of Economic Advisors, the DNC Research Division not only provided policy facts and speech outlines for the separate whistle-stop campaigns of Adlai Stevenson and Harry Truman. It also conducted and disseminated statistical research on voting behavior projections for key states in the electoral college.[148] It also compiled substantial research and speech outlines for defending Truman's Korean War policy and a multivolume collection entitled, "Twenty Years of Progress," which detailed and praised domestic policy accomplishments during the Roosevelt and Truman administrations.[149] In addition to being located within DNC headquarters and having regular contact with the DNC chairman and other DNC staff, the researchers in the 1952 Research Division also provided Democratic congressional candidates with policy facts and speeches to counteract Republican publicity.[150]

After the 1952 campaign, DNC chairman Stephen Mitchell ended the Research Division and transferred its various research functions to the Publicity Division.[151] While the DNC headquarters only operated the Research Division during the presidential campaigns of 1948 and 1952, it continuously operated a Publicity Division during the Truman presidency, although a larger, more active one during presidential campaigns. Later, noticing the irony of the Democratic and Republican national committees' greater devotion to publicity than to research in their organizations and use of resources, political scientists Cornelius Cotter and Bernard Hennessy commented, "Research is vital to the national committees, but it is public relations that is appreciated."[152]

Ever since 1929, when the DNC hired Charles Michelson as a publicity director while the Democratic party was the "out party," the DNC understood the importance of constantly maintaining a Publicity Division. Throughout the presidencies of Herbert Hoover and Franklin D. Roosevelt, though, the DNC only maintained a large, active Publicity Division during presidential campaigns. Succeeding Sam O'Neal as the DNC's publicity director in 1947, Jack Redding wanted to permanently increase the size of the Publicity Division and its func-tions.[153] However, due to the paucity of DNC funds following the Republican sweep of the 1946 congressional elections and the need to raise funds for the 1948 presidential campaign, DNC treasurer George Killion, opposed Redding's plans.

Upon consultation with departing DNC Chairman Bob Hannegan, Gael Sullivan, and his assistant publicity director, Sam Brightman, Redding decided to focus the Publicity Division's limited resources on defending Truman's record and castigating Republican Senator Robert A. Taft.[154] Since most major daily newspapers were pro-Republican in their editorials and endorsements, Redding decided to focus the DNC's publicity efforts on radio commercials attacking the Republican-controlled Eightieth Congress as pro–big business and insensitive to inflation's impact on consumers. Redding also sought to inform voters about policy issues by distributing DNC newsletters through Democratic precinct organiza-tions in major cities.[155] He wanted to revitalize local Democratic organizations by making them more direct partners in DNC publicity operations.

Strapped for funds and facing the daunting task of helping the beleaguered Truman win in 1948, the DNC Publicity Division was impressively innovative in devising ingenious methods for promoting Truman's candidacy and inextri-cably linking moderately liberal Thomas E. Dewey with the most conservative members and legislative behavior of the Republican-controlled Eightieth Con-gress. Produced by its Publicity Division, but officially sponsored by its Women's Division, "Headaches for House Wives" was a series of DNC radio commer-cials that used sardonic humor to ridicule Republican opposition to Truman's anti-inflation proposals. Perhaps the most effective segment quoted part of Sena-tor Taft's reply to a reporter's question about how American families should cope with rising food prices, "Eat less."[156] Other DNC radio commercials in 1948 used parts of popular songs mixed with criticism of Republican policy behavior in the Eightieth Congress. The voice of a ghost representing the Re-publican record in the Eightieth Congress would howl and callously laugh about hurting the policy interests of average Americans.[157] In one of these commer-cials, the ghost wailed, "I took Social Security benefits away from 750,000 people."[158]

Also, during the 1948 campaign, the scarcity of funds limited and some-times threatened the implementation of some of the Publicity Division's tac-tics.[159] The DNC Publicity Division intended to print and distribute three million copies of Truman's biography in comic book form, with art work drawn by Malcolm Ator. But this project was delayed and provided fewer copies due to inadequate funding.[160]

Jack Redding's shrewd manipulation of movie producers enabled him to have a documentary-style campaign movie for Truman produced and distributed for free and shown in theaters throughout the nation shortly before election day. After hearing that the Republican National Committee had produced and would later distribute a campaign film for Dewey, Redding realized that the DNC needed to counter this with a film on Truman but lacked the funds to do this. Through Gael Sullivan, executive director of the Theater Owners of America, Redding threatened to organize demonstrations in front of movie theaters unless movie producers made and distributed a film for Truman in order to give the president "equal time" with Dewey on the screens.[161] Redding later referred to this campaign film, which cost the DNC nothing, as "probably the most important and most successful publicity break of the entire campaign."[162] Media scholar Kathleen Hall Jamieson later estimated that "in 1948 over 50,000,000 people paid to view a political ad produced and distributed by the film industry at no cost to the Democratic party or the Truman campaign."[163]

The DNC Publicity Division's successful tactics in the 1948 campaign signified the peak of its efficacy during the Truman administration. After Jack Redding left during the summer of 1950, Charles Van Devander, who succeeded Redding and served as DNC publicity director until 1952, was confronted with the task of stretching limited funds and personnel to counteract growing Republican and media claims of the Truman administration's corruption, cronyism, and misconduct of the Korean War, McCarthyism, and policies leading to the 1950 congressional election losses. During this period, the DNC Publicity Division diligently but mostly ineffectively reacted to such criticism and charges through press releases and literature defending Truman's foreign and domestic policies and repeating hackneyed Roosevelt-era portrayals of the Republicans as isolationist pawns of big business.[164] In a DNC pamphlet for the 1950 campaign, the Publicity Division accused the Republicans of opposing nearly "every attempt to curb a selfish interest in order to preserve the freedom of all the people."[165]

As Van Devander's successor, Samuel Brightman had the unenviable task of serving as the DNC's publicity director during the 1952 presidential campaign. Brightman was confronted with the daunting task of devising and implementing a publicity strategy that could contribute to the defeat of the well-funded, professionally advertised Republican campaign of Dwight Eisenhower, an immensely popular war hero with a suprapartisan appeal to the voters.[166] The DNC Publicity Division was also burdened by the simultaneous tasks of defending the Truman administration's record and promoting the more independent image that Adlai Stevenson projected.

Consequently, the Publicity Division's strategy was two-tiered. It worked closely with the Research Division to provide statistics, press releases, and advertising emphasizing economic progress and reform during the twenty years of the Roosevelt and Truman administrations. Secondly, it arranged radio and television commercials to enable Stevenson to attract large audiences through his naturally eloquent speaking style.[167] But the Eisenhower campaign spent approximately $800,000, compared to $77,000 by the DNC, on television advertising and reached larger audiences.[168]

The increasingly televised publicity strategy of both Democratic and Republican presidential campaigns became more candidate-centered and independent of national party publicity divisions after 1952. Consequently, throughout the history of its existence, the DNC Publicity Division probably provided its most significant source in contributing to a Democratic presidential victory in the 1948 campaign. Despite scarce resources and a widely held belief that Harry Truman could not win, this division developed and utilized effective publicity tactics that generated greater public support for both Truman and the Democratic party in general. As a result, Sam Brightman later commented that the DNC's publicity efforts helped to characterize the Democratic electoral success in 1948 as "a test of the basic strength of the party, party philosophy, and party performance."[169]

WOMEN'S DIVISION

During the Truman presidency, the DNC would rapidly create or expand a variety of sub-units within its organization. Often named advisory committees, groups, or divisions, they addressed the particular policy interests and functions of representation, communication, and voter mobilization for a variety of voting blocs—such as foreign language ethnic groups, farmers, youth, union members, blacks, and women—during the presidential campaigns.[170] Some of these voting blocs, namely women, blacks, labor, and youth, were represented by special divisions within the DNC apparatus that continued to exist between presidential election years. Their relative importance and efficacy in contributing to Democratic electoral success varied according to the quality and continuity of their executive directors, the extent and frequency with which these leaders interacted with DNC chairmen and Harry Truman, and the extent of their responsibilities, resources, and influence within the DNC's overall organization and operations.

The Nationalities Division and the Young Democratic Clubs of America were more important as sources of publicity and voter mobilization during the 1948 campaign than they were in previous and successive campaigns. The immediate aftermath of World War II made many ethnic groups, especially Jews and eastern and southern European ethnics, more concerned about the conduct of American foreign policy under Truman. The Marshall Plan for rebuilding western Europe, support for liberalized immigration laws that would admit more war refugees, unequivocal opposition to communist expansion in Europe, and the formal recognition of Israel were among the most crucial Truman administration policies for attracting the votes and campaign contributions of ethnic groups, especially Jews and Slavic Catholics.[171]

The Truman campaign and DNC chairman J. Howard McGrath realized, of course, that policy positions that appealed to these ethnic groups would not be enough to assure enough votes to win a close election. A DNC Nationalities Division with a complex organization would be necessary to communicate with these ethnic blocs, especially those which needed campaign literature printed in their native languages. Consequently, McGrath appointed Senator Theodore F. Green of Rhode Island, his mentor and an expert in building successful multiethnic coalitions, as chairman of the DNC's Nationalities Division.[172] Most of the organizational and communication efforts of the Nationalities Division, though, were conducted by Michel Cieplinski, who was appointed executive director of this division by McGrath. Cieplinski had been a newspaper publisher in Poland and immigrated to the United States due to the Nazi invasion. He organized a national committee for each of twenty-two foreign language groups to promote Truman's candidacy through foreign-language newspapers and radio broadcasts.[173] Cieplinski was especially successful in persuading Charles Rozmarek, president of the Polish National Alliance and the Polish American Congress, to actively support Truman.[174] Historian Richard Kirkendall partially credited the DNC's Nationalities Division with enabling Truman to receive a greater share of the Catholic vote than Roosevelt had in 1944.[175]

The millions of young, newly married World War II veterans and the sharply increasing number of college students represented another crucial voting bloc for Truman in 1948. Although the youngest voters tended to be more Democratic than any other age cohort, voters between the ages of twenty-one and thirty-four also tended to have the lowest voter turnout.[176] Consequently, Roy Baker, president of the Young Democratic Clubs of America (YDCA) during the 1948 campaign, emphasized the recruitment of first-time voters, especially college students. This effort included radio programs, "first voter certificates," and ceremonies highlighting recently registered young Democrats.[177] Shortly after the 1948 election, the *Spotlight,* the YDCA's newspaper, boasted, "The smashing Democratic victory of Nov. 2 found Young Democratic groups at a peak of activity unparalleled in their 16-year history, with approximately 2,000 units joining Democratic Central Committees, women's, labor and farm groups in turning out a heavy Democratic vote."[178]

Following Truman's direction, McGrath in 1948 abolished the DNC's Negro Division, previously named the Colored Division, to attract more black voters to Truman. Following Truman's submission of civil rights legislation to Congress and his executive order requiring equal treatment in the military, Truman and McGrath intended the end of the Negro Division to symbolize racial integration within the DNC's apparatus.[179] The DNC's Publicity Division subsequently hired a black journalist as its liaison with black newspapers.[180] While the DNC's Colored Division had conducted most publicity directed at black voters from 1932 to 1944, such publicity was now conducted by the Publicity Division.[181] DNC communications with black Democratic politicians and civil rights leaders were now mostly maintained during the 1948 campaign by Chicago Congressman William Dawson and White House aides Philleo Nash and David Niles.[182]

Compared to these three special divisions, the Women's Division of the DNC proved to be the most consistently dynamic, innovative, and politically influential of the DNC's special divisions throughout the Truman presidency. Since its establishment in 1922, the Women's Division of the DNC had proven itself to be a vital source of Democratic campaign literature and voter mobilization separate from the Publicity Division and the rest of the DNC apparatus. In particular, the Women's Division published the *Democratic Digest* until 1953 and conducted the Reporter Plan during the 1930s to publicize the benefits of New Deal programs.[183] During Roosevelt's presidency, the Women's Division had proven itself to be especially successful in attracting into the Democratic party younger professional women who were previously inclined to be independents or Republicans.

Much of the innovative activities, growth, and increasing influence within the DNC apparatus that the Women's Division experienced during Roosevelt's presidency could be attributed to Mary W. Dewson. Dewson served as executive director of the Women's Division from 1932 to 1934 and as chairman of its Advisory Committee from 1934 to 1937.[184] A leader of the women's suffrage movement and a close friend of Eleanor Roosevelt and Secretary of Labor Frances Perkins, Dewson shrewdly used her political skills and connections to increase the influence of women within the Democratic party and Roosevelt administration. By impressing President Roosevelt and DNC chairman James A. Farley with her division's ability to distribute campaign literature, solicit campaign contributions, and recruit new Democratic voters and campaign volunteers, Dewson was able to influence noticeable increases in the number of women receiving federal appointments and serving as delegates and alternates at Democratic national conventions.[185]

Mary Dewson had established a strong foundation for India Edwards to further advance the presence, status, and influence of women within the Democratic party and in government service. Having worked as a journalist for the *Chicago Tribune,* Edwards was angered by a speech given by Clare Booth Luce at the 1944 Republican national convention.[186] Edwards's son was an Air Corps pilot who died in the explosion of a bomber plane in 1943, and Edwards was outraged by Luce's statement that if all dead soldiers could vote they would vote against Roosevelt.[187]

Her anger at Luce's statement motivated her to volunteer her services to the DNC's Women's Division at the 1944 Democratic national convention. At this convention, Edwards served as the DNC's liaison with journalists for press releases and helped to prepare radio addresses.[188] She subsequently served as the Women's Division's executive secretary (1945-47), associate director (1947-48), and executive director (1949-50). Edwards was appointed vice chairman of the DNC in 1950 but continued to be a major de facto leader of the Women's Division and a source of influence with the president and DNC chairmen for female Democratic activists. In her autobiography, Edwards stated, "My campaign was to get a lot of jobs for a lot of women instead of a Cabinet post or an ambassadorship for myself, though such a position was offered to me in 1948."[189]

During Truman's presidency, Edwards provided outspoken, creative, dynamic, and stable leadership to the Women's Division. This type of leadership enabled it to be the most consistently prominent and productive special division of the DNC in providing a variety of campaign, publicity, fund raising, and organizational services. This was especially evident during the 1948 presidential campaign in which Edwards revealed her flair for dramatizing campaign issues, especially inflation and price controls. The Women's Division organized "Housewives for Truman" trailers in which household items were exhibited and their increased prices were blamed on the Republican policies of the Eightieth Congress.[190]

In her speech at the 1948 Democratic national convention, Edwards directed her speech on inflation to the television cameras. Throughout her speech, she displayed one grocery item after another—a raw steak, a quart of milk, and a pound of sugar—to illustrate high prices and Republican inertia toward them.[191] Clearly exploiting the presence of television cameras, Edwards also opened a hat box, and a balloon rose into the air to symbolize rising prices.[192]

At a less dramatic yet equally important level, Edwards organized the DNC's School of Politics and increased funding for the DNC's "Headaches for House-wives" radio commercials.[193] In the School of Politics, the wives of most cabinet secretaries explained their husbands' duties and departments to women who would attend the 1948 Democratic national convention. Public speaking lessons were also given to Democratic women who requested them.[194] In an October 20, 1948, report, Edwards estimated that the Women's Division had distributed approximately one hundred thousand Truman-Barkley windshield stickers, eight hundred thousand "Dewey Unity" fliers, and one million fliers based on Truman's recent speech in St. Paul.[195]

The activities and responsibilities of Edwards and the Women's Division subsided little after Truman's unexpected victory. Truman delegated publicity responsibilities on two major policy proposals, the Brannan Plan for reforming agricultural policies and his national health insurance plan.[196] She and her division tried to counteract the aggressive, ultimately successful lobbying and publicity efforts of the American Medical Association (AMA) and the American Farm Bureau, which opposed these proposals. Referring to Truman's proposed national health insurance plan, Edwards later commented, "I always considered it a great compliment to the women of the nation that President Truman felt if the Women's Division of the Democratic National Committee explained his plan, our efforts would help to enact it into law."[197] Georgia Cook Morgan, a biographer of Edwards, concluded, "Belief in party loyalty and in utilization of the DNC probably formed the basis of the Truman-Edwards relationship."[198]

Although Edwards declined Truman's offer to become DNC chairman in 1951, she relentlessly pursued her mission of using the Women's Division's various efforts on behalf of the Truman administration and the Democratic party to persuade or pressure Truman to appoint women to high-level federal positions.[199] Partially due to Edwards's recommendations, Truman respectively appointed Perle Mesta and Eugenie Anderson as ambassadors to Luxembourg and Denmark.[200] In general, mostly due to the efforts of Edwards, Truman appointed more women to regulatory commissions than Roosevelt had.[201] Edwards claimed that she had persuaded Truman to appoint federal Circuit Court Judge Florence Allen to the Supreme Court. But Truman deferred the decision to Chief Justice Fred Vinson, who rejected the prospect of a female justice.[202]

Nominated for vice president at the 1952 Democratic national convention, Edwards soon had frequent conflicts with the policies of the new DNC chairman, Stephen A. Mitchell. She opposed his decision to have DNC research director Philip Stern and DNC publicity director Clayton Fritchey assume control of the *Democratic Digest* after the 1952 election.[203] Suspecting that Mitchell intentionally blocked her access to Truman, Edwards complained to Truman after the election that she resented "the continual, whether intentional or thought- less, bypassing of women when policy is to be discussed."[204]

In January 1953, Mitchell announced the abolition of the Women's Divi- sion to signify that Democratic women now had an equal, integrated status within the DNC apparatus. He appointed Katie Louchheim as director of women's activities.[205] By October 1953, Edwards resigned in frustration from her now meaningless position as executive director of the defunct Women's Division.[206] Later lamenting the end of the DNC's Women's Division, Edwards remarked, "In spite of the progress women have made in the elective field, it often has seemed to us oldtimers that women in the Democratic National Committee are not as much full partners as Molly Dewson and I were in the Roosevelt and Truman administrations."[207]

Within only a few years, the DNC's Women's Division went from being the most vital special division of the DNC and a crucial vehicle for Democratic women seeking to enhance their power and status in party affairs and govern- ment service to being a nonentity. Officially, the Women's Division had been abolished for the same reason that the Negro Division had been terminated in 1948, to symbolize integration and equality for a certain voting bloc within the DNC's organization. In general, though, all of the remaining DNC special divi- sions suffered a decline in their organizational status and level of campaign ac- tivities during and after the 1952 presidential election. Estes Kefauver's presidential campaign in the primaries and Adlai Stevenson's general election campaign revealed that the increasingly independent, media-oriented, candidate-centered presidential campaigns would rely less on organizational units for specific blocs of voters than Roosevelt and Truman had.

DNC FINANCES

During Harry Truman's presidency, the DNC experienced changes in the amounts of expenditures and receipt of contributions, methods of fund raising, and sources of funds that revealed changes in the electoral strength of the na- tional Democratic party and in the purposes of DNC expenditures. Political scientist Louise Overacker studied and compared the contributions and expen- ditures of the Democratic and Republican national committees from 1928 to 1944. Overacker found that more than 90,000 individuals contributed to the DNC and more than 140,000 to the RNC in 1928, and that the expenditures of the RNC exceeded those of the DNC by more than $1,000,000. She found, though, that in 1928, the DNC was more dependent than the RNC on receiving a high proportion of its funds from a small number of large donors.[208] Overacker learned that 135 Democrats gave half of the total DNC campaign funds in 1928 and that 52.7 percent of the DNC funds were derived from contributions of $5,000 or more, compared to 45.8 percent of RNC funds from this monetary category.[209] Also, the percentages of DNC and RNC funds contributed by bankers and stockbrokers in 1928 were very similar, at 25.8 percent and 28.2 percent, respectively.[210]

The 1936 presidential campaign, however, revealed the growing differences between DNC and RNC finances as certain business interests, especially banks and investment firms, and wealthy individual contributors became hostile to Roosevelt and the more liberal, prolabor Democratic party during the New Deal era. While RNC expenditures exceeded DNC expenditures by approximately $650,000 in 1932, they exceeded DNC spending by nearly $4,000,000 in 1936.[211] The DNC received 24.2 percent of its funds from bankers and stock brokers in 1932 but only 3.3 percent in 1936.[212]

The Hatch Act of 1940 included two major provisions that affected how both the RNC and DNC collected and expended campaign funds. One provision stated that an interstate political committee could not receive or spend more than $3,000,000 annually. Another provision imposed a limit of $5,000 for each individual contribution to a national political committee.[213] Under DNC Chairman James A. Farley, the DNC had begun to focus its fund-raising efforts on raising small contributions from large numbers of Democrats before this law was enacted. The DNC earned about $250,000 by selling advertising space in the 1936 convention books and selling different editions of this book ranging in cost from $2.50 to $250.[214] Since this practice was prohibited in 1939, the DNC focused even more after 1936 on using $100-a-plate Jefferson-Jackson Day dinners to raise funds.[215] The greater emphasis on fund-raising dinners held in Washington, D.C., and throughout the nation enabled the DNC during the Roosevelt and Truman administrations to partially compensate for the decline in the number and amount of large individual contributions and to make fund raising a more broad-based, participatory process that tried to use the president's broadcasted dinner speeches to nationally strengthen intraparty unity.

The $3,000,000 limit mandated by the Hatch Act of 1940 combined with the $5,000 limit impelled the DNC and RNC to rely more on state and local party committees and on nominally independent, candidate-centered organizations, such as the Truman-Barkley Clubs, to receive and expend campaign contributions and to provide campaign services.[216] Consequently, Roosevelt and then Truman became increasingly dependent on organized labor, especially the politically active, rapidly growing CIO unions, for campaign finances and such services as voter mobilization and the production and distribution of campaign literature.[217] Total expenditures by labor unions toward the campaigns of Democratic presidential nominees increased from more than $770,000 in 1936 to nearly $1.3 million in 1948 and more than $2 million in 1952.[218]

The Five-Dollar Certificate Plan was a creative yet ultimately disappointing DNC fund-raising method used during the 1952 presidential campaign. Beardsley Ruml, the DNC's finance director, introduced the Plan as a way to simultaneously generate grassroots voter participation for Adlai Stevenson, especially among the youngest voters, independents, undecided voters, and disaffected liberal Democrats, and to reduce the substantial fund-raising advantages enjoyed by the Eisenhower campaign.[219] The goal of the Plan was to collect one million $5 contributions by October 15, 1952. Of the $5 million raised through this plan, 60 percent would be kept by the DNC and 40 percent by the Democratic state committees that participated in its implementation. Coordinated by the DNC and Democratic state committees, Ruml's Plan established a complex, decentralized pyramid-shaped organization so that the processes of receiving $5 contributions in exchange for certificates expressing support for Stevenson would arouse broad electoral support for his candidacy.[220]

Unfortunately for the DNC, Ruml's plan encountered several problems. Total contributions yielded only about $600,000, while the total cost of implementing the Plan was over $100,000.[221] The participation of most Democratic state committees was disappointing. Political scientist John Van Doren discovered that, except for Kentucky, "not a single state put the full weight of its regular party organization behind the $5 Plan."[222] Van Doren also found that inadequate accounting procedures resulted in the loss of thousands of certificate booklets.

Despite the failure of the Five-Dollar Certificate Plan in 1952, the DNC fared fairly well in attracting contributions between the time of Harry Truman's startling victory in the 1948 election and the 1952 general election campaign, when Republican presidential nominee Dwight D. Eisenhower was widely regarded as the inevitable victor. But even in 1952 the total contributions received by the DNC were only about $200,000 less than those received by the RNC.[223] By contrast, in 1948, when it appeared that Truman would definitely lose the election and many conservative wealthy southern Democrats and southern Democratic state committees refused to contribute to the DNC, the DNC received $1,861,746 in contributions compared to the RNC's receipt of $2,507,396.[224] The total DNC figure for 1948, however, would have been lower if the DNC had not received about $50,000 in predated checks following Truman's victory during November and December of 1948.[225] These post–election day contributions enabled DNC treasurer Joseph L. Blythe to report the elimination of the DNC's deficit and a surplus of approximately $100,000.[226]

The DNC's receipt of these predated checks was a harbinger of a three-year period from 1949 to 1951 in which contributions received by the DNC substantially exceeded those received by the RNC. The DNC received $1,477,427 in 1949, $1,085,697 in 1950, and $1,318,574 in 1951. The RNC, however, received only $661,804 in 1949, $657,107 in 1950, and $679,157 in 1951.[227]

After analyzing the 1949 DNC and RNC figures, journalists Joseph and Stewart Alsop surmised that the impressive Democratic electoral performance in 1948 was convincing more and more businessmen to contribute to the Democratic party in order to gain influence to benefit their interests. The stark differences between DNC and RNC finances "clearly suggest that an important faction of American business is turning from the traditional business party and flirting with the self-styled defenders of the underprivileged."[228] The Alsops concluded: "It is clear that a powerful, aggressive faction of American business is now betting on the Democrats. The reason is simple—the Democrats have been winners for a long time, and it is always pleasant to bet on a winner."[229]

The dramatic improvement of DNC finances during this period was also evident in attendance at the $100-a-plate Jefferson-Jackson Day dinners in Washington, D.C. Attendance at these dinners increased from approximately two thousand Democrats in 1947 to more than fifty-three hundred in 1952.[230] Like Roosevelt, Truman used his broadcast speeches at these dinners to address one, two, or all of these three basic themes: the promotion of intraparty harmony by stressing historical principles or figures broadly shared by Democrats, the advocacy of major policy proposals, and the further clarification of the Democratic party as a distinctly liberal party.[231] At the 1948 dinner, which was conspicuously boycotted by several southern Democrats angered by Truman's civil rights message to Congress, the president asserted that the 1948 presidential campaign would provide American voters with a "choice between progressive liberalism and conservatism."[232] At the 1949 dinner, Truman told a larger and more enthusiastic audience, "The central issue of the past campaign was the privileged few versus the welfare of all the people."[233] While defending his policies in the Korean War at the 1951 dinner, the president identified a link between the Fair Deal's domestic policy goals and his foreign policy. "A fair deal today means an equal sharing of responsibilities and sacrifices for our defense program."[234]

In 1952 Truman delivered what was perhaps the most momentous Jefferson-Jackson Day dinner speech. After providing an aggressive, detailed defense of his administration's record against Republican charges of corruption, softness on communism, and stalemate in the Korean War and a reaffirmation of liberal domestic policy accomplishments and objectives, Truman stunned most of his listeners by announcing, "I shall not be a candidate for reelection."[235] Truman claimed in his memoirs that he had written a private memo on April 16, 1950, stating that he would not run for president in 1952.[236] A few weeks before the 1952 Jefferson-Jackson Day dinner, Truman conferred with Adlai Stevenson and was confident that Stevenson would eventually accept the Democratic nomination for president. Consequently, Truman carefully timed his public announcement for the Jefferson-Jackson Day dinner because "I felt that in Stevenson I had found the man to whom I could safely turn over the responsibilities of party leadership."[237]

As a party regular, Truman hoped that such a traditional transition of party leadership and the twenty-year Democratic control of the presidency to Stevenson would be smooth and consensual. New forces of campaign politics emerged in 1952 that destroyed Truman's objectives.[238] Estes Kefauver's impressive, initial performance in Democratic presidential primaries, the willingness of key southern conservative Democrats to openly support the Republican presidential nominee, and the ability of the Eisenhower campaign to use television advertising and modern marketing tactics much more effectively than the Stevenson campaign rapidly eroded the fund-raising and vote-getting benefits that Truman and the DNC apparatus had gained since the 1948 victory.

THE DNC AFTER 1952

Harry Truman's criticism of Adlai Stevenson as a campaigner and as the next titular party leader following his nomination overlooked certain fundamental and apparently inevitable and irreversible political trends that would make presidential campaigns more open to public participation and, thus, more dependent on the efforts of "amateurs" and less dependent on the private machinations of the elites among party regulars.[239] It was not surprising, therefore, that Stevenson's two presidential campaigns stimulated the formation of "amateur" Democratic clubs, which often opposed local Democratic machines and party regulars.[240] Although most states in 1952 did not require binding primaries for the selection of delegates to national party conventions, Truman failed to realize the precedent that Estes Kefauver had established when he won twelve of fourteen presidential primaries, including an unexpected, decisive defeat of Truman in the New Hampshire primary.[241] More significantly, Kefauver's 1952 campaign for the Democratic presidential nomination demonstrated that it was now possible for a previously obscure senator, still serving his first Senate term, to quickly gain national name recognition through regular television coverage and use that as a resource to conduct a serious challenge to his party's leadership.

These new political forces did not bode well for the vitality and intraparty influence of DNC headquarters during the years immediately after Truman's presidency. The terms of Stephen A. Mitchell (1952-54) and Paul M. Butler (1955-60), as DNC chairmen were generally periods of budget cuts, deficit reduction, and a downsizing of the DNC headquarters's staff and organizational units.[242] Harry Truman often criticized Paul Butler's performance as chairman, claiming that Butler was detrimental to intraparty unity and sided with Sam Rayburn in Rayburn's conflicts with Butler. But he did agree to serve on the Democratic Advisory Council (DAC), a council created by Butler to formulate and propose clearly liberal Democratic proposals that moderate and conservative congressional Democrats like Sam Rayburn and Lyndon Johnson often opposed.[243] These Texans perceived the DAC as a threat to their party leadership and disruptive of intraparty cooperation in Congress.

In short, former President Harry Truman continued to express, through his words and his political behavior as a party elder, his increasingly outdated values and perceptions about political processes as a party regular, while trying to combine them with his forward-looking values as a liberal reformer on public policy matters. Throughout his presidency, Truman provided a degree of stewardship to the DNC apparatus and a constant concern for its welfare, efficacy, and vitality that greatly exceeded those of future Democratic presidents.[244] Until the DNC apparatus's revitalization in the 1980s and 1990s, the relationship between a Democratic president and the DNC chairman during most of the Truman presidency represented a "last hurrah" for a significant role of the DNC's chairmen, apparatus, fund-raising efforts, and various political operations within the Democratic party.[245]

4

☆ ☆ ☆ ☆ ☆

HAD ENOUGH?
REPUBLICAN RESURGENCE,
1946-1948

On April 13, 1945, the day after Franklin D. Roosevelt died and Harry S. Truman became president, Republican Senator Arthur H. Vandenberg of Michigan wrote that Truman's presidency, unlike Roosevelt's, would mean "that the days of executive contempt for Congress are ended; that we are returning to a government in which Congress will take its rightful place."[1] A few days later, Republican Senator Robert A. Taft of Ohio, a stridently anti–New Deal conservative and de facto spokesman for Senate Republicans, expressed his assumption that, if the Democratic party divides, then Truman "will go with the conservative side."[2] Also, on April 18, 1945, former vice president and conservative Democrat John N. Garner assured Speaker of the House Sam Rayburn that Truman "has a head full of good horse sense" and "can be made into a good President."[3]

Republicans and conservative Democrats in Congress were clearly relieved that Harry S. Truman, instead of Henry A. Wallace, had succeeded Roosevelt.[4] They regarded Wallace as being politically inept, eccentric, dangerously naive about the Soviet Union, and a political captive of CIO unions and communist sympathizers. By comparison, Truman appeared to be a cautious moderate who would restore a relationship of equality on both foreign and domestic policy matters and cooperate with a Congress controlled by the bipartisan conservative coalition since 1939.[5]

ORIGINS OF THE 1946 VICTORY

While conservatives in Congress hoped that Truman would abandon the pursuit of Roosevelt's postwar liberal policy goals, stated in his 1944 Economic

Bill of Rights speech, many liberal activists, journalists, and Roosevelt appointees lamented Truman's presumed lack of commitment to New Deal liberalism and willingness to defer to the conservative-controlled Congress.[6] Liberal critics of Truman were especially dismayed by his decision to replace such New Deal liberals as Attorney General Francis Biddle and Secretary of Labor Frances Perkins with more conservative appointees, especially former moderate and conservative members of Congress, such as Fred Vinson as secretary of the treasury and James Byrnes as secretary of state.[7] In comparing the Truman administration unfavorably with the Roosevelt administration, the iconoclastic, leftist columnist I.F. Stone wrote, "FDR had attracted to the capital a wonderful collection of idealists, liberals and radicals, human spark plugs of various kinds."[8] He characterized Truman's appointees as "Wimpys who could be had for a hamburger."[9]

The new president, though, whose cabinet appointments generally aggravated Roosevelt-worshipping liberals and satisfied the conservative-dominated Congress, sent his Twenty-one Point Plan of policy proposals to Congress on September 6, 1945. Truman's message to Congress included an explicit determination to achieve the postwar liberal policy goals stated by Roosevelt's 1944 Economic Bill of Rights speech.[10] They included the "rights" of Americans to full employment, adequate medical care, and a "decent home."[11] To the disgust of economic conservatives in general and southern whites in particular, Truman also asked Congress to pass legislation to create a permanent Fair Employment Practices Committee (FEPC) to investigate and punish racial discrimination in hiring. After requesting Congress to pass other legislation in both foreign and domestic policy, Truman concluded his message on a Twenty-one Point program by stating that he would soon send to Congress recommendations for a "national health program" and an expanded "social-security system."[12]

Congressional conservatives in both parties were stunned and angered by these proposals. House minority leader Joseph W. Martin Jr., complained that Truman was "out–New Dealing the New Deal."[13] A southern conservative magazine denounced Truman's policy proposals as "the whole program of the CIO Political Action Committee and . . . the negro organizations."[14] Republican Representative Charles A. Halleck of Indiana remarked that Truman's message to Congress was the "kick-off" for the 1946 congressional campaigns.[15]

It was now clear to the Republicans in Congress that Harry S. Truman, despite the end of the Great Depression and World War II, was determined not only to protect the policy legacy of the New Deal but also to expand the federal bureaucracy, regulations, and budgetary responsibilities to include the programmatic goals of the postwar liberals in new controversial areas, such as racial discrimination and national health insurance. In his memoirs, Truman proudly asserted that these proposals "were designed to be as liberal and as far-reaching as the prewar 1940 Democratic campaign."[16]

Truman's proposed Twenty-one Point Plan enabled Republicans to unequivocally and convincingly portray Truman as a big-government liberal determined to continue wartime controls on wages, profits, and consumer goods for the 1946 campaign. But it failed to silence Truman's liberal critics. While fewer New Deal liberals in labor unions, the media, Congress, and activist organizations such as the NAACP doubted the sincerity of Truman's expressed liberalism, they still questioned the efficacy of his leadership and lamented his rhetorical inability to inspire the public to pressure Congress to pass his legislation. In criticizing the emphasis of Truman's liberal detractors on style over substance in evaluating Truman's performance, historian Alonzo L. Hamby wrote, "The assumption that a strong, eloquent president could achieve their objectives revealed also the almost pathetic dependence of the liberals upon FDR."[17]

Other events antagonized the relationship between Truman and the liberal and labor elements of the Democratic party, thus weakening and dividing their party even further as the 1946 midterm elections approached. Two prominent Roosevelt appointees in Truman's cabinet, Secretary of the Interior Harold L. Ickes and Secretary of Commerce Henry A. Wallace, resigned in 1946. Ickes was ethically outraged by Truman's nomination (later withdrawn) of Edwin Pauley, a wealthy California oil executive and Democratic fund raiser, as undersecretary of the navy, a position with jurisdiction over oil reserves.[18] On September 20, 1946, less than two months before the midterm elections, Truman requested and received Wallace's resignation after Wallace delivered a speech implicitly criticizing Truman's foreign policy toward the Soviet Union.[19]

CIO labor activists had been among the most vociferous advocates of Wallace's renomination as vice president in 1944. Truman's request for Wallace's resignation simply added to the bitterness and alienation that they held toward Truman due to conflicts between them and the president over strikes and federal wage controls. AFL and CIO unions in the coal, steel, automobile, and meat packing industries conducted strikes and forced the Truman administration to secure compromises on wages, which often disappointed labor and weakened Truman's wage- and price-control policies.[20] Truman's dramatic request to Congress for authority to draft striking railroad workers on May 25, 1946, led AFL President William Green to accuse Truman of fascism and Republican Senator Taft to accuse him of seeking the power of a dictator.[21]

A Gallup public opinion poll released on June 23, 1946, indicated that 41 percent of the poll's respondents believed that the Republican party would be more effective in reducing strikes and labor unrest while 33 percent favored the

Democratic party. What was even more significant is that this poll revealed that manual laborers, mostly Democratic in their voting behavior, favored the Democratic party over the Republican party on this issue by a margin of only 6 percent.[22] A July 10 poll revealed that union members opposed Truman's strike policy by 56 percent, the same percentage as members of business and professional occupations.[23]

Truman's price-control policies made him and his party even more unpopular with voters. Conservatives in both parties had long been hostile toward the Office of Price Administration (OPA), which established and administered wage- and price-control regulations, and its director, Chester Bowles, a New England patrician and New Deal liberal.[24] The bipartisan conservative coalition in Congress drafted and passed a bill in June 1946 that would have renewed the OPA but would also significantly weaken its regulatory power. Truman vetoed this bill, which, he stated, "would have encouraged the false impression" that the OPA would still protect consumers from high inflation.[25] The end of OPA price controls led to high prices and then shortages of major consumer items, especially meat. A Gallup poll released on August 3, 1946, disclosed that 46 percent of those polled cited inflation as the most important policy problem while 20 percent referred to shortages of food and other goods.[26] The tumultuous domestic political events and divisive policy decisions of Truman provided valuable ammunition for the Republican congressional campaign strategy.

REPUBLICAN STRATEGY

The Republican strategy to gain control of Congress in 1946 went beyond the exploitation of divisions within Democratic ranks and Truman's unpopularity. Herbert Brownell, RNC chairman from 1944 to 1946, prepared for the 1946 elections by significantly increasing the size of the staff at RNC headquarters, creating five new RNC divisions, carefully coordinating the RNC campaign efforts with those of the Republican Congressional Campaign Committee, and raising $750,000 in campaign funds.[27] After establishing a well-funded, vibrant structure for the RNC's campaign, Brownell, closely identified with Governor Thomas E. Dewey of New York and the moderate eastern internationalists wing of the GOP, tactfully resigned as RNC chairman on April 6, 1946, partially to avoid alienating more conservative anti-Dewey Republicans.[28] B. Carroll Reece, a Tennessee congressman, replaced Brownell as RNC chairman.

Brownell evidently wanted to maximize the prospects for a Republican sweep in the midterm elections of 1946 by minimizing the discord that had chronically plagued the GOP. As political scientist Nicol C. Rae has illustrated, there have been three sources of intraparty conflict for the GOP since the beginning of the twentieth century: region, ideology, and the differences between purists, or stalwarts, who stressed conservative principle in campaign rhetoric and party professionals who emphasized centrism to attract more votes.[29] Key western progressive Republicans in Congress, such as Hiram Johnson of California and George Norris of Nebraska, had openly opposed the big business-dominated eastern wing of the GOP and supported Roosevelt and the early New Deal in order to reform and stimulate the agricultural economy.[30] After 1936, though, there were fewer pro-Roosevelt agrarian liberals among congressional Republicans. Also, those who remained became more hostile to Roosevelt as the New Deal became more oriented toward urban and union policy interests and as the president's foreign policy threatened their isolationism.[31]

In addition, greater Republican cohesion and solidarity against Roosevelt were achieved through impressive Republican victories in the midterm elections of 1938 and 1942. The Republicans gained eighty-one seats in the House of Representatives and eight seats in the Senate in 1938 and forty-six House seats and nine Senate seats in 1942.[32] When the Seventy-eighth Congress convened in 1943, the Democrats held a majority of only ten seats in the House but then succeeded in gaining twenty-four House seats in the presidential election year of 1944.[33] This pattern of electoral results clearly indicated that once Roosevelt's presidency ended the Republicans had the potential to win control of Congress in a midterm election.[34]

Despite their commonly shared desire to achieve their greatest electoral victory against the Democrats since 1928, the Republicans still held substantial intraparty differences, especially over foreign policy and the relationship between the federal government and the economy. Although a midwesterner, an anti–New Deal conservative, and a staunch isolationist before American entry into World War II, Senator Arthur H. Vandenberg of Michigan led the mostly eastern metropolitan moderate-to-liberal Republicans in Congress who supported a bipartisan, internationalist foreign policy.[35] In particular, Vandenberg and other internationalist Republicans supported an active leading role for the United States in the newly established United Nations and American economic aid for rebuilding war-ravaged western Europe.[36] By contrast, Senator Robert A. Taft expressed the views of isolationist and unilateralist Republicans who generally opposed a bipartisan foreign policy in peacetime. They were hostile to the prospect of substantial, continuing American economic aid to Europe , the loss of American autonomy, and the greater prospect of military commitments because of future collective security agreements.[37] Fortunately for the Republicans' national strategy to win control of Congress in 1946, Vandenberg and Taft were careful in their campaign and press statements not to publicize and exacerbate these foreign policy differences within the GOP.[38]

An especially important division within the Republican party existed over the extent to which Republicans in Congress should oppose or support the so-cial welfare programs, labor reforms, and business regulations created by New Deal liberalism, which Truman sought to continue and expand. The mostly east-ern moderate and liberal Republicans, represented by presidential nominees Wendell Willkie in 1940 and Thomas E. Dewey in 1944, avoided philosophical questions about whether these Democratic programs should exist.[39] Assuming that such major New Deal policies as Social Security, farm subsidies, and legal rights for labor unions were permanent and accepted by most voters, the moder-ate and liberal GOP candidates after 1936 stressed that Republicans could man-age liberal domestic policies more efficiently while castigating the Democra-tically controlled Congress and administration for fiscal waste, incompetence, and corruption.[40] This pragmatic, nonideological approach seemed especially necessary to win congressional elections in metropolitan areas of the Northeast; it would attract the votes of previously pro-Roosevelt Republicans, indepen-dents, and disaffected Democrats.

Disdaining the moderate and liberal wing's acceptance of basic Democratic programs as "Me Tooism," conservative ideologues and party regulars in the GOP firmly believed that Republicans could win congressional majorities and presidential elections after the war and Roosevelt's presidency by stressing a conservative philosophy and policy agenda that would roll back much of the New Deal and wartime economic policies—especially higher taxes, increased business regulations, and pro-union laws—and reemphasize free enterprise and greater states' rights and state fiscal responsibilities on social welfare.[41] During the 1944 campaign, House minority leader Joseph W. Martin Jr., summarized such ideological antipathy to the New Deal by comparing it to fascism. Accord-ing to Martin, the New Deal, like fascism, "is the conception of the regimented and planned society, living upon vast streams of government debt and taking its shape and destiny from the directives of a bureaucratic elite under the command of a self-inspired leader."[42]

But these ideological and tactical squabbles within the GOP were generally muffled by the RNC's strategy during the 1946 campaign. Republican candi-dates of all types could benefit from the well-funded RNC campaign, which shrewdly realized that a simple, widely publicized slogan, "Had Enough? Vote Republican!" could maximize the voter appeal of a broad variety of Republican candidates. It was previously suggested in a longer form by advertising executive Karl Frost to the Massachusetts Republican state committee.[43] "Had Enough?" was a two-word rhetorical question that conveyed empathy for the grievances and frustrations of a broad range of voters toward economic problems, ranging from the meat shortage to labor unrest, and, apparently, Democratic policies that had either caused them or failed to solve them. "Had Enough? Vote Republican!" was useful to liberal Republican candidates, likely to believe that most voters wanted better management of federal policies. It had equal facility for most conservative Republican candidates, often inclined to believe that most voters finally wanted a systematic rejection of the ideology and much of the policy legacy of New Deal liberalism.[44]

DOMESTIC COMMUNISM

Voter frustration with the various economic problems that they confronted in 1946 seemed to be the major asset of the Republican congressional campaign committee. But if the Republicans wanted to effect a realignment in voting behavior that would return the GOP to the type of longterm majority status that it had enjoyed among voters and in control of Congress and the presidency before the Roosevelt administration, they needed a powerful issue that could permanently diminish, shrink, and weaken the Democratic coalition. As American relations with the Soviet Union worsened and communist parties in France and Italy rapidly grew after World War II, the issue of communist infiltration in the United States held far greater potential for serving the GOP's short-term and long-term electoral purposes in 1946 than it had during Roosevelt's presidency. Conservative Republicans had frequently denounced Roosevelt and liberal, union-endorsed Democratic congressional candidates for formulating and implementing economic policies that were dictated by communist-controlled CIO unions. But Republican charges of communist influence in Democratic campaigns and policies were generally not decisive factors in congressional campaigns before 1946.

By 1946 the campaign rhetoric of more Republicans perceived little or no difference between New Deal liberalism and the totalitarian systems and theories of fascism and communism. The typically bland, taciturn Republican House minority leader, Joseph W. Martin Jr., vociferously promised a Republican audience in 1946 that a Republican Congress would "guarantee to the people of America that Communism, Fascism or any other form of State Socialism will not flourish here!"[45] Near the end of the 1946 campaign, Martin vowed in a radio address, "The Republican Party stands pledged to take the meddling hands of subversionists and petty political despots out of the kitchens of America."[46] The cerebral, dignified Senator Robert A. Taft likewise accused Truman and the Democratic party of appeasing the Soviet Union, seeking communist political support for the midterm elections, and trying to promote communistic policies domestically.[47]

Public opinion polls in 1946 indicated that the GOP could successfully tap into a growing public fear of domestic communism. A Gallup poll released on July 6, 1946, stated that 36 percent of those interviewed, a plurality, believed that American communists should be killed or imprisoned. This plurality was especially significant since 25 percent of the poll's respondents expressed no opinion, and this plurality was virtually the same for all occupational categories.[48] Gallup polls published in August showed that 60 percent of those interviewed believed that the Soviet Union wanted to rule the world while 78 percent of the respondents of another poll were convinced that there were Soviet spies in the United States.[49]

Ironically, membership in the American Communist party had declined from approximately one hundred thousand in 1939 to fifty thousand in 1946.[50] While a noticeable minority of CIO labor organizers were Communists during the 1930s, political scientist Guenter Lewy estimated that only about 15 percent of all CIO union members belonged to unions controlled by Communists in 1945.[51] Another serious blow to American Communists occurred when Walter Reuther, a former Socialist and militant anti-Communist, was elected president of the United Automobile Workers in 1946.[52] Partially due to Reuther's pressure, CIO President Philip Murray began to gradually reduce the power and status of Communist CIO officials until he engineered a resolution in 1949 to formally expel CIO unions suspected of Communist domination.[53]

Despite evidence that the presence and influence of American Communists in labor unions and union-supported Democratic campaigns were exaggerated by Republicans, polls indicated that most Americans perceived a growing domestic Communist presence that was serving threats to national security posed by Soviet foreign policy.[54] In particular, mostly Democratic Catholic voters were concerned about the dangers of domestic and international communism. An October 18, 1946, article in U.S. News found that Catholics "are spearheading the drive against Communism" and that "Republicans are overlooking no opportunities to link the Democratic Party with the [CIO's] Political Action Committee, which, in turn, is charged with being infiltrated with Communists."[55]

With Catholic prelates like Francis Cardinal Spellman of New York emphasizing militant anticommunism as church dogma and with Polish Americans and other Catholics of East European ancestry suspecting that Democratic diplomacy had "sold out" their ancestral nations to communist expansion, the 1946 congressional campaign appeared to be an opportunity for the GOP to co-opt a significant number of Catholic Democrats and union members through an adroit use of the communist issue.[56] This was especially evident in the 1946 Senate campaign of Joseph R. McCarthy. McCarthy was a thirty-six-year-old marine veteran and a former Democrat. He won an upset victory against Senator Robert M. La Follette Jr., in Wisconsin's Republican primary on August 13, 1946, by a margin of 5,378 votes.[57]

La Follette was an agrarian liberal who had been a staunch isolationist prior to American entry into World War II, supported most of the early New Deal, and rejoined the GOP in 1946 after having been a Progressive for twelve years. McCarthy repeatedly denounced La Follette's foreign and domestic policy legislative behavior for "playing into the hands of the Communists" and contributing to the spread of communism in Eastern Europe.[58] Since this primary was an open primary, mostly Democratic Catholic voters from Milwaukee County and other industrial areas along Lake Michigan were crucial to McCarthy's razor-thin victory since La Follette carried most heavily Protestant rural counties.[59]

Despite being the Republican nominee for senator in a mostly Republican state in a year clearly favorable to Republicans nationally, McCarthy still found it necessary to portray his underfinanced, poorly organized Democratic opponent, Howard McMurray, as the pawn of Communist-controlled CIO unions. In his radio broadcasts, McCarthy claimed that agricultural experts from the Truman administration were trying to "communize or Sovietize" Wisconsin farms and that Communist infiltration was widespread in American government, labor, and industry. McCarthy was elected senator with 61.3 percent of the votes and carried all but one of Wisconsin's counties.[60]

A more elaborate use of domestic communism as a campaign tactic against a Democratic opponent was made by Richard M. Nixon. Nixon was a thirty-three-year-old navy veteran and Republican nominee for U.S. representative in California's twelfth congressional district. After easily winning the Republican primary, Nixon faced a more formidable Democratic opponent than McCarthy had. Jerry Voorhis, a former Socialist, had first been elected in 1936 as the twelfth district's congressman. Although Republican voter registration in his district had increased after its boundaries were gerrymandered by the Republican-controlled state legislature in the early 1940s, Voorhis was reelected with 56.8 percent of the votes in 1942 and 55.3 percent in 1944.[61] Voorhis was an ardent, consistent supporter of such major New Deal measures as the Fair Labor Standards Acts of 1938, soil conservation, and rural electrification. He advocated his own proposal for nationalizing the banks of the Federal Reserve system.[62]

Voorhis's policy positions were more liberal than those of the increasing number of Republicans, especially small businessmen and ranchers in his district. But he had been able to cultivate electoral support beyond his Democratic base to include some Republicans and independents who appreciated his diligent constituent service and responsiveness to the needs of low-income farmers.[63] Also, Voorhis was an internationalist on foreign policy and a vigorous anticommunist. As a member of the Dies Committee, which investigated "un-American" organizations like the American Communist party, he sponsored the Voorhis Act of 1940, which required American Communist and fascist organizations "to make a public record of all pertinent facts concerning themselves."[64]

Despite his generally pro-union legislative record, the CIO-PAC (the CIO's political action committee) refused to endorse Voorhis in 1946, although it had supported him in 1944. Communists and other leftists within the CIO-PAC refused to agree to endorse Voorhis, partially because of his anti-Soviet foreign policy record and his support of antiracketeering legislation directed at labor unions.[65] The CIO's nonunion political organization, the National Citizens Political Action Committee (NC-PAC), was divided over whether to endorse Voorhis and did not formally do so.

Nevertheless, Nixon, who labeled himself a "liberal" Republican who avoided attacks on New Deal programs, concentrated his well-researched, aggressively articulate rhetorical attacks on exposing correlations between CIO policy positions and Voorhis's voting record on legislation. Nixon thus claimed that the Communist-infiltrated CIO-PAC and NC-PAC dominated Voorhis's legislative decisions and must be giving him its de facto support.[66] Nixon's publicity revealed that Voorhis voted for thirty-six of forty House bills that the CIO-PAC supported. These bills included the federal school lunch program, abolition of poll taxes, and a postwar loan to Great Britain.[67]

With words uncannily similar to those of Joseph McCarthy, Nixon warned an audience that Communists and their supporters increasingly held positions in the federal bureaucracy and were plotting to "gradually give the American people a Communist form of government."[68] A Nixon advertisement warned the residents of the twelfth district that Voorhis's "voting record in Congress is more Socialistic and Communistic than Democratic."[69] Stunned by Nixon's charges and smear tactics, Voorhis was always on the defensive and belatedly tried to invalidate Nixon's charges of being a dupe of Communists through rambling explanations of legislative processes.[70] Nixon defeated the ten-year incumbent and received 56 percent of the votes.[71]

Reflecting on the use of domestic communism as a smear tactic by some Republican candidates against their Democratic opponents, historian Stephen

E. Ambrose commented: "Thus in the Republican analysis, men like Voorhis were more dangerous than the Communists themselves. It did not matter if Voorhis and his friends were well-meaning dupes or conscious agents of a Communist conspiracy, the effect was the same."[72] Domestic communism would reappear as an effective Republican campaign tactic in the 1950 midterm elections, especially when it was used to defeat conservative southern Democratic Senator Millard Tydings of Maryland, and more so in 1952. This issue proved to be essential to the meteoric advancement in the power and status of Joseph McCarthy and Richard Nixon in Congress and within the Republican party. It would also become a major legislative priority for the Republican-controlled Eightieth Congress.

DEMOCRATIC DEFENSE

Even before Harry Truman and DNC chairman Robert E. Hannegan could prepare a strategy for the 1946 congressional campaign, they found it impossible to unite and harmonize congressional Democrats. Conservative Democrats in Congress, mostly from the South, had been as vociferous and vigorous as Republicans in their opposition to Truman's vetoes of the Case labor disputes bill, which would have virtually repealed the Norris-LaGuardia Anti-Injunction Act of 1932, and of the bill that would have reauthorized a greatly weakened OPA. On April 2, 1946, the 109 southern Democrats who voted for the Case bill passed a resolution demanding a formal apology from Hannegan for a *Democratic Digest* article that referred to passage of the Case bill as "a vote against the American people."[73]

More detrimental to the Democratic party, several southern conservatives used the incident to denounce what they perceived as Communist-dominated CIO influence at DNC headquarters and in the White House since the CIO opposed the Case bill.[74] Shortly thereafter, an eleven-member committee of Democratic representatives was formed to serve as a liaison between all House Democrats and the DNC chairman in order to reduce intraparty discord. But this effort was useless for quickly healing the sharp, apparently irreconcilable policy differences between conservatives and liberal Democrats.

The futility of this symbolic harmonizing motion was especially obvious as Truman planned to purge Representative Roger Slaughter, a conservative, antiadministration Kansas City Democrat who supported the Case bill, in the Missouri primary.[75] As a member of the House Rules Committee, Slaughter had obstructed other administration bills. On May 21, 1946, one day after a *Washington*

Post article explained a meeting between Hannegan and the liaison committee to reconcile intraparty differences for the campaign, Truman wrote to James Pendergast, the late machine boss's nephew: "The meanest partisan Republican has been no more anti-Truman than has Slaughter. . . . Slaughter is obnoxious to me and you must make your choice."[76]

With both conservative Democrats in Congress and such key liberal interest groups as the CIO-PAC alienated from Truman by the fall of 1946, Hannegan desperately tried to defend Truman and rally his fragmented party by emphasizing Democratic domestic and foreign policy accomplishments since 1932 in a 104-page campaign booklet published by the DNC. Entitled *Campaign Issues . . . 1946,* this booklet provided tables of statistics to assert that Truman's continuation and expansion of Roosevelt's policy accomplishments were necessary to maintain international peace and extend domestic prosperity. The DNC publication also portrayed Republican opposition as selfish, backward, and reactionary. It confidently concluded that Americans "have no wish to return to the Republican pattern of timidity, indecision and inaction."[77]

Another DNC pamphlet warned voters about the "Hoover Depression," bank failures, mass unemployment, and other economic miseries of 1932 that would return if the Republicans won control of Congress.[78] Hannegan's publicity effort failed to address the fact that an increasing proportion of voters were currently skeptical of the liberal Democratic emphasis on federal regulations, a prolabor bias, and price controls. In a Gallup poll conducted in mid-October, 77 percent of its Republican respondents and 60 percent of its Democratic respondents agreed that the Congress elected in November should pass new legislation to control labor unions.[79] A Gallup poll conducted in late October revealed that 58 percent of its respondents intended to vote Republican and 42 percent would vote Democratic in the congressional elections.[80] Hannegan, though, told Truman at a cabinet meeting on October 11, 1946, that the Democrats would retain control of Congress after the election.[81]

The most prominent feature of Hannegan's campaign strategy was Truman's absence from the campaign trail. Harry S. Truman does not explain in his memoirs why he did not campaign for Democratic congressional candidates, conduct a whistle-stop speaking tour, or discuss the campaign in his press conferences. According to Margaret Truman, her father accepted the advice of Bob Hannegan. "Mr. Hannegan seemed to think that the less the voters saw of the President, the better it would be for the party."[82] Considering the fact that Truman's public approval rating had plunged from 87 percent in June 1945 to 32 percent by September 1946, it seems probable that Hannegan would have given Truman such advice.[83]

The desperate, nearly pathetic dependence of Democratic electoral fortunes on Franklin D. Roosevelt in 1946 was symbolized by Hannegan's radio broadcasts of taped speeches by Roosevelt during the final days of the campaign. While Hannegan broadcast some tape recordings of Truman's speeches, Truman declined to deliver an election eve broadcast. He also had Sam Rayburn speak as his substitute at a Democratic rally in Independence before he voted.

ELECTION RESULTS

The 1946 congressional elections devastated the Democratic party and Truman's status as presidential party leader. The Republicans gained fifty-seven House seats and thirteen Senate seats. The GOP would have a fifty-seven seat majority in the House and a six-seat majority in the Senate when the Eightieth Congress convened in 1947.[84] The bipartisan conservative coalition that opposed Truman's liberal legislation in the Seventy-ninth Congress was now even more powerful since all southern and most border state Democratic incumbents, the regional sources of Democratic conservatives, were reelected. The Republicans won fifty-seven of the 138 nonsouthern Democratic House seats and seven of the eight Senate seats up for reelection that were held by nonsouthern Democrats with clearly liberal legislative records.[85]

In preparing for the 1948 presidential and congressional elections, Truman, DNC headquarters, and congressional Democrats could take some comfort in the fact that 34 million voters (37 percent of all eligible voters) turned out to vote in 1946, compared to 48 million voters (a 54 percent rate of turnout) in 1944.[86] Low voter turnout had also been essential to the substantial Republican gains in the midterm elections of 1938 and 1942.[87] Political scientist Samuel Kernell concluded that midterm elections are expressions of public opinion on presidential popularity and the condition of the economy while political scientist Matthew Soberg Shugart found that "the electoral cycle is only part of the explanation for divided government in the United States, but it is a big factor."[88]

The Democratic congressional and presidential campaigns of 1948 executed a major effort to mobilize Democratic-inclined voting blocs, which tended to have relatively low rates of voter turnout, such as the youngest voters, blacks, blue-collar workers, and foreign-born citizens. It was also apparent that Truman and pro-union, liberal Democratic congressional candidates needed to develop campaign rhetoric and tactics that would effectively counteract Republican charges of serving the interests of American and Soviet Communists.[89] But, as the Democrats pondered the best strategy for regaining control of Congress and retaining the presidency in the 1948 elections, key questions and differences about how to succeed electorally remained. Should Truman be the party's presidential nominee in 1948? If so, should Truman's party leadership and domestic policy approach to the Republican-controlled Congress be combatively liberal or consensually moderate? Major events of the Republican-controlled Eightieth Congress would help to provide the answers.

THE EIGHTIETH CONGRESS

Harry Truman had to accomplish two major objectives in his relationship with the Eightieth Congress. First, he needed to maintain bipartisan cooperation on foreign policy with the more moderate, internationalist Republicans in general and with Senator Arthur Vandenberg, chairman of the Senate Foreign Relations Committee, in particular. Such cooperation was necessary to secure passage of legislation concerning economic aid to Europe, the unification of the armed forces, and the reduction of tariffs for reciprocal trade agreements. It was also vital to Senate ratification of treaties with Italy, Hungary, Bulgaria, and Romania.[90] Besides being careful to regularly consult such key Republicans as Vandenberg and Speaker of the House Joseph W. Martin Jr., Truman appointed Gen. George C. Marshall to replace James F. Byrnes as secretary of state in January 1947. In addition to appointing this highly respected, nonpartisan war hero as the chief spokesman of his foreign policy, Truman appointed Republicans to key foreign and defense policy positions.[91] Most prominently, Republican business executive Paul Hoffman served as the first administrator of the European Recovery Program, commonly known as the Marshall Plan.[92]

Truman's efforts to further develop and continue a bipartisan consensus during the Eightieth Congress on major foreign and defense policy issues were also aided by Senator Robert A. Taft's focus on domestic, rather than foreign, policy. Taft's domestic policy focus in 1947 and 1948 was partially influenced by his deference to Vandenberg's leadership on foreign policy and his own position as chairman of the Republican Policy Committee and the Senate Labor Committee. Busy formulating and shepherding his own housing, labor, and education legislation during the Eightieth Congress, Taft publicly criticized various aspects of the Marshall Plan and legislation providing military and economic aid to Greece and Turkey. But he ultimately voted for both policies. On such major foreign policy measures favored by Truman and Vandenberg, Taft abstained from rallying isolationist Republicans to obstruct them.

Truman's most dramatic speech seeking bipartisan cooperation on foreign policy was his appeal to Congress for $400 million in military and economic aid to Greece and Turkey, whose governments were respectively threatened by a Communist-supported civil war and Soviet expansion.[93] Influenced by Vandenberg's advice to "scare hell" out of Congress and the public, Truman's special message to Congress of March 12, 1947, firmly requested the appropriation of $400 million in aid to Greece and Turkey within the broader context of an American responsibility to protect its own security and that of other "free peoples who are resisting attempted subjugation by armed minorities or by outside pressures."[94] The appropriations bill for Greek-Turkish aid was passed by broad majorities in both houses of Congress in May.[95]

By contrast, congressional passage of $17 billion for the Marshall Plan in 1948 proved to be more controversial and divisive within the Republican party. The most conservative Republicans in Congress vigorously opposed the Marshall Plan's enactment or sought significant cuts in the amount of the proposed four-year economic aid because of budgetary concerns or suspicions that Truman's foreign policy was subservient to British interests.[96] A combination of George C. Marshall's patriotic stature, a communist coup d'état of the Czech government, Vandenberg's active lobbying of his fellow Republicans and Taft's abandonment of his initial opposition, partially due to his presidential ambition for 1948, all contributed to congressional passage of appropriations for the Marshall Plan.[97]

Although Congress rejected Truman's request for universal military training, it passed the Truman-recommended National Security Act of 1947, which created the Department of Defense to provide greater coordination and unity among the branches of the armed forces.[98] Truman's victories in foreign and defense policy legislation yielded increases in his public approval ratings and a greater, more public exposure of the foreign policy differences among the Republicans in Congress.[99] In particular, these intraparty conflicts over Truman's foreign policy proposals revealed stark ideological and programmatic differences between the more moderate, internationalist Republicans of the Senate and the more conservative, isolationist Republicans of the House. In a tone of moral outrage, Senator Vandenberg publicly denounced the budget-cutting tactics of House Appropriations Committee Chairman John Taber toward the Marshall Plan as an action that "inevitably undermines that confidence and morale abroad upon which recovery, independent freedoms and peace so heavily lean; and that it serves the alien critics who plot to have these peace plans fail."[100]

Thus, Truman's achievement of his first goal for the Eightieth Congress had forged a bipartisan consensus on major foreign policy issues while internally weakening the Republicans in Congress. Truman's second purpose was to defend and promote liberal domestic policies, especially in the areas of hous-ing and labor, as a combatively partisan liberal Democrat. Truman's liberal rheto-ric and behavior toward Congress in 1947 and 1948 concerning public housing, wider Social Security coverage, a higher minimum wage, civil rights, federal aid to elementary and secondary education, national health insurance, and Re-publican-sponsored income tax cuts, aroused opposition from both Repub-licans and mostly southern, conservative Democrats in Congress.[101] In a May 19, 1947, message to Congress, Truman concluded that until national health insurance "is a part of our national fabric, we shall be wasting our most pre-cious national resource and shall be perpetuating unnecessary misery and hu-man suffering."[102] In his April 2, 1948, message to Congress explaining his veto of an income tax cut bill, Truman criticized the bill as "an evil in disguise" and "inequitable."[103]

Congress, however, overrode Truman's veto, and this bill became the In-come Tax Reduction Act of 1948. Throughout the 1947-48 sessions of Con-gress, Truman aggressively used his veto power against Republican-created domestic policy legislation. Congress overrode only twelve of the 258 vetoes that Truman issued throughout his presidency, but seven overrides occurred during the Eightieth Congress, when Truman issued seventy-four regular and pocket vetoes.[104] When Truman signed domestic policy bills into law, he occa-sionally complained that the legislation did not accomplish enough. After sign-ing the Housing and Rent Act of 1948, the president stated that while this law "does not carry out all the recommendations I have made to the Congress for stronger rent control legislation, and will not give tenants all the protection they should have during the present housing shortage," it "is better than no rent con-trol at all."[105]

Truman's most effective use of a veto to express his economic liberalism, contrast himself with the Republican-controlled Congress, and prepare for the 1948 presidential campaign by galvanizing a key Democratic interest group was his veto of the Taft-Hartley Act of 1947. Determined to reduce the legal rights and powers that labor unions had gained from the Wagner Act of 1935, a bipartisan coalition of Republicans and conservative Democrats led by House Education and Labor Committee Chairman Fred Hartley secured House pas-sage of a bill significantly limiting the power of labor unions over their mem-bers and in their relations with management.[106] The Hartley bill's provisions included the prohibition of closed shops, secondary boycotts, mass picketing, jurisdictional strikes, and recognition by the National Labor Relations Board to unions whose officials refused to sign affidavits stating that they were not com-munists.[107] Only twenty-two Republicans in the House—including freshman

Congressman Jacob Javits of New York, who denounced it as "legislation driven by fear and vindictiveness"—voted against the Hartley bill when the House passed it on April 17, 1947.[108]

As chairman of the Senate Labor Committee and the Republican Policy Committee, Robert A. Taft led the Senate effort to develop a more moderate labor bill that could attract large enough majorities in both houses to override a veto.[109] In particular, the compromise bill had to attract the support of liberal Republicans such as Senator Irving Ives of New York, a member of the Senator Labor Committee who was endorsed by the American Federation of Labor (AFL) in 1946. The Taft-Hartley bill, therefore, did not include the Hartley bill's provisions on industry-wide bargaining, employers' contributions to welfare funds, restrictions on conditions for union shops, and the application of antitrust laws to labor unions.[110]

The House passed the Taft-Hartley bill by a vote of 320 to 79 on June 3, 1947.[111] On June 5, 1947, the Senate followed by a vote of 57 to 17.[112] On June 20, 1947, Truman vetoed the measure and referred to it in a radio address as a "shocking piece of legislation" that "will take fundamental rights away from our working people" and "would threaten fundamental democratic freedoms."[113] By June 23, both houses of Congress had overridden Truman's veto.[114] Twenty of the forty-five Democrats in the Senate and 107 of the 188 Democrats in the House voted to override Truman's veto.[115]

Despite substantial Democratic support in Congress for the Taft-Hartley Act, Truman chose to emphasize this law enacted over his veto as a major difference in ideology and domestic policy between the Democratic and Republican parties during his 1948 campaign. More specifically and significantly, Truman's veto was instrumental in gaining the active campaign support of labor unions, especially CIO unions, that were alienated from him in 1946 and might have broadly supported the Progressive presidential candidacy of Henry A. Wallace in 1948.[116] The Taft-Hartley Act of 1947 would have the distinction of being the only major law made by the Eightieth Congress that weakened the provisions of a major New Deal law (the Wagner Act of 1935.)

Widely known as "Mr. Republican" and often perceived as the spokesman of the most conservative Republicans in Congress, Robert A. Taft was actually moderate on the issue of public housing and willing to cooperate with Democrats and liberal Republicans on housing legislation. Since 1945, he had cosponsored legislation with Democratic Senators Robert Wagner of New York and Allen Ellender of Louisiana to provide public housing for low-income residents, federal funds for slum clearance, easier FHA mortgage terms, and the creation of a National Housing Agency.[117] Although the Senate passed the Taft-

Ellender-Wagner housing bill and a Taft-sponsored federal aid to education bill in 1948, the more conservative House Republicans killed both bills.[118]

The deaths of these two Taft-sponsored bills in the House of Representatives provided Truman with two major political advantages for his presidential campaign. They accentuated ideological and programmatic conflicts between Republicans in the House and Senate and partially motivated Republican presidential nominee Thomas E. Dewey to avoid defending Republican legislative behavior.[119] They also helped Truman to justify calling Congress into special session in July 1948 in order to recommend the passage of the Taft-Ellender-Wagner bill, federal aid to education, and major domestic policy proposals that he had recommended to Congress in 1947 and 1948.[120]

Suggested by the DNC's Research Division and endorsed by White House special counsel Clark M. Clifford, Truman's dramatic call for a special session of Congress during his nomination speech at the Democratic national convention elicited Republican charges that he was cynically abusing a constitutional power for campaign purposes.[121] Truman's official reason for stating the necessity of a special session was the need for immediate legislative action on inflation and passage of the Taft-Ellender-Wagner housing bill in both houses of Congress.[122] Although these were Truman's two priorities, his message to Congress also included requests for increased Social Security benefits, a higher minimum wage, bank credit controls, federal aid to education, and civil rights legislation.[123] Truman's political intention was to have the "Turnip Day" session of late July and early August expose the stark contrast between the moderate liberalism represented by the GOP's platform and presidential ticket and the conservatism of most Republicans in Congress, especially those in the House of Representatives.

By sending the special session of Congress a list of liberal domestic legislation, Truman bolstered his credibility and campaign support from liberal Democrats and labor unions. Yet he also risked further alienating southern Democrats, especially due to his repeated submission of civil rights legislation. Representative John Rankin of Mississippi used the occasion of the special session "to extend a challenge to President Truman and to Gov. Thomas E. Dewey, of the State of New York, to engage in a Nation-wide radio debate with me on this FEPC, the most dangerous communistic piece of legislation with which the American people have ever been threatened."[124]

During the special session of the Eightieth Congress, the *New Republic* commented, "Truman is the candidate on a Democratic platform that makes it practically a labor party, but the majority of the members of his party in Congress are conservative."[125] It was not surprising, therefore, that Congress did not pass most of Truman's recommended legislation during this special session. Among the relatively minor items that Congress passed were additional executive powers to control consumer and bank credit, a $65 million loan to the United Nations for the construction of its headquarters, and a $5 million appropriation to buy automobiles for disabled veterans.[126] More ominous for the Truman administration, House and Senate committees continued investigations of current and previous communist infiltration in the federal bureaucracy, which would later focus on former State Department official Alger Hiss.[127] During his news conference of August 12, 1948, Truman agreed with a reporter that the special session proved that the Republican-controlled Congress was a "do-nothing" Congress and reaffirmed his earlier comment that this congressional probe of internal communism was a "red herring."[128]

Fortunately for Truman, Republicans were unable to make domestic communism an effective campaign issue against Truman in 1948. The development of a bipartisan foreign policy against communist expansion, Truman's conduct of the Berlin airlift, the use of Henry Wallace's Progressive party as the target of Democratic rhetoric against domestic communism, and Truman's establishment of loyalty review boards to investigate allegations of communist federal employees combined to weaken the electoral impact of Republican charges of Democratic softness on communism, despite the dramatic developments of the Alger Hiss investigation from August 1948 until election day.[129]

Frustrated by their inability to successfully capitalize on the communist issue against Truman and by Dewey's apparent unwillingness to aggressively defend their legislative record, congressional Republicans issued a 118-page campaign book, *The Story of the 80th Congress*.[130] Written by the Republican Policy Committee, this campaign publication expressed indignation at Truman's constant denunciation of the Eightieth Congress for doing nothing on domestic policy and for being callous to the interests of average Americans. After providing extensive statistics and tables to specify the policy accomplishments of the Republican majorities and their cooperation with Truman on foreign policy, this Republican campaign book concluded that "the Republican Congress and not the President will receive the laurels for cooperation and for a real constructive job in meeting the nation's problems."[131]

THE AFTERMATH

Long after Truman's unexpected electoral victory and the less surprising resumption of Democratic control of both houses of Congress after the 1948 elections, the Republican party continued to experience conflicting interpretations of the role of the Republican-controlled Eightieth Congress in the Democratic electoral success of 1948. Herbert Brownell, the RNC chairman (1944-46) who laid the foundation for the Republican resurgence of 1946 and was Dewey's campaign manager in 1948, unequivocally told political scientist Nicol C. Rae in 1984, "The Eightieth Congress defeated Dewey, not the Democrats."[132] Liberal Republican Senator Irving Ives of New York also attributed Truman's victory and the Democratic sweep of the congressional elections to "the inability of the Eightieth Congress to get together on a forward-looking, liberal program."[133]

Conservative Republicans in Congress, though, partially or entirely attributed Dewey's defeat and the election of a Democratically controlled Congress to Dewey's inability or unwillingness to aggressively defend the legislative record of the Eightieth Congress against Truman's vitriolic, often misleading rhetoric.[134] Outgoing Speaker of the House Joseph W. Martin Jr., later wrote that the Republican-led Eightieth Congress was "a particularly constructive and progressive Congress."[135] Martin also assumed, "If Dewey had been elected in 1948, we never would have experienced the McCarthy era, because Republican energies would have been working in a different direction, discharging the responsibilities of administering the government."[136] Senator Robert A. Taft would likewise claim that if Dewey had equalled Truman's aggressive, partisan rhetoric in refuting Truman's charges about the Eightieth Congress he could have won the election and retained Republican control of Congress.[137]

Regardless of the lingering disagreements within the GOP over whether the Republican record in the Eightieth Congress was an asset or a liability for Dewey's campaign, Susan Hartmann, a leading scholar of the Eightieth Congress, concluded: "Truman shrewdly used the Eightieth Congress to demonstrate the public's continuing attachment to New Deal reform, assured his own and his party's ascendancy, and in so doing gained the admiration and support, if not the love, of liberals in the United States."[138] The *New Republic,* which had previously questioned Truman's commitment to New Deal liberalism, commented shortly after the 1948 election, "Truman is well to the left of the Roosevelt New Deal."[139] In short, the Republican leadership and domestic policy record of the Eightieth Congress provided Truman with a framework that enabled him to combine his values as a party regular and a liberal reformer into rousing, electorally successful campaign rhetoric. His partisan, ideological interpretation and rhetorical manipulation of the Republican legislative behavior and record of the Eighieth Congress, though, proved to be only one of several factors in the Democratic resurgence in the 1948 elections.

5

☆ ☆ ☆ ☆ ☆

MAINTAINING THE
MAJORITY PARTY, 1948

Two days after the 1948 election, White House aide Eben A. Ayers wrote in his diary that, because of Harry Truman's unexpected electoral victory, he "owes no one anything and is in the position of being perhaps the most independent president elected in many years."[1] Historian Donald R. McCoy and journalist Jules Abels both referred to Truman's electoral success as a "personal triumph."[2] Columnist Arthur Krock likewise described it as a "miracle of electioneering" by Truman.[3]

Truman himself was modest and more accurate. Instead of referring to the 1948 electoral results as a personal victory, he described his victory and the election of a Democratic Congress as a party victory. In his memoirs, Truman wrote, "The fundamental purpose of the campaign in 1948 was to put the Democratic party on its own feet and to leave it intact."[4] More specifically and significantly, Truman intended his campaign strategy in 1948—which included social welfare proposals more liberal than Roosevelt's, defiance toward most southern Democrats on civil rights, and a foreign policy toward the Soviet Union repugnant to many leftists who had supported Roosevelt—to permanently direct the ideology and policy agenda of the national Democratic party toward a more coherently and comprehensively liberal and internationalist identity by alienating the most reactionary southern whites and voters on the left who were most hostile to his foreign policy. In specifying this significance of the 1948 election results, Truman wrote, "The greatest achievement was winning without the extreme radicals in the party and without the Solid South."[5]

A PARTY VICTORY

In campaigning for election as president in his own right, Truman was not satisfied to merely maintain the status of the Democratic party as the majority party among voters, retain Democratic control of the presidency, and regain his party's control of Congress. He evidently hoped that the demographic, coalitional, and ideological nature of his electoral support and his staunchly liberal domestic policy proposals, including divisive positions favoring national health insurance, civil rights legislation, and repeal of the Taft-Hartley Act, would enable him to transform the Democratic party among the voters and eventually in Congress into a party liberal enough to accomplish these and other liberal policy goals.[6] In a 1966 interview, Samuel C. Brightman, the DNC's associate publicity director in 1948, substantiated Truman's post-election analysis: "Now, '48 was, in my opinion, a test of the basic strength of the party, party philosophy, and party performance."[7]

More precisely and importantly for Truman's party leadership, though, Truman's strategy, tactics, rhetoric, policy proposals, and interaction with DNC headquarters and key Democratic interest groups comprised and demonstrated the clearest and most politically effective mixture of his two-value systems as a party leader. Truman the party regular stimulated and supervised the revitalization of the DNC headquarters and certain special divisions as innovative, vigorous campaign organizations. DNC chairman J. Howard McGrath claimed that in preparing for the 1948 campaign "the Democratic National Committee's effort was wholly one of organization and building the party to operational efficiency at all levels in spite of the tremendous diversions and divisions which beset it."[8] Truman's experience as a machine politician and his ethos as a party regular taught him that a well-coordinated, party-centered campaign conducted by an efficient campaign organization, rather than a candidate-centered suprapartisan campaign, was essential for a party victory, rather than a personal triumph.

Truman's value system as a liberal reformer motivated him to adopt divisively liberal policy positions and combatively liberal campaign oratory that portrayed apparently sharp ideological and programmatic differences between the two major parties by contrasting Truman's liberalism with the conservatism of the Republican record in the Eightieth Congress. Occasionally during the 1948 campaign, there was a correlation between Truman's liberal policy behavior and the organizational behavior of the DNC apparatus. For example, in 1947, union leaders appreciated how Truman and McGrath used the DNC headquarters to develop a consensus among DNC members and Democratic state chairmen opposing the Taft-Hartley Act and then to lobby Democratic members of Congress against it.[9]

But, before Truman could use the 1948 campaign and election results to make a lasting impact on the Democratic party's ideology and policy agenda, he first had to assure his own nomination and unite most Democrats behind his candidacy. Following the Democratic debacle in the 1946 midterm elections, dispirited Democrats throughout the party—southern conservatives, machine bosses, liberal activists, and union leaders—were seeking a more attractive presidential candidate than Truman.[10] The president consequently needed a campaign strategy that could best combine his regular and reformer characteristics while persuading most skeptical Democrats that he would be a competitive presidential nominee in 1948.

CLIFFORD-ROWE STRATEGY

Harry Truman did not need his White House staff or DNC headquarters to persuade him to adopt aggressively liberal rhetoric and domestic policy positions for the 1948 campaign.[11] It is clear that Truman's liberal beliefs were, according to White House aide and speech writer Charles S. Murphy, "based on practical knowledge from earlier experiences and on his study of history; they were views he held with deep conviction."[12] Truman, though, did need advice on how to maximize the political efficacy of his liberalism for campaign purposes. A group of Truman's White House aides proved to be crucial in providing this necessary strategic advice.

In his study of White House staffs, Patrick Anderson found that Truman and his special counsel, Clark M. Clifford, shared a "pragmatic liberalism" and "a belief that many of the New Dealers were dreamers who had little understanding of politics."[13] After the 1946 elections, Clifford and several other White House aides and cabinet department officials began to meet regularly in the apartment of Oscar Ewing, vice chairman of the DNC and administrator of the Federal Security Agency. Known collectively as the Monday Night Group, these officials discussed and formulated ways to strengthen and clarify the Truman administration's policy identity and agenda as being liberal and to develop this liberalism as an effective strategy for the 1948 presidential campaign.[14]

The Monday Night Group initially focused its efforts on the development of liberal policy positions and their advocacy against more conservative officials in the Truman administration. Thus, the general outline of a campaign strategy that would incorporate and exploit liberal policy positions and rhetoric was provided by someone who did not belong to the Monday Night Group or to the Truman administration at all. It was submitted to budget director James Webb by James H. Rowe Jr., an administrative assistant to Franklin D. Roosevelt and a prominent Washington lawyer.[15] Entitled "The Politics of 1948" and dated

September 17, 1947, Rowe's thirty-three page memorandum explained and suggested a comprehensively liberal campaign that would energize the support of blacks, western progressives, urban ethnics, labor unions, and liberal activists while retaining the South in the electoral college.[16] Rowe assumed, "It is inconceivable that any policies initiated by the Truman Administration no matter how 'liberal' could so alienate the South in the next year that it would revolt."[17]

The Monday Night Group revised, expanded, and updated the Rowe memorandum. Clifford then submitted this forty-three page document to Truman on November 19, 1947.[18] In addition to repeating Rowe's emphasis on domestic policy liberalism to appeal to a variety of Democratic voting blocs and his assumption that the South would not rebel in 1948 over any liberal positions, the Clifford memorandum urged Truman to devote his 1948 State of the Union address to a list of liberal policy recommendations of the Republican-controlled Congress.[19] Clifford shrewdly speculated, "There is little possibility that he will get much cooperation from the Congress but we want the President to be in position to receive the credit for whatever they do accomplish while also being in position to criticize the Congress for being obstructionists for failing to comply with other recommendations."[20]

Most of Truman's foreign policy toward Western Europe and the Soviet Union received bipartisan support and was overseen by his highly respected secretary of state, George C. Marshall. So Clifford urged Truman to use his foreign policy record to counter criticism by Henry A. Wallace, whom Clifford assumed would run as a third-party presidential candidate. Part of Truman's campaign strategy toward Wallace must be "to identify him and isolate him in the public mind with the Communists."[21] While portraying Wallace as a dupe of American Communists and an apologist for Soviet foreign policy interests, Truman could take on Thomas E. Dewey, the probable Republican nominee, on domestic issues. Clifford urged him to continue appointing liberals to key administration positions and to especially address the domestic policy interests of rural western states, such as the expansion of federal electric power and soil reclamation projects, because this region was most receptive to Robert M. La Follette, Sr.'s Progressive presidential candidacy in 1924.[22]

The Clifford memorandum also made recommendations for the style and conduct of Truman's campaign. It suggested that the president launch an officially "non-political" train trip to the West before the Democratic National Convention.[23] This would be followed by a highly partisan whistle-stop speech-making trip after the convention. The Monday Night Group assumed that an extensive speaking trip in which Truman addressed domestic issues that most concerned average Americans, such as high food costs and the housing shortage, in his own informal, folksy speaking style would project Truman's most appealing qualities, his blunt sincerity and unassuming amiability.[24]

The final pages of the Clifford memorandum criticized the Democratic national and state committees for currently lacking the resources, and even the political judgment and foresight, to support such a well-researched, issue-oriented campaign by Truman. "The Chairman of the Illinois Democratic Committee may brag that his committee has no financial worries . . . and the Democratic National Committee may have relaxed in the assurance it can get sufficient funds to finance the 1948 campaign. Both organizations seem to have forgotten that the money-raising is after all only the means for a desirable end."[25] In short, Clifford and other members of the Monday Night Group already suspected that current DNC officials and party regulars in general lacked the creativity, initiative, and intellectual orientation toward issues, policies, and ideas that Truman's whistle-stop campaign needed to succeed.

Partially because of this perspective toward DNC headquarters, the Clifford memorandum suggested that a "working committee," be established and funded by the DNC chairman but that it actually serve and be subordinate to the president's campaign staff on his train.[26] This "working committee," which became the DNC's Research Division, would provide Truman and his speech writers on the train with the facts on all of the policy issues that he would address.[27] It would also provide him with facts on the politics, economics, history, demography, and recent events unique to each community in which Truman would speak. According to William L. Batt Jr., the director of this division, these facts enabled Truman to maximize the local appeal of each whistle-stop speech "so when he went into James Whitcomb Riley's home town, he was quoting from Riley's poetry about the old swimming hole."[28]

The suggestion of a research unit was probably the most innovative practical and organizational recommendation of the Clifford memorandum. Clark M. Clifford later claimed that the Research Division was the only part of the DNC's apparatus that helped Truman's whistle-stop campaign.[29] The research efforts of this DNC staff division enabled Truman to deliver campaign speeches that contained an appealing mixture of strident partisanship, humor, local color, and specific policy positions on issues relevant to his audiences' immediate interests. In his memoirs, Clifford states that Truman generally liked the suggestions of the memorandum, which the president "kept in his desk drawer throughout the campaign for handy reference."[30]

The Rowe-Clifford strategy proved to be an excellent blueprint for planning and executing Truman's whistle-stop campaign. But before Truman could focus on his general election campaign, he had to address two intraparty revolts, the Progressive party candidacy of Henry A. Wallace and later the States' Rights Democratic (SRD), or "Dixiecrat," presidential campaign of Governor J. Strom Thurmond of South Carolina. The Rowe and Clifford memoranda anticipated Wallace's campaign and had already prepared a shrewd research and publicity strategy to discredit his candidacy.[31] Truman and his staff, though, were surprised at the severity to which some southern Democrats reacted to his civil rights message to Congress and were initially uncertain about the best response to this defection.

THE WALLACE CAMPAIGN

Henry A. Wallace's public announcement of his presidential candidacy on December 29, 1947, was certainly not surprising to Truman's White House staff and DNC headquarters.[32] In his broadcast address, Wallace emphasized his opposition to the "bipartisan reactionary war policy."[33] Until the end of 1947, Wallace had denied that he would run for president as a minor party's candidate. He claimed that he only wanted to pressure Truman and the Democratic party to change their foreign policy toward the Soviet Union.[34]

On December 17, 1947, the Progressive Citizens of America (PCA) announced its formation of the Progressive party for the 1948 campaign and its preference for Wallace as its presidential nominee.[35] Founded mostly by members of two recently dissolved CIO-affiliated organizations, the National Citizens Political Action Committee and the Independent Citizens Committee of the Arts, Sciences, and Professions, the PCA did not exclude communists as members. The public image and electoral prospects of the Progressive party and Henry A. Wallace, however, were damaged in 1948 by the fact that only two major CIO unions, the United Electrical Workers union and the International Longshoremen's and Warehousemen's union, supported Wallace.[36] In New York, expected to be Wallace's potentially strongest state, the Liberal party opposed his candidacy after the American Labor Party (ALP) endorsed him, partially because of the antagonism between these two parties.

But the ALP's largest labor voting bloc, the Amalgamated Clothing Workers Union, had withdrawn from the ALP and the only significant newspapers that offered editorial support for the Progressive party were the Communist party's *Daily Worker* and the York, Pennsylvania, *Gazette.*[37] Consequently, the vacuum left in the PCA and, shortly thereafter, in Wallace's presidential campaign was filled with zealous American Communists experienced in organizing campaigns and political movements.[38] Analyzing the influence of the American Communist party, or "C.P.," in Wallace's 1948 campaign, political scientists Harvey Klehr and John Earl Haynes concluded, "The indirect relationship between Wallace and the C.P. and the concealed role of Communist activists in the labor movement and in local liberal organizations led Wallace to misjudge support for a new party."[39]

The extent of Communist influence in the Progressive party later became evident in 1948 in the similarities between its platform and the American Communist party's platform regarding American foreign policy toward the Soviet Union.[40] More specifically, most delegates at the Progressive party's 1948 convention rejected the Vermont Resolution.[41] This proposed platform plank stated that the Progressive party did not give "blanket endorsement" to the foreign policy of the Soviet Union or any other nation.[42]

While these later developments in the Wallace campaign helped to reduce its voter appeal and provided credibility to Democratic charges of Communist domination of the Progressive party, Truman and DNC Chairman J. Howard McGrath were initially apprehensive about the divisive impact of Wallace's candidacy on normally Democratic liberal voters. A few days before Wallace announced his presidential candidacy, McGrath stated that Wallace was welcome in the Democratic party.[43] McGrath and other Truman campaign strategists feared that Wallace could attract enough popular votes in New York, California, Illinois, and Michigan to enable the Republicans to carry these large states in the electoral college.[44]

Immediately after Wallace announced his candidacy, the Truman campaign's public rhetoric abruptly shifted from vaguely soothing statements to denunciations of Wallace's candidacy as a tool of Soviet foreign policy and an asset in electing a "reactionary" Republican president.[45] The potential electoral threat that the Wallace candidacy posed to Truman in New York was evident in a special congressional election in the Bronx held on February 17, 1948. Leo Isacson, a pro-Wallace ALP candidate, won the election with 56 percent of the votes in a four-candidate race.[46] Karl Propper, the Democratic nominee slated by Bronx Democratic boss and former DNC chairman Edward J. Flynn, received only 31 percent.[47] Truman, though, "seemed pleased at the result. He said maybe this would be the 'year of decision' after all," according to White House aide Eben A. Ayers.[48]

Confident that he could discredit Wallace as a dupe of American and Soviet communists, Truman told an Irish-American fraternal organization in New York

City on Saint Patrick's Day that he unequivocally would not seek or accept the electoral support of Henry A. Wallace and his followers because "any price for Wallace and his Communists is too much for me to pay."[49] Some liberal Democrats, however, questioned whether anti-Communist rhetoric by Truman against Wallace would be enough to minimize his leftist movement's political strength.[50]

Democratic senatorial candidate Hubert H. Humphrey warned DNC Executive Director Gael Sullivan that communists were sending organizers and funds into Minnesota in order to dominate the proceedings of the April 30 caucuses of the Democratic Farmer Labor party. Humphrey was angry and frustrated with the inertia and apparent complacency of the DNC headquarters toward the Wallace campaign. Humphrey stated to Sullivan: "We're fighting with everything we've got out here. Where does the National Committee stand?"[51]

Fortunately for Truman and DNC headquarters, the Americans for Democratic Action (ADA) emerged to conduct a vigorous publicity campaign against Henry A. Wallace and the Progressive party. The ADA's extensive research and regularly published reports on Henry Wallace and his minor party were effective in discrediting and marginalizing them in the 1948 campaign. Representing DNC headquarters, Gael Sullivan conferred with Paul Porter, an ADA official and former DNC publicity director, and several other members of the ADA's executive committee on January 29, 1948. Sullivan promised the DNC's financial aid to the ADA and Truman's public expression of interest in the ADA if the ADA waged a vigorous campaign against Wallace.[52]

The ADA's militant campaign against Wallace enabled Truman and the DNC's apparatus to concentrate their attention and resources on the Republicans. While the ADA shared a mutual interest with Truman and DNC officials in destroying the Wallace campaign, it opposed Truman and supported Dwight Eisenhower for the Democratic presidential nomination until the Democratic national convention nominated Truman in July 1948. Organized on January 3, 1947, the ADA committed itself as a nonpartisan organization to an anticommunist, internationalist foreign policy favorable to the Marshall Plan, Truman Doctrine, United Nations, and the recognition of Israel; and liberalism in domestic policy, especially toward civil rights for blacks.[53] Doubting the sincerity and political efficacy of Truman's liberalism, the ADA and its predecessor, the Union for Democratic Action, were outspoken critics of some of Truman's appointments and his perceived lack of commitment on civil rights.[54]

Although it did not devote the bulk of its political efforts to promote Truman's candidacy until the last few weeks of the 1948 campaign, the ADA conducted a research and publicity campaign against Wallace, which proved to be a key asset in Truman's campaign.[55] An ADA report entitled, "Henry A. Wallace: The

First Three Months," claims that American Communist leader William Z. Foster helped to create the Progressive party as a "broad united-front demanded by the CP" in order to disintegrate the Democratic party.[56] The ADA also sought to discredit Wallace's portrayal of himself as the most pro–civil rights, antiracist presidential candidate by disclosing that Wallace had not promoted racial integration within his jurisdiction as secretary of commerce and that Walter White, executive secretary of the NAACP, and Lester Granger, chairman of the National Urban League, opposed Wallace's candidacy.[57]

Written during the 1948 campaign, Arthur M. Schlesinger Jr.'s book, *The Vital Center,* was probably the most theoretical, comprehensive argument for an anticommunist, Cold War liberalism in the United States that would not only avoid political associations with American Communists but would also actively minimize their role in American politics and government.[58] Schlesinger, a leading ADA member, referred to Henry A. Wallace as a "well-intentioned, woolly-minded, increasingly embittered man who was made to order for Communist exploitation; his own sense of martyrdom was swiftly generalized to embrace all friends of Soviet totalitarianism."[59] Schlesinger also emphasized an argument that would often be used by Truman and other liberal Democratic candidates in 1948.[60] According to this argument, the American Communist party "has been a great ally of the American conservatives because of its success, for a season, at least, in dividing and neutralizing the left" and "it is in the survival of the free left . . . that the answer to Communism lies."[61]

Although the ADA remained an officially nonpartisan organization—which included Republican Senator Wayne Morse of Oregon as a member and endorsed Republican Representative Jacob Javits of New York—it emerged as a major force in promoting liberalism within the Democratic party during and after the 1948 campaign. Joseph Rauh, Andrew Biemiller, and other ADA members attending the Democratic national convention of 1948 successfully pressured Truman, McGrath, and other Democrats to adopt the ADA-sponsored civil rights plank, which was more specific and controversial than Truman's proposal.[62] Appreciating the ADA's assistance in attacking Wallace's candidacy, Truman asked ADA chairman Wilson Wyatt to serve again as chairman of the Washington, D.C., Jefferson-Jackson Day Dinner in 1949.[63] Of the Democrats first elected to Congress in 1948, two senators, Hubert Humphrey of Minnesota and Paul Douglas of Illinois, and nine representatives were ADA members.[64] Even more prominent, Adlai Stevenson, the governor-elect of Illinois and the 1952 Democratic presidential nominee, was an ADA member.[65]

The ADA's campaign against Henry A. Wallace and the Progressive party was not the only factor limiting Henry A. Wallace to 1,157,057 votes, fewer

than most analysts expected, in 1948.[66] Wallace's own clumsy campaign rhetoric, inadequate campaign funds, the failure to place his name on the Illinois
ballot, increases in Cold War tensions, and the lack of substantial labor support
also contributed to Wallace's modicum of voter appeal.[67] For the ADA, its effort
to undermine Wallace's candidacy was a crucial opportunity for gaining influence in the White House and among liberal Democrats in Congress after the
1948 election and in the articulation of anti-Communist liberalism.[68]

Anticipating Wallace's candidacy, the Truman campaign, as outlined by
the Rowe and Clifford memoranda, was able to convert a potentially serious
intraparty defection into a voter-appealing asset. With Wallace as the recipient
of charges of communist domination from the ADA, the DNC's Publicity Division, and the media, the Truman campaign was able to simultaneously focus
more of its resources on the Republicans, undermine the credibility of Republican charges that Truman's policies toward domestic and foreign communism
were dangerously soft and ineffective, and increase Truman's attraction to the
most anticommunist Catholic voters.[69]

THE DIXIECRAT REVOLT

The Clifford-Rowe strategy confidently assumed that no matter how liberal Harry Truman's domestic policy proposals and behavior were in 1948, they
could not alienate southern whites. For Clifford and Rowe, it was inconceivable
that southern whites—no matter how much they might resent Truman's support
for a permanent FEPC, federal voting rights, and antilynching legislation—
would defect to the Republican party or form a minor party. The growth of the
black population and black voting power in big states—New York, Michigan,
Ohio, Illinois, and California—and the appeal of the probable Republican presidential nominee, liberal Governor Thomas E. Dewey of New York, with a strong
civil rights record and platform, motivated Truman and his staff to make civil
rights a major component of his 1948 State of the Union Address.[70]

Truman spoke of the need for "effective Federal action" to ensure equal
opportunity in jobs, education, and voting in his January 7, 1948, State of the
Union Address. He stated that he would soon send a special message to Congress on civil rights that would be based on the recommendations of the
President's Committee on Civil Rights.[71] Truman's special message of February
2, 1948, advanced fewer than one-third of this committee's recommendations
on civil rights.[72] Truman's civil rights proposals included a permanent FEPC,
voting rights, and antilynching legislation, but not the advocacy of federally

enforced racial integration in public housing and education, which his committee recommended. The reaction of most southern Democratic members of Congress and governors was swift, hostile, and somewhat surprising to Truman.[73]

The Southern Governors Conference was held on February 7-8, 1948, and focused on how to oppose Truman's civil rights message. Governor Fielding Wright of Mississippi was the only governor at the conference who openly advocated a meeting to consider formally leaving the national Democratic party.[74] Governor J. Strom Thurmond of South Carolina persuaded his colleagues to adopt a more moderate approach for expressing their opposition to Truman's civil rights proposals.[75] During a forty-day period, a committee of southern governors would assess the impact of Truman's civil rights proposals on the South, meet with DNC Chairman J. Howard McGrath, and would then issue a report to all of the members of the Southern Governors Conference.[76]

Meanwhile, some southern DNC members, Democratic state committees, governors, and members of Congress symbolically expressed their dissatisfaction with Truman's civil rights position by refusing to attend the Jefferson-Jackson Day Dinner of February 19, 1948, in Washington, D.C., and to send contributions to the DNC's treasury.[77] In Mississippi, Alabama, and South Carolina, Democratic state and local committees voted to sever formal relations with the DNC. In Arkansas, Governor Ben Laney and Democratic state chairman Arthur Adams failed to persuade their state's Democratic committee to end its relationship with the DNC.[78] But by mid-March, Democratic state chairman Gessner T. McCorvey of Alabama secured pledges from Democratic candidates for electors so that his state could deny Truman its electoral-college votes.[79]

Faced with the prospect of Truman losing southern electoral-college votes, McGrath tried to soothe Thurmond and the other southern governors during their February 23 meeting by assuring them that Truman's civil rights plan did not include federally coerced racial integration of public schools and that he would try to soften the wording of the civil rights plank at the Democratic national convention.[80] Representing the other southern governors, Thurmond was not satisfied with McGrath's diplomacy. In a prosecutorial tone, Thurmond asked McGrath, "Will you now . . . use your influence as Chairman of the Democratic National Committee, to have the highly controversial civil-rights legislation, which tends to divide our people, withdrawn from consideration by the Congress?"[81]

Although McGrath had hoped to reach a rapprochement with the southern governors, he firmly refused Thurmond's request that he seek an abandonment of Truman's proposals. The most ardent southern Democratic opponents of civil rights and Truman's party leadership held a States' Rights Conference in Jackson,

Mississippi on May 10, 1948.[82] The purpose of this conference was not to establish a minor party.[83] Instead, Governor Fielding Wright, the chief organizer of this conference, and other participants wanted to establish regional solidarity against Truman's civil rights proposals and his nomination. They still did not want to formally leave the Democratic party in the election of 1948. At this juncture, Wright, Thurmond, and the other participating southern Democrats wanted to devise a strategy for opposing the nomination of Truman or any other pro–civil rights candidate and a strong civil rights plank at the Democratic national convention in July.[84] If the Democratic national convention did not satisfy their demands, the conferees resolved that they would hold a convention in Birmingham, Alabama, on July 17, 1948, to nominate candidates who would be their states' official Democratic presidential and vice presidential nominees for receiving popular and electoral college votes.[85]

After the Democratic national convention nominated Truman and adopted an ADA-sponsored civil rights plank even stronger than Truman and McGrath preferred, the States' Rights Democrats (SRD) met in Birmingham and recommended J. Strom Thurmond and Fielding Wright as respective presidential and vice presidential nominees to Democratic state parties in the South. The conferees also established a statement of principles that opposed "the totalitarian, centralized, bureaucratic government and the police state called for by the platforms adopted by the Democratic and Republican conventions."[86]

They were soon nicknamed "Dixiecrats" by the media and were generally perceived as a minor party that had bolted from the national Democratic party.[87] But, throughout the 1948 campaign, Thurmond, Wright, and their supporters regarded themselves as bona fide Democrats who were conducting a movement within the national Democratic party.[88] They regarded themselves as Democrats who were making a national, rather than a regional, effort to return the national Democratic party to its Jeffersonian ideological origins with an emphasis on maximizing the discretionary authority of state and local governments and minimizing federal intervention on both racial and nonracial domestic policy issues.[89] The SRD movement's participants and supporters included southern businessmen who were vehemently anti-union, supported the Taft-Hartley Act, opposed higher minimum wages and any further federal social welfare benefits, and wanted state control of tidelands oil, while Truman wanted federal control of it.[90]

As a campaigner and party leader, Harry Truman dealt with the Dixiecrat revolt by avoiding public statements denouncing the SRD movement and promoting his civil rights proposals.[91] He waited until after the Democratic national convention to issue Executive Orders 9980 and 9981 on July 26, 1948.

Executive Order 9980 prohibited racial, religious, and ethnic discrimination in the federal civil service and authorized the appointment of fair-employment officers in all federal agencies and the establishment of a Fair Employment Board within the U.S. Civil Service Commission to enforce the prohibition of discrimination.[92] Executive Order 9981 required "equality of treatment and opportunity for all persons in the armed services without regard to race, color, religion, or national origin," which "shall be put into effect as rapidly as possible."[93] But this second executive order did not specifically mention the racial integration of military units.[94]

Truman relied on McGrath to be his campaign's spokesman to the media regarding his position on the SRD movement. To avoid offending southern Democrats who opposed Truman's civil rights program but also opposed the Dixiecrats, McGrath carefully limited his criticism to the Dixiecrats' efforts to deny Truman's designation as the official Democratic presidential nominee on several states' ballots.[95] William Primm, McGrath's executive assistant and an Alabama native, conducted the DNC's unsuccessful legal challenges to the ballots of Mississippi, Alabama, South Carolina, and Louisiana, the four states whose ballots named Thurmond and Wright as the official Democratic presidential and vice presidential candidates.[96]

Truman also did not deliver campaign speeches in these states and spoke only a few times in the entire South during his general-election campaign. He did not deliver a campaign speech on civil rights until Oct. 29, 1948, a few days before the election. On that day, he became the first Democratic presidential nominee to deliver a campaign speech in Harlem.[97] There Truman praised the contributions to civil rights made by the President's Committee on Civil Rights and explained the provisions of his two executive orders prohibiting racial discrimination.[98] He did not mention, of course, the almost unanimous opposition of southern Democrats in Congress to his legislative proposals on civil rights.

Truman's tactic of aloof reticence toward the SRD movement helped anti–civil rights, anti-SRD southern Democrats, despite the variety of ideological and factional differences among themselves, to effectively minimize the growth and impact of Thurmond's presidential candidacy and this intraparty revolt. Senator James Eastland of Mississippi was the only senator who campaigned for the Thurmond-Wright ticket. Senator Richard Russell of Georgia, who received delegate support for his presidential candidacy at the Democratic National Convention from southerners who later joined the SRD movement, refused to join the States' Rights Democrats and eventually endorsed Truman.[99] Governor Beauford Jester of Texas was initially sympathetic to the SRD movement because of its states' rights position on tidelands oil. But Jester later welcomed

Truman during the president's train tour of Texas and publicly promised his support in the election.[100] Thurmond accused southern Democratic members of Congress who opposed Truman's civil rights policies but refused to join the SRD campaign of being "willing to barter away the rights of the South for a mess of political pottage."[101]

Since Truman seemed doomed to lose the election, concern among southern Democrats in Congress for continued cooperation with Truman on federal patronage after the election does not appear to have been the primary reason for their refusal to join the Dixiecrats.[102] For conservatives such as Russell and Senator Harry Byrd of Virginia, the SRD movement appeared to be not only a futile, quixotic campaign but one that would be disruptive of their regular state Democratic organizations.[103] This was especially a concern for Byrd, who ran a tightly controlled machine and had to be concerned about the electoral consequences of a divided Democratic electorate because of Virginia's significant Republican minority.[104]

Byrd's self-interested pragmatism was followed by Democrats in North Carolina and Tennessee, two other southern states with strong pockets of Republican voting strength, who feared that a formal split in their ballots between Dixiecrats and pro-Truman Democrats could lead to upset Republican victories in congressional, state, and local elections in 1948.[105] The most outspoken and effective opposition to the SRD movement in the South, though, came from pro-union, economically liberal Democrats like Senators John Sparkman and Lister Hill of Alabama, Governor James Folsom of Alabama, and Democratic gubernatorial nominee Sid McMath of Arkansas.[106] These Democrats opposed Truman's civil rights positions but supported his candidacy and generally agreed with Truman on economic issues. Consequently, economically liberal Democrats in the South often portrayed Thurmond and the other Dixiecrats as pro–big business economic reactionaries, funded by and serving the interests of oil tycoons by trying to help Dewey be elected.[107]

These pro-Truman, economically liberal Democrats in the South were assisted by major daily southern newspapers in discrediting the SRD movement. Edited by Ralph McGill, the *Atlanta Constitution* was the most nationally prominent southern newspaper to claim that the Dixiecrats were pawns of the oil industry and were exploiting racial fears in order to serve their economic interests.[108] McGill, although an opponent of Truman's civil rights programs, also disseminated the image of the Dixiecrats as backward-looking "Klaghorns" who were obstacles to the continuing development of a New South that was more culturally, politically, and economically assimilated with the rest of the nation.[109]

Except for the four states of the Deep South where Thurmond was designated as the Democratic nominee, polls showed little voter enthusiasm in the South for the SRD movement. Despite widespread disapproval of Truman's job performance and civil rights program among southern whites, a Gallup poll released on August 20, 1948, indicated that 41 percent of the southern voters questioned intended to vote for Truman.[110] Thirty-four percent of the respondents supported Dewey and only 14 percent supported Thurmond.[111] Gallup's October 28, 1948, poll indicated that nine of the ten states in which Truman held a lead of 8 percent or more were in the South.[112]

Just as Truman was able to generally ignore Wallace's candidacy during his whistle-stop campaign, he was also able to ignore the SRD movement because of this multilateral opposition to the Dixiecrats from these southern Democratic politicians and newspapers as well as the apathy and distrust that most southern white voters expressed toward the Dixiecrat campaign.[113] Like the Wallace campaign, the SRD movement was also undermined internally by poor planning, meager campaign funds, and insufficient advertising.[114]

Although Wallace and Thurmond contended that their campaigns were national efforts, each received about 2.4 percent of the popular votes nationally, and their electoral support was disproportionately concentrated in a few areas. Thurmond received 17.4 percent of the votes cast in the South, and 99.8 percent of the 1,169,134 votes that he received nationally came from eleven southern states. Nearly half of Wallace's national total of 1,157,057 votes came from New York.[115]

As the general election campaign progressed, therefore, the Wallace and Thurmond campaigns became mild distractions rather than serious electoral threats to Truman's candidacy and party leadership. In addressing Henry A. Wallace and the Progressive party, Truman tended to emphasize his more ideological, unyielding ethos as a liberal reformer.[116] He was determined to articulate and solidify aggressive anticommunism as a permanent element of the national Democratic party's liberalism, thus discouraging American Communists and other leftist activists antagonistic toward the containment policy from participating in the Democratic party.[117]

By contrast, Truman's approach to the SRD movement and Thurmond's candidacy during the campaign clearly represented his values as a party regular. Truman the regular emphasized the promotion of intraparty harmony and healing among southern Democrats and avoided the divisive issue of civil rights in his postconvention campaign rhetoric until his October 29 speech in Harlem. Truman's silence on civil rights during most of his campaign and his restraint from public denunciations of Thurmond facilitated the return of most southern Democratic politicians and voters to his candidacy and their repudiation of

Thurmond and the other Dixiecrats.[118] After the election, however, Truman's party leadership would have to decide whether to punish the Dixiecrats for their intraparty revolt and, if so, exactly how to punish them.[119]

THE DEWEY CAMPAIGN

One of the beneficiaries of the 1946 Republican sweep was Thomas E. Dewey, the forty-four-year-old governor of New York. Dewey was reelected with 57 percent of the votes and a margin of 687,151 votes over his Democratic opponent, Senator James M. Mead, the nominee of both the Democratic and American Labor parties.[120] A Gallup poll released on November 1, 1946, indicated that 40 percent, a plurality, of the Republican voters preferred Dewey as the GOP's presidential nominee in 1948. Dewey's closest rival was a former Minnesota governor, Harold Stassen, preferred by 22 percent of the poll's respondents. Despite media prominence as "Mr. Republican," Senator Robert A. Taft of Ohio was ranked fifth, with only 6 percent.[121] A Gallup poll released on December 8, 1946, revealed that 52 percent of the Republicans chose Dewey as their party's presidential nominee, 17 percent favored Stassen, and only 2 percent preferred Taft.[122]

These electoral and polling statistics help explain why Dewey's wide margin of victory in 1946 and favorable poll results influenced the strategy and rhetoric of Dewey's 1948 presidential campaign. Whenever some of his campaign aides or other Republicans urged him to harshly respond to Truman's hyperbolic, scalding charges against the GOP, Dewey repeatedly emphasized that a positive campaign that did not counterattack would be more likely to win the election than his more rhetorically aggressive, unsuccessful 1944 presidential campaign.[123] Most of the content and tone of Dewey's preconvention and general election presidential campaign of 1948 reflected the confident, vague promises of honest, efficient management of government and casual perfunctory dismissals of his Democratic opponent's charges that characterized his 1946 gubernatorial campaign.[124]

The repeated emphasis on "unity" throughout Dewey's campaign speeches was first evident in the New York governor's strategy for receiving the GOP's presidential nomination with as little intraparty rancor as possible. Dewey and Taft shared a strong personal dislike of each other. Taft regarded Dewey as a "Me Too" New Deal–esque Republican who was too quick to abandon conservative principles in order to adapt to public opinion.[125] Dewey perceived Taft as a backward-looking conservative whose ideological rigidity and acerbic language would doom the GOP to electoral defeat.[126]

Fortunately for Dewey, Taft's pursuit of their party's presidential nomination failed to pose a serious threat to his candidacy.[127] John Bennett, a political operative for Taft, found that Taft's strongest base of delegate support for the 1948 Republican national convention was the South, the GOP's weakest region.[128] Revealing Taft's paucity of support in the delegate-rich Northeast, Bennett reported in 1947 that Taft's potential delegate support from New Jersey "is at best precarious."[129]

Because bipartisan cooperation between Truman and the Eightieth Congress had distinguished several major foreign policy initiatives, the widespread public perception of Taft as an isolationist would be a serious liability since a victorious Republican presidential nominee would need to attract some internationalist, independent and Democratic voters. The only formidable opponent of Dewey within the GOP, therefore, was Harold Stassen. Elected governor of Minnesota at the age of thirty-one in 1938, Stassen, like Dewey, was a youthful, dynamic, moderately liberal Republican committed to an internationalist foreign policy. Stassen's foreign policy credentials were bolstered by his combat service in the navy during World War II and his role as a delegate at the founding conference of the United Nations.[130]

Benefiting from Dwight Eisenhower's January 23, 1948, announcement that he would not seek the presidency, Dewey defeated Stassen in the March 9 Republican primary in New Hampshire by winning six of that state's eight delegates.[131] Stassen, however, conducted intense door-to-door campaigns in Wisconsin and Nebraska, which contributed to decisive victories over Dewey in both primaries.[132]

Stassen's progress was slowed when Taft's defeated him in the Ohio Republican primary, but his candidacy's threat to Dewey's nomination ended in the Oregon primary of May 21.[133] Determined to crush Stassen's candidacy, which was favored to win in Oregon's polls, Dewey conducted a well-financed, tightly organized primary campaign in Oregon that combined exhaustive personal campaigning by Dewey, specific policy positions on public power, agriculture, and foreign policy toward Europe, co-opting key local Republican leaders, and saturating the state with radio, newspaper, and billboard advertising.[134]

Dewey's speeches against Stassen employed a pugnacious, prosecutorial style unlike later campaigning against Truman. Dewey especially criticized Stassen's proposal to outlaw the American Communist party. In a nationally broadcast radio debate in Oregon, Dewey eloquently combined militant anti-communism with a Lincolnesque defense of civil liberties by denouncing Stassen's proposal as both ineffective against the communist threat and unconstitutional. Though winning the Oregon primary by nearly ten thousand votes,

Dewey still had to secure the presidential nomination at the Republican national convention.[135]

Dewey entered the Republican National Convention in Philadelphia, begun on June 2, 1948, with nearly three hundred committed delegates.[136] He needed 548 delegate votes to receive the GOP's presidential nomination.[137] Although Taft had performed poorly in the primaries, Dewey's lead was slim and precarious, since Taft had a base of delegate support from nonprimary states in the South and Midwest. Stassen, however, repeatedly rejected Taft's request that he support the Ohio senator's candidacy as part of a "stop Dewey" campaign.[138] Dewey's candidacy then gained momentum at the convention, especially due to delegate support from Indiana, New Jersey, and Pennsylvania. His support increased from 434 votes on the first ballot to a unanimous nomination on the third ballot with 1,094 votes.[139]

Dewey's acceptance speech at the Republican national convention was a harbinger of the style, tone, and basic content of most of his fall campaign speeches. In his rich baritone voice, Dewey repeatedly stressed that he and his fellow Republicans were primarily seeking a spiritual unity of their party in order to provide such unity in national and international leadership.[140] He expressed no partisan aggression or criticism toward Truman or the Democratic party in this speech.

In his rigorous campaign to defeat Stassen in the Oregon primary and his earlier efforts to deal with Eisenhower (a potentially unbeatable rival for the Republican nomination), Dewey concentrated on maximizing his appeal to moderate and liberal internationalist Republicans. He continued this factional focus in choosing a running mate. He refused to appease the conservative, midwestern, isolationist wing of the GOP by offering the vice presidential nomination to House Majority Leader Charles Halleck of Indiana, who thought that a Dewey aide had promised it to him, or any other member of this faction.[141]

Dewey, moreover, did not choose any Republican member of Congress. Instead, he chose a fellow governor, former prosecutor, and liberal internationalist, Earl Warren of California.[142] In his successful campaigns for district attorney, attorney general, and governor, Warren had proven himself to be attractive to Republican, Democratic, and independent voters in California.[143] Dewey hoped that Warren's vice presidential nomination would make him more attractive to independent and Democratic voters and recognized that New York and California provided 72 of the 266 electoral college votes needed to win the election.[144]

Despite his regional, ideological, and programmatic identification with the moderate-liberal, eastern internationalist wing of the GOP, Dewey received broad support within the party for himself and his moderate, consensual platform and campaign style. Although isolationism was still evident among the more conservative, midwestern delegates, the 1948 Republican platform called "for strengthening the United Nations and primary recognition of America's self-interest in the liberty of other peoples."[145] In addition to its support for an internationalist foreign policy and for "stopping partisan politics at the water's edge," the broad wording of the GOP platform on domestic policy reflected Dewey's desire to equal and even exceed Truman's proposals in such areas as civil rights, public health, and housing while balancing domestic policy promises with pledges of more efficient management and coordination with state and local governments.[146]

The breadth of Dewey's delegate support and the general acquiescence of the more conservative, isolationist delegates and party leaders to a moderate platform oriented toward Dewey were mostly caused by the perception of Dewey throughout the GOP as a certain winner.[147] While Dewey's policy positions and progressive record as governor attracted eastern internationalists, conservative party regulars were more attracted to his aggressively eloquent campaign against Roosevelt in 1944. Dewey had castigated Roosevelt's conduct of the war effort, association with machines and the leftist CIO-PAC, and management of the wartime economy and gained the best electoral results of any Republican presidential nominee since 1928.[148]

Dewey's reputation throughout the Republican party as a unifying vote getter assured of defeating Truman was enhanced by his well-known success as a party builder and meticulous campaign organizer in New York.[149] As governor and titular leader of New York's Republican party, Dewey shrewdly combined patronage, a reformist policy agenda, modernization of the party's voter mobilization and polling activities, and constant publicity to solidify Republican strength in upstate rural areas while attracting significant numbers of normally Democratic urban Catholics, Jews, and blacks.[150] Since Herbert Brownell managed Dewey's 1944 presidential campaign and was chosen by Dewey to serve as RNC chairman, much of Brownell's success in preparing the RNC's apparatus, funds, and publicity for the GOP's successful 1946 efforts was indirectly attributed to Dewey as his mentor and sponsor in New York.[151]

Two major flaws of Dewey's campaign were excessive planning and a candidate-centered approach, often aloof from Republican congressional and state campaigns and from RNC headquarters. Dewey and Elliott V. Bell, Dewey's chief speech writer and de facto campaign manager, decided to consistently execute a campaign stressing statesmanlike "unity" and ignoring Democratic attacks. The Dewey campaign was too inflexibly prepackaged and reassured by favorable poll ratings to adapt to Truman's harsh rhetoric and such unexpected issues as Truman's call for a special session of Congress, the controversial, aborted Vinson mission to Moscow, and the Commodity Credit Corporation's inadequate storage facilities as grain prices fell due to bumper crops for wheat and corn.[152] Influenced by John Foster Dulles's bipartisan advice on foreign policy, Dewey never used "Democratic Duplicity and Appeasement in Foreign Policy," an extensively researched document virulently critical of the Roosevelt and Truman administration's foreign policy decisions.[153]

Besides excessive planning, the Dewey campaign also suffered from a distended, uncoordinated organization. Elliott V. Bell exerted the strongest influence over Dewey's campaign decisions and in maintaining communications between Dewey's campaign train, named the "Dewey Victory Special," and the Albany campaign advisers. Herbert Brownell, the nominal campaign manager, was located in a campaign office in Washington, D.C. Brownell's primary function was to serve as a liaison between the Dewey campaign and RNC headquarters, headed by RNC Chairman Hugh Scott.[154] With such agricultural issues as the CCC grain storage bins, rural electrification, and farm price supports becoming more prominent by the fall, Dewey still failed to have Scott establish an RNC special division for farmers.[155] In general, Dewey and the campaign staff led by Bell ignored Brownell and Scott, who both increasingly advocated tough retorts to Truman's charges that a Dewey administration and Republican Congress would weaken or end federal programs benefiting farmers.[156]

The strategic and organizational distance of Dewey's campaign from Republican congressional campaigns was also evident in Dewey's whistle-stop campaign. Unlike Truman, Dewey did not strive to integrate his whistle-stop appearances and campaign speeches with his party's nominees for congressional, state, and local offices.[157] Often Dewey did not mention other Republican candidates or issues peculiar to the whistle-stop community in his speeches and sometimes refused to meet them in his train.[158] Contrasting Truman's and Dewey's different treatments of their parties' candidates in their whistle-stop campaigns, Victor Harding, the director of the Democratic Congressional Campaign Committee, later remarked to journalist Frank McNaughton, "Truman talked grass roots language to grass roots people. Dewey never caught the language on the level on which the people were talking."[159]

The lofty, vague, platitudinous tone and content of Dewey's whistle-stop campaign rhetoric were especially obvious in his address delivered in Des Moines, Iowa, on September 20, 1948. Two days before, Truman had delivered a speech in Dexter, Iowa, focusing on the specific issues of falling farm prices, the Eightieth Congress's failure to authorize adequate grain storage facilities for the Commodity Credit Corporation (CCC), and soil conservation programs. He acerbically accused the Republicans of being "gluttons of privilege" who "already stuck a pitchfork in the farmer's back" and would return the agricultural economy to the condition of the Great Depression if they won the presidency and retained control of Congress.[160]

In his Des Moines speech, however, Dewey did not respond to Truman's accusations and promised to "rediscover the essential unity of our people" and "a Government of team-work."[161] In the conclusion of this speech, Dewey expressed only an obscure, indirect refutation of Truman's frank appeals to the special interests of farmers, union members, and other voting blocs. Dewey vowed that his policy proposals "will not set faction against faction or group against group. They will aim to join us together as a whole people in a more perfect union."[162]

In his October 30 Madison Square Garden speech, which was his last campaign speech, Dewey concluded his campaign with this same bland issueless theme. Dewey pontificated that the United States of America "is called to renew its faith so that the world can begin to have hope again; to renew its strength so that the world can be of good courage again; to renew its vision so that the world can begin to move forward again out of this present darkness toward the bright light of lasting peace."[163] Analyzing Dewey's stunning defeat a few days after the 1948 election, conservative columnist H.L. Mencken referred to such rhetoric by Dewey as "the worst bombast of university professors."[164]

Toward the end of the 1948 campaign, Dewey sensed that public support for Truman was increasing and that his "unity" speeches were unable to stop Truman's gains in public opinion polls.[165] Dewey's campaign, though, was so carefully and rigidly planned and executed around the statesmanlike high road of "unity" that it could not adapt to the growing plausibility of a Democratic upset.[166]

THE TRUMAN CAMPAIGN

The Clifford-Rowe strategy provided Truman's campaign staff and the DNC apparatus with a broad, adaptable campaign outline, instead of a paralyzing, immutable formula. Thus, Truman's strategy was loose enough for him to adopt and successfully utilize such later recommendations as the exploitation of the grain-storage issue and Truman's unexpected call for a special session of Congress. In addition to its strategic flexibility, the Truman campaign, unlike the Dewey campaign, also benefited from smoothly interactive, symbiotic organizational relationships among the White House campaign staff on the president's train, various units of the DNC's apparatus, and the Democratic Congressional Campaign Committee directed by Victor Harding and chaired by Representative Michael Kirwan of Ohio.[167]

The fact that Truman was an underdog also motivated his campaign strategy and organization to assume risks and launch an offensive campaign in which Dewey and the Republican leadership of Congress were treated like incumbents. Truman's use an exhaustive whistle-stop speaking tour as a way to circumvent the mostly pro-Republican major newspapers and enable Truman to communicate directly to the public.[168] To test the efficacy of a postconvention whistle-stop campaign, Truman's White House staff arranged an officially "nonpolitical" train trip to Berkeley, where Truman would accept an honorary degree at the University of California and deliver a commencement address on June 12, 1948. Anticipating a barrage of press criticism of this trip as crassly political, Truman's staff made sure that DNC Chairman J. Howard McGrath did not go along.[169]

Though financed by the president's travel allowance rather than scarce DNC funds, Truman's June tour was obviously a preliminary campaign trip. He delivered four major speeches and several brief whistle-stop speeches in addition to his address at Berkeley.[170] While his Berkeley address emphasized a bipartisan foreign policy with an active United Nations as a key element, his impromptu remarks in Santa Barbara, California, referred to the controversy over the purpose of his "non-political" train trip. "If you are on my side, it's non-political; if you are not, it's a low-down political trip, to come out and tell the people what they ought to hear."[171]

On June 14, 1948, Truman delivered a prepared, lengthy address in Los Angeles, focusing on the "do-nothing" Eightieth Congress. He stated that the purpose of his current speaking tour was "to inform the people what I believe is good for the country" and to give members of Congress "the opportunity to find out what the people think of those things that they have not done."[172] Although less militantly partisan than his postconvention whistle-stop speeches, Truman's Los Angeles speech critically specified the opposition or inertia of Congress toward his policy proposals on price controls, his Twenty-one Point Plan, housing, labor relations, Social Security, health care, and agricultural subsidies.[173] The anti–Wall Street, class conflict tone of Truman's later whistle-stop speeches was indicated in his concluding accusation that Congress had "passed a rich man's tax law" and "passed a lot of special legislation that helps special classes."[174]

In briefer speeches in the Pacific Northwest and West Coast, Truman continued lambasting Congress for being obstructionist and favorable to the economic interests of big business and the wealthiest taxpayers.[175] The president experimented with another theme that would typify his postconvention whistle-stop campaign. He periodically scolded his audiences for a low voter turnout in 1946, resulting in the election of a Republican-controlled Congress, and urged them to vote straight Democratic tickets in 1948. After telling an audience in Olympia, Washington, that the election of a Republican Congress in 1946 "is your fault," Truman concluded, "Then if you people want to continue the policies of the Eightieth Congress, that will be your funeral."[176]

The White House staff believed that Truman's preconvention whistle-stop tour, which used materials from the DNC's Research Division, had generally been a success in preparing the president's rhetorical strategy for the general election campaign.[177] But the president first had to secure his party's nomination and unite its members behind his candidacy at the Democratic national convention in July. Both the Democratic and Republican national conventions would be held in Philadelphia in order to reduce costs and to geographically maximize television coverage of their proceedings.[178] Truman risked facing a televised, dispirited Democratic convention that was sharply divided over his nomination.

The most serious threat to his nomination was the "draft Eisenhower" movement. A wide, diverse spectrum of southern Democrats supported Dwight Eisenhower for their party's presidential nomination. Gessner McCorvey, Alabama's Democratic state chairman and later one of the founders of the States' Rights Democrats movement, and Claude Pepper, a previously pro-Wallace liberal senator from Florida who regarded Truman's foreign policy as antagonistic toward the Soviet Union, both supported Eisenhower.[179] Machine bosses Jacob Arvey, William O'Dwyer, and Frank Hague also joined ADA activists in urging Eisenhower to run for president. All three of these major blocs of delegate support for Eisenhower shared the nonideological, pragmatic perception of Eisenhower as the most likely candidate to unite the party and win the election.[180] The ADA activists further hoped that if Eisenhower became the Democratic presidential nominee then he would accept liberal Supreme Court Justice William O. Douglas as his vice presidential nominee.[181] It is especially ironic that future Dixiecrats and ADA activists each perceived Eisenhower as sympathetic to their position on civil rights.[182]

Fortunately for Truman, Eisenhower issued a message to Claude Pepper on July 9, five days before the Democratic national convention began, unequivocally stating that he would not seek or accept the Democratic presidential nomination.[183] The only remaining, significant opposition to Truman's nomination was the presidential candidacy of Senator Richard B. Russell of Georgia. Nominated by Georgia's delegates as "the foremost exponent of States Rights in the United States today," Russell received 263 votes, all from southern states, on the second ballot, while Truman was nominated with 947½ votes.[184] Having previously failed to defeat the ADA's civil rights plank, southern delegates also failed to restore the two-thirds rule for presidential nominations and to nominate Russell for vice president.[185]

With few delegates enthusiastic about his nomination and with many southern delegates increasingly hostile toward the convention's decisions, Truman wanted to satisfy both the ADA-led liberal activists and the more moderate southerners. He hoped to satisfy the ADA by persuading William O. Douglas to become his running mate, but Douglas rejected Truman's offer.[186] Despite his friendship with Senate Minority Leader Alben W. Barkley and his respect for Barkley's liberal record and legislative skills, Truman assumed that the seventy-year-old Kentuckian would add little strength to his presidential candidacy because of his age and the fact that he also hailed from a border state.[187] But Barkley's rousing, populist-style keynote address and the broad delegate support at the convention for Barkley convinced him to accept Barkley as a running mate.[188]

While Truman the reformer had hoped that a Democratic vice presidential nomination would co-opt younger liberal activists, Truman the regular hoped that a brief, vaguely worded civil rights plank, similar to the party's 1944 plank, would satisfy most southern delegates. Like the 1944 plank, Truman's proposed civil rights plank for the 1948 Democratic platform broadly stated the "belief that racial and religious minorities must have the right to live, the right to work, the right to vote," but did not specify the exact legal methods by the federal government to secure these civil rights.[189] It also called "upon Congress to exert its full authority to the limit of its constitutional powers to assure and protect these rights."[190] The "limit" of Congress's constitutional powers on civil rights could, of course, be interpreted as a concession to the states' rights doctrine of anti–civil rights Democrats.

The credentials committee of the Democratic national convention had accepted South Carolina's all-white delegation, despite the request of black South Carolina Democrats for eight of their state's twenty delegate seats and evidence that their state's Democratic party violated the federal district court decision of *Elmore v. Price*.[191] This court decision forbade the requirement that South Carolinians swear an oath opposing civil rights in order to vote for delegates in the Democratic primary. Thus, it appeared that Truman's mild civil rights plank would be adopted by the Platform Committee, especially since Senator Francis Myers of Pennsylvania, the committee's chairman, and a black committee member, Representative William Dawson of Chicago, supported it.[192]

Myers managed to induce most of the Platform Committee's members to approve Truman's civil rights plank, but a minority of the committee's members led by ADA members Hubert Humphrey and Andrew Biemiller opposed this plank as a capitulation to civil rights opponents.[193] Although initially reluctant to lead the ADA's fight for the convention's adoption of a stronger civil rights plank because of his Senate campaign, Hubert Humphrey agreed to deliver a speech supporting the ADA's plank. Meanwhile, Joseph Rauh and other ADA members gained support for their plank from delegates controlled by machine bosses—especially Jacob Arvey, David Lawrence, and Edward Flynn—who hoped that a stronger civil rights plank would motivate more black voters to support their local Democratic tickets.[194] The biggest undivided bloc of votes for the ADA plank, though, was controlled by John Shelley, a Teamsters' union official and chairman of the California delegation. Shelley warned convention Chairman Sam Rayburn, "If you don't give us a roll call, I'll climb the podium with the entire California delegation."[195]

Known as the Biemiller resolution, the ADA-sponsored amendment specified that the Democratic support for civil rights included protection from lynching and mob violence, equal job opportunities, equal political participation, and equal treatment in the armed forces.[196] Following the defeat of states' rights planks sponsored by the Texas, Tennessee, and Mississippi delegations, the convention's delegates adopted the ADA's civil rights amendment by a vote of 651½ to 581½.[197] Ironically, David Niles, the president's adviser on minority affairs, had previously lobbied the delegates to oppose the ADA's amendment and had warned Rauh, "Joe, you're not going to get fifty votes."[198]

Watching the convention's proceedings on television, Truman referred to the adopted ADA-sponsored civil rights amendment as "the crackpot amendment to the Civil Rights Plank" in his diary.[199] Truman the regular was chagrined that the more specifically worded civil rights plank had, as he feared, antagonized the southerners enough so that delegates from Mississippi and Alabama left the convention in protest and other southern delegates supported the nomination of Richard Russell.[200] In his autobiography, Paul Douglas, who led a demonstration at the convention in support of the Biemiller resolution, claimed that it "breathed new life into the party and brought the Negro and sections of the liberal vote into our ranks."[201]

Accepting the ADA-amended civil rights plank, Truman traveled to Philadelphia to deliver his acceptance speech at 2:00 A.M. on July 15.[202] Truman began his speech with an implicit reference to the recent platform battle on civil rights. Despite internal differences of "the beliefs of the Democratic Party," these "differences have been settled by a majority vote, as they should be."[203]

With the delegates divided on civil rights and pessimistic about victory in November, Truman energized them into a raucous frenzy by castigating the Republican legislative record in the Eightieth Congress, revealing contradictions
between this record and the Republican platform, and calling Congress into
special session on July 26.[204] Truman concluded his acceptance speech by explicitly equating 1948 to 1932, "when the Nation lay prostrate and helpless as a
result of Republican misrule and inaction" and quoting Franklin D. Roosevelt's
1932 acceptance speech in requesting the help of his fellow Democrats.[205]

The next phase of Truman's campaign was to appear before the special
session of Congress, specify the legislation that he wanted it to pass, and to then
repeatedly express his dissatisfaction with the performance of the Republican-
controlled Congress. In his press conference of August 12, 1948, Truman remarked that "it was entirely a 'do-nothing' session."[206] One week before this
press conference, White House appointments secretary Matthew Connelly wrote
to Truman, "The labor boys believe firmly that if the session is continued it will
be politically useful and will also bring good legislation for which the Administration will get credit."[207]

The necessity of fully mobilizing the political resources of organized labor
behind Truman's candidacy was obvious in Truman's first major, prepared campaign speech in his post-convention whistle-stop tour. In a Detroit rally sponsored by the rival AFL and CIO union organizations, Truman delivered an address
on September 6, 1948. He stressed the gains that labor unions and wage earners
had made during the New Deal, such as passage of the Wagner Act and Social
Security Act, and how the recent and potential actions of a Republican-controlled Congress threatened to weaken or destroy these reforms.[208] More specifically and dramatically, Truman warned his listeners, "If the congressional
elements that made the Taft-Hartley law are allowed to remain in power, and if
these elements are further encouraged by the election of a Republican President, you men of labor can expect to be hit by a steady barrage of body blows."[209]

Truman's Detroit speech illustrated one type of campaign address in his
rhetorical strategy. It appealed to the economic self-interest of a specific voting
bloc that was dominant in a given state or region.[210] Consequently, Truman's
speeches in urban industrial areas of the Northeast, Midwest, and West Coast
stressed repeal of the Taft-Hartley Act, his proposals benefiting wage earners,
such as higher minimum wages and national health insurance, and dire warn-
ings about how Republican control of both Congress and the presidency would
exploit labor to benefit big business. In agricultural areas of the Midwest and
West, Truman emphasized how farmers prospered under Democratic agricultural policies and how current and future Republican legislative behavior threat-

(Above) February 26, 1944. Senator Harry S. Truman, DNC Chairman Robert E. Hannegan, Representative Lyndon B. Johnson, and Texas Democratic Chairman Harry L. Seay at the Washington Birthday Dinner in Dallas. *Dallas Daily Times,* Feb. 27, 1944; photo courtesy of William P. Hannegan. *(Below)* January 19, 1948. Speaker of the House Sam Rayburn, Truman, and Senator Alben Barkley gather in Washington for a luncheon meeting of the DNC's finance committee as part of the inaugural festivities leading up to Truman's swearing in the following day.

(Above) February 19, 1948. Wilson Wyatt, Truman, and Howard McGrath gather at the Statler Hotel in Washington before the Jefferson-Jackson Centennial Dinner. *(Below)* Truman and Alben Barkley at the Democratic National Convention in Philadelphia after the 1948 nomination for president and vice president.

(Above) September 18, 1948. Accompanied by Senator Alben Barkley of Kentucky and daughter Margaret, Truman prepares to "give 'em hell" on a state campaign tour in New York. *(Below)* September 1948. Senator Earle Clements of Kentucky introduces Truman at a campaign stop in Louisville.

(Above) 1948. Sam Rayburn, John Pastore, John McCormack, Lyndon Johnson, Earle Clements, Truman, Alben Barkley, and several unidentified men. *(Below)* 1949. Truman and his cabinet at Blair House. Front: Louis A. Johnson, Dean Acheson, Truman, Vice President Alben Barkley, John W. Snyder, and Tom Clark; back: Julius A. Krug, Jesse M. Donaldson, Charles F. Brannan, Charles Sawyer, and Maurice Tobin.

(Above) 1952. The first meeting of what Truman called "the Big Four." Front: Alben Barkley, Truman, and Sam Rayburn; back: Ernest W. McFarland and John McCormack. *(Below)* July 23, 1952. Alben Barkley receives an ovation at the Democratic National Convention in Chicago. He gave a similar "fighting" speech at the convention in 1948 before becoming vice president.

(Left) With the 1952 campaign in full swing, Adlai Stevenson arrives in New York to make a speech to the American Legion. *(Below)* A meeting of the Stevenson campaign committee at the Illinois governor's mansion in 1952. Left to right: George Ball, Senator Clinton Anderson, Mike Monroney, DNC Chairman Stephen Mitchell, Senator John Sparkman, Adlai Stevenson, Wilson Wyatt, Vice Chairman of the DNC India Edwards, Secretary of Commerce Oscar Chapman, Speaker of the House John McCormack, and Senator Earle Clements.

(*Above*) Chief Justice Fred M. Vinson and Truman on their way to the Army-Navy game at Philadelphia. (*Below*) July 18, 1952. In Chicago, Democratic presidential hopefuls W. Averell Harriman, Vice President Alben Barkley, Senator Estes Kefauver, Senator Robert Kerr, and Senator Richard Russell gathered for a televised debate.

(Above) October 12, 1952. Maurice Tobin, Wilson Wyatt, and Governor Stevenson discuss campaign strategy. *(Below)* Vice presidential candidate Alben Barkley makes a speech in San Francisco. Left to right: Jefferson-Jackson Victory Dinner Committee Chair George Killion, Democratic State Central Committee Chair Oliver J. Carter, Barkley, and Elinor R. Heller, DNC.

ened them.[211] Since the Clifford and Rowe strategy had identified the West as "the 'Number One Priority' for the Democrats," the president focused his western whistle-stop speeches on improving federal efforts in public power, reclamation, irrigation, and flood control projects.[212] Information provided by the DNC's Research Division to the speech writers on Truman's train enabled the president to further tailor his speeches to policy interests peculiar to each community that he addressed.[213]

Another rhetorical tactic that Truman repeatedly used proved to be his most histrionic and controversial. Truman portrayed a direct link between his prolabor, liberal domestic policy proposals and an effective foreign policy against Communist aggression.[214] He concluded that Republican opposition to his domestic policy agenda helped communism. In Indianapolis on October 15, 1948, Truman charged that Republican economic policies would create another depression, so communists "are doing all they can in this election to bring about a Republican victory."[215] In his Chicago speech of October 25, Truman claimed that the Republicans and the business interests they served were "powerful reactionary forces which are silently undermining our democratic institutions."[216] An antidemocratic dictatorship, like those of fascist Italy, Nazi Germany, and Communist Czechoslovakia, "could happen here" if Republicans controlled Congress and the presidency and implemented pro–big business policies.[217]

Instead of responding to Truman's shrill charges with equal vigor, Dewey simply expressed regret that Truman was waging a negative campaign.[218] Assisted by Dewey's tepid reply and refusal to exploit Chief Justice Fred Vinson's aborted diplomatic mission to Moscow, Truman's decision to conduct a constant airlift of supplies to the Soviet-blockaded city of Berlin during the fall and summer enabled him to dramatically demonstrate decisive foreign-policy leadership.[219] Thus, willingness to use diplomacy and a military response short of war helped Truman to portray himself as a rational, capable leader in foreign policy.[220]

A Gallup poll released on November 1, 1948, revealed that 49.5 percent of its respondents intended to vote for Dewey while 44.5 percent would vote for Truman.[221] A Crossley poll conducted in mid-October also showed Dewey defeating Truman by a 5 percent margin.[222] Also assuming that Dewey would win, *Kiplinger Magazine* prepared a thirty-two-page special report entitled "What Dewey Will Do."[223]

These poll figures, though, do not measure the differences in organizational vitality between the Dewey and Truman campaigns by the middle of October. Dewey campaign aides Herbert Brownell and John Burton were worried about the size and enthusiasm of Truman's whistle-stop crowds compared to those that appeared for Dewey's speeches.[224] Sensing that Republican campaign workers and voters were overconfident of victory, RNC Chairman Hugh Scott was disturbed by the fact that the RNC had raised only $2.5 million of the $4 million limit allowed by federal law.[225]

Although the DNC was plagued even more by inadequate contributions, the Truman campaign's most powerful and useful organizational ally in providing last-minute campaign funds, additional campaign literature, huge crowds for Truman's major speeches, and voter mobilization in November was organized labor. With the remaining urban Democratic machines less effective as sources of presidential campaign services than they were during Roosevelt's campaigns, organized labor filled the vacuum. It was determined to elect Democratic majorities to Congress, even if Truman appeared doomed to defeat.[226] The newly created Labor's League for Political Education (LLPE) of the AFL was directed by Joseph Keenan, who periodically rode on Truman's campaign train to organize crowds for his speeches.[227] The CIO-PAC and LLPE each spent more than $1 million in this campaign. To support Truman, the CIO-PAC also paid for about one thousand radio speeches and advertisements, distributed ten million campaign leaflets, and later claimed to have fielded 250,000 campaign workers on election day.[228]

The indispensable role of organized labor in Truman's successful campaign was dramatically illustrated in the arrangements for one of Truman's last major campaign addresses. Truman was scheduled to speak at Madison Square Garden on October 28, 1948.[229] Paul Fitzpatrick, Democratic state chairman, however, had failed to schedule and finance the appearance because of inadequate state party funds.[230] David Dubinsky, president of the International Ladies Garment Workers Union and a founder of New York's Liberal party, ensured that the sports arena was made available for Truman's speech and that enough tickets were purchased to fill the seats.[231] It is not surprising that on the day after the election Truman laconically explained the reason for his victory: "Labor did it."[232]

ELECTION RESULTS

Truman's tribute to labor, though, obscured other factors that contributed to a victory in which he received 49.51 percent of the popular votes, and Dewey 45.12 percent.[233] Victory in the electoral college was more pronounced, 303 votes to 189.[234] In congressional elections, the Democrats gained nine Senate seats and seventy-five House seats, providing them with majorities in both houses.[235] The number of Democratic congressional candidates elected from northern urban districts increased from forty-one in 1946 to seventy-four in 1948.[236] Nationally, the Democratic percentage of votes cast in elections for House seats increased from 45.7 percent in 1946 to 53.7 percent in 1948.[237]

Political scientists Norman H. Nie, Sidney Verba, and John R. Petrocik estimated that 70 percent of all union members voted Democratic in 1948 and that 27 percent of the Democratic voters in 1948 were union members.[238] The votes of union members were especially important for Truman's narrow popular vote margins in Illinois and Ohio.[239] The electoral college votes of Illinois and Ohio totaled fifty-three for Truman, nearly half of his margin over Dewey in the electoral college.[240]

But the votes of union members represented only one part of the coalition that elected Truman in his own right and returned Congress to Democratic control. John R. Petrocik found that in "the 1948 election, perhaps the last election of the New Deal era, almost 85 percent of Truman's vote was cast by Southern whites, Jews, blacks, Catholics, and union members."[241] The percentage of voters who identified themselves as Democrats increased from 41 percent in 1944 to 45 percent in 1948.[242] The percentage of voters who identified themselves as Republicans declined from 39 percent in 1944 to 35 percent in 1948.[243] The percentage of independent voters who claimed that they voted Democratic in a presidential election declined only slightly from 62 percent in 1944 to 57 percent in 1948.[244]

These statistics indicate that the 1948 campaign intensified partisan and socioeconomic divisions in favor of the Democratic party and, thus, Truman's candidacy.[245] Truman's victory and the more electorally impressive Democratic gains in nonsouthern congressional elections in 1948 are especially notable as a reaffirmation of the Democratic party as the majority party since voter turnout among voting-age Americans declined from 54 percent in 1944 to 52 percent in 1948.[246] Most analysts had assumed that a relatively low voter turnout among the entire voting-age population would further ensure Dewey's victory since nonvoters were more likely to be Democrats.[247] While a lower voter turnout than that of 1944 did not lead to Truman's defeat, the president also benefited from the fact that two-thirds of the voters surveyed who were undecided in October voted for Truman in the November election.[248]

These statistics and the consensus of most scholars and analysts persuasively indicate that Truman's victory, especially when coupled with nonsouthern Democratic congressional victories, was a party-oriented, maintaining election for the Democratic party rather than a personal victory for Truman.[249] In Truman's campaign rhetoric, he clearly appealed to the most loyal and liberal voting blocs of the New Deal coalition. His constant vilification of the Republican party, symbolized by the Republican control of the Eightieth Congress and emphasis on economic class conflict to portray party differences may partially explain why his electoral appeal among independents and eastern, metropolitan Republicans was weaker than Roosevelt's had been.[250]

Organizationally, Truman's campaign, unlike Dewey's, closely cooperated with his party's congressional and gubernatorial campaigns and relied on the efforts of the national committee's apparatus to mobilize a party-centered, rather than a candidate-centered, voter turnout. This rhetorical and organizational strategy helped Truman benefit from the "reverse coat tails" of victorious Democratic congressional and gubernatorial nominees in several key nonsouthern states.[251] In Iowa, for example, Truman received 50.3 percent of the popular votes compared to 57.8 percent for Guy Gillette, the Democratic senatorial nominee.[252] Truman carried Illinois with 50.1 percent of the popular votes while Democratic senatorial nominee Paul Douglas and Democratic gubernatorial nominee Adlai Stevenson respectively received 55.1 percent and 57.1 percent.[253] Among the major states that Truman carried in the electoral college, the most striking difference occurred in Ohio.[254] There Truman received a margin of 7,107 votes while Democratic Governor Frank J. Lausche was reelected by a plurality of 221,261 votes.[255]

While the Democratic percentages of the votes of union members in presidential elections remained virtually the same, from 72 percent in 1944 to 70 percent in 1948, the Republican percentages of the votes of farmers declined from 52 percent in 1944 to 48 percent in 1948 (see table 1).[256] The campaign activities of organized labor helped Truman to maintain the same levels of electoral support from union members that Roosevelt received in urban, industrial areas of Illinois and Ohio, but the greater voter appeal that Truman enjoyed among farmers enabled him to carry Illinois and Ohio by narrow margins and to especially receive the electoral votes of Iowa, which voted mostly Republican in 1940 and 1944.[257] Truman's policy positions and rhetoric on agricultural issues helped him to appeal to farmers who wanted to ensure the well-funded continuation of Democratic-created farm programs that enriched them.[258] Uncertainty about the future of federal farm programs that benefited southern agriculture if Republicans controlled both the presidency and Congress also helped to solidify Truman's voter appeal among southern farmers and to limit the attraction of J. Strom Thurmond's candidacy.[259]

In Ohio, Illinois, and Wisconsin, states that had significant numbers of voters from both rural and urban areas, Truman's stronger appeal among rural voters helped him to offset the decline in the total Democratic margins in the nation's twelve largest cities from the 1944 to the 1948 presidential elections.[260] The

TABLE 1. Democratic Percentages of
Popular Votes in Farm States Carried by Dewey
in 1944 and by Truman in 1948.

	1944	*1948*
Ohio	49.8	49.5
Iowa	47.5	50.3
Wisconsin	48.6	50.7
Colorado	46.4	51.9

Source: Congressional Quarterly, *Guide to U.S. Elections* (Washington, D.C.: Congressional Quarterly, Inc., 1985), 356-57.

Democratic margins in the twelve largest cities, which included Chicago, Cleveland, and Milwaukee, declined from a total of approximately 2,230,000 votes in 1944 to 1,481,000 votes in 1948.[261] But, while 62 percent of Roosevelt's total national plurality of votes came from these cities, 69 percent of Truman's did.[262]

With black, Jewish, and Catholic voters concentrated in major cities, the Democratic share of votes cast by blacks in presidential elections increased from 68 percent in 1944 to 77 percent in 1948.[263] The Democratic share of votes cast by Jews in presidential elections decreased from 91 percent in 1944 to 72 percent in 1948, with most of the Democratic decline attributed to Henry A. Wallace's appeal among the most liberal Jewish voters.[264] Approximately two-thirds of white, nonsouthern Catholics voted Democratic in the presidential elections of 1944 and 1948, but analyst Samuel Lubell found sharp increases in the number of Catholic Democratic votes cast in several cities in 1948 compared to 1944.[265]

In the South—that is, the eleven states of the former Confederacy and the border states of Kentucky and Oklahoma—Truman received 52.9 percent of the popular votes, compared to Roosevelt's receipt of 69.1 percent of the South's popular votes in 1944.[266] Even though J. Strom Thurmond's States' Rights Democratic candidacy received 17.4 percent of the South's popular votes, the Republican percentage of southern votes in presidential elections decreased only marginally from 30.1 percent in 1944 to 29.7 percent in 1948.[267] In seven of the nine southern states that Truman carried in the electoral college, his percentage of popular votes was smaller than Roosevelt's percentage in 1944.[268]

In addition to the fact that Truman received proportionately smaller pluralities than Roosevelt in seven of the nine southern states carried by both (see table 2), the Republican share of votes in presidential elections cast by southern whites living in metropolitan areas increased from 34 percent in 1944 to 46 percent in 1948.[269] Finally, if the Republican percentage of votes cast in the South in the

1944 presidential election and the combined percentages of Republican and States' Rights Democratic (SRD) votes in the 1948 presidential election are interpreted as expressions of opposition to the national Democratic party, then the percentage of southerners voting against the national Democratic party's presidential nominee increased from 30.1 percent in 1944 to 47.1 percent in 1948.[270]

These analyses of various southern voting statistics indicate growth in Republican voting strength in presidential elections in the South that would become more evident in 1952.[271] Then, Republican presidential nominee Dwight Eisenhower carried Florida, Texas, Tennessee, and Virginia in the electoral college and received 48.9 percent of the South's popular votes.[272] Harry Truman's pursuit of liberal policy objectives after the 1948 election, especially his efforts on civil rights and the repeal of the Taft-Hartley Act, and his mild, occasional efforts to punish former Dixiecrats through his party leadership helped to accelerate the seemingly inexorable increase in southern Republican voting strength after 1948. Political scientist Barbara Sinclair concluded that the growth of industrialization and the weakness of labor unions in the South during and after World War II contributed to greater southern opposition to more liberal economic and social welfare policies.[273]

Harry Truman's campaign strategy, liberal domestic policy agenda, and rhetoric in 1948 reflected his reformist and regular value systems and helped the Democratic party to assert itself as the majority party through the results of the presidential and congressional elections.[274] The prospect of the future passage of Truman's major domestic policy proposals initially appeared to be enhanced by the fact that nearly half of the Democratic gains in House seats were in northern urban congressional districts and that the newly elected Democratic senators included such prominent liberals as Hubert Humphrey of Minnesota, Paul Douglas of Illinois, and Estes Kefauver of Tennessee.[275] After assessing the Democratic sweep of the 1948 congressional elections, *U.S. News and World Report* commented, "On the basis of these figures, it would appear that a sizable majority in support of the New Deal point of view exists in both the Senate and the House."[276]

Truman's fiery populist rhetoric on economic issues and shared Democratic fears of Republican control of Congress and the White House had united most Democrats under Truman's candidacy and party leadership during the general election campaign of 1948. The broad regional, ethnic, economic, and interest-group diversity of the national Democratic party also proved to be a major Democratic advantage in the 1948 election. But while this pluralism was crucial to the party's electoral success, it plagued Harry Truman's party leadership and presi-

TABLE 2. Democratic Percentages of
Popular Votes in Southern States Carried by
Roosevelt in 1944 and Truman in 1948.

	1944	*1948*
Arkansas	70.0	61.7
Florida	70.3	48.8
Georgia	81.7	60.8
Kentucky	54.5	56.7
North Carolina	66.7	58.0
Oklahoma	55.6	62.8
Tennessee	60.5	49.1
Texas	71.4	65.4
Virginia	62.4	47.9

Source: Congressional Quarterly, *Guide to U.S. Elections* (Washington, D.C.: Congressional Quarterly, Inc., 1985), 356-57.

dency as he tried to both benefit the nation and entrench liberalism as the definitive ideology of the Democratic party by seeking passage of liberal legislation.[277] Instead, Truman's Fair Deal proposals would exacerbate intraparty differences during the Eighty-first Congress.[278]

6

☆ ☆ ☆ ☆ ☆

THE FAIR DEAL
AND THE DEMOCRATIC PARTY

A few weeks before the 1948 election, Harry Truman wrote to his sister Mary Jane. Win or lose, he said, "people will know where I stand and a record will be made for future action by the Democratic Party."[1] In his Twenty-one Point Plan, announced on September 6, 1945, his advocacy of the Employment Act of 1946, his various other domestic policy proposals, and his campaign speeches of 1948, Truman had committed himself and his party to protecting and expanding such New Deal policies as the minimum wage, Social Security benefits, public power and reclamation projects, and union rights. By the 1948 campaign, though, it was evident that Truman's presidency and party leadership wanted Democratic liberalism to extend beyond protecting the policy legacy of the New Deal from the hostility of a Republican-controlled Congress and its bipartisan conservative coalition. In particular, Truman's liberal policy agenda sought to achieve three especially difficult policy goals: civil rights laws, national health insurance, and federal aid to elementary and secondary education. Even though he failed to achieve congressional passage of these proposals, Truman's persistent rhetoric and efforts on their behalf permanently ingrained them into the ideology and policy goals of the liberal wing of the Democratic party, thus influencing the policy priorities of future Democratic presidents and liberal Democrats in Congress.[2]

ORIGINS OF THE FAIR DEAL

In the period immediately after the 1948 election, Truman repeatedly asserted that the voters had provided a mandate for this liberal policy agenda, which he identified as the platform of the Democratic party rather than as his own personal initiatives.[3] But less than half, 49.3 percent, of the voters had supported Truman in the election, and it was impossible to discern if most of them had voted for him because of his liberal policy positions—especially his more controversial positions, such as repeal of the Taft-Hartley Act and national health insurance. Gallup polls conducted during the first few months of 1949 revealed that a plurality of Americans questioned opposed Truman's health insurance proposal and believed that, if it were enacted, the quality of health care would decline.[4] More significantly, only 35 percent of one poll's respondents agreed with Truman's position on the Taft-Hartley Act.[5]

Despite the lack of evidence of strong public support for new, major liberal domestic policies and the absence of an atmosphere of national emergency— such as the Great Depression during Roosevelt's first hundred days—Truman devoted his 1949 State of the Union Message to what he called the Fair Deal.[6] The domestic policy proposals that collectively became known as the Fair Deal reiterated Truman's Twenty-one Point Plan of 1945 and included such major campaign promises as proposals for national health insurance, federal aid to education, a comprehensive federal housing policy, and repeal of the Taft-Hartley Act.[7] In contrast to his slashing, combative rhetoric of the 1948 campaign, Truman's words and tone were more conciliatory. The president emphasized in his concluding paragraphs that he hoped "for cooperation from farmers, from labor, and from business" and needed the cooperation of Congress in enacting this liberal legislation.[8]

According to Clark M. Clifford, Truman coined the term *Fair Deal* when he revised the draft of his State of the Union Message.[9] Clifford also claimed that the Fair Deal was intended to be an "analysis" or refinement of the New Deal, instead of merely a continuation of Roosevelt's policies.[10] Ironically, while some parts of the Fair Deal agenda, such as civil rights and national health insurance, were more liberal than the New Deal in that they sought greater federal intervention in these policy areas, the rhetoric and approach to Congress that Truman and his administration officials used were often more moderate and compromising than those of Roosevelt and his New Dealers.[11]

There were several reasons for the relative moderation of the Fair Deal's style in its articulation by Truman and his submission of its policy proposals to Congress. One was that while Truman wanted to increase federal spending in such domestic policy areas as education, health care, and housing, he also wanted to regularly reduce the national debt and maintain balanced budgets, which he accomplished three times during his presidency.[12] Leon H. Keyserling, a member of the Council of Economic Advisers who became its chairman in 1950, was the chief articulator of and influence on Fair Deal economics.[13] Like Raymond Moley, Rexford Tugwell, and other economic advisers in the early New Deal's "Brain Trust," he sought to encourage both economic growth and a broader, more equitable distribution of wealth and economic unity through economic planning and greater cooperation among government, business, and labor.[14] Keyserling was critical of the Keynesian economists' dogmatic emphasis on trust-busting and deficit spending later in the Roosevelt administration.

The influence of Keyserling on Truman and the Fair Deal was evident in a speech that Truman delivered in Kansas City on September 29, 1949. At a Democratic dinner honoring William M. Boyle Jr., as the new DNC chairman, Truman used Keyserling's economic figures and policy recommendations to state that the national income could be increased to $300 billion and minimum family incomes of $4,000 per year through economic growth stimulated and guided by cooperation and planning between the public and private sectors.[15] If the Democratic party succeeded in achieving these economic goals and enacting the other Fair Deal proposals, such as national health insurance and federal aid to education, then, according to Truman, "we will win with that program in 1950, and we will win with that program in 1952."[16]

Besides the emphasis on consensus and cooperation in Keyserling's economic philosophy, another moderating influence on Truman's tactics in promoting the Fair Deal to Congress was his departure from Roosevelt's approach. Roosevelt appealed directly to the public through radio addresses and had White House aides like Thomas Corcoran and administration officials like Harry Hopkins aggressively lobby and pressure Democratic members of Congress to support his legislation.[17] As a senator, Truman resented how Roosevelt treated him and his fellow Democrats in Congress.[18] As president, he refused to appoint a formal White House liaison staff on legislation and usually relied on department heads to submit legislation to Congress.[19]

Truman the party regular wanted to forge greater intraparty harmony in Congress, despite his submission of divisive liberal legislation, by being more deferential to Democratic party leaders and committee chairmen than Roosevelt had been.[20] Truman, moreover, believed that there should be a truly equal balance of power between the president and Congress in the legislative process, rather than presidential domination.[21] Partially because of Truman's perceived passivity in congressional relations concerning Fair Deal legislation, ADA members and other liberals would later question the efficacy and even the sincerity of Truman's leadership of the Fair Deal.[22]

Truman also had a more pragmatic, specific reason for his cautious approach in submitting his Fair Deal legislation to the Democratically-controlled Eighty-first Congress. Truman could not afford to risk alienating Speaker of the House Sam Rayburn or Senate Majority Leader Scott Lucas. He was relying on them to shepherd his legislation through the complexities and obstacles of the bicameral legislative processes and to overcome the implacable opposition of southern conservative Democrats led by Richard Russell in the Senate and Eugene Cox in the House, who were likely to coalesce with Republican allies to kill the Fair Deal. Both Rayburn and Lucas were moderates who accepted some parts of the Fair Deal but opposed its most controversial, liberal proposals.[23]

In particular, both Rayburn and Lucas opposed repeal of the Taft-Hartley Act, a top priority of Truman and organized labor. Rayburn also opposed such key Fair Deal legislation as civil rights and federal aid to education.[24] Senate Democrats had elected Lucas as majority leader because they regarded him as a compromise candidate acceptable to southern conservatives.[25] Lucas's conservatism in his future legislative behavior included his opposition to two major features of the Fair Deal, national health insurance and the Brannan Plan, Truman's proposed reform of agricultural subsidies that had been formulated by Charles Brannan, his secretary of agriculture.[26]

Because of their party loyalty and personal respect for Truman, Rayburn and Lucas avoided making public statements against Fair Deal proposals that they opposed. During the Eighty-first Congress, Rayburn and Lucas would simply allow Fair Deal legislation that they opposed or found too divisive within their party and difficult to pass to die in committees or elsewhere in the legislative process.[27] Hoping that compromise and conciliation with these party leaders would eventually produce at least modest, partial victories for Fair Deal legislation, Truman the party regular refrained from public criticism or aggressive, private pressure toward Rayburn and Lucas.[28] In a confidential 1952 memo, however, Truman the reformer acerbically claimed that Lucas was defeated for reelection in 1950 because of his "half hearted approach" toward the Fair Deal.[29]

INTRAPARTY PROCEDURAL CONFLICTS

In his diary entry of January 5, 1949, columnist Drew Pearson wrote, "Not since the early days of the New Deal has there been such a group of youngsters elected on a clear-cut liberal platform."[30] One liberal Democrat elected to the Senate in 1948 was Representative Estes Kefauver of Tennessee. His 1947 book urged the adoption of various procedural reforms in Congress so that the majority party "will be able to put into effect its platform pledges."[31] Two weeks after Truman's 1949 State of the Union message, the New Republic confidently proclaimed, "The Liberal Majority of the Eighty-first Congress is acting with extraordinary determination to carry through the President's program."[32] In proposing a "strategy for liberals" shortly after the 1948 election, journalist

Irwin Ross noted, "As liberal strength increases within and without the Democratic Party, the weight of dependence can eventually shift—and the liberals can end as masters in the house in which they were originally uneasy guests."[33]

Liberal observers of the Eighty-first Congress were initially optimistic concerning the passage of Fair Deal proposals because of the sharp increase in the number of union-endorsed, nonsouthern Democrats in Congress, especially in the House of Representatives, and in the prominence of determined liberal reformers such as Hubert Humphrey, Paul Douglas, and Estes Kefauver among the freshman senators. Liberals, though, were especially emboldened by a procedural victory in the House Rules Committee. The power and ability of southern conservative Democrats and Republicans on this committee to kill or delay liberal legislation were weakened by the adoption of a new rule. This rule allowed the chairman of any standing committee, upon recognition by the speaker, to require the House Rules Committee to call up any bill that his committee has approved after it has been before the House Rules Committee for at least twenty-one days.[34] In particular, southern conservatives opposed to this rule's reform warned that it would expedite the passage of civil rights legislation, exactly what the liberals intended. The House Rules Committee, furthermore, was now chaired by Representative Adolph Sabath, a Chicago Democrat committed to civil rights and the rest of the Fair Deal.[35]

Supporters of civil rights and other Truman policy goals, though, were discouraged by the failure of the Senate to amend cloture rules.[36] Vice President Alben W. Barkley, Senator Francis Myers of Pennsylvania, and other Truman allies tried but failed to make cloture easier to invoke in order to prevent or end anticipated filibusters against civil rights and other major Fair Deal proposals.[37] Liberals such as ADA member Joseph Rauh blamed Lucas for the narrow, 46-41 vote that defeated this procedural reform in the Senate.[38]

The Senate's failure to make cloture easier served as a harbinger of the later filibusters against Truman's civil rights legislation, including House-passed bills to create a permanent FEPC and to prohibit poll taxes.[39] Other procedural factors that hampered congressional passage of major Fair Deal bills were the timing and order in which Truman submitted Fair Deal legislation.[40] In particular, organized labor pressured Truman to make repeal of the Taft-Hartley Act a top priority while the NAACP and ADA insisted that Truman and their allies in Congress immediately and aggressively seek passage of civil rights measures. By March 1949, Leslie Perry, the NAACP's lobbyist in Washington, D.C., bluntly asserted that Truman owed his narrow electoral victory to black voters and that now it was his responsibility to "get prompt and speedy hearings on the House and Senate calendars before spring."[41]

What further complicated Truman's position procedurally were his poorly-scheduled vacations in Key West, Florida, in November 1948 and March 1949.[42] He and several of his key White House aides were out of Washington while anti–Fair Deal members of Congress and interest groups coalesced and plotted their strategy.[43] Union and civil rights leaders intensified their determination that their legislation be considered first.[44]

Especially after his civil rights proposals seemed to be dead in the Senate because of filibusters, Truman's public statements on the current state of his civil rights legislation in Congress were often curt.[45] By contrast, Truman thought that repeal of the Taft-Hartley Act was more feasible and regularly employed tough rhetoric and threats of denying federal patronage to Democratic congressmen who opposed him. Truman stated at a press conference on April 28, 1949, that a congressional Democrat's position on the Taft-Hartley Act would be one test of his party loyalty and a consideration in granting federal patronage.[46]

In a Labor Day speech in Pittsburgh, Truman accused "an organized conspiracy of the selfish interests" of preventing repeal of the Taft-Hartley Act.[47] He vowed, "We are going to continue to fight for the repeal of that repressive law until it is wiped off the statute books."[48] Truman, the AFL, the CIO, and their allies in Congress had failed to secure congressional passage of acceptable repeal legislation two months before the Pittsburgh speech.[49]

In his determination to discipline and pressure Democrats in Congress to support repeal of the Taft-Hartley Act, Truman the reformer had publicly stated his willingness to use federal patronage to reward or punish Democrats in Congress according to their voting records on repeal legislation and other planks of the 1948 Democratic national platform, which was the basis of the Fair Deal. In a November 30, 1948, letter to J. Howard McGrath, liberal Democratic Congressman John Dingell Sr. of Michigan told the DNC chairman that anti-Truman Democrats should be denied federal patronage because they "will have to do some penance for their lack of faith and cowardly abandonment of the President before being restored to good standing."[50] Throughout the first session of the Eighty-first Congress, columnists, liberal activists, Eleanor Roosevelt, and organizations including the ADA, CIO-PAC, and NAACP urged Truman to use the denial of patronage as just one of several weapons for punishing both the Dixiecrat members of Congress who formally joined the SRD movement and the regular, southern Democrats who opposed most Fair Deal legislation.[51]

But Senator James Eastland of Mississippi, an outspoken supporter of the SRD movement, kept his seat on the Senate Judiciary Committee and could hamper Justice Department patronage and hearings on judicial appointments.[52] Truman's ethos as a party regular eventually prevailed, and he formulated a moderate, compromise policy on patronage. He and his White House aide on personnel, Donald Dawson, would give less consideration toward Dixiecrats than for pro-Truman Democrats on patronage decisions within a state.[53] Truman's compromised policy for using patronage as a tool of party leadership in rewarding loyalty to his administration's policy goals was criticized by liberals for being too soft and ineffective and by southern conservatives as vindictive and unjustified.[54]

On May 3, 1949, Utah Representative Walter K. Granger, a pro-Truman Democrat, chastised former Dixiecrat Representative F. Edward Hebert of Louisiana for complaining about patronage refusals and delays because of his opposition to Fair Deal legislation. According to Granger, "patronage is just about the most persuasive argument that a President has with Congress."[55]

Truman might have relied more on his reformer ethos by aggressively and systematically using patronage in an attempt to persuade or pressure southern conservative Democrats to support Fair Deal legislation. However, it is highly unlikely that such pressure (involving relatively few federal appointments) would have motivated southern conservatives—and southern economic liberals—to support civil rights legislation and other major, divisive Fair Deal proposals.[56] A more powerful procedural tactic within Congress would have been to deny former Dixiecrats their preferred committee seats. The Democratic majorities in the Eighty-first Congress had a larger percentage of southern conservatives in the Senate than in the House. The Democratic Steering Committee did not punish Dixiecrat senators through the denial of their previously held committee seats. Since all Senate chairmen were chosen entirely because of seniority, ten of the fifteen Senate committees were chaired by senators from southern and border states.[57]

Once again, the House of Representatives appeared more likely to adopt procedural reforms that would weaken the power of the bipartisan conservative coalition and promote the passage of liberal legislation. Most members of the House Committee on Committees, which assigned Democrats to committees, were now nonsouthern liberals and moderates. Liberal columnists and editorials urged Truman and pro–Fair Deal Democrats in Congress to abolish the seniority system and elect committee chairmen according to secret ballots and their loyalty to the Fair Deal.[58] The *New York Star* argued that "it is perfectly proper and desirable for Mr. Truman to exercise the party leadership which the people have entrusted to him. It is perfectly proper and desirable that those members of Congress who support his program . . . should organize both houses along lines that will at least minimize the chances of outright obstruction."[59]

During Truman's November 1948 vacation in Key West, he consulted Sam

Rayburn about the possibility of denying seniority and committee assignments to Representative John Rankin of Mississippi and other southern Democratic representatives who had openly supported the Dixiecrat presidential nominee J. Strom Thurmond or had been nominated on SRD slates.[60] Rayburn, however, convinced the president that such presidential intervention in House procedures would arouse the resentment of even pro-Truman Democrats. Truman agreed.[61]

Despite Rayburn's later public announcement that there would be no reprisals against former Dixiecrats in making committee assignments, the Democratic Committee on Committees changed the membership rules of the House Un-American Activities Committee (HUAC) in order to intentionally exclude Dixiecrats John Rankin of Mississippi and F. Edward Hebert of Louisiana as members. The Democratic Committee on Committees had ruled that HUAC members had to be lawyers and could not chair other committees.[62] Hebert was not a lawyer, and Rankin chaired the Veterans' Affairs Committee.

To the dismay of Truman and most liberal House Democrats, HUAC was allowed to continue as a standing committee under the chairmanship of an anti-administration conservative Democrat, Representative John Wood of Georgia. In general, though, the chairmen of major House committees were more liberal and more likely to support Truman's policy proposals than the Senate committee chairmen. Urban ethnic liberals Adolph J. Sabath of Chicago and Emmanuel Celler of Brooklyn would respectively chair the House Rules Committee and Judiciary Committee. Ailing eighty-four-year-old Robert L. Doughton of North Carolina chaired the House Ways and Means Committee during the Eighty-first Congress, but he often deferred the shaping of legislation in his committee to two generally pro-Truman liberals, Jere Cooper of Tennessee and John Dingell Sr. of Michigan.[63]

These modest procedural changes in the House—combined with its greater proportion of pro-Truman liberal Democrats and the experienced leadership of Speaker Sam Rayburn and Majority Leader John McCormack—meant that Fair Deal legislation often succeeded in the House. The Senate was a different matter. There, conservative Democrats exerted greater control in committees, the more successful bipartisan cooperation of conservativesopposed Truman's domestic policy proposals, and the majority leader, Scott Lucas, proved to be less skillful and reliable in promoting Fair Deal bills. Thus the Housing Act of 1949 was the only major Fair Deal proposal to become law. The failed efforts to repeal the Taft-Hartley Act and pass civil rights legislation early in the Eighty-first Congress endangered passage of other controversial Fair Deal legislation, especially in the Senate. Intraparty conflicts over federal aid to education, the Brannan Plan for agricultural reform, and national health insurance further exposed and exacerbated intraparty regional, racial, and ideological differences and demonstrated the power of lobbyists to kill Fair Deal legislation.

THE HEALTH CARE BATTLE

Compared to his support for the Brannan Plan and federal aid to education, Truman's advocacy of compulsory national health insurance had earlier roots in his presidency and political career. As a county judge, Truman oversaw the construction of a county hospital for the indigent.[64] As a senator, he believed that the Social Security Act of 1935 "was a move in the right direction, although it lacked health insurance for hospitals and doctor bills."[65] Like Roosevelt, Truman was alarmed by the millions of young men rejected for military service during World War II.[66]

As Cold War tensions worsened, Truman emphasized improving public health through a federally administered system of compulsory national health insurance as an essential contribution to national defense.[67] Also, since millions of Americans could neither afford private health insurance nor qualify for charitable care given to the very poor by private and public hospitals, Truman hoped that national health insurance would receive the same broad political support that the old age pension and unemployment insurance provisions of the Social Security Act had received. In a 1949 letter to a retired Missouri businessman who opposed Truman's health insurance proposal, Truman asserted that he did not seek to impose "socialized medicine."[68] Instead, he was "trying to fix it so the people in the middle income bracket can live as long as the very rich and the very poor."[69]

In his Twenty-one Point speech of September 6, 1945, Truman supported laws that would fulfill Roosevelt's economic bill of rights. These included the rights "to adequate medical care and . . . good health" and "to adequate protection from the economic fears of old age, sickness, accident, and unemployment."[70] More significantly, on November 19, 1945, Truman became the first president to deliver a special message to Congress entirely devoted to health care. He identified his administration's five basic goals in health care policy as the construction of more hospitals and related facilities, expansion of public health services (especially for maternal and children's health), improvement and expansion of medical education and research, prepayment of medical costs, and protection against lost income due to illness and disability.[71]

Truman realized that his fourth goal, prepayment of medical costs through compulsory national health insurance, was the most controversial. He repeatedly emphasized in this speech that his health program was not socialized medicine. "Socialized medicine means that all doctors work as employees of government. . . . No such system is here proposed."[72]

It is not surprising, therefore, that the first goal was achieved most successfully during the Truman administration. Sponsored by Democratic Senator Lister Hill of Alabama and Republican Senator Harold Burton of Ohio, the Hospital Construction Act of 1946 enjoyed broad bipartisan support in Congress and the endorsements of organized labor and the American Medical Association (AMA). The broad support for the Hill-Burton statute and the relative ease with which it passed both houses were mostly due to the widespread recognition that there was a serious shortage of hospitals and the fact that this law's content consisted of federal aid to states and nonprofit hospitals.[73] The federal government under this law, therefore, supplemented, rather than superseded, state health care policies and did not threaten the AMA's interest in preventing federal dominance in health care.

While Truman did not conduct a regular rhetorical campaign to promote the passage of national health insurance legislation in 1946, he generally supported the health insurance legislation sponsored by Democratic Senators Robert Wagner of New York and James Murray of Montana and Democratic Representative John Dingell Sr. of Michigan.[74] Having failed to persuade Roosevelt to include national health insurance in the Social Security Act of 1935, Wagner submitted his first health insurance bill in 1939. Compared to the legislation that he cosponsored in 1943 and 1945, its health insurance provision was fairly modest.[75] Wagner's 1939 proposal wanted to amend the Social Security Act of 1935 so that federal grants would be given to states to develop state health insurance plans.[76]

Wagner's 1939 bill, though, aroused the opposition of the AMA, which suspected it could lead to compulsory, nationwide, federally controlled health insurance.[77] Roosevelt, furthermore, did not champion this bill. The bill seemed destined to defeat in Congress, due to the significant loss of liberal legislative strength following the 1938 elections, and Roosevelt needed to gain the support of conservative Democrats and Republicans for his foreign policy and defense legislation after World War II began in Europe.[78]

Because of the medical needs of military personnel, American entry into World War II led to a sharp increase in federal involvement in medical care. Military needs during the war facilitated the enactment of federal aid for medical research and education in addition to the vast construction of veterans hospitals.[79] With servicemen's wives and children also receiving federally provided medical care and many Americans fearing a postwar depression, a 1943 Gallup poll indicated that 59 percent of its respondents favored national health insurance.[80]

Encouraged by the apparently widespread public support for compulsory national health insurance, Wagner, Dingell, and Murray also concluded that only a federally administered system with compulsory membership assured coverage for all Americans.[81] The Wagner-Murray-Dingell legislation on health insurance submitted in 1943 and 1945, therefore, was explicit in its provisions on federal control and compulsory membership.[82] The determination of these three pro-union, liberal Democrats to refuse to abandon these provisions of their legislation was solidified by the active support of the AFL and CIO for compulsory national health insurance administered by the federal government.[83] Their insistence on federal control and compulsory membership already minimized the possibility of bipartisan support in Congress, especially since Robert A. Taft was a key Republican member of the Senate Education and Labor Committee chaired by Murray in 1945. Taft supported limited federal aid for health care for the poor.[84] Even while Taft was chairman of this committee during the Eightieth Congress, Murray, Wagner, and Dingell sponsored legislation that gained congressional support only from the most liberal Democrats.[85]

Truman was also determined to ensure that national health insurance was compulsory and federally administered to assure universal coverage and adequate medical care.[86] In addition to his belief that his 1948 campaign platform and upset victory gave him a public mandate to seek passage of such legislation, Truman also felt politically obligated to organized labor and the NAACP, two of the most prominent interest groups endorsing compulsory national health insurance.[87] Truman's liberal position on national health insurance was strengthened and articulated by Oscar Ewing, administrator of the Federal Security Agency. Besides being head of the agency that would administer a compulsory national health plan, Ewing had briefly served as acting DNC chairman in 1946 and was a key member of Truman's campaign staff.[88]

An outspoken liberal ideologue committed to a comprehensive welfare state, Ewing had his report to Truman, *The Nation's Health,* published toward the end of the 1948 campaign.[89] This was the most detailed document representing the Truman administration's position on national health insurance.[90] This report concluded "that the voluntary insurance plans can never do the job that the national interest requires to be done" and that national health insurance is the only "possible way of bringing adequate medical service to fully half of the American people."[91] The major provisions of Truman's national health insurance plan in 1949 were contained in Senate bill 1679, introduced by Senator Elbert Thomas of Utah.[92]

Truman's deference to Ewing as his administration's chief spokesman and advocate for compulsory national health insurance proved to be a tactical error.

Ewing had a reputation among Republicans and conservative Democrats in Congress as a highly partisan liberal ideologue who had a bureaucratic self-interest in simultaneously promoting the elevation of the Federal Security Agency, which would administer Truman's health plan, to cabinet status.[93] A special House committee would later investigate Republican charges that Ewing and Secretary of Agriculture Charles Brannan engaged in improper lobbying activities to promote Fair Deal proposals under their purview.[94]

Moreover, the advocacy of compulsory national health insurance by the Truman administration, the DNC apparatus, and their allies in Congress and among interest groups (especially organized labor, the National Farmers Union, and the Committee for the Nation's Health) were pitifully inferior to the lobbying and publicity of their primary opponent, the American Medical Association.[95] The AMA conducted the most expensive, well-planned, sophisticated, and systematic lobbying and publicity effort of any Fair Deal opponent. It had already been aroused to political opposition of national health insurance by Wagner's 1939 bill and was encouraged by its success in defeating Governor Earl Warren's proposal for a state-run, compulsory health insurance program in California in 1945.[96] Between 1940 and 1945, the National Physicians' Committee spent nearly $1 million on publicity against the Wagner-Murray-Dingell legislation.[97] The AMA raised a $3.5 million fund and paid the public relations firm of Whitaker and Baxter more than $8,000 a month to defeat congressional passage of national health insurance.[98]

The AMA shrewdly realized that it could not appear to be merely obstructionist and callous toward the medical needs of the poor and uninsured.[99] Since 1938, it publicly supported the formation and mass enrollment in Blue Cross and later Blue Shield private, voluntary health insurance plans throughout the nation.[100] Partially because of AMA advocacy, the number of Blue Cross and Blue Shield health insurance policies increased from approximately 28 million in 1945 to more than 61 million by the end of Truman's presidency.[101] The AMA's interest group allies included the United States Chamber of Commerce, American Legion, National Grange, and American Farm Bureau.[102]

As early as April 1949, Gallup polls revealed that a plurality of Americans agreed with the AMA's assertion that the quality of medical care would decline under national health insurance.[103] One poll also indicated that 47 percent of its respondents supported the AMA proposal that the federal government provide grants to states to help provide needed care for Americans who could not afford private health insurance. Only 33 percent supported Truman's plan.[104]

Despite the lack of strong public support for compulsory national health insurance, Truman stated in his special message to Congress on April 22, 1949,

"The only fair and effective means to assure adequate medical care through insurance is to build on the pattern of our existing social insurance plans"—that is, the Social Security system.[105] Truman then specified flaws and inadequacies in voluntary private health insurance plans in meeting this national need.[106] A few days after this speech, though, Senator James Murray of Montana, chairman of the Senate Labor and Public Welfare Committee, failed to convince a majority of his committee's members to support and report out of committee Senate bill 1679's provision for compulsory national health insurance.[107] Senate bill 1679 thus did not receive a floor vote while the Senate considered three compromise health care bills that did not include compulsory national health insurance.[108] The House version of Senate bill 1679 sponsored by Representative John Dingell Sr. likewise died in the Committee on Interstate and Foreign Commerce in 1950.[109]

Besides the paucity of Democratic support within Congress for compulsory national health insurance, the intensification of the issues of domestic and international communism also contributed to the defeat of Truman's health insurance proposal, the most liberal, controversial, and revolutionary Fair Deal social welfare measure. The Alger Hiss controversy, the fall of China to communism, the rise of McCarthyism, the Soviet explosion of an atomic bomb, and the outbreak of the Korean War heightened public concern about the ideas and actions of American and foreign communists during the Eighty-first Congress. Such fear was receptive to the AMA's charges of socialism against Truman's health insurance plan.[110] In a 1950 speech, Senator Robert A. Taft specified Truman's proposal for compulsory national health insurance as one of the most dangerous examples of "socialist" Fair Deal legislation, which threatened to destroy liberty and ultimately lead to communism in the United States.[111] In the 1950 congressional campaigns, such prominent Democratic supporters of compulsory national health insurance as Senators Claude Pepper of Florida and Elbert Thomas of Utah and Representatives Andrew Biemiller of Wisconsin and Eugene O'Sullivan of Nebraska were defeated, partially because of AMA publicity against them and Republican charges linking "socialized medicine" to softness on communism.[112]

Despite the controversy, intraparty divisiveness, and electoral defeats that his failed health insurance plan promoted, Truman continued to advocate a federally administered, compulsory national health insurance program during and after his presidency.[113] His refusal to abandon compulsory national health insurance prevented the enactment of any of the compromise health care bills in the Senate. The president's persistent refusal to compromise on this issue was partially motivated by his programmatic belief that only a compulsory national health insurance program that was part of the Social Security system would ensure adequate coverage. As a matter of political principle, he also did not want to yield to the policy position of the AMA, which he bitterly and suspiciously perceived as a selfish, reactionary interest group callous to the medical needs of uninsured Americans.[114]

Truman's ideological, programmatic, and partisan inflexibility about compulsory national health insurance was also a product of his campaign obligation to organized labor, which was adamant about this position on health care. Unfortunately for Truman's party leadership, his vigorous pursuit of this policy commitment to organized labor, like his early effort to repeal the Taft-Hartley Act, was not shared by most Democrats in Congress and was not supported by public opinion. As political scientist Richard Neustadt convincingly argued, however, Truman's tenacity on this issue pressured Congress to pass two less controversial elements of his health care agenda, more federal aid to hospital construction and medical research.[115] This issue's long-term programmatic and partisan impact, was the partial fulfillment of Truman's policy goal of universal health coverage through the Kennedy and Johnson administrations' advocacy of Medicare for the elderly and Medicaid for the poor and their enactment in 1965.[116]

THE BRANNAN PLAN BATTLE

Unlike the health insurance component of the Fair Deal, the Brannan Plan initially appeared to hold a stronger possibility of enactment because of Truman's campaign success in attracting the votes of farmers who had supported Dewey in 1944. Among Truman's cabinet members, Secretary of Agriculture Charles F. Brannan was the most active, adroit campaigner for Truman in 1948. Brannan delivered more than eighty speeches directed at farmers.

Having proven himself to Truman as both an able, experienced administrator of federal agricultural programs since 1935 and a shrewd political strategist, Brannan was one of the most influential architects of the Fair Deal in the Truman administration.[117] He held a strong, personal and ideological commitment toward formulating and implementing policies that would save family farms and politically unite small farmers and the urban working class.[118] This commitment was strengthened by his close political relationship with James Patton, president of the National Farmers Union. In contrast to the larger, more prosperous, and conservative membership of the American Farm Bureau, the National Farmers Union's members were mostly lower-income small farmers from the Great Plains and western states. Under Patton's leadership, the National Farmers Union endorsed Truman's health insurance proposal and forged an alliance with the CIO.[119]

It was not surprising that Patton played a major role in formulating the provisions of the so-called Brannan Plan for changing the system of agricultural price supports in 1949 and in assuring that his farm organization, the AFL, and the CIO endorsed the Brannan Plan. The Brannan Plan intended to simultaneously ensure high, stable incomes for farmers and lower food prices for consumers, while fewer surpluses of grains would need to be stored by federal facilities. The Brannan Plan encouraged farmers to reduce grain production by subsidizing greater production of milk and livestock. The more specific methods of the Brannan Plan included the abolition of acreage allotments for price-support payments, replacing them with direct payments to the farmers, based on units of production.[120] Intending to benefit small family farmers while limiting government subsidies to large, commercial farmers, the Brannan Plan limited this federal aid to the first $27,500 of production.[121]

With confidence in Brannan's political acumen and agricultural expertise, Truman publicly deferred to Brannan as his administration's spokesman and advocate of this Fair Deal proposal.[122] Brannan conducted an extensive speaking campaign, and he was assisted by the efforts of the DNC's Publicity Division and Women's Division. The DNC sponsored a regional Democratic conference in Des Moines, Iowa, on June 12-13, 1949, primarily to organize support in the Midwest.[123]

The Brannan Plan seemed to have a good chance of becoming law after Democratic Representative Stephen Pace of Georgia, chairman of the House Agriculture Committee, drafted a bill that contained its key elements and a majority of his committee's members voted to report it out by late June.[124] Fearing that the Brannan Plan would damage future farm prices, especially for cotton and tobacco, most southern Democrats in the House opposed the Pace bill and supported a substitute bill sponsored by Democratic Representative Albert Gore Sr. of Tennessee, which rejected the Brannan Plan.[125] Assisted by aggressive lobbying by the American Farm Bureau, a coalition of southern Democrats and Republicans passed the Gore bill by a vote of 239 to 170.[126]

The Brannan Plan also died in the Senate by late July 1949. Although Democratic Senator Elmer Thomas of Oklahoma chaired the Senate Agriculture and Forestry Committee and supported the plan, Democratic Senator Clinton Anderson of New Mexico held more influence with Democratic senators.[127] As Brannan's predecessor as secretary of agriculture, Anderson dealt a fatal blow to the Brannan Plan by publicly opposing it.[128]

Shortly before the House floor vote on the Gore bill, the Senate Agriculture and Forestry Committee unanimously voted to reject the Brannan Plan.[129] Anderson submitted a substitute bill that provided price supports on a sliding scale from 75 percent to 90 percent of parity, depending on the type of commodity. Combined with the Gore bill's provision of 90 percent parity for basic commodities, the Anderson bill became the basis of the Agriculture Adjustment Act of 1949. This law modified the formula for acreage allotments and the use of marketing quotas but mostly updated the price support and commodity storage systems established during the New Deal.[130] It continued 90 percent price supports for two more years.[131]

Although Truman reluctantly signed the Gore-Anderson bill into law, he and Brannan still hoped that elements of the Brannan Plan could be reintroduced to Congress in 1950.[132] But their two chief congressional supporters, Stephen Pace and Elmer Thomas, were retiring in 1950. Any lingering, remote possibility that most Democrats in Congress would support the Brannan Plan was ended by the outbreak of the Korean War. Military food purchases raised farm prices and reduced stored, government-purchased surpluses. The results of the 1950 congressional elections indicated that most prosperous midwestern and western farmers who supported Truman in 1948 had returned to their typically Republican voting behavior, partially because of their hostility toward the Brannan Plan.[133]

Truman thought that the 1948 election gave him a public mandate to propose an agricultural policy that intended to satisfy both farmers and consumers, but he failed to realize that normally Republican farmers who voted for him in 1948 wanted to maintain federal agricultural policy rather than revolutionize it.[134] Despite the populist desire of Truman and Brannan to formulate an agricultural policy intended to politically unite and economically benefit small farmers, wage-earners, and consumers, the methods of the Brannan Plan failed to adequately address and satisfy the different policy interests of farmers, especially cotton and tobacco farmers, represented by southern Democrats in Congress. Since the general public tended to be more aloof and apathetic about the legislative conflicts over the Brannan Plan than those regarding national health insurance, agricultural interest groups led by the American Farm Bureau were especially significant in preventing passage or even serious committee consideration of the Brannan Plan by the Democratic-controlled Congress.[135]

FEDERAL AID TO EDUCATION BATTLE

Unlike compulsory national health insurance and the Brannan Plan, there seemed to be broad public and congressional support for federal aid to elementary and secondary education. During the 1948 campaign and in his 1949 budget message to Congress, Truman proposed $300 million in federal educational grants to the states.[136] A Gallup poll released on January 10, 1949, the same day that Truman submitted his budget message to Congress, revealed that a plurality of its respondents supported this amount of federal aid to education.[137] What was even more encouraging for advocates of federal school aid is that 55 percent of this poll's respondents expressed a willingness to pay higher taxes for this purpose while only 30 percent were unwilling to do so.[138]

Among Democrats in Congress, there was also broad support for at least the concept of federal aid to education. Democrats from a broad range ideologies and regions wanted some federal role in improving the quality and quantity of teachers and school facilities in their states.[139] Just as Senator Robert A. Taft of Ohio was essential in providing bipartisan leadership to assure passage of the Housing Act of 1949, his qualified support for some type of federal aid to education provided the prospect of significant Republican support for Fair Deal legislation on federal aid to elementary and secondary education.[140] The Senate Education and Labor Committee's 1945 hearings on the conditions of public schools provided disturbing evidence of such worsening problems as teacher shortages, overcrowded, aging school buildings, and inadequate salaries that motivated many teachers to seek defense-industry jobs.[141]

There was enough bipartisan support for federal aid to education in 1948 that the Republican-controlled Senate passed a bill authorizing $270 million in aid in 1948.[142] The bill was sponsored by Taft and Democratic Senators Elbert Thomas of Utah and Lister Hill of Alabama, but it subsequently died in the House of Representatives.[143] Following Truman's 1949 budget message to Congress, the Senate drafted a federal aid to education bill, which easily passed the Senate by a vote of 58 to 15 on May 5, 1949.[144]

Truman and, to a lesser degree, most Senate supporters of federal aid to elementary and secondary education did not expect this issue to become so bitterly divisive in the House of Representatives, the media, among interest groups, and throughout the general public in 1949. The Senate bill scrupulously avoided the explosive issues of race and religion. It remained silent on the issue of whether states that practiced de jure racial segregation in public education should be denied federal funds and thus made all states eligible for federal aid. It also allowed each state to decide whether any of this federal aid would be given to parochial schools.[145]

In contrast to the Senate's consensus-building approach, the proceedings of the House Education and Labor Committee tended to exacerbate religious and racial differences and make House passage of a compromise bill impossible.[146] Democratic Representative John Lesinski of Michigan chaired this committee and was determined that the wording of an education bill assured federal aid to parochial schools.[147] The subcommittee of the House Education and Labor Committee, which drafted the House bill, was chaired by Democratic Representative Graham A. Barden of North Carolina.

Barden was equally adamant that the bill's wording must specifically prohibit any federal aid to parochial schools.[148] Consequently, the bill that Barden's subcommittee drafted and submitted to the full committee on July 7, 1949, limited federal aid to public schools and eliminated the wording of the Senate bill that states must distribute this federal aid in a "just and equitable" manner.[149] The "just and equitable" provision of the Senate bill was included by its cosponsors as a compromise to the pro-civil rights liberals who insisted that the Senate bill at least require southern states to allocate an adequate share of federal aid to black public schools.[150]

The possibility of compromise within the entire House Education and Labor Committee evaporated when Lesinski and Barden engaged in a rancorous, public quarrel over this bill. Lesinski denounced Barden's bill for being racist and anti-Catholic and vowed that it would die in his committee.[151] On June 19, one week before Lesinski's diatribe, Francis Cardinal Spellman of New York also accused the Barden bill of anti-Catholic bigotry.[152] Four days later, Eleanor Roosevelt expressed her disagreement with the cardinal in her "My Day" newspaper column.[153]

The prolonged public dispute that ensued between Eleanor Roosevelt and Spellman broadened and inflamed the issue from federal aid to education to the separation of church and state. In a publicized letter, the cardinal accused Roosevelt of having a "record of anti-Catholicism" that was "unworthy of an American mother."[154] Her calm yet scolding refutation of Spellman's charges and the public and editorial outcry against the cardinal stiffened the determination of the National Education Association, Protestants and Other Americans United for Separation of Church and State, and several Protestant and Jewish organizations to ensure that any federal aid policy should not benefit the mostly Catholic parochial schools.[155] To many Americans, Spellman's intervention on this public policy issue raised anxieties about a perceived growth in the secular power and influence of the Catholic hierarchy in both domestic and foreign policy.[156]

Renewed efforts on federal aid to education in 1950 also failed. A majority of the House Education and Labor Committee's members again voted to reject the Senate bill and opposed any form of even indirect federal aid to parochial schools, including the use of federal funds to subsidize the bus transportation for both public and nonpublic school students.[157] Following the death of John Lesinski in May 1950, Graham A. Barden became chairman of the full committee and held this position until 1961.[158] During his tenure as chairman, he was determined that any federal aid to elementary and secondary education must not benefit parochial schools at all or coerce racially integrated schools in the South.[159] The issue of federal aid to education was further complicated and polarized by race. In the 1950 session, Representative Adam Clayton Powell Jr., of New York, a black Democrat nationally recognized by many blacks as a spokesman for their policy interests in the House Education and Labor Committee, introduced an amendment to prohibit federal educational grants to states that maintained legally segregated school systems. The NAACP had previously advised Powell to make sure that the wording of his amendment specifically denied federal aid to segregated public schools and did not just vaguely state that federal aid should be given in a nondiscriminatory manner.[160] The Powell amendment simply strengthened the determination of Barden and other southern Democrats to oppose any federal aid bill that threatened the continuation of racially segregated schools.

Privately, Truman wanted to limit federal aid to public schools and hoped that the civil rights and federal aid to education aspects of the Fair Deal could have been maintained as separate issues.[161] In an unsent letter addressed to John Lesinski and written in August 1949, Truman complained, "I certainly didn't expect the Chairman of the Committee on Education and Labor to join in a filibuster on one of the main bulwarks of the Democratic Platform."[162] During the remainder of the Eighty-first Congress, Truman continued to express the need to provide federal aid to elementary and secondary education while avoiding references to the religious and racial dimensions of this issue.[163]

Following the outbreak of the Korean War, Truman articulated a correlation between his proposals for federal aid to elementary and secondary education and for national defense needs in his 1951 and 1952 budget messages to Congress.[164] But even this rhetorical linkage between foreign and domestic policies during a war failed to stimulate passage of broad-based federal aid to elementary and secondary education. Truman's only minor legislative success was congressional passage of a revision and expansion of a 1940 program to provide aid to public school districts that were "adversely impacted" by large numbers of military personnel and defense industry workers.[165]

THE FAIR DEAL'S INTRAPARTY LEGACY

Harry Truman's legislative leadership of the Fair Deal has often been regarded as a failure because the most prominent, controversial, and pioneering Fair Deal proposals—civil rights legislation, repeal of the Taft-Hartley Act, compulsory national health insurance, the Brannan Plan, and federal aid to elementary and secondary education—were not enacted into law.[166] Historian Richard O. Davies recognized the Housing Act of 1949 as the only major Fair Deal proposal to become law.[167] But even the Housing Act of 1949 was not a truly original Fair Deal initiative. To a great extent, it was a refinement and expansion of the Housing Act of 1937 and passed because it received extensive bipartisan support, most notably from Republican Senator Robert A. Taft.[168]

The passage of the Housing Act of 1949 was indicative of the factors that enabled the more minor, less controversial Fair Deal proposals to be passed by Congress. Like the Housing Act of 1949, most Fair Deal legislative successes were revisions, expansions, or consolidations of New Deal programs that were widely accepted by the public and by most Democrats and a significant number of Republicans in Congress. While Gallup polls in 1949 indicated that most Americans opposed Truman's health insurance proposal and only 43 percent supported his recommendation of $300 million in federal aid to education, 68 percent supported the Fair Deal proposal to raise the minimum wage to 75 cents an hour, and 69 percent supported the legislation that became the 1949 Housing Act.[169] It is not surprising that Truman succeeded in persuading Congress to pass legislation raising the minimum wage and expanding Social Security coverage.[170] Congress likewise passed at least compromise versions of Truman's Fair Deal recommendations to expand or modernize programs for rural electrification, soil conservation, reclamation, and flood control.[171]

By the end of the Eighty-first Congress, it was evident that Truman would never achieve the enactment of the Fair Deal's most ground-breaking and controversial policy goals.[172] Democratic losses in the 1950 congressional elections, allegations of corruption in the Truman administration, Truman's declining public approval rating, the nation's focus on the Korean War and its impact on the civilian economy, and McCarthyism would all combine to negate any possibility of a major Fair Deal proposal being enacted during Truman's presidency. The legislative successes of the Fair Deal, therefore, were generally limited to an extension, consolidation, and revision of the New Deal policy foundation. This limited success reflected the parameters of public opinion and bipartisan support in Congress and the hostility that they posed to any innovative domestic legislation that threatened this consensus during the immediate postwar era.

Neither the legislative success of more obscure, moderate Fair Deal policies nor the failure of major divisive liberal Fair Deal proposals to be enacted should be underestimated in their significance for the long-term impact of Truman's party leadership. The success of the Fair Deal in protecting and updating the policy legacy of the New Deal demonstrated the political fact that such

New Deal policies as rural electrification, minimum wage laws, and agricultural price supports were not the vulnerable, ephemeral products of the emergency atmosphere of the Great Depression and Franklin D. Roosevelt's personal leadership. These New Deal policy accomplishments were deeply ingrained as the domestic policy expectations of most Americans and as the policy identity of the national Democratic party. The presidential and congressional election results of 1948 indicated that most voters wanted to protect the New Deal policy foundation and that the Republican sweep of the 1946 congressional elections did not express a public mandate to repeal it.

Harry Truman's exaggerated, inaccurate perception of the 1948 election results as an ideological and programmatic mandate motivated him to futilely lead his party in Congress in a direction that most Democrats rejected. Truman's efforts to unite and lead Democrats in Congress behind most Fair Deal initiatives were further weakened by his own abstention from aggressively lobbying Congress, the continued success of the bipartisan conservative coalition in manipulating legislative procedures against the Fair Deal, particularly in the Senate against civil rights legislation, and the sophisticated, effective tactics of anti–Fair Deal interest groups.[173] Especially in the Fair Deal's priorities of passing civil rights legislation and repealing the Taft-Hartley Act, Truman's party leadership pursued policy goals that seemed unattainable from the beginning of the Eighty-first Congress. Truman's liberal, reformist ethos and his sense of campaign obligations to blacks, the ADA, and organized labor were more influential in the conduct of his party leadership than his more pragmatic, cautious ethos as a party regular.

Although Truman's party leadership failed to persuade a Democratic-controlled Congress to pass the most ambitious, groundbreaking Fair Deal proposals, it provided a blueprint for future action by Democratic presidents, liberal Democrats in Congress, and liberal interest groups during a political era more conducive to their enactment.[174] Shortly before leaving the presidency, Truman complained that Adlai Stevenson lost the 1952 presidential election partially because Stevenson as the titular leader of the Democratic party failed to express a strong commitment to "Roosevelt's New Deal and the President's Fair Deal."[175] Stevenson's campaign rhetoric was more moderate and ambiguous than Truman preferred, but it did not express an abrupt abandonment of the Fair Deal's policy agenda. Stevenson, Truman, the Democratic Advisory Council, liberal Democrats in Congress, and the ADA articulated and advocated the principles and unattained, major policy goals of the Fair Deal during the Eisenhower administration. The Kennedy and Johnson administrations would partially or fully achieve them.[176]

7

☆ ☆ ☆ ☆ ☆

DEMOCRATIC DISSENSUS, 1950-1952

On November 1, 1949, Harry Truman wrote the following entry in his diary to express his frustration and irritation with the Democratically controlled Eighty-first Congress as it neared the end of its first session, "Trying to make the 81st Congress perform is and has been worse than cussing the 80th. . . . I've kissed and petted more consarned S.O.B. so-called Democrats and left wing Republicans than all the Presidents put together. I have very few people fighting my battles in Congress as I fought F.D.R.'s."[1]

GROWING INTRAPARTY DISCORD

Franklin D. Roosevelt had succeeded in stimulating a programmatic consensus within the Democratic party during his first term. Through New Deal policies, he addressed the policy interests of a broad variety of interest groups and voting blocs. As Roosevelt's party leadership and additional liberal policy proposals became more controversial and divisive, this intraparty consensus withered, and the bipartisan conservative coalition became stronger and larger after the 1938 congressional elections. During the rest of Roosevelt's presidency, the bifurcation in Congress and at national party conventions between mostly southern conservative Democrats and mostly northern liberal Democrats became more rigid, antagonistic, and irreconcilable.

Upon his assumption of the presidency and especially after the presentation of his Twenty-one Point Plan to Congress in 1945, Truman's party leadership and domestic policy goals were also hampered and often obstructed by this division among Democrats. The exasperation that Truman expressed in his diary presaged the emergence of internal, Democratic differences that were more complex and multifaceted than the clearer dualistic distinctions along northern-southern, urban-rural, and liberal-conservative parameters. During the last three years of Truman's presidency and party leadership, the national Democratic party increasingly experienced *dissensus*.

Dissensus is a condition of intraparty political behavior in which party members increasingly lack a shared ideology and policy agenda and become alienated from each other multilaterally, rather than just bilaterally, as they are confronted by new types of issues. In domestic policy during the remaining three years, Truman's party leadership and presidency were forced to address a greater diversity and complexity of issues beyond economic policies, civil rights for blacks, and social welfare programs. Truman had to respond to accusations and congressional investigations of alleged corruption in the federal bureaucracy and among some of his closest White House aides. Liberal, moderate, and conservative Democrats in Congress would be among his critics. Likewise, when Truman created the President's Commission on Internal Security and Individual Rights in 1951, he was criticized on the left for threatening civil liberties and on the right for a weak, inadequate response to the danger of communist subversion of the federal bureaucracy.[2]

Truman, like Roosevelt, sought to develop intraparty unity and bipartisan cooperation in foreign policy.[3] But such unity and cooperation became more difficult to achieve regarding the conduct of American foreign policy toward Western Europe, the Soviet Union, and Asia. Democratic ranks in Congress became more fragmented over the details of American participation in NATO, defense appropriations, the fall of China to communism, and Truman's pursuit of a limited war strategy in the Korean War, which influenced his controversial removal of Gen. Douglas MacArthur.[4]

While Truman's foreign policy decisions and approach to domestic communism intensified opposition from conservative Democrats led by Senator Patrick McCarran of Nevada, the president's unwavering loyalty to White House aides accused of ethical conflicts of interest and his belated efforts to address proven corruption in particular federal agencies dismayed and alienated some of the most reliably pro–Fair Deal liberal Democrats.[5] Senator Paul Douglas of Illinois chaired a special Senate committee to investigate ethics in government in 1950 and later claimed that Truman then indirectly denied him senatorial courtesy regarding vacancies on the federal bench in Illinois.[6] According to Douglas, his continuing loyalty to Truman on most major domestic and foreign policy issues never "softened Truman's personal dislike and opposition" toward the Illinois Democrat.[7]

During the last two years of Truman's presidency, conservative Democrats in Congress coalesced more with Republicans to oppose Truman, and liberal

Democrats distanced themselves further from Truman following the electoral defeats of nonsouthern Democratic incumbents in the 1950 congressional elections, and congressional investigations that raised questions about the ethical climate of his administration and the stalemate in the Korean War. All of these factors contributed to the dissensus within the national Democratic party that influenced Truman to promote Adlai Stevenson as the Democratic nominee for president in 1952, even though Stevenson was a moderate who did not clearly adhere to several major policy positions of Fair Deal liberalism.[8] More than two years before Stevenson succeeded Truman as the titular leader of the national Democratic party, an ambitious, maverick freshman Democratic senator recognized the potential of this growing dissensus within his party to provide him with the opportunity to secure its presidential nomination and leadership.[9]

THE KEFAUVER COMMITTEE

Senator Estes Kefauver of Tennessee was in the second year of his Senate career when he submitted a resolution to conduct a Senate committee investigation of interstate organized crime.[10] During the first three months of 1950, Kefauver was careful to generate enough newspaper publicity and favorable public opinion for such an investigation so that he attracted bipartisan support for his resolution to pressure Senator Patrick McCarran, chairman of the Senate's Judiciary Committee, to allow its adoption and authorization.[11] Having donned a coonskin cap during his victorious primary campaign in 1948 to symbolize his defiant independence from the Crump machine, Kefauver had already proven his shrewdness in using symbolism and news coverage to promote his name recognition and to help him fulfill his ambition for higher office.[12] His decision to launch an investigation of organized crime was influenced by *Washington Post* publisher Philip Graham. Graham suggested such an investigation to Kefauver as an effective vehicle toward Kefauver's nomination for vice president in 1952.[13]

When the Senate approved the authorization and appropriations for the Special Committee to Investigate Organized Crime in Interstate Commerce in May 1950, no one was surprised that Alben Barkley appointed Kefauver as the chairman of this special committee. It became known simply as the Kefauver committee.[14] There was nothing novel about a legislative committee or executive commission conducting investigations of and public hearings on organized crime. After World War II, major investigations of organized crime by state and local governments, most notably in Chicago, Los Angeles, and Miami, had been conducted.[15]

The Kefauver committee's investigation, however, was unique in several ways. It was the first congressional committee to travel throughout the nation, conducting hearings in fourteen cities and televising some of them.[16] In choosing witnesses, conducting research, and making recommendations for further federal action, Kefauver and the other senators on this committee were influenced by the premise that organized crime was a nationwide network, rather than a diffusion of independent, local criminal gangs.[17] In particular, the committee's efforts focused on illegal gambling and collusion between gangsters and public officials. The Kefauver committee claimed that the political influence of gangsters was gained not only through bribery but more commonly "through the acquisition of political power by contributions to political organizations or otherwise by creating economic ties with apparently respectable and reputable businessmen and lawyers, and by buying public good will through charitable contributions and press relations."[18]

During its hearings in 1950 and 1951, the Kefauver committee often found that state and local law enforcement officials and other politicians who were questioned and under suspicion were, at best, lackadaisical and lethargic in their efforts against organized crime, and, at worst, personally enriching themselves by protecting and even engaging in illegal gambling.[19] Especially for the residents of such selected cities as New York, Chicago, New Orleans, and Kansas City, it certainly was not shocking to learn about apparent or definite cooperation between government officials and gangsters in gambling operations.[20] But the constant nationwide media attention given to the Kefauver committee hearings and the televising of hearings in New Orleans, Detroit, St. Louis, and New York elevated this issue above local politics. An estimated twenty to thirty million Americans watched the committee's New York hearings, which provided the most suspense and drama when former Mayor William O'Dwyer and gangster Frank Costello were questioned.[21]

The Kefauver committee hearings yielded several political consequences for the remainder of Truman's presidency and party leadership. The losses of several Democratic congressional and senatorial seats in 1950, especially that of Senate Majority Leader Scott Lucas of Illinois, were partially attributed to the Kefauver Committee's hearings, since they revealed collaboration with gangsters by mostly Democratic politicians and party organizations.[22] Truman was again forced to defend his appointment of William O'Dwyer as ambassador to Mexico, since his testimony about political relations with Costello and the gangster's domination of Tammany Hall further tarnished the ambassador's already tainted reputation.[23] The committee's investigation of the correlation between organized crime and Democratic politics in Kansas City likewise revived the belittling perception of Truman as a machine hack whose earliest political environment was characterized by cooperation between gangsters and machine politicians.[24]

In addition to weakening Truman's stature as titular head of the Democratic party, the Kefauver committee's hearings contributed to more dissensus among Democrats by making the freshman senator from Tennessee the leading challenger for the Democratic presidential nomination by the end of 1951. Even after Kefauver's chairmanship ended in 1951, the senator continued to receive favorable media coverage.[25] His image as a courageous, folksy, maverick reformer was further enhanced by his receipt of a "Father of the Year" award in 1951, his ranking as the second best senator by a poll of Washington correspondents, and his committee's receipt of an Emmy award for the televising of its hearings.[26]

The most significant political result of Kefauver's television-generated national name recognition and viability as a presidential candidate was his upset victory over Truman in New Hampshire's Democratic presidential primary of March 11, 1952. Kefauver won 55.4 percent of the votes and received all twelve of New Hampshire's delegates to the Democratic National Convention.[27] According to historian Joseph B. Gorman, the symbolic importance of Kefauver's underdog victory was magnified by the fact that the president "had been rejected by a majority of his own party in a New England state that preferred a Southern, freshman United States senator to the titular leader of the national party—a man who had almost unanimous backing from higher officials of the state Democratic party and organized labor."[28]

More than a month before the New Hampshire primary, Truman had dismissed all presidential primaries as "eyewash" since most states did not commit their delegates to presidential candidates through primaries.[29]

Truman claimed in his memoirs that he had written a memo to himself on April 16, 1950, stating that he would not seek another term as president in 1952.[30] His announcement on March 29, 1952, that he would not seek another term, however, was widely perceived as a reaction to his embarrassing loss to Kefauver in the New Hampshire primary.[31]

Truman's flippant dismissal of the presidential primaries as "eyewash" proved to be accurate in that Kefauver won twelve of the fourteen primaries that he entered but failed to be nominated since only 227.5 of the primary states' 482 delegate votes were cast for Kefauver on the first ballot at the Democratic National Convention.[32] Wielding enough influence over blocs of delegates to ensure the nomination of Adlai Stevenson for president at the convention, Truman was motivated to prevent Kefauver's nomination because of his intense dislike and distrust of the Tennessee senator. Truman believed that Kefauver, or "cow fever," was so deceitfully opportunistic that he was willing to "discredit his own President" and weaken the Democratic party's electoral strength for the 1950 and 1952 elections.[33]

For Truman the party regular, it was intolerable that a Democratic presidential candidate, whom he believed had "no sense of honor," could receive his party's nomination by exacerbating dissensus within his party by holding highly publicized hearings that dramatized and exaggerated the extent of collaboration and corruption between Democratic politicians and gangsters.[34] Except for Truman's persistent, public defense of William O'Dwyer and his refusal to remove O'Dwyer as ambassador to Mexico, there was no evidence obtained by the Kefauver committee that directly linked Truman or high-level administration officials with the gamblers and public officials who were investigated.[35] This Senate investigation, therefore, was not an investigation of alleged corruption within the Truman administration.

The public, however, had a different perception of the relationship between the revelations of the Kefauver Committee hearings and the ethics of the Truman administration. Despite the Kefauver committee's focus on state and local officials, a Gallup poll released on April 27, 1951, revealed that 76 percent of its respondents perceived a "tie-up between gamblers and persons in government in Washington."[36] The televised hearings had the effect on public opinion of nationalizing and generalizing an issue that had previously and chronically been an issue that the public had identified with specific state and local officials and party organizations, rather than with a president and the national level of his party. As the Kefauver committee hearings continued, the print media published articles exposing alleged or proven corruption, or at least legal yet ethically questionable conflicts of interest, by some Truman administration officials.

The complexities and distinctions between the Kefauver committee investigation and Senate investigations of alleged corruption within certain executive branch agencies blurred and merged so that any congressional investigation of corruption and media stories of cronyism and favoritism in the federal government formed an organic whole known as "the mess in Washington" for many Americans.[37] The public and media image of Harry Truman and his party was further tarnished when his values and behavior as a party regular influenced him to be so unconditionally loyal to his appointees under investigation. Such stubborn loyalty increasingly made him appear to be a crass machine politician tolerant of cronyism and corruption.[38]

THE 1950 ELECTIONS

In a February 20, 1950, speech given to fellow Republicans at a Lincoln Day dinner in Detroit, House Minority Leader Joseph W. Martin Jr., stated, "The Truman Administration is a prisoner of socialistic advisers, thinkers, and planners."[39] Two months later, Martin publicly stated, "Until an Administration is installed in Washington which will adopt policies that will block a communist infiltration at home, no American can feel secure."[40] Two weeks before Martin's speech in Detroit, a conference held by the RNC and House and Senate Republicans announced that the Republican campaign theme for the 1950 elections would be "Liberty Against Socialism."[41] Like Martin's speeches, Republican campaign rhetoric in general gradually evolved from denouncing Fair Deal legislation as creeping socialism to condemning the Truman administration and the Democratic party for incompetence, softness, and even treason in their response to the threats of domestic and international communism. Much of the escalated inflammation of Republican rhetoric would be attributed to Republican Senator Joseph McCarthy's accusation of communist infiltration in the State Department and to the outbreak of the Korean War.[42]

The more skillful and lethal use of anti-Communism as a campaign tactic during the 1950 campaigns, was not limited to Republican campaign strategy and the ideological and legislative behavior of the GOP's right wing in Congress. The intensification of the issue of internal and international communism also contributed to dissensus within the Democratic party following the conviction of Alger Hiss, the fall of China to communism in 1949, and questions arising from Truman's conduct of the Korean War. Democratic Senator Patrick McCarran of Nevada, chairman of the Senate Judiciary Committee, greatly contributed to dissensus within his party on communism and foreign policy in general. A maverick, conservative Democrat, McCarran became the most outspoken Democratic supporter of McCarthy in the Senate.[43]

In 1949 McCarran joined Republican senators in accusing the State Department of "white washing" its role in the fall of China to Mao Zedong.[44] Following the 1950 elections, McCarran chaired hearings by a subcommittee of the Senate Judiciary Committee that mostly supported McCarthy's charges.[45] Furthermore, McCarran's internal security bill of 1950 and his 1952 legislation restricting immigration from communist-dominated nations became law despite Truman's vetoes and the vigorous opposition of liberal Democrats in Congress.[46]

The potential for anticommunism to further divide and weaken the Democratic party was more dramatically illustrated during the 1950 Democratic senatorial primaries in Florida and North Carolina. In both primaries, conservative

Democratic candidates combined red baiting and race baiting to defeat liberal incumbents. Two days after Senator Claude Pepper was defeated for nomination in Florida's May 2 Democratic primary, Harry Truman was asked by a reporter if Pepper's defeat was a defeat for the Fair Deal or his administration. He curtly replied, "No."[47] Less than a week after the November 7 election, though, Truman remarked to his staff that North Carolina Senator Frank P. Graham's defeat for renomination represented one of the "most serious losses for the administration."[48]

Symbolically, the primary defeats of both Pepper and Graham were serious losses for Truman's party leadership and Fair Deal liberalism. They were among the most liberal southern Democrats in the Senate in their support of most of Truman's social welfare and economic policy proposals. Pepper was one of the few senators to vigorously support compulsory national health insurance.[49] Graham, a former president of the University of North Carolina and a nationally recognized educational reformer, was a staunch supporter of federal aid to primary and secondary education despite the racial and religious conflicts surrounding this issue during the Eighty-first Congress.[50]

Unlike other southern Democrats in Congress who had fairly liberal legislative records on social welfare and economic issues, such as Lister Hill of Alabama and Olin D. Johnston of South Carolina, Graham and Pepper did not strive to regularly and actively balance their economic liberalism with an emphasis on white supremacy.[51] Graham and Pepper hoped that liberal educational and economic policies combined with voting rights for blacks in their states would gradually diminish racial discrimination and segregation without coercive federal civil rights laws.[52] They avoided discussing racial issues until they felt compelled to rebut the charges of their primary opponents.

Although Graham had been appointed to the Senate in 1949 while Pepper had served in the Senate for nearly fourteen years, Pepper's defeat was less surprising and less disappointing to Truman. Truman and Pepper had developed a tense, mutually suspicious relationship ever since Pepper's unwavering support for Henry Wallace's renomination as vice president in 1944.[53] A prominent ADA member, he was a die-hard advocate of drafting Dwight Eisenhower for the Democratic presidential nomination in 1948 and briefly offered himself to the Democratic delegates as a presidential candidate. He primarily alienated Truman through his criticism of Truman's early foreign policy toward the Soviet Union and his opposition to military aid to Greece and Turkey.[54]

Even without the exploitation of racial and anticommunist themes by George Smathers, Pepper's victorious opponent in the Democratic primary, the Florida senator had been a chronically controversial figure in his state's Democratic politics.[55] In his 1938 primary race, he needed Franklin D. Roosevelt's intervention to help him defeat two conservative opponents who were supported by Florida business interests angered by Pepper's support of minimum-wage legislation.[56] Despite an inept primary campaign in 1944 by his leading opponent, Ollie Edmunds, an obscure, inarticulate county judge, Pepper was renominated by a surprisingly narrow margin after the Florida AMA and business interests aggressively opposed him.[57]

Consequently, Smathers's use of a sophisticated smear campaign against Pepper facilitated, rather than entirely caused, the defeat of the already beleaguered incumbent and mostly ensured Smathers's victory by a wider margin.[58] Pepper was also slow to respond to Smathers's well-financed, vitriolic campaign because of his surprise at the ferocious and scurrilous nature of these attacks. George Smathers had been one of Pepper's campaign managers in 1938 and had been appointed as a U.S. attorney because of Pepper's use of senatorial courtesy. Regarding Smathers as a liberal protégé, Pepper supported Smathers's nomination and election as a U.S. representative in 1946.[59]

Branding his opponent as "Red Pepper," Smathers widely distributed copies of a booklet entitled *The Red Record of Senator Claude Pepper.* Besides linking Pepper to Fair Deal "socialism," the Smathers campaign accused the senator of being a leading member of a "red network."[60] Using superimposed photographs and headlines from the communist *Daily Worker,* Smathers's campaign literature claimed that Pepper admired Joseph Stalin and was supported by communist front organizations.[61] The AMA waged its own campaign against Pepper and made him one of its top priorities for defeat in 1950.[62]

According to a Florida newspaper editor interviewed by political analyst Samuel Lubell, the most decisive single factor in Smathers's victory was a pro-Pepper CIO effort to register blacks to vote.[63] Although black suffrage in Florida had been steadily growing since the end of World War II, photographs of lines of blacks being led to registration as voters by a "radical" organization were printed in anti-Pepper newspapers and Smathers's campaign publicity.[64] Such photographs aroused white fear and antagonism toward the prospect of a growing black voting bloc manipulated by communist front organizations and radical candidates.

Pepper made a quixotic effort to defend himself against the charges of Smathers and independent organizations that simply wanted to defeat him. He later estimated that Smathers outspent him by a ratio of ten to one.[65] Smathers defeated Pepper in the May 2 primary with 387,215 votes to 319,754, a margin of over 67,000 votes.[66]

Truman remained neutral during the Florida primary, although columnist Drew Pearson later claimed that DNC Chairman William M. Boyle Jr., secretly funneled $25,000 to the Pepper campaign.[67] But Truman's high regard for Frank P. Graham motivated him to indirectly intervene in the North Carolina Democratic primary. He quietly assisted Graham by directing more federal funds and pork barrel projects, especially a new naval facility for Wilmington, toward North Carolina and hoped that Graham's constituents would be impressed with his influence with the Truman administration.[68]

Truman's admiration of Graham and desire to keep him in the Senate were bolstered by the capable, courageous service that Frank P. Graham had provided Truman as one of only two southern members of the President's Committee on Civil Rights and as a special diplomat in Indonesia.[69] Furthermore, Charles S. Murphy, Truman's special counsel and a native of North Carolina, and Jonathan Daniels, the president's first press secretary and now a North Carolina newspaper publisher, were enthusiastic supporters of Graham.[70]

More importantly, Graham was actively supported by Governor W. Kerr Scott, who had appointed him to fill a vacant Senate seat in 1949. Scott was a pro-Truman southern liberal who emphasized educational reforms and road building in his policies and whose coalition included black voters.[71] With the help of Daniels's intervention, he persuaded the reluctant Graham to accept the appointment.

Although he was widely respected in North Carolina for his expansion of the state university system and its role in public health, Graham had never campaigned for elective office and had no existing, statewide organization. Also, Graham's political activism and involvement in a variety of social reform activities led him to join or support a number of organizations, some of which, like the American Civil Liberties Union and the Southern Council on Human Welfare, were infiltrated by American Communists.[72] Finally, in appointing Graham to the Senate and assuming that the educator could easily be nominated and elected to a full term in 1950, Scott had underestimated the extent to which Graham's image among more conservative Democrats had been damaged by his service on Truman's civil rights committee and a recently publicized revelation that Graham had been initially denied security clearance by the Atomic Energy Commission because of his record of leftist associations.[73]

With the help of Scott's political organization, Daniels's constant editorial support, and a CIO-sponsored voter mobilization effort, Graham received a plurality of the votes, 49.1 percent, in the May 27 primary. His closest rival, Willis Smith, received 40.5 percent.[74] Since Graham did not receive a majority of the votes, he and Smith ran against each other in a runoff primary on June 24, 1950.

Despite his nearly 9 percent margin of victory over Smith in the first primary, Graham was already losing ground as he defended himself against Smith's claims that he supported a compulsory FEPC. Graham repeatedly responded that he opposed a compulsory FEPC and wrote a minority report while on Truman's civil rights committee to criticize its proposed methods of enforcement, but he failed to discredit the growing public perception that he was a threat to racial segregation and white supremacy.[75] In early June, the Supreme Court made three decisions against racial segregation that heightened white fears about coerced racial integration and attracted more attention to Smith's charges.[76]

Like Smathers's campaign, Smith's attributed Graham's alleged support of federally enforced race mixing to his "radical" political associations.[77] Smith's supporters, also like Smathers's, used superimposed photographs. They showed Graham's wife apparently dancing with a black soldier and lounging blacks watching whites work in fields.[78] Highly publicized CIO efforts to organize both black and white textile-mill workers behind Graham had the effect of driving more white mill workers to the Smith campaign.[79]

To a lesser degree, Smith's frequent charges that Graham supported Fair Deal "socialism" through the Brannan Plan and compulsory national health insurance, which Graham repeatedly denied, also played a role.[80] But it was Smith's effective combination of race baiting and red baiting that alienated white laborers and lower-income farmers from Graham's campaign and intimidated many of Graham's campaign volunteers.[81] With such rapid momentum behind his campaign and Graham reeling from his charges, Willis Smith won the runoff primary with 51.8 percent of the votes to Graham's 48.2 percent. Graham received more than forty thousand fewer votes than he had in the first primary just a month before.[82]

In the North Carolina and Florida primaries, conservative Democratic candidates had used red baiting as a means of intensifying their major tactic—that is, arousing the racial fears of white voters in order to defeat liberal incumbents. In California's 1950 Senate campaign, both Democratic and Republican candidates used red baiting alone to defeat an already vulnerable, inept liberal Democratic candidate in a race for an open seat. Senator Sheridan Downey of California, a conservative Democrat with close ties to his state's oil industry, withdrew from his campaign for renomination in April 1950, citing ill health.[83]

Downey had chafed under the accusations of U.S. Representative Helen Gahagan Douglas, his leading opponent for the Democratic senatorial nomination, that he was a "do nothing" senator and a pawn of business interests, especially the oil industry, because of his opposition to federal control of tidelands oil, favored by Truman.[84] Downey publicly accused Douglas of using "vicious and unethical propaganda" against him.[85] In a radio address broadcast throughout California, Downey asserted that Douglas's softness toward, and possible conspiracy with, communists was evident in her voting with Vito Marcantonio, New York's controversial left-wing congressman, to deny appropriations to the House Un-American Activities Committee (HUAC).[86]

Endorsed by Downey, Manchester Boddy, publisher of the *Los Angeles Daily News,* entered the campaign as Douglas's chief Democratic rival. Boddy frequently linked Douglas to Marcantonio and claimed that she belonged to "a small subversive clique of red-hots" who were conspiring to infiltrate and then control the California Democratic party.[87] Perhaps Boddy's most damaging tactic against Douglas was to label her as "the pink lady."[88]

California Congressman Richard M. Nixon, the presumptive Republican senatorial nominee, followed the advice of his campaign managers and refrained from red baiting Douglas until after the June 6 primary. The Nixon campaign did not want to interrupt Boddy's barrage against Douglas and also wanted to ensure that the liberal, controversial Douglas, not Boddy, would be the Democratic nominee for the general election.[89] Douglas, strongly supported by CIO unions, enjoyed statewide name recognition strengthened by her and her husband's acting careers. She defeated Boddy by a margin of over 350,000 votes in the primary.

Since Democrats enjoyed an advantage in voter registration in California, Nixon realized that he needed to attract a significant number of Democratic votes in order to defeat Douglas. While Downey and Boddy denounced Douglas for voting against appropriations for HUAC and aid to Greece and Turkey and questioned her patriotism, the Nixon campaign organized an elaborate network of Democrats for Nixon clubs throughout California for mobilizing Democratic voters in November.[90] Nixon also benefited from ample campaign funds sent to him by Downey's supporters in the oil industry, who feared Douglas's support for federal control of tidelands oil. According to the memoirs of Nixon and Thomas P. "Tip" O'Neill Jr., Democratic tycoon Joseph Kennedy and his son, Massachusetts Congressman John F. Kennedy, respectively contributed $150,000 and $1,000 to Nixon's campaign.[91] Although he was still a supporter of the Taft-Hartley Act, Nixon used moderate rhetoric on labor relations and gained the endorsement of the Teamsters Union.[92] While he repeatedly criticized the Fair Deal and Douglas's support of it as socialism, Nixon was careful not to attack popular New Deal programs, such as Social Security and minimum-wage laws.

Building upon Manchester Boddy's characterization of Douglas as "the pink lady," the Nixon campaign distributed a "pink sheet" showing that Douglas and Marcantonio voted the same on 354 legislative issues, especially those pertaining to foreign policy and HUAC.[93] A prominent supporter of the anticommunist Nationalist Chinese and a harsh critic of Truman for "losing" China to communism, Nixon benefited politically from the aggressive Chinese attack against American troops in Korea in late October. He never directly and explicitly accused Douglas of treason but charged her with supporting the Truman administration's "appeasement" of communism in Asia and its efforts to cover up evidence of communist infiltration in general.[94] This latter charge was strengthened by the conviction of Alger Hiss for perjury, which motivated Nixon to rhetorically associate Douglas with Hiss.[95]

Douglas's responses to Nixon's charges were often belated, clumsy, and ineffective. Claiming that her policy behavior addressed the threat of domestic and international communism better than Nixon's, Douglas charged that Nixon voted with Vito Marcantonio to deny aid to South Korea and to reduce appropriations for the Marshall Plan.[96] Nixon adroitly responded that he only voted against the initial bill for Korean aid because, unlike the later, compromise bill that he supported, it did not include aid to the Nationalist Chinese. The Republican nominee likewise claimed that he voted for a one-year, not a two-year, appropriation for European aid, not a reduction in total aid under the Marshall Plan.[97]

Such reckless, duplicitous charges and an attempt to mimic red baiting tactics simply weakened Douglas's effort to portray herself as the victim of an unprincipled smear campaign.[98] Although Harry Truman personally disliked Douglas, once commenting to his aides that she "was one of the worst nuisances," he sent Vice President Alben W. Barkley several cabinet members to California to campaign for Douglas.[99] Despite her opposition to military and economic aid for Greece and Turkey, Truman praised Douglas's foreign policy record at a press conference held five days before the election. Truman stated that, as a member of the House Foreign Affairs Committee, Douglas "is wholeheartedly in accord with the President's foreign policy, which is more than can be said for most California papers."[100] In a campaign address that was broadcast three days before the election, Truman denounced red-baiting Republican candidates such as Nixon for having "maliciously and falsely made charges of disloyalty against some of our finest and ablest public servants—in Congress and in the executive branch."[101]

Nixon trounced Douglas, receiving 59.2 percent of the votes and nearly seven hundred thousand more votes than Douglas.[102] Nixon's anti-Communist strategy against the congresswoman was not the only or even the major factor for her defeat. Like Claude Pepper, Douglas had a liberal record on economic policies that aroused the opposition of a variety of business and agricultural interests and the AMA. Democrats Sheridan Downey and Manchester Boddy

had previously established the rhetorical foundation for Nixon's graphic portrayal of her as soft on communism. With such bitter Democratic dissensus
producing a battered senatorial nominee already discredited from the perspective of many Democratic voters, Nixon merely exploited the situation to gain a
wider margin of victory. Shortly after the election, Nixon stated in a magazine
interview that he received at least 750,000 Democratic votes.[103]

Among all of the 1950 Senate races, the defeat of Democratic Senator Millard
E. Tydings of Maryland was the most significant and surprising. It was the campaign that involved the greatest degree of personal intervention by Senator Jo-
seph McCarthy, who was determined to ensure Tydings's defeat by Republican
John M. Butler. As chairman of a subcommittee of the Senate Foreign Relations
Committee that investigated McCarthy's charges of communists in the State
Department, Tydings dismissed McCarthy's charges as reckless and lacking
evidence.[104] Perceiving Tydings as a dangerous obstacle to his crusade and career, McCarthy provided Butler with a campaign staff and strategy to smear
Tydings as soft on communism and attempting a cover up of Communist infiltration in American foreign policy. Moreover, McCarthy waged a speaking campaign against Tydings throughout Maryland.[105]

Like Helen Gahagan Douglas, Tydings became more vulnerable to Republican red baiting because of a bitterly divisive Democratic primary in which his
Democratic opponents accused him of appeasing and even promoting communism. Endorsed by AFL and CIO unions, former Democratic Congressman John
Meyer accused Tydings of a "complete white wash" of McCarthy's investigation.[106] More severely, Democratic senatorial candidate Hugh M. Monaghan II
equated Tydings's dismissal of McCarthy's accusations of communist infiltration with a "green light to Stalin's agents in this country to gnaw at the founda-
tions of our national security."[107]

With the Maryland Democratic party already splintered by a fractious gubernatorial primary, Tydings mostly ignored these Democratic attacks and promoted his record of constituency service and legislative accomplishments during
his four terms in the Senate. Tydings received 66 percent of the votes in the
primary of September 18.[108] But Monaghan refused to endorse Tydings after the
primary, and Tydings wasted valuable time and attention trying to dissuade
George Mahoney, who narrowly lost the Democratic nomination for governor,
from suing for a recount.[109]

Initially, it appeared that Tydings's legislative record and status as a member of the bipartisan conservative coalition in the Senate would make him im-
mune to red baiting. During the Roosevelt administration, Tydings was one of
the most outspoken and persistent Democratic opponents of New Deal legisla-

tion.[110] In particular, his opposition to the Wagner Act of 1935, Social Security Act of 1935, and such early civil rights proposals as antilynching legislation and a permanent FEPC earned him the animosity of organized labor, blacks, and liberal Democrats in Maryland.[111] Roosevelt tried but failed to defeat Tydings's renomination in 1938.[112]

During Truman's presidency, Tydings continued to oppose liberal domestic policy legislation and cooperated with the Republican-controlled Eightieth Congress on such measures as tax and spending cuts and passage of the Taft-Hartley Act. Truman, though, valued Tydings's judgment on foreign and defense policy, especially after Tydings became chairman of the Senate Armed Services Committee.[113] Tydings, likewise, generally supported Truman on foreign and defense policy issues, including aid to Greece and Turkey, NATO, the Marshall Plan, and the National Security Act.[114] Consequently, Tydings's conservatism on domestic policy and internationalism on foreign policy made him seem impervious from an effective smear campaign based on complicity with communism.

Politically, Tydings had chronically been in a tenuous position within the Maryland Democratic party. He avoided allying himself with any machine or party organization. He built his own statewide personal following through patronage jobs and favors to business interests, such as defense contracts.[115] He rarely coalesced with the rest of Maryland's Democratic congressional delegation, and his conservatism on economic and civil rights issues alienated the growing number of blacks, Catholics, and union members among Maryland Democrats. Most leading Democratic politicians, such as Baltimore Mayor Thomas J. D'Allesandro and Senator Herbert R. O'Conor, did not vigorously defend Tydings until late in the campaign, when the momentum of the Republican smear campaign was irreversible.[116]

John M. Butler's campaign against Tydings was the most sophisticated smear campaign to employ red baiting in 1950. It used composite photography to produce widely distributed photos of Tydings apparently listening attentively to American Communist party leader Earl Browder.[117] Upon the advice of the publisher of the *Washington Times-Herald,* which editorially supported Butler, Butler hired a Chicago public relations executive, Jon M. Jonkel, to manage his campaign. Senator Joseph McCarthy and his staff provided material from the reports of Tydings's subcommittee, campaign funds, campaign literature, and voter mobilization assistance. Maryland's proximity to Washington, D.C., enabled McCarthy to regularly give speeches and supervise Butler's campaign.[118] Besides his own vigorous campaigning, using McCarthy-inspired red baiting against Tydings, Butler was also assisted by conservative radio commentator Fulton Lewis Jr. His broadcasts repeated charges that Tydings was helping the Truman administration in covering up evidence of communist influence in American foreign policy.[119]

Confident of reelection, Tydings did not begin to actively and regularly refute these charges of ineptitude toward, and even collaboration with, communism until late October. In a radio broadcast denouncing the accusations of Fulton Lewis Jr., Tydings sounded more condescending than sincere.[120] Throughout the remainder of his general election campaign, Tydings futilely defended himself against Butler's smear campaign while the Republicans focused on mobilizing typically Democratic black, Catholic, and conservative rural voters behind Butler.[121] In this mostly Democratic border state, Butler defeated Tydings with 53 percent of the votes and a margin of 43,111 votes.[122]

Following this defeat, Tydings asked the Senate's committee on Rules and Administration to have its subcommittee on privileges and elections to investigate and hold hearings on Butler's campaign, especially on alleged illegal campaign funds, fraudulent campaign literature, and illegal intervention from outside of Maryland.[123] At the end of its investigation in 1951, the subcommittee agreed with most of Tydings's charges. The subcommittee's report only blamed Senator Butler for not exercising greater control over technically independent organizations and individuals who smeared Tydings and violated Maryland campaign laws.[124] The subcommittee reprimanded Butler and McCarthy, but Butler kept his seat and neither one was formally censured or punished by the Senate.[125]

Did Truman exercise any party leadership during the 1950 midterm elections, especially against red baiting employed by both Democratic and Republican candidates? Before American entry into the Korean War, Truman concerned himself with the nomination of a Democratic senatorial candidate in Missouri. One of Missouri's two Republican senators, Forrest C. Donnell, was among the most strident Republican critics of Truman's policies. The president was determined that a strong Democratic candidate be nominated who could unite the feuding Missouri Democratic party and defeat Donnell.

After conferring, Democratic Governor Forrest Smith and the president agreed to publicly favor state Senator Emery W. Allison for the nomination and to dissuade attorney general J.E. Taylor from entering the primary.[126] Partially because of Smith's equivocation, Thomas Hennings Jr., entered the primary.[127] Truman wrote a letter to Smith chastising the governor. "I sincerely hope that you will find a way to get Hennings out of this race, so that the Governor of Missouri and the President of the United States can get behind a man who will support the policies of the Democratic Party in the Senate."[128] Hennings defeated first Allison and then Forrest Donnell, the only incumbent Republican senator to lose his reelection bid in 1950. Fortunately for Truman, Hennings then distinguished himself as a persistent opponent and critic of Senator Joseph McCarthy.[129]

During his press conference of February 16, 1950, Truman told reporters that he would conduct a whistle-stop campaign. His offer was warmly received by several Democratic senators seeking reelection.[130] On that night, Truman addressed a Jefferson-Jackson Day dinner. He dismissed Republican charges of socialism against the Fair Deal. He confidently concluded that if the Democratic party presented "its program to the people so plainly that it cannot be misunderstood," then "the people will again voice their approval of the principles which lead to increased prosperity, welfare, and freedom" at home and abroad.[131]

Before the outbreak of the Korean War in late June, Truman and his White House staff were confident that the Democrats could minimize the number of congressional seats that the president's party typically loses in a midterm election, especially since the brief recession of 1949 had ended. After analyzing several public opinion polls and recent voting behavior, political statistician Louis Bean concluded that "no major depression will develop before November and that no major upheavals in international affairs will create regional and nationality cleavages in the United States . . . the 1950 mid-term battle opens with public opinion definitely favorable to the Democrats, with a majority believing that the Democrats will win."[132] Truman, therefore, planned a whistle-stop speaking tour of midwestern and western states in which he would stress the maintenance of prosperity through economic liberalism and of peace through an active leading American role in international affairs.[133]

White House aide Ken Hechler and DNC research director Philip Dreyer were primarily responsible for funding research for Truman's whistle-stop speeches. Hechler had been dismayed that the DNC did not continue its highly successful Research Division after the 1948 election. He believed that the DNC should have a full-time, multimember Research Division for Truman's 1950 whistle-stop campaign. In a 1950 journal entry, Hechler expressed his exasperation with DNC Chairman Boyle's refusal to create such a division. "I spent the morning at the Democratic National Committee, pawing through their files on the Republican Party and Republican campaigns. I am shocked at the skimpy and poorly organized material they have on the Republican party. . . . Are we going to have to do all this at the White House, in addition to other duties?"[134]

Most of the research and speech-writing efforts for Truman's 1950 whistle-stop campaign were performed by George Elsey on the president's train and Hechler and Dreyer, who usually communicated to Elsey through telegraph, in

Washington, D.C.[135] As in the 1948 train trip, Truman's staff provided him with facts peculiar to each whistle-stop community so that he could tailor each speech to each community within the broader context of his administration's policies on hydroelectric power, soil reclamation, farm programs, international trade, and foreign policy.[136] Toward the end of his whistle stop tour, Truman addressed a Democratic dinner in Chicago. In contrast to his class conflict themes and tone in 1948, Truman defended his administration's policies in consensual, unifying terms: "The Democratic Party knows that the prosperity of all groups within the country is interwoven: the prosperity of business is linked with the prosperity of the white collar workers and farmers, and industrial workers. And we believe that the Government must work with all these groups and plan for the future."[137]

During the 1950 campaign, the DNC's Publicity Division generally devoted its efforts to providing fact-filled pamphlets to substantiate the president's consensus-building rhetorical strategy. On economic and social welfare issues, the DNC's Publicity Division, as it did during the 1946 and 1948 campaigns, portrayed the Republican party as backward-looking, reactionary and subservient to big business. In one pamphlet, the DNC dismissed the Republican tactic of labeling all "progressive' legislation as "socialism." It stated, "Nearly every attempt to curb a selfish interest in order to present the freedom of all the people has been attacked as an alien idea or an attempt by 'little men' to change our form of government."[138]

Furthermore, Jack Redding, the DNC's publicity director, sought to maximize the amount of free air time that Democratic members of Congress and administration officials received through radio and television interviews to explain, defend, and promote administration policies.[139] On January 5, 1951, Charles Van Devander, Redding's successor, reported to the White House that Democratic officials appeared on 394 national radio and television programs in 1950. If the DNC had purchased the same amount of air time, it would have cost $2.5 million.[140]

The beginning of the Korean War in late June, however, abruptly halted any further, significant participation by Harry Truman in the 1950 elections. Truman's quick deployment of American ground troops eventually increased, rather than mitigated, Republican criticism of Truman's foreign policy toward communist expansion as weak, incompetent, and possibly influenced by a communist conspiracy in the State Department.[141] Open disputes between Secretary of State Dean Acheson and Secretary of Defense Louis Johnson over American policies in Korea combined with bipartisan congressional criticism of Johnson's prior cuts in defense spending induced Truman to force Johnson to resign in September.[142]

Truman's replacement of Johnson with the highly respected George C. Marshall combined with the successful American invasion of Inchon on September 15, 1950, did little to improve the status of Truman and his party in public opinion polls as election day neared.[143] Public frustration and uncertainty with Truman's foreign policy made red baiting rhetoric, used by both Republican and Democratic candidates, more credible while the continuing Senate investigation of organized crime made the electorate more likely to express its dissatisfaction by voting Republican.[144] The publicity strategy of DNC headquarters then concentrated on trying to persuasively explain the president's conduct of the Korean War, especially after China's military intervention two weeks before the elections.[145] In his first and last major campaign speech since his spring-whistle stop tour, Truman delivered a nationally broadcast speech on November 4, 1950. After defending the war effort in Korea, Truman asserted his confident belief "that the rank and file of the Republican Party must be ashamed of the reckless tactics of some of their leaders, and I believe they will repudiate them at the polls."[146]

Any hope that Truman may have had that a significant number of disaffected Republican voters would vote Democratic was squelched by the congressional elections. The Democrats lost twenty-eight House seats and five Senate seats.[147] The Democratic majority in the Senate fell to a margin of two seats. Defeated incumbents included Majority Leader Scott Lucas of Illinois and Majority Whip Francis Myers.[148] Although Truman was often frustrated by Lucas's cautious centrism and ineffective leadership skills, Lucas was replaced by Ernest McFarland of Arizona, an even more cautious and ineffective majority leader.[149] As in the 1946 midterm elections, the congressional Democrats most likely to be defeated for reelection, especially in the House, were nonsouthern liberals.[150]

The defeat of Senator Elbert Thomas of Utah was especially discouraging, given the liberal policy goals that Truman hoped to instill in the Democratic party.[151] Truman respected Thomas for his staunch liberalism in supporting and promoting controversial Fair Deal proposals, especially national health insurance and repeal of the Taft-Hartley Act.[152] In addition to his economic liberalism, Thomas was also a vocal critic of HUAC and cosponsored a resolution, directed at McCarthy, to end Senate authority over investigations of subversion.[153] His victorious Republican opponent, Wallace Bennett, smeared Thomas as the "darling of several un-American organizations" and blanketed Utah with literature falsely accusing Thomas of communist associations.[154]

Besides the defeats of prominent liberal Democrats such as Elbert Thomas and Claude Pepper, the DNC and organized labor were especially embarrassed by Republican Senator Robert A. Taft's margin of victory in his reelection bid.

With the DNC providing research assistance and AFL and CIO unions devoting substantial campaign funds, publicity, and voter mobilization drives of union members to the Democratic campaign, Taft defeated Joseph T. Ferguson, the Democratic senatorial nominee, with 57.5 percent of the votes.[155] Taft's wide margin was attributed to his support from normally Democratic Catholics, Jews, and union members who resented organized labor's aggressive promotion of Ferguson.[156]

In his postelection analysis, Truman wrote to a Missouri Democrat that he regretted "that our national labor leaders used very poor judgment in their approach to the campaign in Ohio, Illinois, and Indiana."[157] After expressing his concern about the McCarthyistic smear tactics used in several campaigns, Truman concluded his letter by asking his fellow Missourian to "take a hand in preventing a revival of hysteria which might result in a Ku Klux Klan worse than the one we were visited with in 1922."[158]

With no hope of achieving passage of major Fair Deal legislation during the Eighty-second Congress, Truman focused on the conduct of his foreign policy and tried to mollify the anticommunist hysteria fueled by McCarthy. Democratic dissensus deepened as congressional Democrats from a diverse range of ideological hues criticized his foreign policy and distanced themselves from him during the investigations of bureaucratic corruption and his steady decline in public approval ratings.[159] Having vowed to himself in 1950 that he would not seek reelection in 1952, Harry Truman faced a formidable task as a party leader. He had to assure the nomination of a Democratic presidential candidate who could unite and energize a fragmented, dispirited Democratic party and win the 1952 presidential election while assuring the continuation of New Deal–Fair Deal liberalism as its ideological and programmatic identity in national politics and public policy.

THE MESS IN WASHINGTON

Within Congress and the media, "the mess in Washington" was associated with a pattern of favoritism, cronyism, influence peddling, and the use of governmental and DNC positions and influence to benefit private, and sometimes criminal, interests.[160] Although Harry Truman was never personally implicated in any of the apparent or actual scandals detailed by congressional investigations and news coverage, he was widely perceived as being, at best, sluggish and ineffective in addressing this ethical quagmire or being, at worst, consciously obstructionistic toward any investigations and prosecutions of illegal behavior within his administration.[161] Even some of Truman's harshest critics conceded that the "mess in Washington" partially resulted from the sharp growth in such federal activities as income tax collection, subsidies to business, and contractual relationships.[162]

This systemic perception by both Democratic and Republican members of Congress was evident in a Senate investigation of the Reconstruction Finance Corporation (RFC) that was chaired by Democratic Senator J. William Fulbright of Arkansas from 1950 to 1951. Two other prominent members of this subcommittee of the Senate Banking and Currency Committee were Democratic Senator Paul H. Douglas of Illinois and Republican Senator Charles W. Tobey of New Hampshire. Although Fulbright was a vocal supporter of Truman's controversial removal of Gen. Douglas MacArthur from his command in Korea in 1951, Fulbright and Truman had had a distant, strained relationship ever since he had suggested that Truman resign from the presidency.[163] Sensing that Truman regarded both Fulbright and himself as "overeducated s.o.b.'s," Douglas believed that Truman's hostility and petty vindictiveness toward him began when the ADA liberals supported Dwight Eisenhower for president at the 1948 Democratic national convention.[164] He concluded that Truman had tried to harass and intimidate him during this subcommittee's proceedings by having the RFC investigate his previous communications with this agency and then having the Bureau of Internal Revenue (BIR) audit his income tax returns.[165]

Besides his affiliation with the opposition party, Tobey had indulged in the most stridently moralistic rhetoric when he served on the Kefauver committee and denounced the collusion between Democratic politicians and gangsters. As a member of the Senate Naval Affairs Committee in 1946, Tobey enraged Truman by questioning the ethics of Edwin Pauley and preventing his appointment as undersecretary of the navy. Tobey had also chaired the Senate Banking and Currency Committee during the Eightieth Congress and focused on an investigation of the RFC's loan policies toward the Baltimore and Ohio Railroad.[166] Truman was already suspicious of the motives, investigatory practices, and policy recommendations of this bipartisan trio.[167]

Although it was not abolished until the Eisenhower administration, the policy purpose, cost effectiveness, and even the political ethics of the RFC had been increasingly scrutinized by Congress since the last year of the Roosevelt administration. Created by the Hoover administration in 1932, the RFC's original purpose was to serve as a temporary agency that would grant low-interest loans to such businesses as banks, railroads, and insurance companies in order to help them survive the most severe period of the Great Depression. During World War II, the RFC expanded its bureaucracy and variety of activities in order to help finance the war effort, especially by buying and storing such military supplies as synthetic rubber and metals.[168] The prestige and power of the RFC were further enhanced by the fact that its director from 1932 to 1945 was Jesse H. Jones, a conservative Texas banker who generally enjoyed wide bipartisan respect in Congress.[169]

Following the departure of Jones, the authority over the RFC devolved to a less experienced, multimember board of directors. Despite the end of the Great Depression and World War II, the RFC retained its vast accumulation of funds, personnel, and diversity of lending and subsidy activities. It now used its authority to grant attractive, low-interest loans to such businesses as resort hotels, night clubs, and gambling casinos.[170] Such RFC activities and its more decentralized administrative structure made this agency more susceptible to fiscal waste, political favoritism, and even illegal activities.

The Fulbright subcommittee's hearings were often tedious and complex. They extensively questioned RFC employees and board members and the recipients of RFC loans about the RFC's decision-making processes and the wisdom of certain RFC loans.[171] The subcommittee questioned Donald Dawson, the White House personnel director and former RFC director, about whether he had improperly accepted a free room at the Saxony Hotel in Florida, which had applied for and later received an RFC loan.[172] Dawson admitted that he had accepted a free hotel room but did not know that it was from an applicant for an RFC loan and did not intervene on its behalf. The subcommittee eventually conceded that it had no conclusive evidence against Dawson and thanked him for his testimony.[173] The only high-level Truman associate to resign apparently because of this Senate investigation was William M. Boyle Jr. The Fulbright subcommittee and another Senate subcommittee investigated the possibility that Boyle helped the American Lithofold Corporation, a former client of his law firm, to receive an RFC loan in exchange for a fee.[174] Boyle resigned as DNC chairman shortly after the second subcommittee's hearings.[175]

For the purposes of media dramatization and attracting public attention, the most significant aspect of the Fulbright subcommittee's investigation of the RFC was the evidence of influence peddling and conflicts of interest by E. Merl Young. Young was an RFC examiner who was suspected of obtaining an RFC loan for the Instrom Corporation in exchange for a well-paying job with this company.[176] A Missourian and former Senate aide to Truman, Young gave his wife Lauretta, a White House stenographer, a mink coat worth nearly $10,000. It was a gift from Samuel I. Rosenbaum, an attorney for a company that had received an RFC loan.[177]

Previously, a 1949 Senate investigation of "five percenters"—that is, lobbyists who used their actual or apparent political influence to secure federal contracts or favorable bureaucratic treatment for their business clients—revealed that businessmen Harry Hoffman and David Bennett had given deep freezers to Harry Vaughan, Truman's military aide and close friend, and several other Truman administration members. Bennett was a business associate of John Maragon, a former aide to Vaughan and now a prominent "five percenter."[178] Truman staunchly and publicly defended Vaughan and rejected Vaughan's offer to resign.[179]

The mink coat and deep freezers were powerful, memorable symbols for the general public, media, and Republicans. The Republicans, developed a strategy for the 1952 presidential campaign that emphasized these gifts as examples of Democratic corruption. Truman's staunch, assertive defense of Vaughan and Dawson were unable to discredit the hardening, increasingly irreversible impression that a "Missouri Gang" indulged in favoritism, cronyism, and influence peddling, just as an "Ohio Gang" had dominated the scandal-ridden administration of Warren G. Harding.[180] Even liberals who had praised Truman's combative liberalism now began to reconsider their earlier assumptions that the transition from Roosevelt to Truman meant a transition from New Deal idealism to self-serving cronyism and influence peddling in the executive branch.[181]

Appearing to be oblivious and obstinate toward the concerns of liberal Democrats in Congress that the appearance of pervasive unethical behavior in his administration was damaging the party's public image, Truman persisted in his assumption that these Senate investigations were the results of bipartisan personal attacks on him and a strategic effort by the Republican party and Republican-owned newspapers and magazines to discredit his administration for the 1952 campaign.[182] Truman's skepticism of the sincerity of the Fulbright subcommittee's investigation was strengthened by its interim report's conclusion.[183] Entitled *Favoritism and Influence,* this report suggested that there was an appearance of unethical conflicts of interest by some current and former administration officials but did not accuse anyone of criminal behavior.[184] Truman referred to this report as "asinine" at a press conference.[185] Nevertheless, he eventually adopted its recommendation that he submit a reorganization bill to Congress that would eliminate the RFC board and create a single administrator.[186]

Truman responded to House subcommittee investigations of the Bureau of Internal Revenue (BIR) and the tax division of the Department of Justice more quickly and vigorously in his proposed reform and reorganization.[187] This response was prompted by the severity of charges that some BIR collectors clearly engaged in unethical and even criminal behavior in granting favorable treatment to gamblers being investigated for income tax violations and by the fact that J. Howard McGrath, his attorney general and former DNC chairman, was suspected of preventing a thorough investigation of favoritism by the tax division.[188] The House investigation of the BIR led to either the forced resignations or criminal convictions of BIR officials on charges that included tax evasion, accepting bribes for "fixing" tax delinquencies, embezzling, and backdating tax receipts.[189]

The House investigation of the tax division of the Justice Department focused on the behavior of Theron Lamar Caudle, the head of this division since 1947. It revealed that Caudle had accepted favors from tax attorneys and businessmen under investigation for tax violations in the form of mink coats, free airplane trips to Florida, a sales commission, and a new car.[190] Despite the evidence that Caudle apparently tried to obstruct or delay federal prosecution of some of these people, McGrath defended Caudle. In 1956 Caudle and Matthew J. Connelly, Truman's former appointments secretary, were convicted and subsequently imprisoned on charges of conspiring to defraud the federal government by trying to "fix" the tax case of Irving Sachs, a shoe manufacturer from St. Louis.[191] At least in Connelly's case, Truman and his White House staff were convinced that this prosecution by the Eisenhower administration was simply a continued Republican effort to discredit the Democratic administration.[192]

Compared to Truman's initial reactions to the Senate investigations of the RFC and the "five percenters," the response of Truman, his White House staff, and DNC headquarters to the congressional hearings on the BIR and Justice Department was quicker, more sophisticated, and multifaceted.[193] Shortly after replacing William M. Boyle Jr., as DNC chairman, Frank E. McKinney announced that he would not accept a salary from the DNC, would ensure that DNC staff personnel did not peddle influence with federal agencies to lobbyists, would reduce the patronage functions of the DNC chairman, and would strengthen the research and publicity activities of DNC headquarters.[194] In particular, McKinney, under pressure from the White House staff, began to fund, staff, and activate a full-time DNC Research Division before the 1952 campaign in order to counteract media stories and RNC publicity emphasizing the corruption investigations.[195]

Truman's rhetorical and legislative strategy was also more pro-active and constructive.[196] Especially after the convictions of several BIR officials, Truman began to concede that there were some dishonest federal officials but emphasized that corruption was personal, not partisan, and was limited to relatively few appointees.[197] Sounding more like a progressive reformer than a defensive party regular, Truman also emphasized his formulation of legislation, recommended by McKinney, to reorganize the BIR in late 1951 and its submission to

Congress in early 1952.[198] Truman's reorganization bill abolished the patronage system in the BIR so that the commissioner of internal revenue was the only appointed official. All other officials and employees would be civil servants. This reformed agency would be "alert to the practices of the influence peddlers and fixers" and "thoroughly inspected and controlled from top to bottom to assure complete integrity and fidelity in its operations."[199] By March 1952 both houses of Congress passed Truman's legislation reforming the BIR.[200]

In both substantive reforms and political damage control, Truman's legislative success with the reorganization of the BIR was the clearest and most effective result of his reformist impulse.[201] On April 10, 1952, shortly after its passage, Truman submitted three bills to Congress that would end the political appointments of postmasters, customs officials, and U.S. marshals and classify these positions under civil service.[202] Congress rejected all three proposals, even though the Hoover Commission had previously recommended the Post Office reform.[203]

In the wake of the BIR plan's legislative success, the congressional defeats of these three proposals were not surprising. Republicans and conservative Democratic opposition to Truman in general intensified on April 8, 1952, when the president announced his controversial seizure of steel mills.[204] Also, the BIR plan had passed the Senate very narrowly, despite the vigorous rhetorical and lobbying efforts of three liberal Democratic senators and the overwhelming public support of Truman's BIR plan that was recorded by Gallup polls.[205] Furthermore, the Post Office, Customs Service, and U.S. Marshals Service, unlike the BIR, had not experienced dramatic, highly publicized scandals exposed by congressional investigations. Finally, while the patronage system in the BIR had become politically intolerable because of the severity of the tax-fixing scandals, most members of Congress wanted to preserve these other positions as political appointments.[206]

The competence and even the sincerity of Truman's reform efforts were again questioned regarding his response to the congressional investigation of the Justice Department's tax division.[207] In addressing allegations that Theron Lamar Caudle and other Justice Department officials had engaged in tax fixing and interference with federal cases on behalf of favored "clients," Truman was more equivocal and hesitant than he had been with the BIR. This more cautious, vacillating approach was partially influenced by a greater conflict between Truman's regular and reformer value systems since this issue involved J. Howard McGrath, his attorney general and former DNC chairman.

By late 1951, the White House staff, and especially special counsel Charles S. Murphy, were pressuring Truman to remove McGrath as attorney general. McGrath indicated that he wanted to remain in office, so Truman agreed to let him continue as attorney general.[208] Truman's ardent personal and partisan loyalty to McGrath impelled him to assume this risk. The president then assumed a greater risk by giving McGrath the discretion to appoint a private attorney to investigate the Justice Department and make any necessary recommendations for reform.

McGrath, later claiming that he obtained Truman's approval first, appointed Newbold Morris as a special assistant for this purpose on February 1, 1952.[209] Morris, a Republican lawyer from New York City prominent in civic affairs, soon suspected that McGrath did not want a serious, independent, thorough investigation.[210] But Morris believed that Truman sincerely wanted a vigorous investigation and would provide cooperation and support for his efforts.[211]

Morris's investigation soon foundered. This inquiry was hobbled by Congress's refusal to grant Morris the authority to grant immunity to key witnesses, Morris's own indecisive leadership and controversial public statements, and the growing friction between him and McGrath.[212] Public, media, and congressional perception of Morris's investigation as being inept and possibly a whitewash by McGrath was strengthened when McGrath told a House subcommittee investigating the Justice Department that he would not require his department's employees to fill out a questionnaire on personal finances that Morris had created and distributed.[213] McGrath had concluded that Morris was a "publicity seeker" who had to be fired.[214]

Special counsel Charles S. Murphy and White House press secretary Joseph Short regarded McGrath as more culpable and as a greater liability to the administration.[215] Despite McGrath's 1955 statement that he had received Truman's approval before he fired Morris on April 3, 1952, Truman told the press on that same day that he had recently received McGrath's voluntary resignation and did not know about McGrath's removal of Morris beforehand. Throughout this press conference, Truman either refused to answer questions about Morris's removal and McGrath's allegedly voluntary resignation or provided no revealing details.[216] The president tried to focus this press conference on his announcement of McGrath's successor, federal district Judge James P. McGranery. By August 1952, McGranery announced that his department had been adequately investigated and that progress had been made in answering ethical misconduct in the executive branch.[217]

Despite McGranery's optimistic statement, Truman, his White House staff, and the DNC publicity efforts failed to significantly diminish the widespread impression reinforced by media and Republican charges that corruption was deeply rooted in the Truman administration.[218] Already irritated with Adlai Stevenson for conducting a presidential campaign that seemed to organizationally and rhetorically distance itself from Truman and his administration, Truman was enraged that Stevenson implicitly agreed with an Oregon newspaper that there was a "mess in Washington." In a publicized letter to the *Oregon Journal,* Stevenson stated that he had solved a similar ethical problem while he was governor and that his sincerity and competence on this issue were further demonstrated by his choice of Stephen A. Mitchell as the new DNC chairman.[219] Instead of being "an old line politician" like his predecessor, Mitchell had served "as counsel to the Congressional committee investigating the Department of Justice."[220] Stevenson issued this letter less than two weeks after McGranery's press statement about a successful conclusion to ethical investigations in his department.

Neither Truman nor the Eisenhower campaign had assumed that Stevenson would unwittingly add further credibility to the Republican focus on corruption as one of the three themes emphasized in the 1952 Republican presidential campaign (along with the Korean War and communism). As the 1952 campaign neared an end, Truman sought to improve the ethical image of his administration in his whistle stop speeches.[221] But few Democratic candidates helped Truman defend his record. Many of them distanced themselves from Truman on this issue, further accelerating the process of dissensus.[222] Thus, the well-entrenched common assumption of an ethical "mess in Washington" was partially strengthened by some of Truman's and his subordinates' mistakes and decisions and by inadequate Democratic support in Congress for most of his proposed reforms.[223] The remaining two elements of the three-pronged Republican campaign strategy for 1952, Korea and communism, were honed and tested by Republican candidates in the 1950 midterm elections.

THE 1952 CAMPAIGN

Initially, though, Truman thought that he had found the most qualified person as president and titular leader of the Democratic party as early as the summer of 1950. From Truman's perspective, Fred M. Vinson, chief justice of the Supreme Court, would be the best candidate for the Democratic presidential nomination in 1952 for several reasons. Firstly, Vinson had the broadest, most diverse range of experience and service among any of the possible candidates in the federal government.[224] Vinson had successively served as a U.S. representative from Kentucky, a judge in the U.S. Court of Appeals in Washington, D.C., director of economic stabilization, federal loan administrator, and director of war mobilization and reconversion.[225] Truman subsequently appointed Vinson secretary of the treasury in 1945 and chief justice in 1946. As secretary of the treasury, Vinson gained diplomatic experience in negotiating a postwar loan to Great Britain and in developing the International Monetary Fund and the International Bank for Reconstruction and Development.[226] Truman's respect for Vinson's negotiating skills was also evident in his controversial proposal that Vinson go to Moscow to negotiate a settlement of the Berlin crisis during the 1948 campaign.

Secondly, unlike Truman's other appointees to the Supreme Court, Vinson remained a close confidante of Truman on political matters and often accompanied Truman on the president's vacations in Key West, Florida. Truman highly valued Vinson's judgment and advice on a wide range of issues.[227] The president continued adamantly to favor Vinson as his successor and in November 1951 again encouraged Vinson to run, despite the fact that Vinson repeatedly had declined.[228]

Thirdly, although Truman never stated this, it seems logical that Truman regarded Vinson as the best candidate to succeed him partially because of the similarities between the two men. Like Truman, Vinson was from a border state and was a New Deal–Fair Deal liberal, although legal scholars later criticized his leadership of the Supreme Court for inadequately protecting civil liberties during the postwar red scare.[229] Truman later described Vinson's "liberalism as broad and deep," and he also perceived Vinson as being, like himself, a political pragmatist who would continue the pursuit of liberal policy goals and the promotion of a liberal identity for the Democratic party while also making the necessary compromises for winning elections and mitigating intraparty conflicts.[230]

By January 1952, Truman realized that he could not persuade Vinson to run and briefly reconsidered running again himself. Charles S. Murphy, Truman's special counsel, later claimed that "at that stage, he would have run himself if that course had been recommended to him by his staff and other advisors. Instead, they uniformly recommended against it."[231]

Despite the contention of columnist Arthur Krock that Truman had offered Dwight Eisenhower the Democratic presidential nomination in November 1951, both Truman and Eisenhower later denied this conversation.[232] With Truman uncertain about a suitable alternative to Vinson, White House aide David Lloyd, who had briefly worked with Adlai Stevenson during World War II, recommended the eloquent, patrician governor of Illinois.[233] Truman did not know Stevenson well, but Stevenson had compiled an impressive record as a reformist governor and had been elected governor by a wide margin in 1948.[234]

Truman had Stevenson see him in Washington on January 23, 1952, for the ostensible purpose of discussing a mine disaster in Illinois.[235] Truman soon directed the conversation toward the 1952 presidential campaign, urged Stevenson to run for president, and assured the governor that he could secure the nomination.[236] Stevenson declined Truman's offer and expressed his desire to serve another term as governor in order to fulfill his policy goals.[237] Truman asked Stevenson to at least consider the offer.

By early March, Truman was concerned and perplexed that Stevenson had not yet answered. When Truman had Stevenson see him again about the presidential nomination, the governor again stated that he did not wish to run for president because of his public commitment to run for a second term as governor.[238] In his diary, Truman noted that he had told Stevenson that "I could get him nominated whether he wanted to be or not. Then I asked him what he'd do in that case. He was very much worried and said that no patriot could say no to such a condition."[239]

Although Truman was frustrated and irritated by Stevenson's apparent indecision, it still seemed that the president could engineer a movement at the Democratic national convention that could pressure Stevenson to accept the nomination, especially since Chicago machine boss Jacob Arvey and other admirers of the governor in Illinois were already promoting him for president.[240] Since there was still uncertainty about who would be the Democratic presidential nominee, especially after Truman publicly announced in late March that he would retire, a number and variety of Democrats sought their party's presidential nomination. In addition to Estes Kefauver, W. Averell Harriman, Alben W. Barkley, Richard B. Russell, and Robert S. Kerr entered the race.

Truman respected Harriman's liberalism and his capable service in his administration as ambassador to the Soviet Union, secretary of commerce, special assistant, and director of the Mutual Security Agency.[241] But Harriman had no prior experience as a campaigner. He managed to defeat Kefauver in the Washington, D.C., presidential primary by running to the left of Kefauver on civil rights and mobilizing that city's black voters, thus making him anathema to southern delegates at the convention.[242]

Robert S. Kerr was a moderate Democratic senator from Oklahoma. He had frequently been in conflict with Truman over policies affecting the oil and gas industry, especially when Truman vetoed Kerr's bill to remove independent natural gas companies from the jurisdiction of the Federal Power Commission (FPC) and when Kerr opposed Truman's renomination of Leland Olds as FPC chairman.[243] Nevertheless, Kerr still publicly stated that he would withdraw his candidacy and support Truman if the president sought reelection.[244] Despite his vigorous, expensive campaign against Kefauver in the Nebraska primary, Kefauver defeated him by more than twenty thousand votes.[245] Hoping for a deadlocked convention that might chose him as a compromise candidate, Kerr managed to receive only 65 votes on the first ballot of the delegates and 5½ votes on the second ballot.[246]

Other than Harriman, Senator Richard B. Russell of Georgia was the only candidate to defeat Estes Kefauver in a presidential primary in 1952. Defeating Kefauver by more than eighty-six thousand votes in Florida's May 6 primary, Russell was still plagued by his national image as a regional candidate.[247] He tried to portray himself as a capable, moderate alternative with significant national experience because of his chairmanship of the Senate Armed Services Committee and his key role in developing a bipartisan, internationalist foreign and defense policy in the Senate, especially concerning NATO and the Marshall Plan.[248]

Most of Russell's delegate support and potential electoral support remained limited to the South. He was a leading member of the anti–Fair Deal, bipartisan conservative coalition in Congress. His vigorous opposition to civil rights for blacks and most policy positions favored by organized labor assured the opposition of these interest groups and most nonsouthern delegates to his candidacy.[249] Despite Russell's exhaustive campaign for delegate support at the convention, the Georgia senator's delegate support peaked at 294 votes on the second ballot. With no primary campaigning at all in 1948, Russell had received 263 votes at the 1948 convention.[250]

On May 29, 1952, Alben W. Barkley publicly stated that he would not actively seek the Democratic presidential nomination but would accept it if it were offered at the convention.[251] Truman had enjoyed a long, warm friendship with his vice president, but Barkley had not been his first choice for vice president. Like Vinson, Barkley was a Kentuckian whose devotion to liberalism in the Democratic party was not questioned by Truman. But Truman did not value Barkley's counsel as much as he did Vinson's, and Barkley, at the age of seventy-four, seemed too old for the presidency.[252]

Barkley was well-known among Democratic party regulars for his rousing, populist speeches at Democratic national conventions and his skills as a humorous, folksy raconteur at Democratic fund-raising dinners. His confidence that he would receive the Democratic presidential nomination, since Stevenson had still expressed no desire for it, was further strengthened by the volume of mail that he received from Democratic well wishers.[253] A few weeks before the Democratic national convention began on July 21, 1952, Truman made one last effort to persuade Stevenson to accept the nomination by having DNC Chairman Frank E. McKinney confer with the governor. Stevenson still refused.[254] Barkley's hopes were further raised when Truman now told Barkley he would support his vice president for the presidential nomination on July 13.[255] Five days before the convention began, Truman wrote to a Democratic delegate from Missouri and asked him to organize the entire Missouri delegation behind Barkley's candidacy.[256]

A Gallup poll released in June had revealed that only 17 percent of the poll's Democratic respondents supported Barkley's candidacy.[257] The question of Barkley's electability was foremost in the minds of organized labor. Despite Barkley's pro-labor legislative record, his age and the commitments of many pro-labor delegates to other presidential candidates motivated several AFL and CIO leaders to inform Barkley that they would not support him.[258] Also, despite Stevenson's public statements that he was not seeking the nomination, the "draft Stevenson" organization was formidable and gaining momentum. In particular, machine bosses Jacob Arvey of Chicago and David Lawrence of Pittsburgh succeeded in committing most of the Illinois and Pennsylvania delegates to Stevenson.[259] Finally, Stevenson's inspiring, eloquent welcoming address to the delegates on the opening day of the Democratic national convention in Chicago attracted more support to the "draft" movement.[260] Barkley then announced the withdrawal of his candidacy.

Barkley's withdrawal had the effect of further accelerating the momentum behind Stevenson, especially among delegates who were determined to unite behind a candidate to prevent Kefauver's nomination. Kefauver and Harriman delegates began to coalesce and oppose the seating of the Virginia delegation because of that state's refusal to accept the Moody resolution. This was a loyalty pledge seeking to ensure that the eventual Democratic presidential and vice presidential nominees would be on all states' ballots. This action motivated more southern delegates to support Stevenson, especially after the Arvey-controlled Illinois delegates supported Virginia.[261] The convention had experienced bitter intraparty conflicts over the wording of its civil rights plank and a dispute over the credentials of the Texas delegates, who were divided between pro-Truman Loyalists and anti-Truman Regulars.[262]

On July 24, the fourth day of the convention, Stevenson called Truman and asked if it would "embarrass" the president if he allowed himself to be nominated. Truman enthusiastically told Stevenson that it would "please him in every way."[263] Truman soon contacted Thomas Gavin, his alternate in the Missouri delegation, and instructed him to vote for Stevenson.[264]

The rules of the 1952 Democratic national convention required 616 votes to nominate a presidential candidate. With Truman adding further strength to the Stevenson bandwagon, Stevenson received 617½ votes on the third ballot on July 25.[265] In his acceptance speech, he sought to instill a unifying theme in the Democratic presidential campaign by stating that "the Democratic Party is the people's party . . . the party of no one because it is the party of everyone. That I think, is our ancient mission."[266] By contrast, in an address that immediately preceded Stevenson's, Truman delivered a shrill, aggressively partisan attack against the Republicans for being "men of little faith and no vision" and opposing "every measure that has made our country prosperous at home, and powerful abroad."[267]

Stevenson's uplifting address and his immediate appeal as a compromise candidate briefly suspended the dissensus that plagued the party and was evident in the convention's proceedings, especially its votes on platform planks and the credentials of several southern delegations.[268] In an attempt to satisfy at least the more moderate southern delegates, Stevenson, upon Truman's suggestion, chose Senator John Sparkman of Alabama as his vice presidential nominee. Sparkman was a consistent opponent of civil rights legislation, but he supported most liberal domestic policies, especially federal housing programs.[269]

Sparkman's nomination angered fifty black delegates, including New York Congressman Adam Clayton Powell Jr., enough that they left the convention.[270] Following the convention, several major southern Democratic politicians, including governors James F. Byrnes of South Carolina, Allen Shivers of Texas, and Robert Kennon of Louisiana, endorsed the Republican presidential nominee, Dwight D. Eisenhower. The DNC headquarters feared that Stevenson's divorce would lead normally Democratic Catholic voters to support Eisenhower.[271] In short, the pace of Democratic dissensus quickened as the general election campaign got under way.

Dissensus was also evident in the lack of coordination and structural integration within the Democratic presidential campaign. There often appeared to be two different Democratic presidential campaigns in terms of campaign organization and rhetorical emphasis, Stevenson's and Truman's. To Truman's dismay and exasperation, the Stevenson campaign tried to project a more independent image by locating its headquarters in Springfield, Illinois, instead of using the DNC headquarters.[272] Replacing Frank E. McKinney with Stephen A. Mitchell as DNC chairman was also an attempt by Stevenson to distance himself from what his campaign manager, Wilson Wyatt, tactfully called the "political phases" of the Truman administration.[273] Stevenson and his staff emphasized style and erudition in Stevenson's speeches, partially to attract undecided and independent voters and favorable media analysis.[274] Unlike the advertising and public relations experts who dominated Eisenhower's campaign, the liberal intellectuals and ADA members on Stevenson's campaign staff reinforced his emphasis on thought-provoking prose.[275]

The DNC headquarters, whose research and publicity division had compiled prodigious amounts of economic statistics and facts citing "twenty years of progress" under Democratic administrations and literature refuting Republican charges, was relegated to a secondary position.[276] Most of its resources and personnel were devoted to defending Truman's foreign and domestic policy record against Republican criticism.[277] Preparing for the possibility that Senator Robert A. Taft would be the Republican presidential nominee, the DNC headquarters had also compiled and then distributed pamphlets warning voters that Taft and "Taft-minded" men would dominate Congress and Eisenhower if the Republicans gained control of the presidency and Congress in the 1952 elections.[278]

The tone and content of Truman's whistle-stop campaign rhetoric in September and October of 1952 generally reflected these DNC materials. While praising Stevenson's record as governor and his potential as a future president, Truman mostly emphasized the economic reforms and prosperity that benefited average Americans under two consecutive Democratic administrations.[279] Truman's whistle-stop speeches often alternated between a defense of his administration's record and a shrill denunciation of Republicans as do-nothing reactionaries in foreign and domestic policies while rarely mentioning Eisenhower. In a September 1 address in Milwaukee, Truman dismissed the Republicans as "the party of the special interests, still the errand boys of the big lobbies, still the ones who want to exploit labor and the farmers and the consumers."[280]

Thus, while Stevenson struggled to broaden the appeal of his candidacy to undecided, better-educated, middle-class voters, Truman, as he did in 1948, often spoke in more divisive language that graphically and bluntly depicted stark class and ideological differences between the two parties on economic issues.[281] The Eisenhower campaign was too shrewd to become entangled in a debate on New Deal–Fair Deal liberalism. Eisenhower had declared that he accepted the basic policy foundation of the New Deal and would not challenge it during the campaign.[282] Instead, the Eisenhower campaign cultivated a suprapartisan, consensus-building image of the Republican presidential nominee as a patriotic war hero who would decisively and victoriously end the war in Korea and Democratic incompetence, corruption, and softness toward domestic and international communism.[283]

Television advertising played a more prominent, sophisticated role in Eisenhower's suprapartisan, candidate-centered campaign that communicated the values of trust, seasoned and proven leadership ability, and empathy with voter concerns about peace and prosperity. In contrast to the Stevenson campaign's use of a relatively small number of thirty-minute commercials in which the Democratic presidential nominee explained his policy platform, the Eisenhower campaign used a larger number of brief commercials that included a promotion of his war hero image, "I like Ike" cartoons, and an "Eisenhower Answers America" series in which Eisenhower provided short answers to the questions of "average Americans" about consumer prices.[284] With Stevenson's tendency to give lengthy, more complex speeches on television, the Democratic campaign relied more on print ads and pamphlets that were party-centered and identified the Democratic party with greater economic security for average Americans and the Republican party with the Great Depression and economic elitism.[285] This Democratic concentration on partisan and economic policy differences also influenced the type of negative publicity that was used. Campaign literature for the DNC headquarters, the Springfield headquarters, and various pro-Stevenson organizations often used guilt by association in which Eisenhower was portrayed as an amiable, attractive facade for the machinations of divisively partisan, ideologically conservative, and controversial Republicans, especially Taft, McCarthy, and Nixon, his running mate.

Television proved to be essential in resolving the biggest crisis of the Republican presidential campaign. Businessmen had contributed to a private fund for Nixon, which the media reported as an ethically questionable "slush fund" in late September.[286] The Eisenhower campaign was now put on the defensive, especially because Nixon had been aggressively denouncing Democratic corruption. The Stevenson campaign's ability to exploit this issue was blunted by the fact that it had to explain a similar private fund, which campaign manager Wilson Wyatt claimed was primarily used to subsidize the modest salaries of the governor's staff.[287]

But Nixon still had to convince Eisenhower that he was not an intolerable liability in the campaign who should be replaced. The Eisenhower campaign purchased $75,000 worth of air time for a speech that would immediately follow the popular comedy show of Milton Berle and attract an audience of approximately 58 million viewers.[288] Nixon shrewdly realized the importance of image and emotional appeal in television communications. His so-called Checkers speech—named after a dog that was given as a gift to him and that he defiantly vowed to keep—portrayed Nixon as a self-made man from a poor background who still struggled to support his family and claimed that the fund was only used for office expenses. He also went on the offensive against the Democratic campaign by challenging Stevenson and Sparkman to disclose their own financial histories and referred to the fact that Sparkman's wife was on the Alabama senator's office payroll.[289] Nixon concluded by asking viewers to contact the Republican National Committee about whether he should be retained as

Eisenhower's running mate. By a margin of 350 to 1, Americans who contacted the RNC supported Nixon.[290]

If the Checkers speech had failed and Eisenhower had replaced Nixon, the Democratic campaign might have more effectively portrayed Eisenhower as a dupe and stalking horse for corrupt, ruthless Republicans. Instead, Gallup polls showed that public support for the Eisenhower-Nixon ticket increased from 51 percent in a poll released on September 22 to 53 percent in an October 1 poll.[291] DNC surveys and reports to DNC headquarters indicated that the Eisenhower campaign was increasingly attracting the support of normally Democratic Catholic ethnic voters concerned about communism.[292] The DNC Research Division tried in vain to counteract this Catholic movement toward Eisenhower by providing fact-filled literature claiming that Democratic domestic, foreign, and defense policies symbiotically benefited immigrant groups, promoted prosperity for lower-income Americans, and fought the spread of domestic and international communism.[293]

Despite Stevenson's choice of an Alabama segregationist as his running mate and the frequent absence of specific rhetorical appeals to blacks on the civil rights issue, polls indicated that black Democratic voters, unlike Catholics and southern whites, were unlikely to support Eisenhower.[294] Polls conducted by Louis Harris indicated that support for Stevenson among black northern voters increased from 56 percent in September to 75 percent in November.[295] Such strong indications of black electoral support for Stevenson were used by some pro-Eisenhower organizations in the South to appeal to the racial fears of white voters. According to a campaign pamphlet entitled, "Death of Decency," the election of Stevenson would lead to "Negro Bosses in the Mills" because the "policies of the Democratic Party are now set by a combination of Northern City Bosses, Crooked Politicians, and Radical College Professors. . . . In order to save our way of life—in order to avoid a racial struggle,—we, the White People of the South, must vote for 'Ike' Eisenhower!"[296]

On the eve of the election, Truman and Stevenson provided nationally broadcast speeches. Again, there was a noticeable difference in the style and substantive emphases of their speeches. Truman stated, "This election may decide whether we shall go ahead and expand our prosperity here at home or slide back into a depression."[297] In a veiled reference to Eisenhower's dramatic announcement of October 25 that he would go to Korea, Truman castigated the Republicans for "playing politics with the sacrifices our men are making on the battleline to protect our freedom and achieve peace."[298] In Stevenson's speech, the governor adopted a lofty tone mostly devoid of partisan attacks. He recalled key moments of campaign trips and ruefully expressed some self-doubt and uncertainty about his rhetoric.[299] He interpreted his campaign as "a great opportunity to educate and elevate a people whose destiny is leadership, not alone of a rich, prosperous, contented country, but of a world in ferment."[300]

THE RESULTS

Privately assuming that Stevenson could not defeat Eisenhower, such key members of the Democratic presidential campaign as Wilson Wyatt and Samuel Brightman, the DNC's publicity director, saw many of their concerns and pessimistic assumptions come to fruition in the election results.[301] Eisenhower was elected president in 1952 with 55 percent of the popular votes and carried thirty-nine states in the electoral college, including Missouri and Illinois and four southern states.[302] Despite the misleading assumption that unusually high rates of voter turnout benefit Democratic candidates, voter turnout in the 1952 presidential election was 61.6 percent, compared to 51.1 percent in 1948.[303] The Republicans also won control of Congress by gaining twenty-two seats in the House and one seat in the Senate.[304] Eisenhower usually received substantially wider margins than victorious Republican congressional candidates because of the fairly high rate of ticket splitting among pro-Eisenhower Democratic and independent voters.[305]

Gallup polls revealed that 23 percent of the Democratic voters and 65 percent of the independent voters surveyed supported Eisenhower.[306] As far as the Democratic electoral base was concerned, Stevenson received 56 percent of the Catholic vote, compared to Truman's 64 percent in 1948.[307] Despite the absence of a significant southern-oriented minor party in the 1952 election, Stevenson received only 51 percent of the popular votes in the South—that is, the eleven states of the former Confederacy—while Truman received 52.9 percent and J. Strom Thurmond received 17.4 percent in 1948.[308] Consequently, the Republican percentage of the popular vote in the South increased from 29.7 percent in 1948 to approximately 49 percent in 1952.[309]

The prospect of a future realignment of southern white voters with the GOP seemed especially favorable in the metropolitan areas of major, growing, prosperous southern cities and in the "peripheral" South (the four southern states that Eisenhower carried: Tennessee, Virginia, Florida, and Texas) and in such southern-oriented border states as Kentucky and Oklahoma.[310] When pollster Louis Harris speculated in 1954 on the prospect of the Republicans becoming the majority party among voters, he noted the greater attraction of higher-income urban and suburban southern whites to the GOP, compared to lower-income rural whites.[311] Contrary to the expectations of many nonsouthern Americans, Harris noted that southern whites who voted Republican for president in 1952 were motivated more by economic issues, the Korean War, and a revulsion against the "mess in Washington" than a fear of civil rights policies for blacks under a Stevenson presidency.[312]

Although the content and tone of Stevenson's campaign rhetoric tended to be less combatively liberal than Truman's, Stevenson's electoral performance among the two most liberal Democratic voting blocs, blacks and Jews, was virtually the same as Truman's in 1948. According to data analyzed by political scientists Everett C. Ladd Jr., and Charles D. Hadley, blacks and Jews respectively gave 77 percent and 72 percent of their votes to Truman in 1948 and 76 percent and 72 percent to Stevenson in 1952.[313] Among union members who voted in presidential elections, support for Democrats declined from 70 percent in 1948 to 60 percent in 1952.[314]

THE AFTERMATH

On December 22, 1952, Harry Truman wrote a memo in which he mused about the significance of the election results. He sardonically referred to Eisenhower supporters as "the Republican Dixiecrat, Shivercrat, anti Korean Bible-belt coalition," thus directing most of his contempt at pro-Eisenhower southern Democrats.[315] For Truman, the Republicans won a decisive victory because of "an appalling campaign made up of lies, misrepresentation and bold demagoguery."[316]

But throughout the lengthy, reflective memo, Truman placed most of the blame on the Stevenson campaign's poor sense of timing and organization and such evidence of Democratic dissensus as Estes Kefauver's campaign and Stevenson's abrupt replacement of Frank E. McKinney with Stephen A. Mitchell as DNC chairman.[317] Truman attributed most of this intraparty conflict over the Democratic presidential nomination and problems in the conduct of the campaign to Stevenson's refusal to let Truman secure the nomination for him in January so that Stevenson "could have been sold to the country before the convention."[318] Truman was still baffled and irritated that Stevenson "did not and does not yet understand the necessity of organization from the precinct to the National Committee."[319]

With his ethos as a party regular stressing the importance of the role of the DNC apparatus and chairman, Truman underestimated the forces changing the American two-party system that were evident in the 1952 election, such as the accelerated movement of southern white voters toward the Republican party, the increase in split-ticket voting, the use of public relations and advertising firms and consequent decline of party organizations in conducting presidential campaigns, and the potential of television to enable suprapartisan, candidate-centered, rather than party-centered, campaigns to succeed and to promote images rather than issues.[320] In retirement, Truman continued to participate in Democratic party affairs, especially as a member of the Democratic Advisory Council (DAC).

Created by DNC chairman Paul Butler as an appendage of the DNC in 1956, the DAC was an excellent forum for Truman's value systems as a party regular and a liberal reformer. The DAC's purpose was to discuss, research, formulate, and promote liberal policy positions for the party in order to avoid a drift toward centrism during the 1950s.[321] But the DAC did not play a significant role in the 1960 presidential campaign, and Truman was disappointed with the party's choice of a presidential nominee and in John F. Kennedy's management of the 1960 Democratic national convention and campaign according to the "new politics" of television imagery, polling, and high spending.[322] The Democratic party, nonetheless, nominated a presidential candidate whose rhetoric and platform were committed to the liberal policy identity that Truman struggled to solidify and enhance during his presidency and party leadership.

At the age of seventy-six, Truman conducted his last whistle-stop campaign for the Democratic party. It was actually a "prop stop," an airplane tour of twelve states in six weeks to promote Kennedy's candidacy.[323] For Truman, it was especially important to elect a Democratic president because, as he stated after the election, the president is "the lobbyist for everybody in the United States."[324]

☆ ☆ ☆ ☆ ☆

Epilogue
TRUMAN'S LEGACY
IN THE DEMOCRATIC PARTY

A few months after he became president, a Gallup poll recorded Harry Truman's public approval rating at 87 percent.[1] As Truman prepared to leave the White House in December 1952, a Gallup poll recorded his public approval rating at 31 percent.[2] For the first time in twenty-four years, the Republicans won control of the presidency and both houses of Congress. With the highest rate of voter turnout for a twentieth-century presidential election, a substantial minority of Democratic voters split their ballots and provided a wide margin of victory for the Republican nominee.[3] Even Truman's home state of Missouri gave Eisenhower a majority.

These statistics provide a measure of the immediate public perception and electoral results of Truman's party leadership. They suggest that Truman was a failure as a party leader. The Democratic party in Congress, the minority party after 1952, was led by Sam Rayburn and Lyndon Johnson, southern moderates who openly cooperated with the Republican president and GOP congressional leaders on major policy issues and would continue to compromise and cooperate with the president after their party regained control of Congress in 1954.[4] Rayburn and Johnson frequently and openly fought with DNC chairman Paul M. Butler as he sought to clarify and express a more distinctly liberal ideological and programmatic identity for the Democratic party.[5] Becoming more cautious and moderate in his rhetoric and policy positions, especially on civil rights, Adlai Stevenson easily defeated the more liberal W. Averell Harriman, whom Truman openly favored, for the Democratic presidential nomination in 1956.[6] As a more moderate, politically savvy nominee in 1956, Stevenson was defeated by a wider margin of votes and received smaller proportions of votes from blacks, Catholics, southern whites, and union members than in 1952.[7]

Since Harry Truman had struggled to maintain and further enhance the Democratic party as a distinctly liberal, electorally successful majority party, what were his major, enduring accomplishments, if any, as a party leader? They were twofold. First, he maintained the programmatic, ideological, and coalitional foundation of the expanded Democratic party and liberal identity that Franklin D. Roosevelt had established. Despite political analyst Samuel Lubell's dismissive conclusion that Truman merely "bought time" and sought "to perpetuate rather than break the prevailing stalemate," Truman's maintenance of Roosevelt's liberal legacy in the Democratic party was not easy.[8] Without Roosevelt's personal leadership, liberal Democrats feared that the New Deal coalition would disintegrate, conservative Democrats would increase their influence over Democratic national platforms and presidential nominations, and such unfulfilled liberal policy goals as civil rights for blacks would be abandoned.[9]

As some liberals suspected and even assumed, Truman could have been a vacillating, cautious centrist quick to compromise with and appease the bipartisan conservative coalition on domestic policy and southern Democrats on civil rights in order to assure his nomination in 1948 and avoid the Dixiecrat revolt. But Harry Truman chose the more difficult, controversial, and politically self-endangering course of continuing and strengthening his party's liberal identity through defiant rhetoric toward conservatives in both parties and divisive policy behavior that included vetoing the Taft-Hartley Act and initiating the desegregation of the military.

Second, Truman went beyond protecting and sustaining his party's New Deal–inspired ideology, coalition, and policy foundation, which was difficult enough, and directed the Democratic party toward more difficult, challenging liberal policy goals through the Fair Deal. The Fair Deal's most liberal and controversial policy objectives—civil rights legislation, federal aid to elementary and secondary education, and national health insurance—created bitter dissensus among Democrats in Congress during and after Truman's presidency. Truman did not desert these Fair Deal principles and goals for the sake of political expediency and intraparty healing during the remainder of his administration. Instead, Truman and liberal Democrats in Congress embedded these three policy goals and ideological characteristics firmly and clearly enough within their party's identity so that they were partially or fully achieved during the more favorable political environment of the Kennedy and Johnson administrations.[10]

During Harry Truman's political career in general and presidential party leadership in particular, he was strongly influenced by his value systems as a party regular and a liberal reformer. He tried to maintain and further develop a Democratic party that would be a symbiosis of these values—that is, a distinctly liberal, internally harmonious, electorally successful, well-organized majority party. Despite the difficulty, if not the impossibility, of developing a Democratic party that combined these often contradictory characteristics during an era marked by increasingly conservative and even reactionary political forces and trends, Truman persevered. His farsighted, combative liberalism as a party leader was partially influenced by his Democratic mentors—Andrew Jackson, William Jennings Bryan, and Woodrow Wilson.[11] These historical relationships solidified Truman's determination to ensure that the Democratic party of the future would always be able to further refine and reshape its liberalism in order to meet new policy needs and political conditions.

While Truman's greatest strengths and accomplishments as a party leader were his efforts for what he perceived to be his party's long-term ideological, programmatic, and electoral welfare, his greatest weaknesses and mistakes often occurred when his ethos as a party regular dominated his choice of methods. In particular, Truman failed to understand the significance and impact of major changes in campaign tactics and rhetoric, voting behavior, and mass communications that were beginning to revolutionize party politics. Truman was often oblivious to the fact that his background, beliefs, methods, and perspectives as a party regular—such as his acceptance of machine politics, staunch loyalty to controversial appointees, straight-ticket voting, indifference to rhetorical style, and rejection of presidential primaries as "eyewash"—were increasingly perceived as anachronistic by Americans toward the end of his presidency.[12] Unlike Estes Kefauver, Adlai Stevenson, and later John F. Kennedy, Harry Truman did not recognize the greater importance of adapting to the more candidate-centered, participatory, and telegenic methods, tactics, and processes of intraparty politics in order to be effective.[13]

Nevertheless, Harry Truman was one of only two post–World War II presidents who exercised a considerable degree of concern and personal attention to developing and revitalizing his party's national organization as a means of influencing its ideological and programmatic identity and strengthening its internal cohesion and electoral welfare. Both of these presidents recognized the importance of closely managing their parties' national organizations through regular contact with national party chairmen and supervision of the political operations of national party headquarters. The second president was one of Harry Truman's most energetic and enthusiastic liberal supporters in Hollywood during the 1948 presidential campaign—Ronald W. Reagan.[14]

☆ ☆ ☆ ☆ ☆

ABBREVIATIONS

CQ	Congressional Quarterly
DNC	Democratic National Committee
FDR	Franklin D. Roosevelt
FDRL	Franklin D. Roosevelt Library, Hyde Park, New York
GPO	Government Printing Office
HLND	Hesburgh Library, University of Notre Dame, Notre Dame, Indiana
HST	Harry S. Truman
HSTL	Harry S. Truman Library, Independence, Missouri
JFKL	John F. Kennedy Library, Boston, Massachusetts
JWMI	Joseph W. Martin Jr. Institute, North Easton, Massachusetts
LOC	Library of Congress, Washington, D.C.
NYT	*New York Times*
OF	Official File
PPF	President's Personal File
PPP	*Public Papers of the Presidents of the United States, Harry S. Truman* (Washington, D.C.: GPO, 1961-66) These eight volumes are cited by year and page number.
PSF	President's Secretary's File
RNC	Republican National Committee
UKL	University of Kentucky Library, Special Collections, Lexington, Kentucky

☆ ☆ ☆ ☆ ☆

NOTES

1. TRUMAN AND HIS PARTY

1. Robert H. Ferrell, ed., *Dear Bess: The Letters from Harry to Bess Truman, 1910-1959* (New York: Norton, 1983), 343, 426. **2.** Andrew Dunar, *The Truman Scandals and the Politics of Morality* (Columbia: Univ. of Missouri Press, 1984), 75-80. **3.** Author's interview with Richard E. Neustadt, Wellfleet, Mass., July 24, 1991. **4.** Frank Mason, *Truman and the Pendergasts* (Evanston, Ill.: Regency Books, 1963), 127-43; and Gene Powell, *Tom's Boy Harry* (Jefferson City, Mo.: Hawthorn, 1948), 34-82. **5.** David McCullough, *Truman* (New York: Simon and Schuster, 1992), 63; and Robert H. Ferrell, *Harry S. Truman, A Life* (Columbia: Univ. of Missouri Press, 1994), 112.

6. Merle Miller, *Plain Speaking: An Oral Biography of Harry S. Truman* (New York: Berkley Medallion, 1974), 67-68, 151-153. **7.** Jonathan Daniels, *The Man of Independence* (New York: J.B. Lippincott, 1950), 70-109. **8.** Merle Miller, *Plain Speaking,* 115. **9.** Gosnell, 66; and McCullough, *Truman,* 58-59. **10.** Richard L. Miller, *Truman: The Rise to Power* (New York: McGraw-Hill, 1986), 68.

11. Daniels, *Man of Independence,* 43-110. **12.** William L. Bradshaw, "The Missouri County Court: A Study of the Organization and Functions of the County Board of Supervisors in Missouri," *University of Missouri Studies* 6 (1931): 1-21; Lyle W. Dorsett, *The Pendergast Machine* (New York: Oxford Univ. Press, 1968), 70-73; William Reddig, *Tom's Town: Kansas City and the Pendergast Legend* (New York: J.B. Lippincott, 1947), 181-84; and Powell, *Tom's Boy Harry,* 2-26. **13.** Powell, *Tom's Boy Harry,* 53. **14.** Dorsett, *Pendergast Machine,* 102-3; and Reddig, *Tom's Town,* 185. **15.** Alfred Steinberg, *The Man from Missouri* (New York: G.P. Putnam's Sons, 1962), 69.

16. Charles P. Blackmore, "Joseph B. Shannon: Political Boss and Twentieth Century 'Jeffersonian'" (Ph.D. diss., Columbia University, 1953). **17.** Ibid., 85-86; and Dorsett, *Pendergast Machine,* 91. **18.** Maurice M. Milligan, *Missouri Waltz: The Inside Story of the Pendergast Machine by the Man who Smashed It* (New York: Scribner's, 1948), 76. **19.** Steinberg, *Man from Missouri,* 62-75. **20.** Richard L. Miller, *Truman,* 170.

21. Ibid., 342. **22.** Thomas J. Heed, "Prelude to Whistlestop: Harry S. Truman the Apprentice Campaigner" (Ed.D. diss., Columbia University, 1976). **23.** Gosnell, 73. **24.** McCullough, *Truman,* 174-179. **25.** Steinberg, *Man from Missouri,* 78-80.

26. Mason, *Truman and the Pendergasts,* 72. **27.** Gosnell, 84. **28.** Lyle W. Dorsett, "Truman and the Pendergast Machine," *Midcontinent American Studies Journal* 7 (Fall 1966): 18. **29.** HST to Bess Truman, May 14, 1934, 6, Pickwick Hotel Papers, PSF, HSTL. **30.** Eugene Schmidtlein, "Truman the Senator" (Ph.D. diss., University of Missouri, 1962), 35-37. **31.** Harry S. Truman, *Memoirs* (New York: New American Library, 1955), 1:161-62; and Ferrell, ed., *Off the Record* (New York: Harper & Row, 1980), 230-31. **32.** Steinberg, *Man from Missouri,* 60; and Reddig, *Tom's Town,* 183-85. **33.** Dorsett, *Pendergast Machine,* 72-73. **34.** Alfred Steinberg, *The Bosses* (New York: Macmillan, 1972), 335. **35.** Dorsett, *Pendergast Machine,* 93; and Margaret Truman, *Harry S. Truman* (New York: Morrow, 1973), 79.

36. Franklin D. Mitchell, "Who Is Judge Truman? The Truman for Governor Movement of 1931," *MidContinent American Studies Journal* 7 (Fall 1966): 3-15. **37.** Lyle W. Dorsett, "Kansas City Politics: A Study of Boss Pendergast's Machine," *Arizona and the West* 8 (Summer 1966): 114-16. **38.** Powell, *Tom's Boy Harry,* 42-54; Richard L. Miller, *Truman,* 247; and Dorsett, *Pendergast Machine,* 166-167. **39.** Steinberg, *Bosses,* 336; Sean J. Savage, *Roosevelt: The Party Leader, 1932-1945* (Lexington: Univ. Press of Kentucky, 1991), 64-65; and John H. Fenton, *Politics in the Border States* (New Orleans: Hauser Press, 1957), 137. **40.** Merle Miller, *Plain Speaking,* 137; Ferrell, *Dear Bess,* 348-49; and Pickwick Hotel Papers, 11, HSTL.

41. Ibid., 4, HSTL. **42.** Daniels, *Man of Independence,* 138-39, 155-56. **43.** Dorsett, *Pendergast Machine,* 112. **44.** Daniels, *Man of Independence,* 174. **45.** Richard L. Miller, *Truman,* 264-65; Timothy K. Evans, "'This Certainly Is Relief!' Matthew S. Murray and Missouri Politics during the Depression," *Bulletin of the Missouri Historical Society* 28 (July 1972): 219-33; T.J. Edmonds to Harry Hopkins, Feb. 6, 1934, and Hopkins to Marvin McIntyre, July 7, 1938, both in Harry Hopkins Papers, FDRL.

46. Eugene Schmidtlein, "Harry S. Truman and the Pendergast Machine," *Midcontinent American Studies Journal* 7 (Fall 1966): 33. **47.** Philip A. Grant Jr., "The Election of Harry S. Truman to the United States Senate," *Missouri Historical Society Bulletin* 36 (1980): 103-9; and Richard S. Kirkendall, "Truman and the Pendergast Machine: A Comment," *Midcontinent American Studies Journal* 7 (Fall 1966): 38. **48.** Daniels, *Man of Independence,* 173. **49.** Gosnell, 100-101. **50.** Dorsett, "Kansas City Politics," 116-17.

51. Powell, *Tom's Boy Harry,* 78. **52.** Daniels, *Man of Independence,* 173-74. **53.** Powell, *Tom's Boy Harry,* 64; and Milligan, *Missouri Waltz,* 229. **54.** Ferrell, *Dear Bess,* 304-5. **55.** Steinberg, *Man from Missouri,* 126; and William Helm, *Harry Truman: A Political Biography* (New York: Duell, Sloan and Pearce, 1947), 64. **56.** Richard S. Kirkendall, "Truman's Path to Power," *Social Science* 43 (1968): 67-73. **57.** McCullough, *Truman,* 213-16. **58.** Ferrell, *Dear Bess,* 415. **59.** Steinberg, 149. **60.** *Congressional Record,* 75th Cong., 2d sess., 1920-22; and Merle Miller, *Plain Speaking,* 152-53.

61. HST, *Memoirs,* 1:173; and James T. Patterson, *Congressional Conservatism and the New Deal* (Lexington: Univ. of Kentucky Press, 1967), 38. **62.** Margaret Truman, *Where the Buck Stops: The Personal and Private Writings of Harry S. Truman* (New

York: Warner, 1989), 221; Robert A. Rutland, *The Democrats from Jefferson to Carter* (Baton Rouge: Louisiana State Univ. Press, 1979), 201-5; Monte M. Poen, ed., *Strictly Personal and Confidential: Letters Harry Truman Never Mailed* (Boston: Little, Brown, 1982), 132; Robert Shogan, *The Riddle of Power* (New York: Dutton, 1991), 13-20; and Alonzo L. Hamby, *Liberalism and Its Challengers: FDR to Reagan* (New York: Oxford Univ. Press, 1985), 54-60. **63.** Cabell Phillips, *The Truman Presidency: The History of a Triumphant Succession* (New York: Macmillan, 1966), 232; and *PPP, 1948,* 406, 552. **64.** Poen, *Strictly Personal and Confidential,* 109. **65.** Steinberg, *Man from Missouri,* 69.

66. Ferrell, *Dear Bess,* 409. **67.** Ibid., 386. **68.** Ibid., 396-97. **69.** Savage, *Roosevelt,* 36-37. **70.** Sister M. Patrick Ellen, "The Role of the Chairman of a Congressional Investigating Committee of the Senate to Investigate the National Defense Program, 1941-1948" (Ph.D. diss., St. Louis University, 1962), 282; and *Congressional Record,* 78th Cong., 1st sess., 39.

71. Donald H. Riddle, *The Truman Committee: A Study in Congressional Responsibility* (New Brunswick, N.J.: Rutgers Univ. Press, 1964), 7-19. **72.** HST, *Memoirs,* 1:210. **73.** Riddle, *Truman Committee,* 21; and Richard L. Miller, Truman, 369-80. **74.** Merle Miller, *Plain Speaking,* 177. **75.** Ibid., 179-80; and Bruce Catton, *The War Lords of Washington* (New York: Harcourt, Brace, 1948), 296-303.

76. Richard L. Miller, *Truman,* 241-42; and Arthur M. Curtis to Harry Hopkins, May 21, 1936, Harry Hopkins Papers, FDRL. **77.** Milligan, *Missouri Waltz,* 150-201. **78.** *Congressional Record,* 75th Cong., 3d sess., 1962-64. **79.** Ibid., 1964. **80.** Burton K. Wheeler, *Yankee from the West* (New York: Doubleday, 1962), 373.

81. V.R. Messall and David Berenstein to Harry Easley, June 10, 1940, Harry Easley Papers, HSTL. **82.** Easley to HST, July 26, 1944, Harry Easley Papers, HSTL; and transcript, Harry Easley Oral History Interview, Aug. 24, 1967, 42-45, HSTL. **83.** Daniels, *Man of Independence,* 198. **84.** Transcript, Easley Oral History Interview, 7. **85.** Ibid., 43.

86. *St. Louis Post-Dispatch* Morgue, 1949, 98, Jonathan Daniels Papers, Part II, HSTL; and 1940 Campaign brochure, "2: Important Messages," Harry Easley Papers, HSTL. **87.** Author's phone interview with William Hannegan, Feb. 24, 1994; and Daniels, *Man of Independence,* 208-09. **88.** Steinberg, *Man from Missouri,* 169-75. **89.** Campaign leaflet, "What the United States Senate Thinks of Harry S. Truman," undated 1940, Harry Easley Papers, HSTL. **90.** Daniels, *Man of Independence,* 203-4.

91. Clipping, *Congressional Record,* 76th Cong., pt. 3, Appendix, 4546, Victor Messall Papers, HSTL. **92.** *Congressional Record,* 76th Cong., pt. 3, Appendix, 5367-5369. **93.** Gosnell, 146; and Fenton, *Politics in the Border States,* 139-40. **94.** Copy of official primary results of Aug. 6, 1940, 4, Victor Messall Papers, HSTL. **95.** Ibid.

96. Ibid., 3; and Daniels, *Man of Independence,* 210-11. **97.** Ferrell, *Dear Bess,* 441. **98.** Ibid., 446. **99.** Dorsey H. Watson to HST, Sept. 5, 1940, Senatorial File, HST Papers, HSTL. **100.** HST to Watson, Sept. 12, 1940, Senatorial File, HST Papers, HSTL.

101. Clipping, *St. Louis Globe-Democrat,* Nov. 30, 1940, Victor Messall Papers, HSTL. **102.** Steinberg, *Man from Missouri,* 196-98. **103.** *Time* 41, no. 10 (March 8, 1943): 15. **104.** Press release, "Statement by Senator Harry S. Truman on the Strike Situation," Aug. 14, 1941, Senatorial File, HST Papers, HSTL. **105.** Catton, *War Lords,* 118-20.

106. Robert S. Allen and William V. Shannon, *The Truman Merry-Go-Round* (New York: Vanguard, 1950), 13. **107.** HST to Edward J. Flynn, Aug. 5, 1941, Senatorial File, HST Papers, HSTL. **108.** HST to Harry Easley, June 9, 1943, Senatorial File, HST Papers, HSTL. **109.** Research notes for *The Man of Independence,* Aug. 30, 1949, 6, Jonathan Daniels Papers, part I, HSTL. **110.** HST to FDR, Sept. 22, 1943, Senatorial File, HST Papers, HSTL; and unsigned manuscript, "Dirt Farmer and Dirt Politician," undated 1946, 10-11, Robert E. Hannegan Papers, HSTL.

111. Clipping, *St. Louis Post-Dispatch,* Jan. 25, 1944, Jonathan Daniels Papers, part II, HSTL. **112.** HST to Herb Graffis, Mar. 2, 1943, Senatorial File, HST Papers, HSTL. **113.** James F. Byrnes, *All in One Lifetime* (New York: Harper, 1958), 221-29; and Ferrell, *Dear Bess,* 505. **114.** Richard L. Miller, *Truman,* 385-86; Allen and Shannon, *Truman Merry-Go-Round,* 13-14; Tyler Abell, ed., *The Drew Pearson Diaries, 1949-1959* (New York: Holt, Rinehart and Winston, 1974), 11; Mason, *Truman and the Pendergasts,* 155-56; and Bert Cochran, *Harry Truman and the Crisis Presidency* (New York: Funk and Wagnalls, 1973), 18-19. **115.** Transcript, Easley Oral History Interview, 99-103; and Cochran, *Truman and the Crisis Presidency,* 18.

116. Transcript, William Wear, Sr., Oral History Interview, Apr. 26, 1990, 58-59, HSTL. **117.** Author's phone interview with William Hannegan, May 28, 1994; Daniels, *Man of Independence,* 238-39; and HST to Harry Easley, May 23, 1944, Senatorial File, HST Papers, HSTL. **118.** David E. Lilienthal, *The Journals of David E. Lilienthal: The TVA Years, 1939-1945* (New York: Harper and Row, 1964), 1:690; Rexford G. Tugwell, *Off Course: From Truman to Nixon* (New York: Praeger, 1971), 179; and index card entry, July 22, 1944, The Secret Diary of Harold L. Ickes, LOC. **119.** Claude D. Pepper, *Pepper: Eyewitness to a Century* (New York: Harcourt, Brace, Jovanovich, 1987), 135. **120.** Margaret Truman, *Harry S. Truman,* 166-67; Allen and Shannon, *Truman Merry-Go-Round,* 13-14; and Merle Miller, *Plain Speaking,* 182-83.

121. Easley to HST, July 26, 1944, Harry Easley Papers, HSTL; research notes for *Man of Independence,* undated 1949, 31; HST to Harry Easley, May 23, 1944, Senatorial File, HST Papers, HSTL; and author's phone interview with William Hannegan, Feb. 24, 1994. **122.** Transcript, George E. Allen Oral History Interview, May 15, 1969, 59, HSTL. **123.** Robert H. Ferrell, *Choosing Truman: The Democratic Convention of 1944* (Columbia: Univ. of Missouri Press, 1994), 35. **124.** Byrnes, *All in One Lifetime,* 216-31; and Samuel Rosenman, *Working with Roosevelt* (New York: Harper, 1952), 202. **125.** Phillips, *Truman Presidency,* 38; Gosnell, *Truman's Crises,* 179; and Steinberg, *Man from Missouri,* 200-203.

126. Savage, *Roosevelt,* 159-63. **127.** Ferrell, *Choosing Truman,* 43-44. **128.** Index card entry, July 9, 1944, The Secret Diary of Harold L. Ickes, LOC; and Jim Bishop, *FDR's Last Year: April 1944–April 1945* (New York: William Morrow, 1974), 87. **129.** Robert Sherwood, *Roosevelt and Hopkins: An Intimate History* (New York: Harper, 1948), 740-41. **130.** Index card entry, July 16, 1944, The Secret Diary of Harold L. Ickes, LOC.

131. George E. Allen, *Presidents Who Have Known Me* (New York: Simon and Schuster, 1950), 125. **132.** Transcript, Allen Oral History Interview, 59. **133.** Josephus Daniels to FDR, Apr. 11, 1944, Robert E. Hannegan Papers, HSTL. **134.** Index card entry in Ickes diary, July 16, 1944, LOC. **135.** Ferrell, *Choosing Truman,* 6.

136. Author's interview with Wilson Wyatt in Louisville, Ky, on June 24, 1993. **137.** Transcript, Allen Oral History Interview, 62; and Daniels, *Man of Independence,* 240-45. **138.** Copy of letter, FDR to Hannegan, July 19, 1944, Robert E. Hannegan Papers, HSTL; Ferrell, *Choosing Truman,* 83-84; and Grace Tully, *F.D.R. My Boss* (New York: Charles Scribner's Sons, 1949), 276. **139.** Sherwood, *Roosevelt and Hopkins,* 881. **140.** Ibid., 882.

141. Richard L. Miller, *Truman,* 383-84. **142.** Cochran, *Truman and the Crisis Presidency,* 18; Alben W. Barkley, *That Reminds Me* (New York: Doubleday, 1954), 189-90; and Wyatt interview. **143.** Press release, Sept. 9, 1941, Senatorial File, HST Papers, HSTL. **144.** DNC, *Official Report of the Proceedings of the Democratic National Convention, 1944* (Washington, D.C.: DNC, 1944), 256-75. **145.** Abell, *Pearson Diaries,* 11.

146. Ferrell, *Dear Bess,* 509. **147.** Gosnell, *Truman's Crises,* 197-99. **148.** HST, *Memoirs,* 1:218-19. **149.** Pamphlet, "The Inside Story," Missouri Republican State Committee, 1944, Victor Messall Papers, HSTL. **150.** Steinberg, *Man from Missouri,* 219-20.

151. Clipping, *Pittsburgh Sun-Telegraph,* Nov. 7, 1944, Senatorial File, HST Papers, HSTL. **152.** Clipping, *Albany Times-Union,* Nov. 6, 1944, Senatorial File, HST Papers, HSTL. **153.** McCullough, *Truman,* 321. **154.** Merle Miller, *Plain Speaking,* 414. **155.** Margaret Truman, *Harry S. Truman,* 73.

156. Steinberg, *Man from Missouri,* 229-30; and Gosnell, *Truman's Crises,* 219. **157.** HST, *Memoirs,* 1:220. **158.** Gosnell, *Truman's Crises,* 210. **159.** Helm, *Harry Truman,* 230-31. **160.** *Congressional Record,* 79th Cong., 1st sess., 679.

161. Marie D. Natoli, "Harry S. Truman and the Contemporary Vice Presidency," *Presidential Studies Quarterly* 18 (1988): 81-84. **162.** Transcript, Edward D. McKim Oral History Interview, Feb. 17 and 19, 1964, 106, HSTL. **163.** Robert J. Donovan, *Conflict and Crisis: The Presidency of Harry S. Truman, 1945-1948* (New York: Norton, 1977). **164.** Transcript, Matthew J. Connelly Oral History Interview, Aug. 21, 1968, 429, HSTL. **165.** Alonzo L. Hamby, *Beyond the New Deal: Harry S. Truman and American Liberalism* (New York: Columbia Univ. Press, 1973), 54-56; author's interview with Joseph Rauh in Washington, D.C., July 10, 1991; transcript, James H. Rowe Jr. Oral History Interview, Sept. 30, 1969 and Jan. 15, 1970, 37, HSTL; and Steven M. Gillon, *Politics and Vision: The ADA and American Liberalism, 1947-1985* (New York: Oxford Univ. Press, 1987), x-22.

166. Harry S. Truman, *Truman Speaks* (New York: Columbia Univ. Press, 1960), 7; transcript, interview with J. Howard McGrath, Mar. 24, 1955, 15, Memoirs File, HST Papers, HSTL; and Dunar, *Truman Scandals,* 7-8. **167.** Transcript, Connelly Oral History Interview, 298; author's interview with Donald Dawson in Washington, D.C., July 11, 1991; and diary entry, Nov. 4, 1948, 188, Eben A. Ayers Papers, HSTL.

2. TRUMAN AND THE MACHINE BOSSES

1. Lyle W. Dorsett, *Franklin D. Roosevelt and the City Bosses* (New York: Kennikat Press, 1977), 114. **2.** Samuel J. Eldersveld, "The Influence of Metropolitan Party Plu-

ralities in Presidential Party Pluralities Since 1920," *American Political Science Review* 43 (December 1949): 1198-1202. **3.** Jack Redding, *Inside the Democratic Party* (New York: Bobbs-Merrill, 1958), 46-51. **4.** Daniels, *Man of Independence*, 235-36. **5.** Dorsett, Franklin D. *Roosevelt and the City Bosses*, 5-77; Steinberg, *Bosses*, 361-63; and George Graham, *Morality in American Politics* (New York: Random House, 1952), 87-88.
  6. Philip J. Funigiello, *The Challenge to Urban Liberalism: Federal-City Relations during World War II* (Knoxville: University of Tennessee Press, 1978), 10. **7.** Ibid., 98-99. **8.** Roger Biles, *Big City Boss in Depression and War: Mayor Edward J. Kelly of Chicago* (DeKalb: Northern Illinois Univ. Press, 1984), 74-80; and John Kincaid, "Political Success and Policy Failure: The Persistence of Machine Politics in Jersey City" (Ph.D. diss., Temple University, 1981), 477. **9.** *PPP,* 1946, 61. **10.** Hal Burton, *The City Fights Back* (New York: Citadel Press, 1954), 85; and Kenneth Fox, *Metropolitan America: Urban Life and Urban Politics in the United States, 1940-1980* (Jackson: Univ. Press of Mississippi, 1986), 51.
  11. Bruce Stave, *The New Deal and the Last Hurrah: Pittsburgh Politics* (Pittsburgh: Univ. of Pittsburgh Press, 1970), 162-192; and Steven P. Erie, *Rainbow's End: Irish-Americans and the Dilemmas of Urban Machine Politics, 1840-1985* (Berkley: Univ. of California Press, 1988), 163-168. **12.** John M. Allswang, *Bosses, Machines, and Urban Voters: An Americna Symbiosis* (New York: Kennikat Press, 1977), 31. **13.** Erie, *Rainbow's End,* 195. **14.** Mark I. Gelfand, *A Nation of Cities: The Federal Government and Urban America, 1933-1965* (New York: Oxford Univ. Press, 1975), 109-12; and Richard O. Davies, *Housing Reform during the Truman Administration* (Columbia: Univ. of Missouri Press, 1966), 12. **15.** Zane L. Miller, *Urbanization of Modern America* (New York: Harcourt Brace Jovanovich, 1973), 164.
  16. U.S. Congress, *Housing Act of 1949: Hearings before the Committee on Banking and Currency, House of Representatives, on H.R. 4009,* 81st Cong., 1st sess. (Washington, D.C.: GPO, 1949), 9-11. **17.** U.S. Congress, *Housing Act of 1949: Hearings before a Subcommittee of the Committee on Banking and Currency, United States Senate, on S. 2246,* 81st Cong., 1st sess., (Washington D.C.: GPO, 1949), 18-19. **18.** Davies, *Housing Reform,* 84-115. **19.** Erie, *Rainbow's End,* 163-68. **20.** Burton, 20-21; and Michael P. Weber, *Don't Call Me Boss: David L. Lawrence, Pittsburgh's Renaissance Mayor* (Pittsburgh: Univ. of Pittsburgh Press, 1988), 194-205.
  21. H.R. 4009 hearings, 43-47; and Robert A. Caro, *The Power Broker: Robert Moses and the Fall of New York* (New York: Vintage Books, 1975), 12, 777-78. **22.** Charles Van Devander, *The Big Bosses* (New York: Howell, Soskin, 1944), 316-17. **23.** Gillon, *Politics and Vision,* 40-46; Irwin Ross, "Big City Machines and Liberal Voters," *Commentary* 10, no. 4 (October 1950): 301-8; DNC Pamphlet, "Who Voted to Strengthen the Free World?" undated 1950, Political File, PSF, HSTL; and Michael J. Cohen, *Truman and Israel* (Berkeley: Univ. of California Press, 1990), 202. **24.** Weber, *Don't Call Me Boss,* 186; and DNC, *National Convention, 1944,* 256-75. **25.** Dawson interview; and Sally Shames, "David L. Lawrence, Mayor of Pittsburgh: Development of a Political Leader" (Ph.D. diss., University of Pittsburgh, 1958), 43.
  26. Thomas J. Donaghy, *Keystone Democrat: David Lawrence Remembered* (New York: Vantage Press, 1986), 121. **27.** Report of the proceedings, DNC Credentials Com-

mittee, Aug. 23, 1949, 237-301, DNC Records, HSTL. **28.** DNC, *National Convention, 1944,* 260. **29.** William D. Miller, *Mr. Crump of Memphis* (Baton Rouge: Louisiana State Univ. Press, 1964), 321. **30.** Dawson interview. **31.** Michael J. Cohen, 215; William O'Dwyer, *Beyond the Golden Door* (New York: St. John's University Press, 1987), 255-360, 317-320; Rauh interview; and John F. Martin, *Civil Rights and the Crisis of Liberalism: The Democratic Party, 1945-1976* (Boulder, CO: Westview Press, 1979), 81-82. **32.** Weber, *Don't Call Me Boss,* 11. **33.** Shames, "Lawrence," 105-7. **34.** C.H. Westbrook, ed., *The Pennsylvania Manual, 1939* (Harrisburg: Commonwealth of Pennsylvania, 1940), 153-56; Richard C. Keller, *Pennsylvania's Little New Deal* (New York: Garland, 1982), 1-23, 230-35; and Paul B. Beers, *Pennsylvania Politics Today and Yesterday* (University Park: Pennsylvania State Univ. Press, 1980), 94. **35.** *NYT,* June 10, 1934, sec. 2:1.

36. Keller, *Pennsylvania's Little New Deal,* 157-285. **37.** James E. Miller, "The Negro in Pennsylvania Politics with Special Reference to Philadelphia since 1932," (Ph.D. diss., University of Pennsylvania, 1945), 240-42. **38.** Keller, *Pennsylvania's Little New Deal,* 303-17; Joseph E. Guffey, *70 Years on the Red-Fire Wagon* (Pittsburgh: privately printed, 1952), 109; and FDR to Michael Francis Doyle, Oct. 26, 1938, OF 300, FDRL. **39.** *NYT,* Feb. 28, 1939, 2, Dec. 9, 1939, 7, and Apr. 13, 1940, 18; Shames, "Lawrence," 32; and Donaghy, *Keystone Democrat,* 155-57. **40.** Donaghy, *Keystone Democrat,* 67.

41. Transcript, David L. Lawrence Oral History Interview, June 30, 1966, 10-15, HSTL. **42.** DNC, *National Convention, 1944,* 256. **43.** Donaghy, *Keystone Democrat,* 74. **44.** HST, *Memoirs,* 1:117. **45.** Author's interview with Samuel C. Brightman in Bethesda, Md., July 12, 1991.

46. DNC, *Democracy at Work: The Official Report of the Democratic National Convention, 1948* (Philadelphia: Local Democratic Political Committee of Pennsylvania, 1948), 2-3. **47.** Weber, *Don't Call Me Boss,* 334; and Beers, *Pennsylvania Politics,* 249. **48.** George Gallup, *The Political Almanac: 1952* (New York: B.C. Forbes and Sons, 1952), 262. **49.** Donaghy, *Keystone Democrat,* 122. **50.** *NYT,* Feb. 16, 1950, 10.

51. Donaghy, *Keystone Democrat,* 151-52; Weber, *Don't Call Me Boss,* 336-37; and Report of the proceedings, DNC Credentials Committee, Aug. 23, 1949, 290-301, DNC Records, HSTL. **52.** Report of the proceedings, DNC Credentials Committee, Aug. 23, 1949, 37, DNC Records, HSTL. **53.** Walter Johnson, *How We Drafted Adlai Stevenson* (New York: Knopf, 1955), 127-28; and Wyatt interview. **54.** Porter McKeever, *Adlai Stevenson: His Life and Legacy, a Biography* (New York: Quill, 1989), 193; and Richard C. Bain and Judith H. Parris, *Convention Decisions and Voting Records* (Washington, D.C.: Brookings Institution, 1973), 54. **55.** Walter Johnson, *How We Drafted Stevenson,* 102-14; and Congressional Quarterly, *Guide to U.S. Elections* (Washington, D.C.: CQ Press, 1985), 205.

56. Hugh A. Bone, *Party Committees and National Politics* (Seattle: Univ. of Washington Press, 1958), 219; and Philip A. Klinkner, *The Losing Parties: Out-Party National Committees, 1956-1993* (New Haven: Yale Univ. Press, 1994), 19-21. **57.** Burton, *City Fights Back,* 20-21. **58.** Ibid., 193. **59.** Alfred Steinberg, "Pittsburgh, A Big City," *National Municipal Review* 44 (March 1955): 126-31; and Jeanne R. Lowe, "Rebuilding Cities—and Politics," *Nation* 186 (Feb. 8, 1958): 118-21. **60.** David L. Lawrence, "Balancing Good Politics and Good Administration," *Public Administration Review* 14 (Spring 1954): 97. **61.** Roger Biles, *Memphis in the Great Depression* (Knoxville: Univ. of Tennessee Press, 1986), 75. **62.** Ibid., 78-79; and Dorsett, *Roosevelt and the City Bosses*, 35-48. **63.** William D. Miller, *Mr. Crump of Memphis*, 42-61. **64.** Ibid., 82-89; and author's interview with William Woolsey in Louisville, Ky., June 24, 1993. **65.** Biles, *Memphis in the Great Depression*, 42.

66. Steinberg, *Bosses*, 125-27; and City of Memphis, *Memphis: Civic Progress, 1940-1944* (Memphis: City of Memphis, 1945), 12-21. **67.** Steinberg, *Bosses*, 113; and Lucy Randolph Mason, *To Win These Rights: A Personal Story of the CIO in the South* (New York: Harper, 1952), 106-7. **68.** Ralph Bunche, *The Political Status of the Negro in the Age of FDR* (Chicago: Univ. of Chicago Press, 1973), 1132-33; David M. Tucker, *Black Pastors and Leaders* (Memphis: Memphis State Univ. Press, 1975), 100-102; and Gloria Brown Melton, "Blacks in Memphis, Tennessee, 1920-1955: A Historical Study," (Ph.D. diss., Washington State University, 1982), 131-32, 143-55. **69.** V.O. Key Jr., *Southern Politics in State and Nation* (Knoxville: Univ. of Tennessee Press, 1985), 60. **70.** Steinberg, *Bosses*, 132.

71. Jennings Perry, *Democracy Begins at Home: The Tennessee Fight on the Poll Tax* (Philadelphia: J.B. Lippincott, 1944), 35. **72.** William D. Miller, *Mr. Crump of Memphis*, 305-6. **73.** Robert H. Ferrell, ed., *Truman in the White House: The Diary of Eben A. Ayers* (Columbia: Univ. of Missouri Press, 1991), 252; and Biles, *Memphis in the Great Depression*, 125-35. **74.** William D. Miller, *Mr. Crump of Memphis*, 325. **75.** DNC, *Democracy at Work*, 277.

76. Woolsey interview; and Gallup, *Political Almanac: 1952*, 276. **77.** Allen Kitchens, "Ouster of Mayor Edward H. Crump," *West Tennessee Historical Society* 19 (1965): 105-20. **78.** Ibid., 123; and Steinberg, *Bosses*, 130. **79.** Kitchens, "Ouster of Crump," 123. **80.** Telegram, Estes Kefauver to Tom C. Clark, Aug. 1, 1948, Tom C. Clark Papers, HSTL. **81.** HST, *Memoirs*, 2:238. **82.** Estes Kefauver to HST, Aug. 30, 1949, OF 300, HSTL. **83.** Estes Kefauver to HST, Dec. 22, 1949, PSF, HSTL, 84. **84.** HST to Estes Kefauver, Jan. 2, 1950, PSF, HSTL. **85.** Charles L. Fontenay, *Estes Kefauver: A Biography* (Knoxville: Univ. of Tennessee Press, 1980), 239.

86. Steinberg, *Bosses*, 132-33; and Tucker, *Black Pastors and Leaders*, 97. **87.** Woolsey interview. **88.** Ralph Whitehead Jr., "The Ward Boss Who Saved the New Deal," *Chicago* 26 (May 1977): 140-42, 176-86. **89.** Biles, *Big City Boss*, 58. **90.** Stanley Frankel and Holmes Alexander, "Arvey of Illinois, New-Style Political Boss," *Collier's* 123 (July 23, 1949): 66.

91. Whitehead, "Ward Boss," 142. **92.** Klinkner, *Losing Parties*, 14-26; Michael J. Cohen, *Truman and Israel*, 202; Rauh interview; and Ralph M. Goldman, *Search for Consensus: The Story of the Democratic Party* (Philadelphia: Temple University Press, 1979), 277. **93.** "No Dog in the Manger," *Time* 48 (Dec. 30, 1946): 17. **94.** Len O'Connor, *Clout: Mayor Daley and His City* (Chicago: Henry Regnery, 1975), 85. **95.** Mike Royko, *Boss: Richard J. Daley of Chicago* (New York: New American Library, 1971), 61-63.

96. McKeever, *Adlai Stevenson,* 108-14. **97.** Martin, *Civil Rights,* 81; and Rauh interview. **98.** DNC, *Democracy at Work,* 202-10. **99.** Rauh interview. **100.** *PPP,* 1948, 853.

101. Ferrell, *Truman in the White House,* 266, 282; and Irwin Ross, *The Loneliest Campaign* (New York: New American Library, 1968), 182. **102.** Congressional Quarterly, *Guide to U.S. Elections* (Washington, D.C.: CQ Press, 1985), 357, 499, 615. **103.** McKeever, *Adlai Stevenson,* 103. **104.** Ibid., 112. **105.** James Lanagan to HST, Feb. 21, 1952, PSF, HSTL.

106. Virgil W. Peterson, *Barbarians in Our Midst* (Boston: Little, Brown, 1952), 248-50. **107.** Estes Kefauver, *Crime in America* (New York: Doubleday, 1951), 88. **108.** O'Connor, *Clout,* 72-73; and Virgil W. Peterson, *Barbarians in Our Midst,* 262-64. **109.** Ferrell, *Off the Record,* 261; and Estes Kefauver to HST, July 20, 1952, PSF, HSTL. **110.** Congressional Quarterly, *Guide to U.S. Elections,* 358.

111. Brightman interview; and Herbert S. Parmet, *The Democrats: The Years after FDR* (New York: Macmillan, 1976), 151. **112.** Ralph M. Goldman, *The National Party Chairmen and Committees: Factionalism at the Top* (New York: M.E. Sharpe, 1990), 458. **113.** Warren Moscow, *The Last of the Big-Time Bosses: The Life and Times of Carmine DeSapio and the Rise and Fall of Tammany Hall* (New York: Stein and Day, 1971), 88; and Alfred Connable and Edward Silberfarb, *Tigers of Tammany: Nine Men Who Ran New York* (New York: Holt, Rinehart and Winston, 1967), 298. **114.** Salvatore LaGumina, *New York at Mid-Century* (Westport, Conn.: Greenwood Press, 1992), 67. **115.** U.S. Senate, Special Committee to Investigate Organized Crime in Interstate Commerce, *The Kefauver Committee Report on Organized Crime* (New York: Didier, 1951), 106-7.

116. Louis Eisenstein and Elliot Rosenberg, *A Stripe of Tammany's Tiger* (New York: Robert Speller & Sons, 1966), 196-197. **117.** Ibid. **118.** Leonard Katz, *Uncle Frank: The Biography of Frank Costello* (New York: Drake, 1973), 178. **119.** Kefauver, *Crime in America,* 286-287. **120.** George Wolf, *Frank Costello: Prime Minister of the Underworld* (New York: Morrow, 1974), 223.

121. Moscow, *Last of the Bosses,* 70. **122.** Ibid., 73. **123.** Ibid., 75. **124.** Ibid., 80. **125.** Ibid., 105.

126. Robert Berdiner, "How Presidents Are Made," *The Reporter* (Feb. 9, 1956), 14. **127.** O'Dwyer, *Behind the Golden Door,* 282. **128.** LaGumina, *New York at Mid-Century,* 100-104. **129.** Ferrell, *Truman in the White House,* 266. **130.** Congressional Quarterly, *Guide to U.S. Elections,* 357.

131. Ferrell, *Truman in the White House,* 366; and Dawson interview. **132.** Moscow, Last of the Bosses, 100-101. **133.** Caro, *Power Broker,* 786-87; and George Walsh, *Public Enemies* (New York: Norton, 1980), 164-65. **134.** Connable and Silberfarb, *Tigers of Tammany,* 317; and Caro, 786. **135.** *Kefauver Committee Report on Organized Crime,* 121-22.

136. Warren Moscow, *What Have You Done for Me Lately?* (Englewod Cliffs, N.J.: Prentice-Hall, 1967), 32; and Jules Abels, *The Truman Scandals* (Chicago: Henry Regnery, 1956), 35. **137.** Moscow, *Last of the Bosses,* 87. **138.** Ferrell, *Truman in the White House,* 366. **139.** Ibid. **140.** *PPP,* 1950, 587.

141. LaGumina, *New York at Mid-Century,* 115. **142.** Ibid., 142. **143.** Ibid., 130. **144.** Richard N. Smith, *Thomas E. Dewey and His Times* (New York: Simon and Schuster, 1982), 573; and Congressional Quarterly, Guide to U.S. Elections, 518, 626. **145.** LaGumina, *New York at Mid-Century,* 142-45.

146. Kefauver Committee Report on Organized Crime, 125. **147.** *PPP,* 1951, 261; and *PPP,* 1952, 306. **148.** Alan Ware, *The Breakdown of Democratic Party Organization, 1940-1980* (New York: Oxford Univ. Press, 1985), 49-50. **149.** Samuel Lubell, *The Future of American Politics* (New York: Harper, 1965), 49. **150.** Ibid.

151. Fox, *Metropolitan America,* 51. **152.** Louis Harris, *Is There a Republican Majority?* (New York: Harper, 1954), 124. **153.** John J. Gunther, *Federal-City Relations in the United States* (Newark: Univ. of Delaware Press, 1990), 158; and O'Dwyer, *Beyond the Golden Door,* 256. **154.** Davies, *Housing Reform,* 136; and Dennis R. Judd, *The Politics of American Cities* (Boston: Little, Brown, 1984), 270. **155.** John J. Grove, "Pittsburgh's Renaissance: Industry's Role in the Rebirth of a City," *U.S.A. Tomorrow* 1 (October 1954): 14-21.

156. Erie, *Rainbow's End,* 163-64; and Paul Kleppner, *Chicago Divided: The Making of a Black Mayor* (DeKalb: Northern Illinois Univ. Press, 1985), 83-84. **157.** Louis Harris, *Is There a Republican Majority,* 1-21; and Edward C. Banfield and James Q. Wilson, *City Politics* (Cambridge: Harvard Univ. Press, 1963), 151-67. **158.** James Q. Wilson, *The Amateur Democrat* (Chicago: Univ. of Chicago Press, 1962), 13-15. **159.** John J. Harrigan, *Political Change in the Metropolis* (Glenview, Ill.: Scott, Foresman, 1989), 112. **160.** Cabell Phillips, "Exit the Boss, Enter the Leader," *New York Times Magazine,* Apr. 15, 1956, 26, 40, 42, 44; Frank J. Sorauf, "Patronage and Party," *Midwest Journal of Political Science* 3 (May 1959): 118-20; and Theodore J. Lowi, "Machine Politics—Old and New," *Public Interest* (Fall 1967): 83-92.

161. Dunar, *Truman Scandals,* 111-16; and Graham, *Morality,* 170. **162.** Ibid., 166-68, 231. **163.** Abels, *Truman Scandals,* 31-32. **164.** Walsh, *Public Enemies,* 222; and Charles W. Tobey, *The Return to Morality* (New York: Doubleday, 1952), 23-34. **165.** Abels, *Truman Scandals,* 36.

166. William D. Miller, *Mr. Crump of Memphis,* 330; David M. Tucker, *Memphis since Crump: Bossism, Blacks, and Civic Reformers, 1948-1968* (Knoxville: Univ. of Tennessee Press, 1980), 56-60; and Kincaid, "Political Success and Policy Failure," 477-78. **167.** Robert L. Heibroner, "Carmine G. DeSapio: The Smile on the Face of the Tiger," *Harper's Magazine* 209 (July 1954): 27-28; and Eugene Kennedy, *Himself! The Life and Times of Mayor Richard J. Daley* (New York: Viking, 1978), 86-88. **168.** Harris, *Is There a Republican Majority?* 5-59; and Angus Campbell and Warren E. Miller, "The Motivational Basis of Straight and Split Ticket Voting," *American Political Science Review* 51 (June 1957): 295.

3. TRUMAN AND THE DEMOCRATIC NATIONAL COMMITTEE

1. Abell, *Pearson Diaries,* 542. **2.** George C. Roberts, *Paul M. Butler: Hoosier Politican and National Political Leader* (Lanham, Md.: Univ. Press of America, 1987),

76-82; and Klinkner, *Losing Parties,* 20-21. **3.** HST, *Truman Speaks,* 7; and Theodore Cousens, *Politics and Political Organizations in America* (New York: Macmillan, 1942), 295, 299-300, 386-88, 405-6. **4.** Ralph M. Goldman, "The American President as Party Leader: A Synoptic History," in *Presidents and Their Parties: Leadership or Neglect?* ed. Robert Harmel (New York: Praeger, 1984), 22; and James W. Davis, *The President as Party Leader* (New York: Praeger, 1992), 106-7. **5.** Ferrell, *Off the Record,* 342.

6. Klinkner, *Losing Parties,* 22-40; and Irving Bernstein, *Promises Kept: John F. Kennedy's New Frontier* (New York: Oxford Univ. Press, 1991), 27. **7.** Ferrell, *Off the Record,* 381. **8.** Goldman, *Chairmen and Committees,* 432. **9.** Ken Hechler, *Working with Truman* (New York: G.P. Putnam's Sons, 1982), 26, 36, 152-53. **10.** Brightman interview; Neustadt interview; and author's telephone interview with George Elsey, Sept. 1, 1991.

11. Research notes for *The Man of Independence,* Aug. 30, 1949, 6, Jonathan Daniels Papers, part I, HSTL. **12.** Ferrell, *Choosing Truman,* 63-88; Hannegan interview, Feb. 24, 1994; and Parmet, *Democrats,* 18-20. **13.** Richard T. Johnson, *Managing the White House* (New York: Harper & Row, 1974), 52. **14.** Sidney M. Milkis, *The President and the Parties: The Transformation of the American Party System since the New Deal* (New York: Oxford Univ. Press, 1993), 152. **15.** Francis H. Heller ed., *The Truman White House: The Administration of the Presidency, 1945-1953* (Lawrence: Univ. Press of Kansas, 1980), 36-37; and author's telephone interview with Ken Hechler, Aug. 27, 1991.

16. Harold F. Bass Jr., "Presidential Responsibility for National Party Organization, 1945-1974" (Ph.D. diss., Vanderbilt University, 1978), 94-95. **17.** Davis, *President as Party Leader,* 104. **18.** V.O. Key Jr., *Politics, Parties, and Pressure Groups* (New York: Thomas Y. Crowell, 1950), 285. **19.** Dawson interview. **20.** Abell, *Pearson Diaries,* 96-97.

21. Eleanor Roosevelt to HST, Sept. 3, 1947, Robert E. Hannegan Papers, HSTL. **22.** Author's interview with William Batt Jr., Middletown, Conn., July 20, 1991. **23.** Author's telephone interview with Bertram Gross, Sept. 21, 1992. **24.** Brightman interview. **25.** India Edwards, *Pulling No Punches* (New York: G.P. Putnam's Sons, 1977), 140-42.

26. Ibid., 140. **27.** *PPP,* 1950, 140. **28.** Marie Chatham, "The Role of the National Party Chairman from Hanna to Farley" (Ph.D. diss., University of Maryland, 1953), 309. **29.** Bass, "Presidential Responsibility," 9. **30.** Research notes for *The Man of Independence,* Aug. 30, 1949, 6, Jonathan Daniels Papers, part I, HSTL.

31. Author's telephone interview with William Hannegan, Feb. 24, 1994. **32.** Parmet, *Democrats,* 68. **33.** Redding, *Inside the Democratic Party,* 94-95. **34.** Drew Pearson, "Hannegan and Wallace," manuscript, undated 1946, 1, Robert E. Hannegan Papers, HSTL. **35.** Fred Rodell, "Robert E. Hannegan," *American Mercury* 63, no. 272 (August 1946): 138.

36. Pearson, "Hannegan and Wallace," 12-13, HSTL. **37.** Ferrell, *Truman in the White House,* 211. **38.** Ibid., 121, 145. **39.** Clipping, Bell Syndicate, Sept. 14, 1946, Robert E. Hannegan Papers, HSTL. **40.** DNC booklet, "Campaign Issues . . . 1946" (Washington, D.C.: DNC, 1946), Clark M. Clifford Papers, HSTL.

41. Margaret Truman, *Harry S. Truman,* 349-50. **42.** Joseph C. Goulden, *The Best Years, 1945-1950* (New York: Atheneum, 1976), 229-30. **43.** David W. Reinhard, *The Republican Right since 1945* (Lexington: Univ. of Kentucky Press, 1983), 15-36. **44.** NYT, Jan. 24, 1947, 5. **45.** R. Alton Lee, *Truman and Taft-Hartley: A Question of Mandate* (Lexington: Univ. of Kentucky Press, 1966), 93.

46. Ibid., 95. **47.** *NYT,* Feb. 13, 1947, 5. **48.** Press release, Aug. 22, 1947, DNC Clipping File, HSTL. **49.** Press release, Dec. 18, 1947, DNC Clipping File, HSTL. **50.** Polls, Gael Sullivan to DNC members, June 6, 1947, PSF, HSTL.

51. Congressional Quarterly, *Guide to U.S. Elections,* 320; and press release on Gael Sullivan's Nov. 20, 1947 speech to the United Democratic Women's Clubs of Maryland, 2-3, HSTL. **52.** Speech by Gael Sullivan to Kansas Democratic Club, Feb. 21, 1948, 1, DNC folder, John M. Redding Papers, HSTL. **53.** Redding, Inside the Democratic Party, 156-65. **54.** Pleas E. Greenlee to HST, Aug. 25, 1947, DNC folder, PSF, HSTL. **55.** Telegrams, Frank McHale to HST, Herbert S. Walters to HST, Melvin E. Thompson to HST, and A.F. Whitney to HST, all dated Aug. 26, 1947, DNC folder, PSF, HSTL.

56. Redding, *Inside the Democratic Party,* 94. **57.** Mike Kirwan to HST, Sept. 12, 1947, 2, PSF, HSTL. **58.** Brightman interview. **59.** Clipping, *St. Louis Post-Dispatch,* July 14, 1947, DNC Clipping File, HSTL; and Redding, *Inside the Democratic Party,* 89-90. **60.** *NYT,* Sept. 28, 1947, 1.

61. Ibid., Oct. 30, 1947, 1. **62.** Transcript, Matthew J. Connelly Oral History Interview, Aug. 21, 1968, 406-7, HSTL. **63.** Goldman, *Chairmen and Committees,* 424; and Allen and Shannon, *Truman Merry-Go-Round,* 98-102. **64.** Transcript, Kenneth M. Birkhead Oral History Interview, July 7, 1966, 36, HSTL. **65.** Pat Brown to Matthew J. Connelly, Dec. 29, 1947, OF 300, HSTL; and Gael Sullivan to Clark M. Clifford, June 2, 1947, Clark M. Clifford Papers, HSTL; and James Roosevelt to J. Howard McGrath, Oct. 29, 1947, J. Howard McGrath Papers, HSTL.

66. United Press clipping, Oct. 29, 1948, DNC Records, J. Howard McGrath Papers, HSTL. **67.** Robert A. Garson, *The Democratic Party and the Politics of Sectionalism: 1941-1948* (Baton Rouge: Louisiana State Univ. Press, 1974), 284-302. **68.** *Providence Bulletin,* Feb. 28, 1948, DNC Records, J. Howard McGrath Papers, HSTL. **69.** *Providence Bulletin,* Jan. 30, 1948, DNC Records, J. Howard McGrath Papers, HSTL. **70.** Ibid.

71. Clark M. Clifford to HST, Nov. 19, 1947, 20, Clark M. Clifford Papers, HSTL. **72.** Elsey interview; and transcript, Birkhead Oral History Interview, 40. **73.** Ferrell, *Truman in the White House,* 285. **74.** HST, *Memoirs,* 2:257. **75.** *PPP,* 1949, 237-38.

76. Jules Abels, *Out of the Jaws of Victory* (New York: Henry Holt, 1959), 284. **77.** Lemuel H. Davis to HST, July 16, 1951, OF 1644, HSTL; and Maury Maverick to Donald Dawson, Oct. 6, 1950, OF 300, HSTL. **78.** Ferrell, *Truman in the White House,* 84-85. **79.** Transcript, interview with J. Howard McGrath, Feb. 24, 1955, 13-15, Memoirs file, HST Papers, HSTL. **80.** Goldman, *Chairmen and Committees,* 430.

81. Proceedings of the DNC's Credentials Committee, Aug. 23 and 24, 1949, DNC Records, HSTL. **82.** Clipping, *Kansas City Times,* June 23, 1949, William M. Boyle Jr. Papers, HSTL. **83.** McCullough, *Truman,* 688-89. **84.** *PPP,* 1949, 439.

85. Joseph P. Harris "The Senatorial Rejection of Leland Olds," *American Political Science Review* 45 (1951): 674-92. **86.** *PPP,* 1949, 502. **87.** Ibid. **88.** Goldman, *Chairmen and Committees,* 430. **89.** Joseph P. Harris, "Rejection of Olds," 674-92. **90.** DNC press release, Oct. 9, 1949, DNC Clipping File, HSTL.
91. Clipping, *Washington Star,* Oct. 11, 1949, DNC Clipping File, HSTL. **92.** Hamby, *Beyond the New Deal,* 335. **93.** *PPP,* 1950, 257. **94.** Allen and Shannon, *Truman Merry-Go-Round,* 74. **95.** DNC press release, Oct. 28, 1949, 4, William M. Boyle Jr., Papers, HSTL. **96.** Ibid. **97.** *PPP,* 1950, 410. **98.** Ibid., 413. **99.** Clipping, *Louisville Courier Journal,* Jan. 4, 1950, Committee Finances 1949-1950 folder, DNC Clipping File, HSTL. **100.** Congressional Quarterly Report (Mar. 23, 1951), 426; and Sean J. Savage, "Conflicts over a Research Division for the Democratic National Committee during the Truman Administration" (paper presented at the annual meeting of the Southwestern Political Science Association, Austin, Texas, Mar. 21, 1992), 30.
101. Clipping, *Washington Post,* Aug. 8, 1950, Committee Finances 1949-1950 folder, DNC Clipping File, HSTL. **102.** Gosnell, *Truman's Crises,* 456. **103.** HST to Clifford Langsdale, Nov. 29, 1950, PSF, HSTL. **104.** Hechler, *Working with Truman,* 169-72; and Murphy to HST, July 11, 1950, DNC folder, Charles S. Murphy Papers, HSTL. **105.** Clipping, *Washington Post,* July 21, 1951, 1951 folder, OF 299-A, HSTL.
106. Dunar, *Truman Scandals,* 94-95. **107.** Copy of U.S. Senate, Interim Report of the Committee on Expenditures in the Executive Departments, 82d Cong., 2d sess., Jan. 31, 1952, Senate Report 1142, 24, UKL. **108.** *PPP,* 1951, 545; and *NYT,* October 14, 1951. **109.** Ibid. **110.** Edwards, *Pulling No Punches,* 141.
111. Clipping, *Washington Post,* Nov. 5, 1951, Frank McKinney folder, PSF, HSTL. **112.** India Edwards to HST, Oct. 30, 1951, Box 56, India Edwards File, HSTL. **113.** Ed Brown to Matthew J. Connelly, Nov. 14, 1951, Miscellaneous folder, OF 299-A, HSTL. **114.** W.O. Edwards to HST, Dec. 11, 1951, Miscellaneous folder, OF 299-A, HSTL. **115.** Transcript, Matthew J. Connelly Oral History Interview, 408-11, HSTL.
116. Goldman, *Chairmen and Committees,* 434. **117.** Clipping, *Washington Star,* Nov. 1, 1951, DNC Clipping File, HSTL. **118.** "McKinney for Boyle," *Newsweek* 38 (Nov. 28, 1951): 28-29. **119.** Frank E. McKinney's acceptance speech, Oct. 31, 1951, Frank E. McKinney folder, DNC Clipping File, HSTL. **120.** Hechler and Gross interviews; and author's telephone interview with Philip Dreyer, Oct. 24, 1991.
121. DNC press release, Dec. 2, 1951, Frank E. McKinney folder, DNC Clipping File, HSTL. **122.** "Final Report of Frank E. McKinney," Aug. 20, 1952, 4, Frank E. McKinney folder, PSF, HSTL; and Goldman, *Chairmen and Committees,* 435. **123.** *NYT,* Dec. 11, 1951. **124.** Clipping, *Philadelphia Inquirer,* Dec. 11, 1951, Frank E. McKinney folder, DNC Clipping File, HSTL. **125.** Clipping, *Washington Post,* May 20, 1952, Frank E. McKinney folder, PSF, HSTL.
126. DNC press release, May 19, 1952, Frank E. McKinney folder, PSF, HSTL. **127.** *PPP,* 1952, 360. **128.** Wyatt interview. **129.** Ferrell, *Off the Record,* 267. **130.** Ibid., 268.
131. HST, *Memoirs,* 2:561-63. **132.** Bass, "Presidential Responsibility," 1-2; and James W. Davis, *President as Party Leader,* 109. **133.** Bone, *Party Committees and National Politics,* 32-33. **134.** Gross interview; and HST, *Memoirs,* 2:561-62.

135. Cornelius P. Cotter and Bernard Hennessy, *Politics without Power: The National Party Committees* (New York: Atherton Press, 1964), 74-75, 88. **136.** Charles S. Murphy to HST, June 4, 1951, Charles S. Murphy Papers, HSTL; and Hechler interview. **137.** Dreyer interview. **138.** Bertram Gross to HST, Jan. 5, 1952, Research Division folder, PSF, HSTL. **139.** Batt interview. **140.** Dreyer interview.
    141. Batt interview; and transcript, Johannes Hoeber Oral History Interview, Sept. 13, 1966, 27-28, HSTL. **142.** Transcript, William L. Batt Jr., Oral History Interview, July 26, 1966, 41, HSTL. **143.** Ibid., 12. **144.** Transcript, Frank K. Kelly Oral History Interview, Apr. 15, 1988, 62, HSTL. **145.** Transcript, William L. Batt Jr., Oral History Interview, 12-13.
    146. Transcript, Frank K. Kelly Oral History Interview, 65. **147.** David Lloyd to George Elsey and Ken Hechler, June 17, 1951, George M. Elsey Papers, HSTL. **148.** Gross interview. **149.** "Local Background and Information for the Stevenson Campaign 1952," report completed by Anthony Lewis, Box 325, Philip Stern Papers, JFKL. **150.** Gross interview.
    151. Bone, *Party Committees and National Politics,* 42-43. **152.** Cotter and Hennessy, *Politics without Power,* 134. **153.** Redding, *Inside the Democratic Party,* 42. **154.** Ibid., 44-45. **155.** Ibid., 46.
    156. Brightman interview; and James T. Patterson, *Mr. Republican: A Biography of Robert A. Taft* (Boston: Houghton Mifflin, 1972), 379. **157.** "Democratic Radio Show: Script #1," 1948, Radio Script folder, India Edwards Papers, HSTL. **158.** Ibid., 10. **159.** Redding, *Inside the Democratic Party,* 146. **160.** Ibid., 237-38.
    161. Ibid., 244-54. **162.** Ibid., 254. **163.** Kathleen Hall Jamieson, *Packaging the Presidency* (New York: Oxford Univ. Press, 1984), 33-34. **164.** DNC pamphlet, "Who Voted to Strengthen the Free World? The Record of the United States Senate on Foreign Policy," 1950, Clinton Anderson folder, PSF, HSTL. **165.** DNC pamphlet, "Scare Words: A Compilation of Republican Attacks on Progressive Legislation since 1882," 1950, 1, Clinton Anderson folder, PSF, HSTL.
    166. Jamieson, *Packaging the Presidency,* 41-42. **167.** George W. Ball, *The Past Has Another Pattern* (New York: Norton, 1982), 143-44. **168.** Jamieson, *Packaging the Presidency,* 43-45. **169.** Transcript, Samuel C. Brightman Oral History Interview, Dec. 7-8, 1966, 14-15, HSTL. **170.** "Final Report of Frank E. McKinney," Aug. 20, 1952, Frank E. McKinney folder, PSF, HSTL.
    171. Max Levin to Green, May 21, 1948; Leonard Lerner to Green, Apr. 26, 1948; and A.M. Grobard to Green, Apr. 14, 1948, Theodore F. Green Papers, LOC; and Lubell, *Future of American Politics,* 201-4. **172.** Allen and Shannon, *Truman Merry-Go-Round,* 98-102. **173.** "Plan of Activities," undated, Box 1130, Theodore F. Green Papers, LOC. **174.** Redding, *Inside the Democratic Party,* 202-7. **175.** Richard S. Kirkendall, "Election of 1948," in *History of American Presidential Elections: 1789-1968,* ed. Arthur M. Schlesinger Jr. and Fred L. Israel (New York: Chelsea House, 1971), 4:3139.
    176. Angus Campbell and Robert L. Kahn, *The People Elect a President* (Ann Arbor: Univ. of Michigan Survey Research Center, 1952), 36-39. **177.** Vincent M. Gaughan to John W. Snyder, Oct. 2, 1948, DNC 1943-1952 folder, John W. Snyder Papers, HSTL; and "Report of Young Democratic National Headquarters Activity, 1948-

1949," HST Papers, HSTL. **178.** *The Spotlight* 6, no. 16 (November 1948): 2, Clark M. Clifford Papers, HSTL. **179.** Clipping, *Washington Star,* Aug. 4, 1948, DNC Clipping File, HSTL. **180.** Brightman interview.

181. DNC pamphlet, "The Truman Record," 1948, DNC file, John M. Redding Papers, HSTL. **182.** John F. Martin, *Civil Rights,* 79-85. **183.** Roger H. Marz, "The Democratic Digest: A Content Analysis," *American Political Science Review* 51 (September 1957): 696-703; and Savage, *Roosevelt,* 91-94. **184.** Susan Ware, *Partner and I* (New Haven: Yale Univ. Press, 1987), 168-72, 182-83. **185.** Mary Dewson to Caroline O'Day, Mar. 15, 1934, DNC Papers, FDRL; chart, "Suggested Programs for Democratic Women's Organizations," Mary Dewson Papers, FDRL; Susan Ware, *Partner and I,* 199-221; chart, "The Favored State Party Set Up for Democratic Women," 1938, PPF 603, FDRL; Henry B. Sirgo, "Women, Blacks and the New Deal," *Women & Politics* 14, no. 3 (1994): 61-63; and Marguerite Fisher and Betty Whitehead, "Women and National Party Organization," *American Political Science Review* 38 (1944): 896.

186. Transcript, India Edwards Oral History Interview, Jan. 16, 1969, 2, HSTL. **187.** Georgia Cook Morgan, "India Edwards: Distaff Politician of the Truman Era," *Missouri Historical Review* 78 (1984): 297. **188.** Transcript, India Edwards Oral History Interview, 3. **189.** Edwards, *Pulling No Punches,* 8. **190.** "Housewives for Truman: A Program Designed to Bring in the Vote," 1948, 4-5, India Edwards Papers, HSTL. **191.** Transcipt, India Edwards Oral History Interview, 19-21. **192.** Ibid., 22. **193.** Morgan, "India Edwards," 300; and Edwards, *Pulling No Punches,* 115. **194.** Transcript, India Edwards Oral History Interview, 18-19. **195.** Edwards to HST, Oct. 20, 1948, India Edwards Papers, HSTL.

196. Reo M. Christenson, *The Brannan Plan: Farm Politics and Policy* (Ann Arbor: Univ. of Michigan Press, 1959), 153-54; Monte M. Poen, *Harry S. Truman versus the Medical Lobby: The Genesis of Medicare* (Columbia: Univ. of Missouri Press, 1979), 178-179; and Edwards, *Pulling No Punches,* 129-140. **197.** Edwards, *Pulling No Punches,* 130. **198.** Morgan, "India Edwards," 299. **199.** India Edwards to HST, Oct. 24, 1951, PSF, HSTL. **200.** Edwards, *Pulling No Punches,* 173-74.

201. Morgan, "India Edwards," 302-3; and transcript, India Edwards Oral History Interview, 89. **202.** Edwards, *Pulling No Punches,* 171-72. **203.** Ibid., 199-203. **204.** India Edwards to HST, Dec. 4, 1952, India Edwards Papers, HSTL. **205.** Bone, *Party Committees and National Politics,* 107-8; and Katie Louchheim, *By the Political Sea* (New York: Doubleday, 1970), 68.

206. Ann Landers to India Edwards, Oct. 8, 1953, India Edwards Papers, HSTL. **207.** Edwards, *Pulling No Punches,* 269. **208.** Louise Overacker, *Presidential Campaign Funds* (Boston: Boston Univ. Press, 1946), 13-14. **209.** Ibid., 14. **210.** Ibid., 15.

211. Key, *Politics, Parties, and Pressure Groups,* 456. **212.** Overacker, *Presidential Campaign Funds,* 15. **213.** Ibid., 36; and Alexander Heard, *The Costs of Democracy* (Chapel Hill: Univ. of North Carolina Press, 1960), 352. **214.** Savage, *Roosevelt,* 87-88. **215.** Ronald F. Stinnett, *Democrats, Dinners, and Dollars* (Ames: Iowa State Univ. Press, 1967), 173.

216. J.W. Lederle, "Political Committee Expenditures and the Hatch Act," *Michigan Law Review* 44 (1945): 294-99; and Louise Overacker, "Presidential Campaign

Funds," *American Political Science Review* 39 (October 1945): 899-925. **217.** Key, *Politics, Parties, and Pressure Groups,* 482-483. **218.** Overacker, *Presidential Campaign Funds,* 59; and Congressional Quarterly, *Politics in America, 1945-1964* (Washington, D.C.: CQ Press, 1965), 82. **219.** John Van Doren, *Big Money in Little Sums* (Chapel Hill: Univ. of North Carolina Press, 1956), 12-13. **220.** Ibid., 15-16.
   221. Ibid., 43, 58. **222.** Ibid., 34. **223.** *CQ Weekly Report* 21, no. 2 (Jan. 9, 1953): 41. **224.** *CQ Weekly Report* 7, no. 3 (Jan. 21, 1949): 71. **225.** Clipping, *Washington Post,* Dec. 30, 1948, DNC Clipping File, HSTL.
   226. Ibid. **227.** Clippings, *Chicago Tribune,* Feb. 27, 1950, and *New York Times Herald,* Nov. 3, 1950, DNC Clipping File, HSTL; and *CQ Weekly Report* 10, no. 3 (Jan. 18, 1952): 42. **228.** Clipping, *New York Herald Tribune,* Feb. 5, 1950, DNC Clipping File, HSTL. **229.** Ibid. **230.** Stinnett, *Democrats, Dinners, and Dollars,* 176, 186.
   231. Savage, *Roosevelt,* 88-89. **232.** Stinnett, *Democrats, Dinners, and Dollars,* 246. **233.** Ibid., 248. **234.** Ibid., 253. **235.** *PPP,* 1952, 225.
   236. *Memoirs,* 2:551-52. **237.** Ibid., 555. **238.** Gary W. Reichard, *Politics as Usual: The Age of Truman and Eisenhower* (Arlington Heights, Ill.: Harlan Davidson, 1988), 77-83. **239.** Nelson W. Polsby and Aaron Wildavsky, *Presidential Elections* (New York: Free Press, 1991), 328. **240.** James Q. Wilson, *Amateur Democrat,* 18-21.
   241. James W. Davis, *President as Party Leader,* 20; and Fontenay, *Estes Kefauver,* 193-98. **242.** Roberts, *Butler,* 56-60; and Bone, *Party Committees and National Politics,* 102-3. **243.** Parmet, *Democrats,* 151-61. **244.** Cotter and Hennessy, *Politics without Power,* 87-89; and Larry J. Sabato, *The Party's Just Begun* (Glenview, Ill.: Scott, Foresman, 1988), 59-60. **245.** Bass, "Presidential Responsibility," 2-14; Milkis, *President and the Parties,* 312-13; Paul S. Herrnson, *Party Campaigning in the 1980s* (Cambridge: Harvard Univ. Press, 1988), 124-30; Sabato, *Party's Just Begun,* 152-60; and John F. Bibby, *Politics, Parties, and Elections in America* (Chicago: Nelson-Hall, 1992), 91-92.

4. HAD ENOUGH? REPUBLICAN RESURGENCE, 1946-1948

   1. Arthur H. Vandenberg Jr., ed., *The Private Papers of Senator Vandenberg* (Boston: Houghton Mifflin, 1952), 167. **2.** Patterson, *Mr. Republican,* 302. **3.** Parmet, *Democrats,* 18. **4.** Reinhard, *Republican Right since 1945,* 12. **5.** David L. Porter, *Congress and the Waning of the New Deal* (New York: Kennikat Press, 1980), 136-43; and Patterson, *Congressional Conservatism and the New Deal,* 333-34.
   6. Rauh interview; Gillon, *Politics and Vision,* x-22; and Hamby, *Beyond the New Deal,* 121-22. **7.** Olin D. Johnston to HST, Apr. 18, 1945, PPF 598, HST Papers, HSTL; and HST to Fred M. Vinson, Aug. 27, 1945, Fred M. Vinson Collection, HSTL. **8.** I.F. Stone, *The Truman Era, 1945-1952* (Boston: Little, Brown, 1972), xxi. **9.** Ibid. **10.** *PPP,* 1945, 279-80.
   11. Ibid., 280. **12.** Ibid., 309. **13.** James R. Boylan, *The New Deal Coalition and the Election of 1946* (New York: Garland, 1981), 21. **14.** Garson, *Democratic Party,* 146. **15.** Donovan, *Conflict and Crisis,* 115.

16. HST, *Memoirs,* 1:535. **17.** Hamby, *Beyond the New Deal,* 85. **18.** Dunar, *Truman Scandals,* 23-30. **19.** Henry Wallace to HST, Sept. 20, 1946, PSF, HSTL. **20.** Boylan, *New Deal Coalition,* 36-42.

21. Ibid., 46; and William S. White, *The Taft Story* (New York: Harper Brothers, 1954), 45. **22.** George H. Gallup, *The Gallup Poll: Public Opinion, 1935-1971* (New York: Random House, 1972), 2:585. **23.** Ibid., 588. **24.** Chester Bowles, *Promises to Keep* (New York: Harper & Row, 1971), 153-54. **25.** *PPP,* 1946, 330.

26. Gallup, *Public Opinion, 1935-1971,* 2:590. **27.** Patrick E. McGinnis, "Republican Party in Congress, 1936-1948" (Ph.D. diss., Tulane University, 1967), 140-44. **28.** Ibid. **29.** Nicol C. Rae, *The Decline and Fall of the Liberal Republicans* (New York: Oxford Univ. Press, 1989), 6-35. **30.** Clyde P. Weed, *The Nemesis of Reform: The Republican Party during the New Deal* (New York: Columbia Univ. Press, 1994), 11-24.

31. Ibid., 188-90. **32.** Joseph W. Martin Jr., *My First Fifty Years in Politics* (New York: Greenwood Press, 1975), 81; and McGinniss, 99. **33.** U.S. Census Bureau, *The Statistical History of the United States from Colonial Times to the Present* (Stamford, Conn.: Fairfield, 1965), 691. **34.** Irwin Gertzog, "The Role of the President in the Mid-Term Congressional Election" (Ph.D. diss., University of North Carolina, 1965), 82; Donald Kingsley, "Election Interlude," *Current History* 3 (December 1942): 300-301; Gary C. Jacobson, *The Electoral Origins of Divided Government* (Boulder, Colo.: Westview Press, 1990), 51; Gary C. Jacobson and Samuel Kernell, *Strategy and Choice in Congressional Elections* (New Haven: Yale Univ. Press, 1981), 17; and David W. Brady, "The Causes and Consequences of Divided Government: Toward A New Theory of American Politics?" *American Political Science Review* 87 (March 1993): 189-94.
35. Arthur H. Vandenberg to Robert E. Hannegan, Oct. 26, 1946, Robert E. Hannegan Papers, HSTL; and J. W. Patterson, "Arthur Vandenberg's Rhetorical Strategy in Advancing Bipartisan Foreign Policy," *Quarterly Journal of Speech* 56 (1970): 284-95.

36. HST, *Memoirs,* 1:601-2; Patterson, *Mr. Republican,* 330-40; and Vandenberg, *Papers of Vandenberg,* 266-67. **37.** George H. Nash, *The Conservative Intellectual Movement in America since 1945* (New York: Basic Books, 1976), 125; and Reinhard, *Republican Right since 1945,* 4-5. **38.** Arthur H. Vandenberg to Robert A. Taft, Apr. 23, 1946, and Taft to Vandenberg, Oct. 20, 1946, Robert A. Taft Papers, LOC. **39.** Russell Kirk and James McClellan, *The Political Principles of Robert A. Taft* (New York: Fleet Press, 1967), 47. **40.** Jouett Shouse to Charles P. Grimes, Sept. 29, 1944, Jouett Shouse Papers, UKL; and Richard N. Smith, *Dewey and His Times,* 419.

41. Reinhard, *Republican Right since 1945,* vii-16. **42.** Martin's speech at the 1944 Republican National Convention, June 27, 1944, 1-13, Joseph W. Martin Jr. Papers, JWMI. **43.** Goulden, *Best Years,* 230. **44.** Reinhard, *Republican Right since 1945,* 17; White, *Taft Story,* 56; and *Human Events* 3 (Nov. 6, 1946): 5. **45.** Martin's speech to Women's Republican Club, Washington, D.C., Feb. 8, 1946, 8, Joseph W. Martin Jr. Papers, JWMI.

46. Martin's radio address, Oct. 24, 1946, 2, Joseph W. Martin Jr. Papers, JWMI. **47.** Patterson, *Mr. Republican,* 313. **48.** Gallup, *Public Opinion, 1935-1971,* 2:587. **49.** Ibid., 591, 594. **50.** Harvey Klehr and John E. Haynes, *The American Communist Movement* (New York: Twayne, 1992), 108-9.

51. Guenter Lewy, *The Cause That Failed* (New York: Oxford Univ. Press, 1990), 216. **52.** Irving Howe and Lewis Coser, *The American Communist Party: A Critical History* (New York: Frederick A. Praeger, 1962), 459. **53.** Lewy, *Cause That Failed,* 218. **54.** Gallup, *Public Opinion, 1935-1971,* 2:593-94. **55.** *U.S. News* 21, no. 16 (Oct. 18, 1946): 22. **56.** Donald F. Crosby, "The Politics of Religion: American Catholics and the Anti-Communist Impulse," in *The Specter: Original Essays on the Cold War and the Origins of McCarthyism,* ed. Richard R. Griffith and Athan Theoharis (New York: New Viewpoints, 1974), 18-39; and Nash, *Conservative Intellectual Movement,* 80-81. **57.** Thomas C. Reeves, *The Life and Times of Joe McCarthy* (New York: Stein and Day, 1982), 92. **58.** Ibid., 85. **59.** Richard H. Rovere, *Senator Joe McCarthy* (New York: Meridian, 1959), 103-4; David M. Oshinsky, *Senator Joseph McCarthy and the American Labor Movement* (Columbia: Univ. of Missouri Press, 1976), 43-45; and Athan G. Theoharis, *The Yalta Myths: An Issue in U.S. Politics, 1945-1955* (Columbia: Univ. of Missouri Press, 1970), 52-53. **60.** Reeves, *Joe McCarthy,* 105; Congressional Quarterly, *Guide to U.S. Elections,* 635; and Louis H. Bean, *Influences in the 1954 Mid-Term Elections* (Washington, D.C.: Public Affairs Institute, 1954), 10-13.

61. Tom Wicker, *One of Us: Richard Nixon and the American Dream* (New York: Random House, 1991), 41; and Congressional Quarterly, *Guide to U.S. Elections,* 952, 957. **62.** Jerry Voorhis, *Confessions of a Congressman* (New York: Doubleday, 1947), 75-182. **63.** William Costello, *The Facts about Nixon: An Unauthorized Biography* (New York: Viking, 1960), 37; and Voorhis, 134. **64.** Ibid., 216-17. **65.** Ibid., 98-99; and Stephen E. Ambrose, *Nixon: The Education of a Politician, 1913-1962* (New York: Simon & Schuster, 1987), 130.

66. Costello, *Facts about Nixon,* 52-55; and Paul Bullock, *Jerry Voorhis: The Idealist as Politician* (New York: Vantage Press, 1978), 253-74. **67.** Ambrose, *Nixon,* 133-134. **68.** Bullock, *Voorhis,* 266. **69.** Fawn W. Brodie, *Richard Nixon: The Shaping of His Character* (Cambridge: Harvard Univ. Press, 1983), 180-81. **70.** Ambrose, *Nixon,* 135.

71. Congressional Quarterly, *Guide to U.S. Elections,* 962. **72.** Ambrose, *Nixon,* 128. **73.** Clipping, *Chicago Tribune,* Apr. 3, 1946, Robert E. Hannegan Papers, HSTL. **74.** *NYT,* Apr. 18, 1946. **75.** Clipping, *Washington Post,* May 20, 1946, Robert E. Hannegan Papers, HSTL; and *PPP,* 1946, 350.

76. Ferrell, *Off the Record,* 88-89. **77.** DNC, *Campaign Issues . . . 1946* (Washington, D.C.: DNC, 1946), 102. **78.** DNC Campaign leaflet, 1946, Clark M. Clifford Papers, HSTL. **79.** Gallup, *Public Opinion, 1935-1971,* 2:606. **80.** Ibid.

81. Notes on cabinet meeting, Oct. 11, 1946, Matthew J. Connelly Papers, HSTL. **82.** Margaret Truman, *Harry S. Truman,* 349. **83.** American Institute of Public Opinion poll, June 30, 1945, 1, HST Papers, HSTL; and Gallup, *Public Opinion, 1935-1971,* 2:604. **84.** U.S. Census Bureau, *Statistical History,* 691. **85.** Boylan, *New Deal Coalition,* 152; "Election Roundup," *New Republic* 115 (Nov. 18, 1946): 639-48; and "Picking Up the Pieces," *The Nation* 163 (Nov. 16, 1946): 543.

86. Bibby, *Politics, Parties, and Elections,* 257; Gertzog, "Role of the President," 89; and Gallup, *Political Almanac: 1952,* 83; and Gary C. Jacobson, *The Politics of Congressional Elections* (New York: Harper Collins, 1992), 104. **87.** McGinnis, "Republican Party in Congress," 174. **88.** Samuel Kernell, "Presidential Popularity and Negative

Voting: An Alternative Explanation of the Midterm Congressional Decline of the President's Party," *American Political Science Review* 71 (1977): 44-56; and Matthew Soberg Shugart, "The Electoral Cycle and Institutional Sources of Divided Presidential Government," *American Political Science Review* 89 (1995): 328. **89.** Copy of radio address by Alben W. Barkley, Aug. 17, 1946, 4, John W. Snyder Papers, HSTL. **90.** Susan M. Hartmann, *Truman and the 80th Congress* (Columbia: Univ. of Missouri Press, 1971), 47. **91.** Dawson interview. **92.** Allen R. Raucher, *Paul G. Hoffmann: Architect of Foreign Aid* (Lexington: Univ. of Kentucky Press, 1985). **93.** Howard Jones, *"A New Kind of War": American Strategy and the Truman Doctrine in Greece* (New York: Oxford Univ. Press, 1989), 11-47; and HST, *Memoirs,* 2:128-36. **94.** Howard Jones, *"New Kind of War,"* 138-44, 168-69; Dean Acheson, *Present at the Creation: My Years in the State Department* (New York: Norton, 1969), 219; and HST's quote from *PPP,* 1947, 178-79. **95.** Reinhard, *Republican Right since 1945,* 31-32.

96. Robert A. Taft to Frank Gannett, Dec. 26, 1947, Robert A. Taft Papers, LOC; Donovan, *Conflict and Crisis,* 342; and H. Bradford Westerfield, *Foreign Policy and Party Politics: Pearl Harbor to Korea* (New Haven: Yale Univ. Press, 1955), 230-267. **97.** Harold L. Hitchens, "Influences on the Congressional Decision to Pass the Marshall Plan," *Western Political Quarterly* 21 (1968): 51-68; Quentin Quade, "The Truman Administration and the Separation of Powers: The Case of the Marshall Plan," *Review of Politics* 27 (1965): 58-77; John Bennett to Robert A. Taft, Oct. 25, 1947, Robert A. Taft Papers, LOC; and Patterson, *Mr. Republican,* 388-89. **98.** Joe R. Dunn, "UMT: A Historical Perspective," *Military Review* 61 (1981): 11-18; and Douglas Kinnard, *The Secretary of Defense* (Lexington: Univ. of Kentucky Press, 1980), 5-21. **99.** Gallup, *Public Opinon, 1935-1971,* 2:623. **100.** Vandenberg, *Papers of Vandenberg,* 398.

101. Donald R. McCoy, *The Presidency of Harry S. Truman* (Lawrence: Univ. Press of Kansas, 1984), 102-7; and David R. Mayhew, *Party Loyalty among Congressmen: The Difference between Democrats and Republicans, 1947-1962* (Cambridge: Harvard Univ. Press, 1966), 123. **102.** *PPP,* 1947, 252. **103.** Ibid., 1948, 202. **104.** Michael Nelson, ed., *Guide to the Presidency* (Washington, D.C.; Congressional Quarterly Press, 1989), 451; and J.S. Kimmitt and Roger K. Haley, ed., *Presidential Vetoes, 1789-1976* (Washington, D.C.: GPO, 1978), 362-75. **105.** Ibid., 196.

106. Gerard D. Reilly, "The Legislative History of the Taft-Hartley Act," *George Washington Univ. Law Review* 29 (1960): 285-300. **107.** Fred A. Hartley, *Our New National Labor Policy: The Taft-Hartley Act and the Next Steps* (New York: Funk and Wagnalls, 1948), 55-70. **108.** Jacob K. Javits, *Javits: The Autobiography of a Public Man* (Boston: Houghton Mifflin, 1981), 138. **109.** Robert W. Merry, "Robert A. Taft: A Study in the Accumulation of Legislative Power," in *First Among Equals,* ed. Richard A. Baker and Roger H. Davidson (Washington, D.C.: CQ Press, 1991), 184-85; and Lee, *Truman and Taft-Hartley,* 71. **110.** Lee, *Truman and Taft-Hartley,* 74-77; and Gilbert Y. Steiner, *The Congressional Conference Committee: Seventieth to Eightieth Congress* (Urbana: Univ. of Illinois Press, 1951), 166-69.

111. *Congressional Record,* 80th Cong., 1st sess., 1947, 6529. **112.** Ibid., 6536. **113.** *PPP,* 1947, 298-301. **114.** Merry, "Robert A. Taft," 186. **115.** Lee, *Truman and Taft-Hartley,* 102; Mayhew, 123; and U.S. Census Bureau, 691.

116. Allen Yarnell, *Democrats and Progressives: The 1948 Presidential Election as a Test of Post War Liberalism* (Berkeley: Univ. of California Press, 1974), 24. **117.** Davies, *Housing Reform,* 25-44. **118.** Merry, "Robert A. Taft," 188; Richard O. Davies, "'Mr. Republican' Turns 'Socialist'": Robert A. Taft and Public Housing," Ohio History 73 (1964): 135-43; and Charles C. Brown, "Robert A. Taft, Champion of Public Housing and National Aid to Schools," *Bulletin of the Cincinnati Historical Society* 26 (July 1968): 225-53. **119.** Richard N. Smith, *Dewey and His Time,* 504-12. **120.** Hartmann, *Truman and the 80th Congresss,* 198.

121. Irwin Ross, *Loneliest Campaign,* 137; Batt interview; and Martin's speech, July 30, 1948, Joseph W. Martin Jr. Papers, JWMI. **122.** *PPP,* 1948, 416-22. **123.** Ibid. **124.** *Congressional Record,* 80th Cong., 2d sess., vol. 94, July 26, 1948, 9377. **125.** Richard L. Strout, *TRB: Views and Perspectives on the Presidency* (New York: Macmillan, 1979), 67.

126. R. Alton Lee, "The Turnip Session of the Do-Nothing Congress," *Southwest Social Science Quarterly* 44 (December 1963): 265. **127.** Goulden, *Best Years,* 320-21. **128.** *PPP,* 1948, 438. **129.** Jules Abels, *Out of the Jaws of Victory,* 156-62; Francis H. Thompson, *The Frustration of Politics: Truman, Congress, and the Loyalty Issue, 1945-1953* (Rutherford, N.J.: Farleigh Dickinson Univ. Press, 1979), 25-78; and Alan D. Harper, *The White House and the Communist Issue, 1946-1952* (Westport, Conn.: Greenwood Press, 1969), 25-34. **130.** RNC, *The Story of the 80th Congress,* 1948, Joseph W. Martin Jr. Papers, JWMI.

131. Ibid., 109. **132.** Rae, *Decline and Fall of Liberal Republicans,* 34. **133.** Richard N. Smith, *Dewey and His Times,* 544. **134.** Reinhard, *Republican Right since 1945,* 54-55. **135.** Joseph W. Martin Jr., *First Fifty Years in Politics,* 194.

136. Ibid., 198. **137.** James T. Patterson, *Mr. Republican,* 424-26. **138.** Hartmann, *Truman and the 80th Congress,* 216. **139.** Strout, *TRB,* 71.

5. MAINTAINING THE MAJORITY PARTY, 1948

1. Ferrell, *Truman in the White House,* 282. **2.** McCoy, *Presidency of Truman,* 162; and Abels, *Out of the Jaws of Victory,* 288. **3.** *NYT,* Nov. 4, 1948. **4.** HST, *Memoirs,* 2:257. **5.** Ibid.

6. Ferrell, *Off the Record,* 150; and Hamby, *Liberalism and Its Challengers,* 91-92. **7.** Transcript, Brightman Oral History Interview, 14-15, HSTL. **8.** Redding, *Inside the Democratic Party,* 7. **9.** Poll, Gael Sullivan to DNC members and Democratic state chairmen, June 6, 1947, HSTL; and transcript, Brightman Oral History Interview, 6, HSTL. **10.** Clifton Brock, *Americans for Democratic Action: Its Role in National Politics* (Westport, Conn.: Greenwood Press, 1985), 87-91; and Pat Brown to Matthew J. Connelly, Dec. 29, 1947, OF 300, HSTL.

11. Yarnell, *Democrats and Progressives,* x; Neustadt 1991; and Abels, *Out of the Jaws of Victory,* 4. **12.** Heller, *Truman White House,* 121. **13.** Patrick Anderson, *The Presidents' Men* (New York: Doubleday, 1968), 93, 124. **14.** Clark M. Clifford, *Counsel to the President* (New York: Random House, 1991), 84-85. **15.** Transcript, James H.

Rowe Jr. Oral History Interview, Sept. 30, 1969, and Jan. 15, 1970, 29, HSTL; and Clifford, *Counsel to the President,* 193.
   16. Transcript, Rowe Oral History Interview, 129-61, HSTL. **17.** Ibid., 130. **18.** Clark M. Clifford to HST, Nov. 19, 1947, Clark M. Clifford Papers, HSTL. **19.** Ibid., 32-33. **20.** Ibid., 33.
   21. Ibid., 6. **22.** Ibid., 23-24. **23.** Ibid., 29. **24.** Donovan, *Conflict and Crisis,* 395-431. **25.** Clifford memo, Nov. 19, 1947, 40, HSTL.
   26. Ibid., 40-41. **27.** Transcript, George M. Elsey Oral History Interview, Feb. 10, 1964, 57-61, HSTL. **28.** Transcript, Batt Oral History Interview, 9, HSTL. **29.** Transcript, Clark M. Clifford Oral History Interview, July 26, 1971, 316-17, HSTL. **30.** Clifford, *Counsel to the President,* 194.
   31. Transcript, Kenneth M. Birkhead Oral History Interview, July 7, 1966, 36, HSTL. **32.** Gael Sullivan to Clark M. Clifford, June 2, 1947, Clark M. Clifford Papers, HSTL. **33.** Henry A. Wallace, "I Shall Run in 1948," *Vital Speeches* 14 (Jan. 1, 1948): 173. **34.** Yarnell, *Democrats and Progressives,* 14-19; and Jerold A. Rosen, "Henry A. Wallace and American Liberal Politics, 1945-1948," *Annals of Iowa* 44 (1978): 462-74. **35.** Karl M. Schmidt, *Henry A. Wallace: Quixotic Crusade, 1948* (Syracuse, NY: Syracuse Univ. Press, 1960), 35.
   36. Bert Cochran, *Labor and Communism: The Conflict That Shaped American Unions* (Princeton: Princeton Univ. Press, 1977), 299-303. **37.** Schmidt, *Henry A. Wallace,* 39-40. **38.** Norman D. Markowitz, *The Rise and Fall of the People's Century: Henry A. Wallace and American Liberalism, 1941-1948* (New York: Free Press, 1973), 311; and Howe and Coser, *American Communist Party,* 475. **39.** Klehr and Haynes, *American Communist Movement,* 115. **40.** Donald B. Johnson, *National Party Platforms* (Urbana: Univ. of Illinois Press, 1978), 1:426, 438-39.
   41. James A. Weschler, *The Age of Suspicion* (New York: Random House, 1953), 232. **42.** Howe and Coser, *American Communist Party,* 473-76; and Klehr and Haynes, *American Communist Movement,* 121. **43.** *NYT,* Dec. 26, 1947, 18. **44.** Clifford memo, Nov. 19, 1947, 29-39, HSTL; Pat Brown to Matthew J. Connelly, Dec. 29, 1947, HSTL; and McKeever, *Adlai Stevenson,* 116. **45.** *Capital Comment,* Jan. 3, 1948, J. Howard McGrath Papers, HSTL.
   46. *NYT,* Feb. 18, 1948. **47.** Ross, *Loneliest Campaign,* 65-66. **48.** Ferrell, *Truman in the White House,* 246. **49.** *PPP,* 1948, 189. **50.** Curtis D. MacDougall, *Gideon's Army* (New York: Marzani and Munsell, 1965), 191; and John E. Haynes, *Dubious Alliance: The Making of Minnesota's DFL Party* (Minneapolis: Univ. of Minnesota Press, 1984), 102-25.
   51. Hubert H. Humphrey to Gael Sullivan, Apr. 19, 1948, Oscar R. Ewing Papers, HSTL. **52.** Gael Sullivan to Paul Porter, Jan. 27, 1948, J. Howard McGrath Papers, HSTL. **53.** Gillon, *Politics and Vision,* 22-39; and Brock, *Americans for Democratic Action,* 51-88. **54.** Rauh interview; and Brock, *Americans for Democratic Action,* 87-88. **55.** Brock, *Americans for Democratic Action,* 101.
   56. ADA report, "Henry A. Wallace: The First Three Months," April 27, 1948, 1-3, Oscar L. Chapman Papers, HSTL. **57.** Ibid., 3; Hanes Walton Jr., *Black Political Parties* (New York: Free Press, 1972), 36; and ADA report, "Henry A. Wallace: The Last Seven

Months of His Presidential Campaign," Oct. 14, 1948, 20, HSTL. **58.** Alonzo L. Hamby, "Henry A. Wallace, The Liberals, and Soviet-American Relations," *Review of Politics* 30 (1968): 153-69; Rosen, "Wallace and Liberal Politics," 462-74; and Torbjorn Sirevaq, "The Dilemma of the American Left in the Cold War Years: The Case of Henry A. Wallace," *Norwegian Contributions to American Studies* 4 (1973); 399-421. **59.** Arthur M. Schlesinger Jr., *The Vital Center* (Boston: Houghton Mifflin, 1962), 115. **60.** *PPP,* 1948, 559, 845; and Gillon, *Politics and Vision,* 53-55.

61. Schlesinger, *Vital Center,* 129-30. **62.** Rauh interview; and John F. Martin, *Civil Rights,* 83-85. **63.** Wilson W. Wyatt Sr., *Whistle Stops* (Lexington: Univ. Press of Kentucky, 1985), 45. **64.** Brock, *Americans for Democratic Action,* 101-8. **65.** Gillon, *Politics and Vision,* 55.

66. Congressional Quarterly, *Guide to U.S. Elections,* 357. **67.** Robert A. Divine, "The Cold War and the Election of 1948," *Journal of American History* 59 (June 1972): 90-110; Lawrence Lader, "The Wallace Campaign of 1948," *American Heritage* 28 (1976): 42-51; and Schmidt, *Henry A. Wallace,* 244-51. **68.** Allen Yarnell, "Liberals in Action: The ADA, Henry Wallace, and the 1948 Election," *Research Studies* 40 (1972): 260-73; Parmet, *Democrats,* 90; and David Lloyd, "Notes in A.D.A. Convention, Chicago, April 8-9-10, 1949," PPF, HSTL. **69.** Jack Redding to J. Howard McGrath, Apr. 20, 1948; and appointment folder, McGrath's appointment with Francis Cardinal Spellman, Oct. 21, 1948, both in J. Howard McGrath Papers, HSTL; and Lubell, *Future of American Politics,* 201-4. **70.** Hechler, *Working with Truman,* 61-62; and Henry Lee Moon, *Balance of Power: The Negro Vote* (New York: Doubleday, 1948), 4-71.

71. *PPP,* 1948, 3. **72.** President's Committee on Civil Rights, *To Secure These Rights* (Washington, D.C.: GPO, 1947); and *PPP,* 1948, 121-26. **73.** Neustadt interview. **74.** Gary C. Ness, "The States' Rights Democratic Movement of 1948" (Ph.D. diss., Duke University, 1972), 39-42. **75.** Nadine Cohodas, *Strom Thurmond and the Politics of Southern Change* (New York: Simon and Schuster, 1993), 132.

76. Ness, "States' Rights Democratic Movement of 1948," 43. **77.** John F. Huss, *Senator for the South: A Biography of Olin D. Johnston* (New York: Doubleday, 1961), 158-59; and Garson, *Democratic Party,* 241-42. **78.** Charles E. Goodman to Matthew J. Connelly, Apr. 20, 1948, of 300, HSTL. **79.** William D. Barnard, *Dixiecrats and Democrats: Alabama Politics, 1942-1950* (University: Univ. of Alabama Press, 1974), 104-20; and Key, *Southern Politics,* 332. **80.** Garson, *Democratic Party,* 238.

81. Redding, *Inside the Democratic Party,* 136. **82.** *NYT,* May 11, 1948. **83.** William B. Hesseltine, *Third Party Movements in the United States* (New York: D. Van Nostrand, 1962), 97. **84.** Ness, "States' Rights Democratic Movement of 1948," 106-7. **85.** Garson, *Democratic Party,* 262.

86. *States' Rights Information and Speakers' Handbook* (Jackson, Miss.: National States' Rights Campaign Committee, 1948), 4. **87.** William G. Carleton, "The Fate of Our Fourth Party," *Yale Review* 38 (March 1949): 449-59; and Clipping, *Raleigh News Observer,* Aug. 17, 1948, DNC Clipping File, HSTL. **88.** Ann Mathison McLaurin, "The Role of the Dixiecrats in the 1948 Election" (Ph.D. diss., University of Oklahoma, 1972), 74-75. **89.** Clipping, *NYT,* Sept. 7, 1948, DNC Clipping File, HSTL; Sarah McCulloh Lemmon, "The Ideology of the 'Dixiecrat' Movement," *Social Forces* 30 (December

1951): 162-71; and Seale Harris, *The Death of the National Democratic Party: The Truth about Truman, Big-City-Machine-Labor-Socialist Party* (Kingsport, Tenn.: Kingsport Press, 1952), 38-65. **90.** Ness, "States' Rights Democratic Movement of 1948," 170; Ernest R. Bartley, "The Tidelands Oil Controversy," *Western Political Quarterly* 2, no. 1 (March 1949): 135-53; and Lucius J. Barker, "The Supreme Court as Policy Maker: The Tidelands Oil Controversy," *Journal of Politics* 24 (1962): 350-66.

91. Harvard Sitkoff, "Harry Truman and the Election of 1948: The Coming of Age of Civil Rights in American Politics," *Journal of Southern History* 37 (1971): 597-616. **92.** Donald R. McCoy and Richard T. Ruetten, *Quest and Response: Minority Rights and the Truman Administration* (Lawrence: Univ. Press of Kansas, 1973), 129. **93.** Barton J. Bernstein and Allen J. Matusow, eds., *The Truman Administration: A Documentary History* (New York: Harper, 1966), 111. **94.** Harvard Sitkoff, "Racial Militancy and Inter-racial Violence in the Second World War," *Journal of American History* 58 (1971): 661-81. **95.** Redding, *Inside the Democratic Party,* 139-42.

96. Ness, "States' Rights Democratic Movement of 1948," 219-25. **97.** John F. Martin, *Civil Rights,* 88. **98.** *PPP,* 1948, 932-25; and Henry B. Sirgo, "Blacks and Presidential Politics," in *Blacks and the American Political System,* ed. Huey L. Perry and Wayne Parent (Gainesville: Univ. Press of Florida, 1995), 82. **99.** Gilbert C. Fite, *Richard B. Russell Jr., Senator From Georgia* (Chapel Hill: Univ. of North Carolina Press, 1991), 241. **100.** McLaurin, "Role of the Dixiecrats," 203.

101. Ibid., 234. **102.** Richard Hofstadter, "From Calhoun to the Dixiecrats," *Social Research* 16 (June 1949): 143. **103.** "Danger from the Dixiecrats," *New Republic* 119 (Aug. 2, 1948): 114. **104.** Garson, *Democratic Party,* 294-96; and Key, *Southern Politics,* 33-34. **105.** Alexander Heard, *A Two Party South?* (Chapel Hill: Univ. of North Carolina Press, 1952), 54-73.

106. Barnard, *Dixiecrats and Democrats,* 108-9; and H.M. Cooley to John W. Snyder, Apr. 30, 1948, PSF, HSTL. **107.** Copy of radio address by Senator Lister Hill, Mar. 11, 1948, J. Howard McGrath Papers, HSTL; Heard, *Two Party South?* 23; and Dewey W. Grantham Jr., *The Democratic South* (Athens: Univ. of Georgia Press, 1963), 78. **108.** Frank W. Ashley, "Selected Southern Liberal Editors and the States' Rights Movement of 1948" (Ph.D. diss., University of South Carolina, 1959); and Ralph McGill, *The South and the Southerner* (Boston: Little, Brown, 1963), 187. **109.** Clipping, *Atlanta Constitution,* July 25, 1948, DNC Clipping File, HSTL; and Emile B. Ader, "Why the Dixiecrats Failed," *Journal of Politics* 15 (1953): 367-69. **110.** Gallup poll, Aug. 20, 1948, American Institute of Public Opinion Papers, HSTL.

111. Ibid. **112.** Gallup poll, Oct. 28, 1948, American Institute of Public Opinion Papers, HSTL. **113.** Ader, "Why the Dixiecrats Failed," 360-61; Cohodas, *Strom Thurmond,* 189-90; and Carleton, "Fate of Our Fourth Party, 449-51. **114.** McLaurin, "Role of the Dixiecrats," 217. **115.** Gallup, *Political Almanac: 1952,* 19; and Congressional Quarterly, *Guide to U.S. Elections,* 357.

116. Jack Redding to J. Howard McGrath, Apr. 20, 1948, J. Howard McGrath Papers, HSTL. **117.** Yarnell, "Liberals in Action," 260-73; and Klehr and Haynes, *American Communist Movement,* 122-33. **118.** Copy of speech by Representative Brooks Hays, July 19, 1948, Southern Revolt—1948 Folder, JFKL. **119.** Abels, *Out of the Jaws of*

Victory, 284-85; William D. Hassett to Rev. Edward Pruden, Nov. 12, 1948, OF 1644, HSTL; and Dawson interview. **120.** Congressional Quarterly, *Guide to U.S. Elections,* 518. **121.** Gallup, *Public Opinion, 1935-1971,* 2:605. **122.** Ibid., 2:612. **123.** Herbert Brownell, *Advising Ike: The Memoirs of Attorney General Herbert Brownell* (Lawrence: Univ. Press of Kansas, 1993), 40; and Richard N. Smith, *Dewey and His Time,* 466-67. **124.** Warren Moscow, *Politics in the Empire State* (New York: A.A. Knopf, 1948), 33-34. **125.** Robert A. Taft to H. Hayes Landon, Sept. 14, 1945, Robert A. Taft Papers, LOC.

126. Richard N. Smith, *Dewey and His Time,* 34. **127.** Richard Rovere, "Taft: Is This the Best We've Got?" *Harper's* 207 (April 1948): 289-92. **128.** John Bennett to Robert A. Taft, July 12, 1947, Aug. 9, 1947, and Oct. 25, 1947, Robert A. Taft Papers, LOC. **129.** John Bennett to Robert A. Taft, May 13, 1947, Robert A. Taft Papers, LOC. **130.** Ross, *Loneliest Campaign,* 37.

131. Ibid., 41; and Malcolm Moos, *The Republicans: A History of Their Party* (New York: Random House, 1956), 436. **132.** Reinhard, *Republican Right since 1945,* 41-43. **133.** *NYT,* May 5-6, 1948. **134.** Ross, *Loneliest Campaign,* 48-49; and Richard N. Smith, *Dewey and His Time,* 489-92. **135.** Richard N. Smith, *Dewey and His Time,* 494.

136. Reinhard, *Republican Right since 1945,* 44. **137.** Bain and Parris, *Convention Decisions,* 271. **138.** Reinhard, *Republican Right since 1948,* 47; and James T. Patterson, *Mr. Republican,* 512. **139.** RNC, *Official Proceedings of the 24th Republican National Convention* (Washington, D.C.: RNC, 1948), 257-76. **140.** *NYT,* June 25, 1948.

141. Henry Z. Scheele, *Charlie A. Halleck: A Political Biography* (New York: Exposition Press, 1966), 120-21. **142.** Robert Shogan, "1948 Election," *American Heritage* 19 (1968): 29. **143.** G. Edward White, *Earl Warren: A Public Life* (New York: Oxford Univ. Press, 1982), 62-95. **144.** Brownell, *Advising Ike,* 79. **145.** Donald B. Johnson, *National Party Platforms,* 450.

146. Ibid., 451-54. **147.** Charles H. Titus, "The Two Major Conventions in 1948," *Western Political Quarterly* 1, no. 3 (September 1948): 253-54. **148.** Reichard, *Politics as Usual,* 236. **149.** Moscow, *Politics in the Empire State,* 31-33; and Brownell, *Advertising Ike,* 43-44. **150.** Moscow, *Politics in the Empire State,* 32-35.

151. Bone, *Party Committees and National Politics, 39;* and Brownell, 72-74. **152.** Goulden, *Best Years,* 410-11. **153.** Abels, *Out of the Jaws of Victory,* 154-55; and Lawrence A. Yates, "John Foster Dulles and Bipartisanship, 1944-1952" (Ph.D. diss., University of Kansas, 1981), 27-142. **154.** James L. Wick, *How Not to Run for President* (New York: Vantage, 1952), 65. **155.** Thomas G. Hall, "The Aiken Bill, Price Supports and the Wheat Farmer in 1948," *North Dakota History* 39 (1972): 13-22, 47; and Oliver P. Williams, "The Commodity Credit Corporation and the 1948 Presidential Election," *Midwest Journal of Political Science* 1 (1957): 111-24.

156. Abels, *Out of the Jaws of Victory,* 231-35; and "Farm Prices: Campaign Dilemma," *U.S. News and World Report* 25 (Sept. 10, 1948): 14-15. **157.** Brightman interview. **158.** Richard N. Smith, *Dewey and His Times,* 528-29. **159.** Frank McNaughton to Don Bermingham and Bob Girvin, Nov. 6, 1948, Frank McNaughton Papers, HSTL. **160.** *PPP,* 1948, 503-508.

161. Kirkendall, "Election of 1948," 3205. **162.** Ibid, 3210. **163.** Richard N. Smith,

Dewey and His Times, 538-39. **164.** Moos, *Republicans,* 447. **165.** Brownell, *Advising Ike,* 83-84; and Gallup, *Public Opinion, 1935-1971,* 2:765-67. **166.** Abels, *Out of the Jaws of Victory,* 243-58; and Gosnell, *Truman's Crises,* 409. **167.** Brightman, Batt, and Elsey interviews. **168.** David Coyle to Bill Hassett, June 28, 1948, Campaign strategy folder, PSF, HSTL. **169.** Ross, *Loneliest Campaign,* 79-80. **170.** Strout, *TRB,* 64-65. **171.** *PPP,* 1948, 348. **172.** Ibid., 349. **173.** Ibid., 349-53. **174.** Ibid., 353. **175.** Boyd A. Martin, "The 1948 Elections in the Eleven Western States," *Western Political Quarterly* 2 (March 1949): 89-91. **176.** *PPP,* 1948, 124. **177.** Ferrell, *Truman in the White House,* 262. **178.** Proceedings of DNC meeting, Oct. 29, 1947, 93-100, DNC Records, HSTL. **179.** Garson, *Democratic Party,* 269-72; and Pepper, *Eyewitness to a Century,* 158-68. **180.** McCullough, *Truman,* 632-33.

181. Rauh interview. **182.** John F. Martin, *Civil Rights,* 81-84. **183.** Arthur Krock, *Memoirs: Sixty Years on the Fighting Line* (New York: Funk & Wagnalls, 1968), 243-44; and *NYT,* July 9, 1948, 18. **184.** DNC, *Democracy at Work,* 232, 280. **185.** Bain and Parris, *Convention Decision,* 273, 276.

186. Ferrell, *Truman in the White House,* 265. **187.** Wyatt interview. **188.** Ferrell, *Off the Record,* 141-42. **189.** Donald B. Johnson, *National Party Platforms,* 404; and copy of HST's proposed 1948 civil rights plank, 12, DNC 1949-50 folder, Clinton Anderson Papers, HSTL. **190.** Ibid.

191. Proceedings of DNC Credentials Committee, July 13, 1948, 4-66, DNC Records, HSTL. **192.** Rauh interview. **193.** Paul H. Douglas, *In the Fullness of Time: The Memoirs of Paul H. Douglas* (New York: Harcourt, Brace, Jovanovich, 1972), 133. **194.** Rauh interview; and Gillon, *Politics and Vision,* 48-50. **195.** Rauh interview.

196. Brock, *Americans for Democratic Action,* 97. **197.** DNC, *Democracy at Work,* 179-82; and Bain and Parris, Convention Decisions, 275. **198.** Rauh interview. **199.** Ferrell, *Off the Record,* 143. **200.** Ibid.; and Richard D. Chesteen, "'Mississippi Is Gone Home!': A Study of the 1948 Mississippi States' Rights Bolt," *Journal of Mississippi History* 32 (February 1970): 49-53.

201. Douglas, *In the Fullness of Time,* 134. **202.** Donovan, *Conflict and Crisis,* 407. **203.** *PPP,* 1948, 406. **204.** Ibid., 406-9. **205.** Ibid., 410.

206. *PPP,* 1948, 438. **207.** Matthew J. Connelly to HST, Aug. 5, 1948, PSF, HSTL. **208.** *PPP,* 1948, 476-77. **209.** Ibid., 477. **210.** Clark M. Clifford to HST, Aug. 17, 1948, Clark M. Clifford Papers, HSTL.

211. Allen J. Matusow, *Farm Politics and Policies in the Truman Years* (Cambridge: Harvard Univ. Press, 1967), 170-90. **212.** Clifford memo, Nov. 19, 1947, 38, HSTL. **213.** Batt interview. **214.** Mary Welek Atwell, "Eleanor Roosevelt and the Cold War Consensus," *Diplomatic History* 3 (1979): 109. **215.** *PPP,* 1948, 802.

216. Ibid., 850. **217.** Ibid., 850-51. **218.** Richard N. Smith, *Dewey and His Times,* 536. **219.** Wilson D. Miscamble, "Harry S. Truman, the Berlin Blockade and the 1948 Election," *Presidential Studies Quarterly* 10 (1980): 306-16. **220.** Philip C. Jessup, "Park Avenue Diplomacy: Ending the Berlin Blockade," *Political Science Quarterly* 87 (1972): 377-400; Fred B. Misse, "Truman, Berlin and the 1948 Election," *Missouri Historical*

Review 76 (1982): 164-73; Hechler, *Working with Truman,* 90-91; and Divine, "Cold War and the Election of 1948," 90-110.
221. Gallup, *Public Opinion, 1935-1971,* 2:766. **222.** Frederick Mosteller et. al., *The Pre-Election Polls of 1948* (New York: Social Science Research Council, 1949), 59. **223.** Copy of Kiplinger Washington Letter, Oct. 30, 1948, 4, Frank McNaughton Papers, HSTL. **224.** Brownell, *Advising Ike,* 84. **225.** Morris L. Ernst and David Loth, *The People Know Best: The Ballots vs. the Polls* (Washington, D.C.: Public Affairs Press, 1949), 54.
226. Transcript, Joseph D. Keenan Oral History Interview, Feb. 2, 1971, 22, HSTL. **227.** Goulden, *Best Years,* 412-13. **228.** Abels, *Out of the Jaws of Victory,* 224-25; and Ross, *Loneliest Campaign,* 223. **229.** *PPP,* 1948, 908-14. **230.** Dawson interview.
231. Redding, 279-80. **232.** *NYT,* Nov. 4, 1948, 1. **233.** Congressional Quarterly, *Guide to U.S. Elections,* 357. **234.** Ibid., 1120. **235.** U.S. Census Bureau, *Statistical History,* 691.
236. Gallup, *Political Almanac: 1952,* 66. **237.** Ibid., 78. **238.** Norman H. Nie, Sidney Verba, and John R. Petrocik, *The Changing American Voter* (Cambridge: Harvard Univ. Press, 1979), 383-84. **239.** Richard O. Davies, "Whistle-Stopping through Ohio," *Ohio History* 71 (1962): 113-23; and McKeever, *Adlai Stevenson,* 117-27. **240.** Congressional Quarterly, *Guide to U.S. Elections,* 304.
241. John R. Petrocik, *Party Coalitions: Realignments and the Decline of the New Deal Party System* (Chicago: Univ. of Chicago Press, 1981), 95. **242.** Gallup, *Political Almanac: 1952,* 37. **243.** Ibid. **244.** Ibid., 38. **245.** Everett C. Ladd Jr., *Transformations of the American Party System: Political Coalitions from the New Deal to the 1970s* (New York: Norton, 1975), 102-3.
246. Gallup, *Political Almanac: 1952,* 83. **247.** Abels, *Out of the Jaws of Victory,* 306; and Louis Harris, *Is There a Republican Majority?* 15-17. **248.** Campbell and Kahn, *People Elect a President,* 8-9. **249.** Ibid., 274-75; Michael Barone, *Our Country* (New York: Free Press, 1990), 221; Kirkendall, "Election of 1948," 3099-3100; Milkis, *President and the Parties,* 155; and V.O. Key Jr., *The Responsible Electorate* (New York: Vintage Books, 1966), 66-67, 77. **250.** Key, *Responsible Electorate,* 44-49; and Gallup, *Political Almanac: 1952,* 38.
251. Warren E. Miller, "Presidential Coattails: A Study in Political Myth and Methodology," *Public Opinion Quarterly* 19, no. 4 (Winter 1954-55): 353-68; Campbell and Miller, "Motivational Basis," 295; Milton C. Cummings Jr., *Congressmen and the Electorate: Elections for the U.S. House and the President, 1920-1964* (New York: Free Press, 1966), 13; and Charles Press, "Voting Statistics and Presidential Coattails," *American Political Science Review* 52 (1958): 1041-1050. **252.** Congressional Quarterly, *Guide to U.S. Elections,* 357, 616. **253.** Ibid., 357, 615, 499. **254.** Lew Wallace, "The Truman-Dewey Upset," *American History Illustrated* 11 (1976): 29. **255.** Congressional Quarterly, *Guide to U.S. Elections,* 357, 521.
256. Nie et al., 383-84; and George H. Gallup, *The Gallup Political Almanac for 1948* (Princeton: American Institute of Public Opinion, 1948), 11. **257.** Matusow, *Farm Politics and Policies,* 177-88; Thomas G. Ryan, "Farm Prices and the Farm Vote in 1948," *Agricultural History* 54 (1980): 389-90; and Wesley McCune, "Farmers in Poli-

tics," *Annals of the American Academy of Political and Social Science* 319 (1958): 41-51. **258.** Oliver P. Williams, "Commodity Credit Corporation," 111-24; Hall, "Aiken Bill," 47; and Lubell, *Future of American Politics,* 160. **259.** Edward L. Schapsmeier and Frederick H. Schapsmeier, "Farm Policy from FDR to Eisenhower: Southern Democrats and the Politics of Agriculture," *Agricultural History* 53 (1979): 365-66; and G. William Domhoff, *Fat Cats and Democrats: The Role of the Big Rich in the Party of the Common Man* (Englewood Cliffs, N.J.: Prentice-Hall, 1972), 92-93, 100-101. **260.** Eldersveld, "Influence," 1193-1200; and Duncan MacRae Jr., and James A. Meldrum, "Critical Elections in Illinois: 1888-1958," *American Political Science Review* 54 (September 1960): 678.

261. Lubell, *Future of American Politics,* 49. **262.** Ibid.; and Congressional Quarterly, *Guide to U.S. Elections,* 356-57. **263.** Ladd, *Transformation,* 112. **264.** Ibid., 115; and Lawrence H. Fuchs, "American Jews and the Presidential Vote," *American Political Science Review* 49 (June 1955): 386-87. **265.** Ladd, *Transformation,* 270; Nie et al., *Changing American Voter,* 383; and Lubell, *Future of American Politics,* 200-203.

266. Gallup, *Political Almanac for 1948,* 281; and Gallup, *Political Almanac: 1952,* 19. **267.** Ibid. **268.** Congressional Quarterly, *Guide to U.S. Elections,* 356-57. **269.** Ladd, *Transformation,* 165. **270.** Gallup, *Political Almanac for 1948,* 281; and Gallup, *Political Almanac: 1952,* 18-19.

271. A.G. Grayson, "North Carolina and Harry Truman, 1944-1948," *Journal of American Studies* 9 (1975): 296-97; Donald Strong, "The Presidential Election in the South, 1952," *Journal of Politics* 17 (August 1955): 364; and Heard, *Two Party South,* 29. **272.** Ladd, *Transformation,* 153-54; and George H. Gallup, *Special 1952 Election Supplement to the Political Almanac, 1952* (New York: B.C. Forbes & Sons, 1952), 3. **273.** Key, *Southern Politics,* 674-75; Louis Harris, *Is There a Republican Majority,* 60; Goldman, *Search for Consensus,* 193-95; *PPP,* 1949, 439; and Barbara Sinclair, "Agenda and Alignment Change: The House of Representatives, 1925-1978," in *Congress Reconsidered,* ed. Lawrence C. Dodd and Bruce I. Oppenheimer (Washington, D.C.: Congressional Quarterly Press, 1981), 230-31. **274.** Kirkendall, "Election of 1948," 3144-45. **275.** Gallup, *Political Almanac: 1952,* 66; and *U.S. News & World Report* 25 (Nov. 12, 1948): 19-20, 40-43.

276. *U.S. News & World Report* 25 (Nov. 12, 1948): 19-20, 40-43. **277.** Barone, *Our Country,* 225-28; and Philip A. Grant Jr., "The 1948 Presidential Election in Virginia: Augury of the Trend Towards Republicanism," *Presidential Studies Quarterly* 8 (1978): 319-28. **278.** James MacGregor Burns, *The Deadlock of Democracy: Four-Party Politics in America* (Englewood Cliffs: Prentice-Hall, 1963), 313-16; and Patrick R. Cotter and James Glen Stovall, "The Conservative South?" *American Politics Quarterly* 18 (January 1990): 110-11.

6. THE FAIR DEAL AND THE DEMOCRATIC PARTY

1. Ferrell, *Off the Record,* 150. **2.** Hamby, *Liberalism and Its Challengers,* 91-92. **3.** *PPP,* 1948, 941, 945. **4.** Gallup, *Public Opinion, 1935-1971,* 2:802. **5.** Ibid., 2:805.

6. *PPP,* 1949, 7. **7.** HST, *Memoirs,* v. 1:530; and *PPP,* 1949, 1-7. **8.** Ibid., 7. **9.** Clifford, 248. **10.** Transcript, Clifford Oral History Interview, 67, HSTL. **11.** Hamby, *Beyond the New Deal,* 196-297; and "The President Charts the Course," *New Republic* 120 (Jan. 17, 1949): 6. **12.** HST, *Memoirs,* 1:47. **13.** Leon Keyserling, "Harry S. Truman: The Man and the President," in *Harry S Truman: The Man from Independence,* ed. William E. Levantrosser (New York: Greenwood Press, 1986): 235-44. **14.** Donald K. Pickens, "Truman's Council of Economic Advisers and the Legacy of New Deal Liberalism," in *Harry S Truman: The Man from Independence,* 245-64; and Alonzo L. Hamby, "The Vital Center, the Fair Deal, and the Quest for a Liberal Political Economy," *American Historical Review* 77 (1972): 653-78. **15.** *PPP,* 1949, 494-495; and Hamby, *Beyond the New Deal,* 302.

16. *PPP,* 1949, 495. **17.** Anderson, *Presidents' Men,* 43; Richard Neustadt, "Presidency and Legislation: Planning the President's Program," *American Political Science Review* 49 (December 1955): 1014. **18.** Hechler and Neustadt interviews. **19.** Heller, *Truman White House,* 228-30. **20.** Curtis A. Amlund, "Executive-Legislative Imbalance: Truman to Kennedy," *Western Political Quarterly* 18 (1965): 640-45; and Reo M. Christenson, "Presidential Leadership of Congress: Ten Commandments Point the Way," *Presidential Studies Quarterly* 8 (1978): 257-68.

21. HST, *Memoirs,* 2:536-37. **22.** Brock, *Americans for Democratic Action,* 112-14. **23.** Edward L. Schapsmeier and Frederick H. Schapsmeier, "Scott W. Lucas of Havana: His Rise and Fall as Majority Leader in the United States Senate," *Journal of Illinois State Historical Society* 70 (1977): 302-20; and D.B. Hardeman and Donald C. Bacon, *Rayburn: A Biography* (Lanham, Md.: Madison Books, 1987), 348-419. **24.** Dwayne L. Little, "The Political Leadership of Speaker Sam Rayburn, 1940-1961" (Ph.D. diss., University of Cincinnati, 1970), 150-51; and Hardeman and Bacon, *Rayburn,* 333. **25.** Douglas, *In the Fullness of Time,* 561.

26. Schapsmeier and Schapsmeier, "Scott W. Lucas of Havana," 316; and Hamby, *Beyond the New Deal,* 305. **27.** Hamby, *Beyond the New Deal,* 314-17; and Brock, *Americans for Democratic Action,* 111-14. **28.** Alfred Steinberg, *Sam Rayburn: A Biography* (New York: Hawthorn, 1975), 359. **29.** Ferrell, *Off the Record,* 283. **30.** Abell, *Pearson Diaries,* 7-8.

31. Estes Kefauver and Jack Levin, *A Twentieth-Century Congress* (New York: Duell, Sloan and Pearce, 1947), 104. **32.** "Congress Clears the Decks," *New Republic* 120 (Jan. 17, 1949): 6. **33.** Irwin Ross, *Strategy for Liberals: Politics of a Mixed Economy* (New York: Harper, 1949), 139. **34.** "Congress Clears the Decks," *New Republic* 120 (Jan. 17, 1949): 6. **35.** Burton A. Boxerman, "Adolph Joachim Sabath in Congress: The Roosevelt and Truman Years," *Journal of the Illinois State Historical Society* 66 (Winter 1973): 442.

36. Floyd M. Riddick, "The Eighty-First Congress: First and Second Sessions," *Western Political Quarterly* 4 (March 1951): 54-55. **37.** Abels, *Out of the Jaws of Victory,* 285. **38.** Hamby, *Beyond the New Deal,* 313. **39.** Riddick, "Eighty-First Congress," 66. **40.** Neustadt interview.

41. "Next Steps in the Fair Deal," *New Republic* 120 (Mar. 7, 1949): 11. **42.** Ferrell, *Truman in the White House,* 283, 297. **43.** Neustadt interview. **44.** Brock, *Americans for*

Democratic Action, 114-15; and Gerald Pomper, "Labor and Congress: The Repeal of Taft-Hartley," *Labor History* 2, no. 3 (Fall 1961): 324-25. **45.** *PPP,* 1949, 480, 484. **46.** Ibid., 237-38. **47.** Ibid., 461. **48.** Ibid. **49.** Pomper, "Labor and Congress," 338. **50.** John Dingell, Sr., to J. Howard McGrath, Nov. 30, 1948, PSF, HSTL. **51.** Clippings, *Chicago Sun,* Nov. 21, 1948, *New York Star,* Dec. 5, 1948, *Chicago Sun-Times,* Nov. 28, 1948, DNC Clipping File, HSTL. **52.** Stephen K. Bailey and Howard D. Samuel, *Congress at Work* (New York: Henry Holt, 1952), 74, 273. **53.** Dawson interview; clipping, *Kansas City Times,* June 23, 1949, William M. Boyle Jr. Papers, HSTL; HST to Donald Dawson, June 25, 1949, PSF, HSTL; Estes Kefauver to HST, Aug. 30, 1949, OF 300, HSTL; and Estes Kefauver to HST, Dec. 22, 1949, PSF, HSTL. **54.** McCoy and Ruetten, *Quest and Response,* 184; and Maury Maverick to Donald Dawson, Oct. 6, 1950, OF 300, HSTL. **55.** Clipping, *Congressional Record,* May 3, 1949, A2785, OF 300, HSTL.

56. Copy of Governor Hugh White's speech to States' Rights Convention, June 26, 1952, 5, PSF, HSTL; and Bailey and Samuel, *Congress at Work,* 138. **57.** Ibid., 81. **58.** Clipping, *Chicago Sun-Times,* Nov. 28, 1948, DNC Clipping File, HSTL. **59.** Clipping, *New York Star,* Dec. 5, 1948, DNC Clipping File, HSTL. **60.** Robert J. Donovan, *Tumultuous Years: The Presidency of Harry S Truman, 1949-1953* (New York: Norton, 1982), 17.

61. Steinberg, *Sam Rayburn,* 250. **62.** Bailey and Samuel, *Congress at Work,* 78. **63.** "Oldsters Take Over," *U.S. News & World Report* 25 (Nov. 12, 1948): 40-42. **64.** HST, *Memoirs,* 2:31. **65.** Ibid., 1:172.

66. Ibid., 2:32. **67.** Frank D. Campion, *The AMA and U.S. Health Policy Since 1940* (Chicago: Chicago Review Press, 1984), 153-57. **68.** Poen, *Strictly Personal and Confidential,* 96. **69.** Ibid., 97. **70.** *PPP,* 1945, 280.

71. Ibid., 482-89. **72.** Ibid., 488. **73.** William S. White, "Medicine Man from Alabama," *Harper's Magazine* 219 (November 1959): 90-94. **74.** *PPP,* 1946, 218; and Poen, *Truman versus the Medical Lobby,* 70-71. **75.** Thomas R. Byrne, "The Social Thought of Robert F. Wagner" (Ph.D. diss., Georgetown University, 1951), 254-55.

76. Campion, *AMA and U.S. Health Policy,* 8-9. **77.** Morris Fishbein, *A History of the American Medical Association* (Philadelphia: W.B. Saunders, 1947), 413. **78.** Kathleen Rivet, "Lost: A National Health Program," *American Labor Legislation Review* 31 (September 1941): 120-22. **79.** Thomas Parron, "The United States Public Health Service in the War," in *Doctors at War,* ed. Morris Fishbein (New York: Dutton, 1945), 249-73. **80.** Fred Cantril, ed., *Public Opinion, 1935-1946* (Princeton: Princeton Univ. Press, 1951), 441.

81. J. Joseph Huthmacher, *Senator Robert F. Wagner* (New York: Atheneum, 1968), 293-94. **82.** FDR to Robert Wagner, June 16, 1943, PPF 1710, FDRL; and U.S. Senate, *National Health Program: Hearings before the Committee on Education and Labor on S. 1601,* 79th Cong., 2d sess., April 2–July 10, 1946, 1439-40. **83.** Harry and the Problem of Medical Care," *Annals of the American Academy of Political and Social Science* 273 (January 1951): 122-30; and Forrest A. Walker, "Compulsory Health Insurance: 'The Next Great Step in Social Legislation,'" *Journal of American History* 56 (September 1969): 290-304. **84.** Poen, *Truman versus the Medical Lobby,* 88-89; and Patterson, *Mr. Republican,* 323. **85.** Watson Miller to John Steelman, Mar. 17, 1947, OF 419-B, HSTL.

86. Ferrell, *Off the Record,* 165-66. **87.** Poen, *Truman versus the Medical Lobby,* 84. **88.** Transcript, Oscar R. Ewing Oral History Interview, April 29-30 and May 1-2, 1969, 115, HSTL; and Hechler, *Working with Truman,* 60-61. **89.** Hamby, *Beyond the New Deal,* 296-97. **90.** Oscar R. Ewing, *The Nation's Health: A Ten Year Program* (Washington, D.C.: GPO, 1948).

91. Ibid., 88, 114. **92.** Stanley Kelley Jr., *Professional Public Relations and Political Power* (Baltimore: Johns Hopkins University Press, 1956), 70. **93.** James G. Burrow, *AMA: Voice of American Medicine* (Baltimore: Johns Hopkins University Press, 1963), 355; and "The Assessment and Public Opinion," *Journal of the American Medical Association* 138 (1948): 1230-31. **94.** Hamby, *Beyond the New Deal,* 325-26; and Karl Schriftgiesser, *The Lobbyists: The Art and Business of Influencing Lawmakers* (Boston: Little, Brown, 1951), 124. **95.** Campion, *AMA and U.S. Health Policy,* 156-57; and Kelley, *Public Relations,* 67-106; pamphlet, "The Truth about Health Programs," 1950, DNC folder, JFK Pre-Presidential Papers, JFKL; and copy of Representative John D. Dingell, Sr.'s speech, Sept. 14, 1950, DNC folder, JFK Pre-Presidential Papers, JFKL.

96. Oliver Garceau, *The Political Life of the American Medical Association* (Hamden, Conn.: Archon Books, 1941), 75-76. **97.** Campion, *AMA and U.S. Health Policy,* 124-36. **98.** Allen and Shannon, *Truman Merry-Go-Round,* 338. **99.** Paul Starr, *The Social Transformation of American Medicine: The Rise of a Sovereign Profession and the Making of a Vast Industry* (New York: Basic Books, 1982), 280-89. **100.** Campion, *AMA and U.S. Medical Policy,* 128; and "Which Medicine," *Time* 53 (June 21, 1949): 48.

101. Herman M. Somers and Anne R. Somers, *Doctors, Patients, and Health Insurance* (Washington, D.C.: Brookings Institution, 1961), 548. **102.** Poen, *Truman versus the Medical Lobby,* 90. **103.** Gallup, *Public Opinion, 1935-1971,* 2:802. **104.** Ibid. **105.** *PPP,* 1949, 227.

106. Ibid. **107.** Poen, *Truman versus the Medical Lobby,* 165. **108.** Kelley, *Public Relations,* 72. **109.** *Congressional Record,* 81st Cong., 2d sess., 1950, vol. 96, pt. 6, 7770. **110.** Kelley, *Public Relations,* 77.

111. *Congressional Record,* 81st Cong., 2d sess., 150, A2530-2532. **112.** Kelley, *Public Relations,* 99-106; Pepper, *Eyewitness to a Century,* 203; and George E. O'Malley to Jake More, Nov. 15, 1950, Iowa folder, PSF, HSTL. **113.** Ferrell, *Off the Record,* 303; *PPP,* 1951, 353; and *PPP,* 1952-1953, 746-47. **114.** *PPP,* 1952-1953, 358; and Ferrell, *Off the Record,* 262. **115.** Richard Neustadt, "Congress and the Fair Deal: A Legislative Balance Sheet," *Public Policy* 5 (1954): 349-81.

116. Irving Bernstein, *Promises Kept,* 25; and Campion, *AMA and U.S. Health Policy,* 277-78. **117.** Ferrell, *Truman in the White House,* 382. **118.** Christenson, *Brannan Plan,* 61. **119.** Ibid., 50-54. **120.** Wayne D. Rasmussen ed., *Agriculture in the United States: A Documentary History* (New York: Random House, 1975), 4:2952-59; Matusow, *Farm Politics and Policies,* 194-99; Christenson, *Brannan Plan,* 68-72; and Schapsmeier and Schapsmeier, "Farm Policy," 366.

121. Robert Griffith, "Forging America's Postwar Order," in *The Truman Presidency,* ed. Michael J. Lacey (New York: Cambridge Univ. Press, 1989), 75. **122.** *PPP,* 1949, 130, 238-39, 292. **123.** Christenson, *Brannan Plan,* 61. **124.** *Congressional Record,*

81st Cong., 1st sess., vol. 95, pt. 7, 9852; and *NYT,* June 29, 1949, 5. **125.** Mayhew, *Party Loyalty among Congressmen,* 49. **126.** Matusow, *Farm Politics and Policies,* 210. **127.** Christenson, *Brannan Plan,* 159-60. **128.** Ferrell, *Truman in the White House,* 324. **129.** Matusow, *Farm Politics and Policies,* 214. **130.** William H. Peterson, *The Great Farm Problem* (Chicago: Regnery, 1959), 120-28. **131.** Rasmussen, 4:2959-71. **132.** *PPP,* 1949, 464-69; and *NYT,* Dec. 13, 1949, 37. **133.** Matusow, *Farm Politics and Policies,* 220-21. **134.** Ross, *Loneliest Campaign,* 256. **135.** Christenson, *Brannan Plan,* 155.

136. *PPP,* 1949, 76. **137.** Gallup, *Gallup Poll,* 2:780. **138.** Ibid., 2:781. **139.** Samuel H. Weaver, "The Truman Administration and Federal Aid to Education" (Ph.D. diss., American University, 1972), 7-123. **140.** Brown, "Taft: Champion of Public Housing," 225-53.

141. U.S. Senate, Committee on Education and Labor, Federal Aid for Education, 79th Cong., 1st sess., 1945, 118-25. **142.** Patterson, *Mr. Republican,* 432. **143.** Donovan, *Tumultuous Years,* 124. **144.** Diane Ravitch, *The Troubled Crusade: American Education, 1945-1980* (New York: Basic Books, 1983) 33; and Richard F. Fenno, "The House of Representatives and Federal Aid to Education," in *New Perspectives on the House of Representatives,* ed. Robert L. Peabody and Nelson W. Polsby (Chicago: Univ. of Chicago, 1963), 195-235. **145.** Fenno, "House and Federal Aid," 201-35; and *NYT,* May 6, 1949, 1.

146. Douglas, *In the Fullness of Time,* 416-17. **147.** Seymour P. Lachman, "The Cardinal, the Congressman, and the First Lady," *Journal of Church and State* 7 (1965): 35-66. **148.** Frank J. Munger and Richard F. Fenno, *National Politics and Federal Aid to Education* (Syracuse: Syracuse Univ. Press, 1962), 122-24. **149.** U.S. Congress, House of Representatives, Special Subcommittee of the Committee on Education Public School Assistance Act of 1949, 81st Cong., 1st sess., 1949, 743-44. **150.** Patterson, *Mr. Republican,* 433.

151. Lachman, "Cardinal, Congressman, First Lady," 43; and Elmer L. Puryear, *Graham A. Barden: Conservative Carolina Congressman* (Buies Creek, N.C.: Campbell Univ. Press, 1979), 86. **152.** Gilbert E. Smith, *The Limits of Reform: Politics and Federal Aid to Education* (New York: Garland, 1982), 317-18. **153.** Joseph P. Lash, *Eleanor: The Years Alone* (New York: W.W. Norton, 1972), 157-58; and Robert I. Gannon, *The Cardinal Spellman Story* (London: Robert Hale, 1962), 311-22. **154.** Quoted in Lash, *Eleanor,* 158. **155.** Ravitch, *Troubled Crusade,* 38.

156. John S. Conway, "Myron C. Taylor's Mission to the Vatican, 1940-1950," *Church History* 44 (1975): 85-99; Paul Blanshard, *American Freedom and Catholic Power* (Boston: Beacon Press, 1958), 322-23; and George J. Gill, "The Truman Administration and Vatican Relations," *Catholic Historical Review* 73 (July 1987): 408-23. **157.** Ravitch, *Troubled Crusade,* 40. **158.** Charles V. Hamilton, *Adam Clayton Powell Jr.: The Political Biography of an American Dilemma* (New York: Collier Books, 1991), 330. **159.** Puryear, *Graham A. Barden,* 227; and Munger and Fenno, *National Politics,* 122-24. **160.** Hamilton, *Adam Clayton Powell,* 226-27.

161. *PPP,* 1950, 141-43. **162.** Poen, *Strictly Personal and Confidential,* 98. **163.** *PPP,* 1950, 386. **164.** Ibid., 1951, 94-95; and Ibid., 1952-1953, 100-101. **165.** Ravitch, *Troubled Crusade,* 41-42.

166. Griffith, "Forging America's Postwar Order," 87-88. 167. Davies, *Housing Reform,* 114. 168. Charles C. Brown, "Taft: Champion of Public Housing," 219-53; and Louis W. Koenig, ed., *The Truman Administration: Its Principles and Practice* (New York: New York Univ. Press, 1956), 165. 169. Gallup, *Public Opinion, 1935-1971,* 2:780-81. 170. Wilbur J. Cohen and Robert J. Myers, "Social Security Act Amendments of 1950," *Social Security Bulletin* 13 (October 1950): 3-14.
    171. Neustadt, "Congress and the Fair Deal," 349-81. 172. Riddick, "Eighty-First Congress," 60-66. 173. Robert Lane, "Notes on the Theory of the Lobby," *Western Political Quarterly* 2 (1949): 154-62; James MacGregor Burns, *Congress on Trial: The Legislative Process and the Administrative State* (New York: Harper, 1949), 31; and Richard W. Gable, "NAM: Influential Lobby or Kiss of Death?" *Journal of Politics* 15 (1953): 254-73. 174. Irving Bernstein, *Promises Kept,* 247; and Allen J. Matusow, *The Unraveling of America* (New York: Harper & Row, 1984), 4, 53, 227. 175. Ferrell, *Off the Record,* 282-83.
    176. William E. Leuchtenburg, *In the Shadow of FDR: From Harry Truman to Ronald Reagan* (Ithaca: Cornell Univ. Press, 1983), 28-31; Hamby, *Liberalism and Its Challengers,* 65-71; James L. Sundquist, *Dynamics of the Party System* (Washington D.C.: Brookings Institution, 1983), 215-17; and Larry Berman, "Lyndon B. Johnson: Paths Chosen and Opportunities Lost," in *Leadership in the Modern Presidency* (Cambridge: Harvard Univ. Press, 1988), 134-35.

7. DEMOCRATIC DISSENSUS, 1950-1952

1. Ferrell, *Off the Record,* 168. 2. Thompson, *Frustration of Politics,* 47-49, 168; and Peter L. Steinberg, "The Great 'Red Menace': U.S. Prosecution of American Communits, 1947-1951" (Ph.D. diss., New York University, 1979), 199-200. 3. Richard Whelan, *Drawing The Line: The Korean War, 1950-1953* (Boston: Little, Brown, 1990), 24-26. 4. Cecil V. Crabb, *Bipartisan Foreign Policy: Myth or Reality?* (Evanston, Ill.: Row, Peterson, 1957), 81-87; Letters to JFK from Edward Cooper, Apr. 12, 1951, Elizabeth Beaumont, Apr. 11, 1951, Ruth O'Neill, Apr. 12, 1951, and John Hogan, Apr. 14, 1951, Box 93, Speech Files 1947-52, JFK Pre-Presidential Papers, JFKL; and D. Clayton James, *Refighting the Last War: Command and Crisis in Korea, 1950-1953* (New York: Free Press, 1993), 213-14. 5. Tobey, *Return to Morality,* 167-68; Paul H. Douglas, *Ethics in Government* (Cambridge: Harvard Univ. Press, 1952), 10-27; and Abell, *Pearson Diaries,* 212-13.
    6. Douglas, *In the Fullness of Time,* 225. 7. Ibid. 8. Bert Cochran, *Adlai Stevenson: Patrician among the Politicians* (New York: Funk and Wagnalls, 1969), 210-23. 9. Fontenay, *Estes Kefauver,* 164. 10. *Congressional Record,* 81st Cong., 2d session, vol. 96, pt. 1, Jan. 5, 1950, 67-68.
    11. Fontenay, *Estes Kefauver,* 167. 12. David Halberstam, *The Fifties* (New York: Villard Books, 1993), 188-94. 13. Fontenay, *Estes Kefauver,* 164; and Joseph B. Gorman, *Kefauver: A Political Biography* (New York: Oxford Univ. Press, 1971), 75. 14. William H. Moore, *The Kefauver Committee and the Politics of Crime: 1950-1952* (Columbia:

Univ. of Missouri Press, 1974), 64. **15.** Ibid., 39-41; and Virgil W. Peterson, *Barbarians in Our Midst,* 252. **16.** U.S. Senate, Special Committee to Investigate Organized Crime in Interstate Commerce, 82d Congress, 1st sess., Report no. 307, 3d Interim Report, 9-10. **17.** Ibid., 174-207; and Kefauver, *Crime in America,* 308-33. **18.** U.S. Senate, Report no. 307, 1-2. **19.** Ibid., 162-73; and Virgil W. Peterson, *Barbarians in Our Midst,* 259-64. **20.** Albert Deutsch, *The Trouble with Cops* (New York: Crown, 1954), 7-8, 12-13. **21.** Moore, *Kefauver Committee,* 184; and Gus Tyler, "The Big Fix," *New Republic* 125 (Oct. 22, 1951): 11-12, 20. **22.** Ferrell, *Off the Record,* 260; and "Protected Gambling in Chicago," *Criminal Justice* 74 (May 1947): 20-23. **23.** Walsh, *Public Enemies,* 221-22. **24.** U.S. Senate, Report no. 307, 18-24; William Bradford Huie, "How to Think about Truman," *American Mercury* 73 (August 1951): 121-28; and "Is President Truman an Honorable Man?" American Mercury 72 (May 1951): 546-50. **25.** "Kefauver in Seattle," *New Republic* 125 (Dec. 17, 1951): 6.

26. Gorman, *Kefauver,* 102; and "Who Are the Nation's Best and Worst Senators?" Pageant 7 (September 1951): 111-17. **27.** Congressional Quarterly, *Politics in America,* 13. **28.** Gorman, *Kefauver,* 129. **29.** *PPP,* 1952, 132. **30.** HST, *Memoirs,* 2:551.

31. *PPP,* 1952, 225; John Robert Greene, *The Crusade: The Presidential Election of 1952* (Lanham: Univ. Press of America, 1985), 128-30; and James W. Davis, *President as Party Leader,* 25. **32.** Stephen J. Wayne, *The Road to the White House* (New York: St. Martin's Press, 1988), 13; Paul T. David, Malcolm Moos, and Ralph M. Goldman, *Presidential Nominating Politics in 1952* (Baltimore: John Hopkins Univ. Press, 1954), 1:64. **33.** Neustadt interview; dictation, Oct. 3, 1953, Memoirs file, Post-Presidential Files, HSTL; and Ferrell, *Off the Record,* 260-261. **34.** Ferrell, *Off the Record,* 269. **35.** Moore, *Kefauver Committee,* 211-13.

36. Gallup, *Public Opinion, 1935-1971,* 2:979. **37.** Author's phone interview with David Stowe, July 8, 1991; Bolles, *How to Get Rich in Washington* (New York: Norton, 1952): 23-27; Abels, *Truman Scandals,* 14; Dunar, *Truman Scandals,* 137-38; and Fletcher Knebel and Jack Wilson, "The Scandalous Years," *Look* 15 (May 22, 1951): 31-37. **38.** "Is President Truman an Honorable Man?" 549-50. **39.** Copy, speech by Joseph W. Martin Jr., Feb. 20, 1950, 2, Box 65, File 117, Joseph W. Martin Jr. Papers, JWMI. **40.** Martin, speech, Apr. 26, 1950, 5, Box 65, File 117, Joseph W. Martin Jr. Papers, JWMI.

41. *NYT,* Feb. 7, 1950. **42.** Rovere, *McCarthy,* 125; Reinhard, *Politics as Usual,* 62-63; Griffith, "Forging America's Postwar Order," 10-20; and Ronald J. Caridi, *The Korean War and American Politics: The Republican Party as a Case Study* (Philadelphia: Univ. of Pennsylvania Press, 1968), 94-95. **43.** Gilman M. Ostrander, *Nevada: The Great Rotten Borough, 1859-1964* (New York: Knopf, 1966), 188-96; and Richard M. Fried, *Men against McCarthy* (New York: Columbia Univ. Press, 1976), 30. **44.** Walter S. Poole, "The Quest for a Republican Foreign Policy, 1941-1951" (Ph.D. diss., University of Pennsylvania, 1968), 355-56. **45.** Fried, *Men against McCarthy,* 160-62.

46. Ambrose, *Nixon,* 164; Ferrell, *Off the Record,* 258; and Douglas, *In the Fullness of Time,* 249. **47.** *PPP,* 1950, 284. **48.** Ferrell, *Truman in the White House,* 380. **49.** Poen, *Strictly Personal and Confidential,* 180. **50.** Warren Ashby, *Frank Porter Graham: A Southern Liberal* (Winston-Salem, N.C.: John F. Blair, 1980), 259.

51. Barnard, *Dixiecrats and Democrats,* 108; William G. Carleton, "The Southern Politician—1900 and 1950," *Journal of Politics* 13 (1951): 221; and Key, *Southern Politics,* 145-46. **52.** Alexander R. Stoesen, "The Senatorial Career of Claude D. Pepper" (Ph.D. diss., University of North Carolina, 1965), 9-121; and Julian M. Pleasants and Augustus M. Burns III, *Frank Porter Graham and the 1950 Senate Race in North Carolina* (Chapel Hill: Univ. of North Carolina Press, 1990), 92-93. **53.** Pepper, *Eyewitness to a Century,* 135-36. **54.** Schmidt, *Henry A. Wallace,* 42-43; and Ferrell, *Off the Record,* 87. **55.** Ralph McGill, "Can He Purge Senator Pepper?" *Saturday Evening Post* 222 (Apr. 22, 1950): 33.

56. Savage, *Roosevelt,* 133-34. **57.** Key, *Southern Politics,* 98; Pepper, *Eyewitness to a Century,* 120-21; and Congressional Quarterly, *Guide to U.S. Elections,* 1093. **58.** Bert Collier, "Pepper v. Smathers," *New Republic* 122 (May 1, 1950): 14-15; Joseph G. LaPalombara, "Pressure, Propaganda, and Political Action in the Elections of 1950," *Journal of Politics* 14 (May 1952): 310; and Lubell, *Future of American Politics,* 113. **59.** Pepper, *Eyewitness to a Century,* 190-93. **60.** Stoesen, "Senatorial Career of Pepper," 329.

61. Fried, 96-98. **62.** Kelley, *Public Relations,* 99. **63.** Lubell, Future of American Politics, 124. **64.** Ibid., 124-25; and Key, *Southern Politics,* 519. **65.** Pepper, *Eyewitness to a Century,* 205.

66. Congressional Quarterly, *Guide to U.S. Elections,* 1093. **67.** Abell, *Pearson Diaries,* 126. **68.** Pleasants and Burns, *Frank Porter Graham,* 159. **69.** Ashby, *Frank Porter Graham,* 207-11, 224. **70.** Pleasants and Burns, *Frank Porter Graham,* 181-82, 211; and HST to Jonathan Daniels, June 17, 1950, PSF, HSTL.

71. Pleasants and Burns, *Frank Porter Graham,* 6. **72.** Daniel J. Singal, *The War Within* (Chapel Hill: Univ. of North Carolina Press, 1982), 191-93; Ashby, *Frank Porter Graham,* 269; and Harvey Klehr, *The Heyday of American Communism: The Depression Decade* (New York: Basic Books, 1984), 276-77. **73.** Pleasants and Burns, *Frank Porter Graham,* 27-28. **74.** Congressional Quarterly, *Guide to U.S. Elections,* 1097. **75.** Pleasants and Burns, *Frank Porter Graham,* 92-93.

76. Augustus M. Burns III, "Graduate Education for Blacks in North Carolina, 1930-1951," *Journal of Southern History* 46 (May 1980): 195-218; and Ashby, *Frank Porter Graham,* 264. **77.** Lubell, *Future of American Politics,* 108-9. **78.** Ashby, *Frank Porter Graham,* 266. **79.** Pleasants and Burns, *Frank Porter Graham,* 214; and Lubell, *Future of American Politics,* 112-14. **80.** Kelley, *Public Relations,* 99; and Pleasants and Burns, *Future of American Politics,* 228.

81. Fried, 99-100. **82.** Congressional Quarterly, *Guide to U.S. Elections,* 1097. **83.** Wicker, *One of Us,* 72. **84.** Ambrose, *Nixon,* 209. **85.** Earl Mazo, *Richard Nixon: A Political and Personal Portrait* (New York: Harper & Brothers, 1959), 74.

86. Wicker, *One of Us,* 72. **87.** Costello, *Facts about Nixon,* 62. **88.** Helen Gahagan Douglas, *A Full Life* (New York: Doubleday, 1982), 301; and Ronald Brownstein, *The Power and the Glitter* (New York: Pantheon Books, 1990), 120. **89.** Ambrose, *Nixon,* 211-13. **90.** Costello, *Facts about Nixon,* 72.

91. Thomas P. O'Neill Jr., *Man of the House* (New York: Random House, 1987), 81; and Richard M. Nixon, *RN: The Memoirs of Richard Nixon* (New York: Grosset and

Dunlap, 1978), 75. **92.** Ambrose, *Nixon,* 213. **93.** Brodie, *Nixon,* 241-42; and Earl Mazo and Stephen Hess, *Nixon: A Political Portrait* (New York: Popular Library, 1968), 71-72. **94.** Mayo, *Nixon,* 141. **95.** Wicker, *One of Us,* 73; and *U.S. News & World Report* 29 (Oct. 27, 1950): 19.

96. Ambrose, *Nixon,* 214-15. **97.** Costello, *Facts about Nixon,* 67-68; and Nixon, *RN,* 77. **98.** Fried, *Men against McCarthy,* 110; and Burton R. Brazil, "The 1950 Elections in California," *Western Political Quarterly* 4 (March 1951): 67. **99.** Ferrell, *Truman in the White House,* 373; and Ambrose, *Nixon,* 219. **100.** *PPP,* 1950, 697.

101. Ibid., 702. **102.** Congressional Quarterly, *Guide to U.S. Elections,* 611. **103.** *U.S. News & World Report* 29 (Nov. 17, 1950): 30. **104.** Caroline H. Keith, *"For Hell And A Brown Mule": The Biography of Senator Millard E. Tydings* (Lanham, Md.: Madison Books, 1991), 75-92. **105.** Ibid., 88.

106. Fried, *Men against McCarthy,* 125-26. **107.** Fenton, *Politics in the Border States,* 182. **108.** Keith, *"For Hell and a Brown Mule,"* 92. **109.** Ibid. **110.** Patterson, *Congressional Conservatism and the New Deal,* 38-41.

111. Fenton, *Politics in the Boarder States,* 183; and J.B. Shannon, "Presidential Politics in the South," *Journal of Politics* 2 (August 1939): 290-95. **112.** Savage, *Roosevelt,* 143-44. **113.** Ferrell, *Truman in the White House,* 364. **114.** Keith, *"For Hell and a Brown Mule,"* 402. **115.** Ibid., 89-90; and Harry W. Kirwin, *The Inevitable Success: Herbert R. O'Conor* (Westminster, Md.: Newman Press, 1962), 509.

116. Fried, *Men against McCarthy,* 124-25. **117.** U.S. Senate, *Maryland Senatorial Election of 1950: Hearings before the Subcommittee on Privileges and Elections of the Committee on Rules and Administration, Pursuant to S. Res. 250,* 82d Cong., 1st sess., 1951, 8-15. **118.** Ibid., 183-201; Kelley, *Public Relations,* 116; and Fried, *Men against McCarthy,* 127. **119.** LaPalombara, "Pressure," 308; and Robert Griffith, *The Politics of Fear: Joseph R. McCarthy and the Senate* (Lexington: Univ. of Kentucky Press, 1970), 62-63. **120.** Fried, *Men against McCarthy,* 135; and Kelley, 131.

121. Lubell, *Future of American Politics,* 153; and Fenton, *Politics in the Border States,* 186. **122.** Congressional Quarterly, *Guide to U.S. Elections,* 619. **123.** Keith, *"For Hell and a Brown Mule,"* 419. **124.** U.S. Senate Committee on Rules and Administration, *Maryland Senatorial Election of 1950* report, 82d Cong., 1st sess., 1951, 2-7, 37-41. **125.** Keith, *"For Hell and a Brown Mule,"* 426-27.

126. Ferrell, *Off the Record,* 171; and *PPP,* 1950, 13. **127.** Alonzo L. Hamby, *Man of the People: A Life of Harry S. Truman* (New York: Oxford Univ. Press, 1995), 481. **128.** Ferrell, *Off the Record,* 173. **129.** Donald J. Kemper, *Decade of Fear: Senator McCarthy and Civil Liberties* (Columbia: Univ. of Missouri Press, 1965), 7-29; and Ernest Kirschten, "Donnell Luck and Missouri Scandal," *Nation* 171 (Oct. 14, 1950): 332-34. **130.** *NYT,* Feb. 17, 1950.

131. *PPP,* 1950, 169. **132.** Louis H. Bean, *The Mid-Term Battle* (New York: Business Press, 1950), 98. **133.** Ken Hechler to Louis Bean, Oct. 17, 1950, and Hechler to Bertram Gross, Oct. 24, 1950, October-December 1950 folder, Ken Hechler Papers, HSTL. **134.** Hechler, *Working with Truman,* 130-31. **135.** Hechler and Dreyer interviews.

136. Hechler, *Working with Truman,* 133-34, 142-43; and *PPP,* 1950, 364-408. **137.** *PPP,* 412. **138.** DNC pamphlet, "Scare Words: A Compilation of Republican Attacks on Programmatic Legislation since 1882," 1950, 1, Clinton Anderson folder, PSF, HSTL. **139.** Jack Redding to Charles G. Ross, June 10, 1950, 1950 folder, OF 299-A, HSTL. **140.** Charles Van Devander to Joseph Short, Jan. 5, 1951, 1951 folder, OF 299-A, HSTL.

141. Halberstam, *Fifties,* 49-59; Crabb, 87; and Kent M. Beck, "American Liberalism and the Cold War Consensus: Policies and Policymakers of the Moderate Democratic Left, 1945-1953" (Ph.D. diss., University of California-Irvine, 1976), 353. **142.** Ferrell, *Truman in the White House: The Diary of Eben A. Ayers,* 361; and Ferrell, *Off the Record,* 191-93. **143.** John E. Mueller, *War, Presidents, and Public Opinion* (Lanham, Md.: Univ. Press of America, 1985), 24, 159-60. **144.** *U.S. News & World Report* 29 (Oct. 27, 1950): 19-21; and George E. O'Malley and Jake More, Nov. 15, 1950, Iowa folder, PSF, HSTL. **145.** Dreyer interview; and DNC booklet, "The Truth about Korea," 1950, Clinton P. Anderson folder, PSF, HSTL.

146. *PPP,* 1950, 702. **147.** Congressional Quarterly, *Politics in America, 1945-1964,* 10. **148.** Neil MacNeil, *Dirksen: Portrait of a Public Man* (New York: World, 1970), 92; and Beers, *Pennsylvania Politics,* 164. **149.** Ernest W. McFarland, *Mac: The Autobiography of Ernest W. McFarland* (privately published, 1979), 140-41; and Ferrell, *Off the Record,* 283. **150.** *U.S. News & World Report* 29 (Nov. 17, 1950): 117.

151. Ferrell, *Truman in the White House,* 380. **152.** Reinhard, *Republican Right since 1945,* 66; and Campion, *AMA and U.S. Health Policy,* 210. **153.** Eleanora W. Schoenebaum ed., *Political Profiles: The Truman Years* (New York: Facts in File, 1978), 542. **154.** Frank H. Jonas, "The 1950 Elections in Utah," *Western Political Quarterly* 4 (March 1951): 88-90; and Frank H. Jonas, "The Art of Political Dynamiting," *Western Political Quarterly* 10 (June 1957): 374-91. **155.** Fred Shutrump to Mike Kirwan, Jan. 5, 1950, Ohio folder, PSF, HSTL; and *U.S. News & World Report* 29 (Oct. 20, 1950): 11-12.

156. Lubell, *Future of American Politics,* 183-87; and Patterson, *Mr. Republican,* 456-73. **157.** HST to Clifford Langsdale, Nov. 29, 1950, Missouri folder, PSF, HSTL. **158.** Ibid. **159.** Little, 225; David B. Truman, *The Congressional Party: A Case Study* (New York: Wiley, 1959), 117; and Gallup, *Public Opinion, 1935-1971,* 2:989, 1040, 1050. **160.** Bolles, *How to Get Rich in Washington,* 3-45; and Helen Fuller, "The Tax Thieves of 1951," *New Republic* 125 (Nov. 12, 1951): 9-10.

161. "Fuller, "Tax Thieves of 1951," 10; Douglas, *In the Fullness of Time,* 188; and Abels, *Truman Scandals,* 314. **162.** Tobey, *Return to Morality,* 87-89; Douglas, *Ethics in Government,* 7-34; and letters, Joseph J. O'Connell to Fred M. Vinson, Aug. 18, 1945, and Sept. 4, 1945, Fred M. Vinson Papers, UKL. **163.** McCullough, *Truman,* 523. **164.** Douglas, *In the Fullness of Time,* 222-23. **165.** Ibid., 223-24.

166. U.S. Senate, Banking and Currency Committee, *Proposed Extension of Reconstruction Finance Corporation: Hearings on $80,000,000 Loan to B&O Railroad,* 80th Cong., 1st sess., May 28–June 5, 1947. **167.** Ferrell, *Off the Record,* 201. **168.** Abels, *Truman Scandals,* 71. **169.** Jesse H. Jones, *Fifty Billion Dollars: My Thirteen Years with the RFC (1932-1945)* (New York: Macmillan, 1951), ix-20, 131-49. **170.** Abels, *Truman Scandals,* 72; and U.S. Senate, Subcommittee of the Committee on Banking and Currency, *Study of Reconstruction Finance Corporation: Hearings on S. Rept. 219,* 82d Cong., 1st sess., Mar. 5, 1951, 1236-58.

171. Ibid., March 7, 1951, 1305-25. **172.** Dunar, *Truman Scandals,* 93. **173.** Dawson interview. **174.** Charles S. Murphy to HST, Aug. 9, 1951, William M. Boyle Jr. folder, Charles S. Murphy Papers, HSTL; and Bolles, *How to Get Rich in Washington,* 152-54. **175.** *Newsweek* 38 (Oct. 22, 1951): 23. **176.** U.S. Senate, *Hearings on S. Rept. 219,* Mar. 8, 1951, 1377-90; and Knebel and Wilson, "Scandalous Years," 36. **177.** Donovan, *Tumultuous Years,* 335-37. **178.** Dunar, *Truman Scandals,* 64-66. **179.** *PPP,* 1949, 425; and Ferrell, *Truman in the White House,* 325. **180.** Abels, *Truman Scandals,* 307-11.

181. Strout, *TRB,* 72-74, 387; Allen and Sherman, *Truman Merry-Go-Round,* 86-88; Hamby, *Beyond the New Deal,* 338-39; and *Nation* 169 (Sept. 10, 1949): 241. **182.** Gallup, *Public Opinion, 1935-1971,* 2:1018; Abell, *Pearson Diaries,* 156-62; Ferrell, *Off the Record,* 268; and Donald Dawson to HST, Dec. 9, 1950, RFC folder, PSF, HSTL. **183.** Haynes Johnson and Bernard W. Gwertzman, *Fulbright: The Dissenter* (New York: Doubleday, 1968), 120-23. **184.** U.S. Senate, Committee on Banking and Currency, *Favoritism and Influence,* 82d Cong., 1st sess., Feb. 5, 1951, Senate Report 75, 7-9. **185.** *PPP,* 1951, 145.

186. Gosnell, *Truman's Crises,* 500. **187.** Dunar, *Truman Scanals,* 128; and *PPP,* 1951, 641-45. **188.** U.S. Congress, House, Subcommittee of the Committee on Ways and Means, *Internal Revenue Investigation: Hearings,* 82d Cong., 1st sess., Sept. 10, 1951–Jan. 29, 1952; and Ibid., Subcommittee of the Committee on the Judiciary, *Investigation of the Department of Justice: Report Pursuant to H. Res. 50,* 82d Cong., 2d sess., Mar. 26–June 27, 1952. **189.** Dunar, *Truman Scandals,* 98-103; Abels, *Truman Scandals,* 158-251; James H. Shelton, "The Tax Scandals of the 1950's" (Ph.D. diss., American University, 1971), 17-119; J. Malcolm Barter, "The Tax Thieves of 1951," *New Republic* 125 (Dec. 10, 1951): 12-13; and William V. Shannon, "The Tax Thieves of 1951," *New Republic* 125 (Dec. 3, 1951): 12-14. **190.** *Newsweek* 38 (Dec. 10, 1951): 21.

191. Dunar, *Truman Scandals,* 150-54; and Brownell, *Advising Ike,* 142, 150. **192.** Dawson interview; Stowe interview; transcript, Matthew J. Connelly Oral History Interview, 451; and Merle Miller, *Plain Speaking,* 439. **193.** Heller, *Truman White House,* 26-27; and William E. Pemberton, *Bureaucratic Politics: Executive Reorganization during the Truman Administration* (Columbia: Univ. of Missouri Press, 1979), 103-17. **194.** Copy, Frank E. McKinney's acceptance speech, Oct. 31, 1951, Frank E. McKinney folder, DNC Library Clipping File, HSTL; and Frank E. McKinney to HST, Nov. 1, 1951, Frank E. McKinney Papers, HSTL. **195.** George M. Elsey to Clark M. Clifford, Dec. 28, 1951, Political File, Clark M. Clifford Papers, HSTL; and Hechler and Neustadt interviews.

196. Michael G. Fullington, "Presidential Management and Executive Scandal," *Presidential Studies Quarterly* 9 (1979): 193-99. **197.** *PPP,* 1951, 641-44; 1952-53, 599-600. **198.** Ibid., 1951, 646; 1952-53, 1161; and Goldman, *Chairmen and Committees,* 435. **199.** Goldman, *Chairmen and Committees,* 1-2. **200.** Pemberton, *Bureaucratic Politics,* 168-72.

201. Koenig, *Truman Administration,* 51-57; and Stephen Hess, *Organizing the Presidency* (Washington, D.C.: Brookings Institution, 1988), 41, 53-55. **202.** *PPP,* 1952-53, 254-58. **203.** Dunar, *Truman Scandals,* 133-34. **204.** *PPP,* 1952-53, 246-48; and

Phillip E. Stebbins, "Truman and the Seizure of Steel: A Failure in Communication," *Historian* 34 (1971): 2-20. **205.** Pemberton, *Bureaucratic Politics,* 167-69; and Gallup, *Public Opinion, 1935-1971,* 2:1037. **206.** Robert E. Hannegan to Fred M. Vinson, Aug. 17, 1945, Fred M. Vinson Papers, UKL; Shelton, "Tax Scandals, 71-113; Abels, *Truman Scandals,* 145-83; and *PPP,* 1952-53, 253, 432. **207.** U.S. Congress, House, Subcommittee of the Committee on the Judiciary, *Investigation of the Department of Justice: Hearings,* 82d Cong., 2d sess., Mar. 26, 1952, 18-30. **208.** Neustadt interview; and Dunar, *Truman Scandals,* 111-12. **209.** Transcript, interview with J. Howard McGrath, Mar. 24, 1955, 24-25, Memoirs File, PPF, HSTL; transcript, Matthew J. Connelly Oral History Interview, 360; and Abels, *Truman Scandals,* 16. **210.** Newbold Morris, *Let the Chips Fall: My Battle against Corruption* (New York: Appleton-Century-Crofts, 1955), 7-8.

211. Ibid., 11-18; and *PPP,* 1952-53, 152-53. **212.** Transcript, Harold D. Seidman, Oral History Interview, July 29, 1970, 81-85, 97-99, HSTL; Morris, *Let the Chips Fall,* 20-26; and *PPP,* 1952-53, 166. **213.** U.S. Congress, House, Subcommittee of the Committee on the Judiciary, *Investigation of the Department of Justice: Hearings,* 82d Cong., 2d sess., Mar. 31, 1952, 55. **214.** Transcript, McGrath interview in Memoirs File, 27, HSTL. **215.** Charles S. Murphy to HST, Apr. 1, 1952, Murphy Files, HST Papers, HSTL; and transcript, Roger Tubby Oral History Interview, Feb. 10, 1970, 142-43, HSTL.

216. *PPP,* 1952-53, 230-32. **217.** Abels, *Truman Scandals,* 19-20. **218.** Stowe interview; Brightman interview; Dunar, *Truman Scandals,* 135-136; Knebel and Wilson, "Scandalous Years," 37; press release from Republican Policy Committee, Mar. 13, 1951, Box 35, Folder 35.82.2, Joseph W. Martin Jr. Papers, JWMI; and DNC, *The Democratic Platform, 1952* (Washington, D.C.: DNC, 1952), 38-40. **219.** Ferrell , *Off the Record,* 267-68. **220.** Ibid., 268.

221. *PPP,* 1952-53, 568-69, 693-94, 847-49. **222.** Ernest Frey to Fred M. Vinson, Dec. 10, 1951, Fred M. Vinson Papers, UKL. **223.** Memos, Donald Dawson to Charles S. Murphy, July 10, 1951, Aug. 6, 1951, and Aug. 14, 1951, all in Charles S. Murphy Papers, HSTL. **224.** HST, *Memoirs,* 2:552-53. **225.** Schoenebaum, *Political Profiles,* 583.

226. Barton J. Bernstein, "Charting a Course between Inflation and Depression: Secretary of the Treasury Fred Vinson and the Truman Administration's Tax Bill," *Register of the Kentucky Historical Society* 66 (1968): 53-64. **227.** Wyatt interview. **228.** Hechler, *Working with Truman,* 242-43; and HST, *Memoirs,* 2:553-54. **229.** James Bolner, "Mr. Chief Justice Vinson and the Communist Controversy: A Reassessment," *Register of the Kentucky Historical Society* 64 (1968): 378-91. **230.** HST, *Memoirs,* 2:553.

231. Charles S. Murphy to Robert L. Dennison, Aug. 18, 1972, Robert L. Dennison Papers, HSTL. **232.** Krock, *Memoirs,* 267-69; Stephen E. Ambrose, *Eisenhower: Soldier, General of the Army, President-Elect, 1890-1952* (New York: Simon and Schuster, 1983), 602; and *PPP,* 1951, 629. **233.** Phillips, "Exit the Boss, Enter the Leader," 417. **234.** McKeever, *Adlai Stevenson,* 149-72. **235.** Neustadt interview.

236. Ibid. **237.** Walter Johnson, *How We Drafted Stevenson,* 18-19. **238.** Ferrell, *Off the Record,* 244-45. **239.** Ibid., 245. **240.** David et al., *Presidential Nominating Politics,* 1:39-40; and John B. Martin and Eric Larrabee, "The Drafting of Adlai Stevenson," *Harper's* 205 (October 1952): 35-43.

241. Hamby, *Man of the People,* 602; and Rudy Abramson, *Spanning the Century: The Life of W. Averell Harriman, 1891-1986* (New York: Morrow, 1992), 464-65. **242.** Abramson, *Spanning the Century,* 494. **243.** Ann Hodges Morgan, *Robert S. Kerr: The Senate Years* (Norman: Univ. of Oklahoma Press, 1977), 43-127. **244.** Fontenay, *Estes Kefauver,* 43-127. **245.** Ibid., 199. **246.** DNC, *Official Report of the Proceedings of the Democratic National Convention, 1952* (Washington, D.C.: DNC, 1952), 456, 484. **247.** Congressional Quarterly, *Politics in America, 1945-1964,* 13; *Newsweek* 39 (May 12, 1952): 28-29; and *Time* 59 (May 19, 1952): 29-32. **248.** Fite, *Russell,* 286-87. **249.** Ibid., 290; and David D. Potenziani, "Striking Back: Richard B. Russell and Racial Relocation," *Georgia History* 65 (1981): 263-77. **250.** DNC, *National Convention: 1952,* 484; and Congressional Quarterly, *Politics in America, 1945-1964,* 98.

251. Greene, *Crusade,* 138-39. **252.** Wyatt interview; and HST, *Memoirs,* 2:558. **253.** Letters to Alben W. Barkley from Lloyd R. Porter, May 27, 1952, Roger G. Branigin, May 31, 1952, W.N. Boaz, Sr., June 13, 1952, and David S. Sinaink, June 14, 1952, all in Political File, Alben W. Barkley Papers, UKL. **254.** Ferrell, *Off the Record,* 244. **255.** Hamby, *Man of the People,* 607-8.

256. Barkley, *That Reminds Me,* 242-43. **257.** Gallup, *Public Opinion, 1935-1971,* 2:1069. **258.** Barkley, *That Reminds Me,* 236-40; and transcript, Joseph D. Keenan Oral History Interview, Febr. 2, 1971, 48, HSTL. **259.** Clipping, *Courier-Journal,* Aug. 10, 1952, Earle L. Clements Collection, UKL. **260.** Adlai E. Stevenson, *Major Campaign Speeches, 1952* (New York: Random House, 1953), 3-6; and Walter Johnson, *How We Drafted Stevenson,* 110-14.

261. David et al., *Presidential Nominating Politics,* 181; Fontenay, *Estes Kefauver,* 218-21; and Allan P. Sindler, "The Unsolid South: A Challenge to the Democratic National Party," in *The Uses of Power: Seven Cases in American Politics,* ed. Alan F. Westin (New York: Harcourt, Brace, and World, 1962), 255-64. **262.** Bain and Parris, *Convention Decisions,* 289; and HST to Harry L. Seay, Apr. 23, 1952, PSF, HSTL; and clipping, *San Antonio Evening News,* May 28, 1952, PSF, HSTL. **263.** Ferrell, *Off the Record,* 262. **264.** Greene, *Crusade,* 159. **265.** DNC, *National Convention, 1952,* 538.

266. Stevenson, *Major Campaign Speeches,* 10. **267.** DNC, *National Convention, 1952,* 541. **268.** Neustadt interview; and Sindler, "Unsolid South," 263-65. **269.** McKeever, *Adlai Stevenson,* 201-2; and Parmet, *Democrats,* 101. **270.** Wil Haygood, *King of the Cats: The Life and Times of Adam Clayton Powell Jr.* (Boston: Houghton Mifflin, 1993), 170-71; and Barton J. Bernstein, "Election of 1952," *History of American Presidential Elections: 1789-1968* (New York: Chelsea House, 1971), 4:3240.

271. Louis Harris, *Is There a Republican Majority?* 65-66; James R. Sweeney, "Revolt in Virginia: Harry Byrd and the 1952 Presidential Election," *Virginia Magazine of History and Biography* 2 (April 1978): 186; and Brightman interview. **272.** Ferrell, *Off the Record,* 281. **273.** Wyatt interview. **274.** Ibid.; Nathan B. Blumberg, *One-Party Press? Coverage of the 1952 Presidential Campaign in 35 Daily Newspapers* (Lincoln: Univ. of Nebraska Press, 1954), 14; McKeever, *Adlai Stevenson,* 250-52; and Jamieson, *Packaging the Presidency,* 60-62. **275.** Kelley, *Public Relations,* 150-56; and Bernstein, "Election of 1952," 3250-51.

276. John Bartlow Martin, *Adlai Stevenson of Illinois* (New York: Doubleday, 1977), 608-41; and DNC Research Division materials provided to the author by Bertram Gross, DNC research director in 1952. **277.** Anthony Lewis, "Local Background Information for the Stevenson Campaign 1952," Philip Stern Papers, JFKL; and Bertram Gross to Matthew J. Connelly, Aug. 2, 1952, OF 299, HSTL. **278.** DNC report, "If Taft Had His Way in Congress," Aug. 5, 1952, provided to the author by Bertram Gross. **279.** *PPP,* 1952-53, 545, 556, 561, 597, and 602. **280.** Ibid., 545.
281. Hamby, *Man of the People,* 614. **282.** Ambrose, *Eisenhower,* 530-31; and Wyatt interview. **283.** Brownell, *Advising Ike,* 123-28; and Jamieson, *Packaging the Presidency,* 48-49. **284.** Jamieson, *Packaging the Presidency,* 81. **285.** DNC booklet, "How to Win in 1952," Box 14, Folder 4, Paul M. Butler Papers, HLND; and DNC booklet, "The Republicans' Platform for 1952: What It Really Means," September 1952, provided by Gross.
286. Arthur E. Rowse, *Slanted News: A Case Study of the Nixon and Stevenson Fund Stories* (Boston: Little, Brown, 1957), 4-29; Leonard Lurie, *The Running of Richard Nixon* (New York: Coward, McCann, and Geohogan, 1972), 120-22; Nixon, *RN,* 92-93; and Mazo, *Richard Nixon,* 107. **287.** John Bartlow Martin, *Stevenson of Illinois,* 691-98; and Wyatt interview. **288.** Jamieson, *Packaging the Presidency,* 70-71; and Ambrose, *Nixon,* 289. **289.** *U.S. News & World Report* 39 (Oct. 3, 1952): 66-70. **290.** Jamieson, *Packaging the Presidency,* 77.
291. Gallup, *Public Opinion, 1935-1971*; 2:1090, 1092. **292.** Lewis Dexter to Ken Hechler, Oct. 11, 1952, and October 26, 1952, Racial Groups folder, Ken Hechler Files, HSTL; and Lubell, Future of American Politics, 214. **293.** DNC Research Division literature provided to the author by Gross. **294.** John F. Martin, *Civil Rights,* 114-15; and Louis Harris, *Is There a Republican Majority?* 152. **295.** Louis Harris, *Is There a Republican Majority?* 156.
296. Pamphlet, "Death of Decency," 1952, OF 300, HSTL. **297.** *PPP,* 1952-53, 1047. **298.** Ibid. **299.** Stevenson, *Major Campaign Speeches,* 314-15. **300.** Ibid., 314.
301. Wyatt and Brightman interviews. **302.** Congressional Quarterly, *Guide to U.S. Elections,* 305, 358. **303.** Ibid., 320. **304.** Congressional Quarterly, *Politics in America,* 13. **305.** Angus Campbell, Gerald Gurin, and Warren E. Miller, "Political Issues and the Vote: November, 1952," *American Political Science Review* 47 (1953): 359-86; and Angus Campbell, Gerald Gurin, and Warren E. Miller, *The Voter Decides* (Evanston, Ill.: Row, Peterson, 1954); and Gary C. Jacobson, "The Incumbency and Competition in Elections to the U.S. House of Representatives, 1952-82," *American Political Science Review* 31 (1987): 126-41.
306. Wayne, *Road to the White House,* 74. **307.** Ibid.; and Nie, Verba, and Petrocik, *Chaning American Voter,* 383. **308.** Gallup, *Political Almanac: 1952,* 19; and Wayne, *Road to the White House,* 74. **309.** Gallup, *Political Almanac: 1952,* 19; and Ladd, *Transformations,* 153. **310.** Strong, *TRB,* 343-89; Sweeney, "Revolt in Virginia," 186; Sundquist, *Dynamics,* 282-92; and Jack Bass and Walter DeVries, *The Transformation of Southern Politics* (New York: Basic Books, 1976), 3-41.
311. Louis Harris, *Is There a Republican Majority?* 68-71. **312.** Ibid., 71. **313.** Ladd, *Transformation,* 112, 115. **314.** Nie, Petrocik, and Verba, *Changing American Voter,* 383; and Louis Harris, *Is There a Republican Majority?* 147. **315.** Ferrell, *Off the Record,* 279.

316. Ibid. **317.** Ibid., 281-82. **318.** Ibid., 282. **319.** Ibid. **320.** David S. Broder, *The Party's Over: The Failure of Politics in America* (New York: Harper & Row, 1972), 1-12; Kelley, *Public Relations,* 150-51; Martin P. Wattenberg, *The Decline of American Political Parties, 1952-1980* (Cambridge: Harvard Univ. Press, 1984), 66-72; Ruth K. Scott and Ronald J. Hrebenar, *Parties in Crisis* (New York: Wiley, 1984), 43; and Eric Barnouw, *Tube of Plenty: The Evolution of American Television* (New York: Knopf, 1975), 9-74. **321.** Klinkner, *Losing Party,* 14-26; Ferrell, *Off the Record,* 381-83; and Parmet, *Democrats,* 151-61. **322.** Merle Miller, *Plain Speaking,* 439; Ferrell, *Off the Record,* 390; and Poen, *Strictly Personal and Confidential,* 136. **323.** Stowe interview. **324.** Merle Miller, *Plain Speaing,* 445.

EPILOGUE: TRUMAN'S LEGACY IN THE DEMOCRATIC PARTY

1. *Gallup Opinion Index* 182 (October-November 1980): 35. **2.** Ibid., 34. **3.** Congressional Quarterly, *Guide to U.S. Elections,* 320, 358; and Wayne, *Road to the White House,* 74. **4.** Nelson W. Polsby, *Congress and the Presidency* (Englewood Cliffs, N.J.: Prentice-Hall, 1986), 25. **5.** Brightman interview. **6.** Abramson, *Spanning the Century,* 532-43. **7.** Congressional Quarterly, *Guide to U.S. Elections,* 359; and Wayne, *Road to the White House,* 74. **8.** Lubell, *Future of American Politics,* 26-27. **9.** Hamby, *Beyond the New Deal,* 53-55; and John F. Martin, *Civil Rights,* 79-85. **10.** Irving Bernstein, *Promises Kept,* 4-6; and Matusow, *Unraveling of America,* 20.

11. Margaret Truman, *Where the Buck Stops?* 289-305, 341-60. **12.** Allen and Shannon, *Truman Merry-Go-Round,* 41-42; *PPP,* 1952, 132; and Ferrell, *Off the Record,* 284-86; and Cornelius P. Cotter and John B. Bibby, "Institutional Development of Parties and the Thesis of Party Decline," *Political Science Quarterly* 95 (Spring 1980): 13-15. **13.** Rodney M. Sievers, "Adlai E. Stevenson and the Crisis of Liberalism," *Midwest Quarterly* 14 (Winter 1973): 135-49; Abraham Holtzman, "Party Responsibility and Loyalty: New Rules in the Democratic Party," *Journal of Politics* 22 (August 1960): 485-501; Wilson, *Amateur Democrat,* 53; and Samuel Kernell, *Going Public* (Washington, D.C.: CQ Press, 1993), 108-9, 115; and Stephen A. Salmore and Barbara G. Salmore, *Candidates, Parties, and Campaigns* (Washington, D.C.: CQ Press, 1985), 46-47. **14.** James W. Davis, *President as Party Leader,* 102-11; James A. Davis and David L. Nixon, "The President's Party," *Presidential Studies Quarterly* 24 (Spring 1994): 363-73; Sabato, *Party's Just Begun,* 60-61; Rhodes Cook, "Reagan Nurtures His Adopted Party to Strength," *Congressional Quarterly Weekly* 43 (Sept. 28, 1985): 1927-1930; and Jo Freeman, "The Political Culture of Democrats and Republicans," *Political Science Quarterly* 101 (1986): 327-56.

☆ ☆ ☆ ☆ ☆

INDEX

Note: Page numbers appearing in italic type refer to pages that contain tables.

Pecora, Ferdinand, 52
Pegler, Westbrook, 22
Pendergast, James M., 3
Pendergast, Mike, 3, 4
Pendergast, Tom: funeral of, 23; and
  Truman, 3-4, 5-8, 11-12, 26, 34
Pendergast machine, 3, 22, 26
Pennsylvania Democratic party, 32-34
Pepper, Claude, 18, 65, 133, 156, 172-73
Perkins, Frances, 92
Perry, Jennings, 39
Perry, Leslie, 148
Petrocik, John R., 139
Pittsburgh Sun-Telegraph, 22
poll taxes, 38-39, 41, 148
Porter, Paul, 62, 118
Powell, Adam Clayton, Jr., 162, 196
presidential elections: of 1948, 45, 109,
  111-43; of 1952, 169-70, 191-201
President's Commission on Internal
  Security and Individual Rights
  (1951), 166
President's Committee on Civil Rights,
  123
Primm, William, 123
Progressive Citizens of America
  (PCA), 116-17
Propper, Karl, 117
Providence Evening Bulletin, 66
public housing, 28-29, 54, 107, 145.
  See also Housing Act (1937);
  Housing Act (1949)
Public Utility Holding Company Act
  (1935), 9
Public Works Administration, 37

Rabbits (Democratic party faction), 4, 5
race: as campaign issue, 19, 20, 33,
  119, 172, 175, 199; and Crump, 38;

and Fair Deal objectives, 29, 160-61,
  162; integration of in DNC, 60, 82;
  Truman on, 123
Rae, Nicol C., 95, 110
Rankin, John, 108, 151
Rauh, Joseph, 45, 119, 135, 148
Rayburn, Sam: and Democratic party,
  57, 58, 90, 203; and Roosevelt, 19;
  and Truman, 17, 103, 146-47, 151
Reconstruction Finance Corporation
  (RFC), 71, 185-87
Redding, Jack, 75, 78-79, 182
*The Red Record of Senator Claude
  Pepper* (Smathers), 173
Reece, B. Carroll, 94
reform initiatives, Truman's, 6, 9-10,
  11, 15-16, 188-89
religion, 123, 160-62
Republican National Committee
  (RNC): campaign strategy of, 94-97;
  finances of, 70, 85-86, 88; publicity
  by, 79
Republican party, 22, 45, 91-110
Reuther, Walter, 98
Riley, James Whitcomb, 115
RNC. *See* Republican National
  Committee (RNC)
Rogers, Hugo, 49
Roosevelt, Eleanor, 60, 69, 149, 161
Roosevelt, Franklin D.: congress
  under, 165; criticism of, 129; and
  machine bosses, 12, 37, 39, 42, 53;
  and New Deal, 164; political
  agendas of, 25-26, 153, 172, 179;
  presidential campaign of, 21-23; and
  Truman, 16-17, 18-19, 20, 58
Roosevelt, Franklin D., Jr., 45, 50
Roosevelt, James, 65
Rosenbaum, Samuel I., 186